Women in Early Modern Ireland

Women in Early Modern Ireland

edited by

Margaret MacCurtain and
Mary O'Dowd

EDINBURGH UNIVERSITY PRESS

© Edinburgh University Press 1991
22 George Square, Edinburgh

Distributed in North America
by Columbia University Press
New York

Set in Linotron Palatino
by Photoprint Ltd, Torquay, and
printed in Great Britain by
Redwood Press Limited,
Melksham, Wilts

British Library Cataloguing
   in Publication Data
Women in early modern Ireland 1500–1800.
   1. Ireland. Society. Role of women, history
   I. O'Dowd, Mary II. MacCurtain, Margaret
305.4209415

ISBN 0 7486 0223 2 (cased)

Contents

Introduction
M. MacCurtain and M. O'Dowd   1

Section I: Law, Politics and War

1. Irishwomen and Property in the Sixteenth Century
   K.W. Nicholls   17

2. Women in Gaelic Society during the Age of Transition
   K. Simms   32

3. Women and Crime in Seventeenth-Century Ireland
   R. Gillespie   43

4. Women and Piracy in Ireland: from Gráinne
   O'Malley to Anne Bonny
   J.C. Appleby   53

5. Political Women and Reform in Tudor Ireland
   C. Brady   69

6. Women and War in Ireland in the 1640s
   M. O'Dowd   91

7. Irish Women Overseas, 1500–1800
   J. Casway   112

8. Women and Eighteenth-Century Irish Republicanism
   N.J. Curtin   133

Section II: Religion and Education

9. Women and Gaelic Literature, 1500–1800
   B. Cunningham   147

10. Women, Education and Learning in Early Modern
    Ireland
    M. MacCurtain   160

11. Women and the Reformation in Seventeenth-Century
    Ireland
    P. Kilroy   179

12. Women and Protestant Minorities in Eighteenth-
    Century Ireland
    D. Hempton and M. Hill   197

13. Women and Religious Practice
    P.J. Corish   212

Section III: Family, Household and Health

14. No Scythians Here: Women and Marriage in
    Seventeenth-Century Ireland
    D. Dickson   223

15. Life after Death: Widows in Carrick-on-Suir, 1799
    L.A. Clarkson and E.M. Crawford   236

16. Women in the Domestic Linen Industry
    W.H. Crawford   255

17. Women and the Preparation of Food in Eighteenth-
    Century Ireland
    N. Cullen   265

18. Family, Love and Marriage: Some Evidence from the
    Early Eighteenth Century
    S. Connolly   276

19. Images of 'Poor' Women in the Writing of
    Irish Men Midwives
    J. Murphy Lawless   291

20. Women in Irish Folklore: the Testimony Regarding
    Illegitimacy, Abortion and Infanticide
    A. O'Connor   304

21. Women and Madness in Ireland, 1600–1850
    E. Malcolm   318

    Index   335

Contributors

DR JOHN APPLEBY: St Michael's Grammar School, London.

DR CIARAN BRADY: Department of Modern History, Trinity College, Dublin.

DR JERROLD CASWAY: Howard Community School, Maryland.

PROF. L.A. CLARKSON & DR E.M. CRAWFORD: Department of Economic and Social History, Queen's University, Belfast.

PROFESSOR P.J. CORISH: St Patrick's College, Maynooth, Co. Kildare.

DR S.J. CONNOLLY: Department of History, University of Ulster, Coleraine.

DR W.H. CRAWFORD: Ulster Folk Museum, Hollywood, Co. Down.

NUALA CULLEN: Blackrock, Co. Dublin.

BERNADETTE CUNNINGHAM: Dublin Diocesan Library.

DR NANCY CURTIN: Department of History, Fordham University, New York.

DR DAVID DICKSON: Department of Modern History, Trinity College, Dublin.

DR RAYMOND GILLESPIE: Drumcondra, Dublin.

DR MYRTLE HILL & DR DAVID HEMPTON: Department of Modern History, Queen's University, Belfast.

PHIL KILROY: Armagh.

DR MARGARET MacCURTAIN: Department of Modern Irish History, University College, Dublin.

DR ELIZABETH MALCOLM: Whitefield, Manchester.

DR JO MURPHY-LAWLESS: Department of Sociology, Trinity College, Dublin.

KENNETH NICHOLLS: Department of Irish History, University College, Cork.

DR ANNE O'CONNOR: c/o Department of Irish Folklore, University College, Dublin.

DR MARY O'DOWD: Department of Modern History, Queen's University, Belfast.

DR K SIMMS: Department of Medieval History, Trinity College, Dublin.

Acknowledgements

The editors would like to thank the following for illustrations: the National Museum of Ireland (nos 1, 2, 16); Heather King (no. 3); Martin Timoney (no. 4); the Office of Public Works, Dublin (nos 5, 6, 8); Anne O'Dowd (no. 9); the Franciscan Convent, Killiney (no. 10); Simon Wingfield Digby (no. 11); the British Library (no. 12); the *Irish Ancestor* (no. 13); the National Trust (no. 14); Irish Architectural Archive (no. 15). We would also like to thank Mairead Dunlevy and Raghnaill O Floinn of the National Museum of Ireland for their advice and assistance; Brenda Mooney for drawing our attention to illustration no. 17; and the Photographic Unit in Queen's University, Belfast for their technical expertise and skill.

Introduction

I

The historiography of women's history in Ireland is largely
a story of neglect with only a small number of pioneers
quietly insisting on establishing the significance of the subject. In
England, critical investigation of women in the past developed
out of the women's suffrage movement of the late nineteenth and
early twentieth centuries. There was a corresponding women's
movement in Ireland but it did not give rise to the same interest
in the history of Irish women. Curiously, this was at a time when
Irish women historians achieved greater recognition and status
than they have ever done since. The first professors of history in
University College, Dublin and University College, Galway were
women: Mary Hayden (appointed in 1911) and Mary Donovan
O'Sullivan (appointed in 1914). Constantia Maxwell was a lec-
turer in Trinity College, Dublin by 1923 and in 1936 she was
appointed professor of economic history. Other women such as
Alice Stopford Green, Eleanor Knott and Ada K. Longfield also
established reputations as historians and scholars in the first
decades of the twentieth century. The research of most of these
women was in economic and social history which occasionally
touched on the role of women in society but none chose to explore
the topic in any depth.[1] The writings of Helena Concannon on the
Women of 'Ninety Eight (Dublin, 1919) and her more general
survey of women in Irish history (*Daughters of Banba* (Dublin,
1922)) were exceptional and are worthy of reconsideration in this
regard.

Another notable exception to the neglect of the study of
women's role in society was the publication in 1936 of a collection
of essays on the position of women in early Irish law, edited by
D.A. Binchy. Published under the discrete title of *Studies in Early
Irish Law* and written partly in German, the volume analysed
frankly and objectively the way in which early Irish law dealt with
such topics as wives (including secondary wives), concubines

(those with and without legal sanction), divorce, adultery and rape. Published a year before De Valera's constitution of 1937, *Studies in Early Irish Law* strongly suggested that woman's role as mother and guardian of the family was not an inviolable characteristic of Irish women. Regrettably, the research and conclusions of the essays were not followed up. It was not until the 1970s that Donncha Ó Corráin made the contents of the book accessible to a wider audience.[2]

In the post-war years, the Irish historical world became – with a few notable exceptions – overwhelmingly male. Historical interest moved away from the economic and social interests of the first generation of women historians and concentrated on political issues and particularly, on the political worlds of London and Dublin. Women's lack of political power for much of the historical period meant that they were rarely of interest in themselves. They might feature in the background as negative or disruptive influences – as for example, Dervogilla O'Rourke, Anna Parnell or Katherine O'Shea; as loyal but passive supporters of men's actions such as the sixteenth century countess of Desmond, Sarah Curran or the mother of Patrick Pearse; or, more generally, as marriage pawns in the men's political game, but attention was rarely focused on women in their own right. Some women were treated more seriously but usually because they had participated in the political world on male terms. The two Irish women who have been the subject of most biographies and historical examination – Gráinne O'Malley and Constance Markievicz – are classic examples of this phenomenon.

The concentration on political history, the lack of interest in economic and social history and a reluctance in mid-twentieth century Ireland to critically explore such sensitive issues as childbirth, marriage and family relations led to a neglect of women's role in society. It also led, it might be added, to an implicit belief that the history of women was not a subject worthy of historical exploration. In short, the revolution in Irish history writing was concerned with the public, political world of Ireland in which women rarely appeared.

Slowly, such attitudes have changed. Some progress was made in the 1960s, mainly by female scholars. Margaret MacCurtain pioneered the history of women's education and her work was followed by a number of postgraduate theses on the topic.[3] But it was not until the 1970s that the history of Irish women began to be investigated in depth. Increasing interest in the history of women in Ireland was a by-product of the women's movement in Ireland and two of the historians involved, Mary Cullen and Margaret MacCurtain, have been active in that movement since its foundation. In the wider historical world in Ireland, the revival of interest in economic and social history in the 1970s also brought women more into focus in the historical record.

The publication of *Women in Irish Society. The Historical Dimension* (Dublin, 1978), edited by Margaret MacCurtain and Donncha Ó Corráin was a landmark in the writing of women's history in Ireland. For the first time, established academic historians were writing and discussing the impact of women on Irish society in the past. The volume has been slowly followed by other publications on women's history, most notably on women and education, the suffrage movement and women's position in nineteenth century Ireland.[4] In 1987 the Women's Studies Forum established the Irish Feminist History Forum and this was followed in the summer of 1988 by the formation of the Irish Association for Research in Women's History which is formally linked to the International Federation for Research in Women's History. Women's history is now one of the most exciting areas of Irish history and the initiation of a debate about the validity of a feminist interpretation of Irish history is already producing many stimulating ideas and research.

There are and always will be obstacles to the investigation of women in past Irish societies. The paucity of source material is an insurmountable barrier. Other countries have similar problems: the historical record is in most western countries male orientated. But the destruction of the Irish national archives in 1922 makes the Irish problem many times more difficult. The surviving transcripts and calendars concentrate almost exclusively on political developments. Documentary material such as local parish records and wills which could have been used to recover the history of many women has disappeared completely.

The source problem explains why most research on Irish women's history has to date concentrated on the nineteenth and twentieth centuries where more manuscript material survives. Little has been written on the period before 1800. The aim of this collection of essays is to try to redress the balance. The contributors were asked to do two things. First, to examine the role of women in their particular area of interest and secondly, to indicate source material which might assist further research on the history of women in Ireland. The editors hope that the collection will thus serve a twin function, i.e. provide an outline of the main developments and changes in the history of Irish women in the early modern period and suggest possible areas for future research.

II

Of all the factors which determined women's position in society, the law was the most powerful. Kenneth Nicholls' opening chapter documents the survival into the late sixteenth century of Gaelic customs relating to marriage and dowry giving. In Gaelic Ireland married women enjoyed the right to hold and administer property independently of their husbands while the customs relating to the dowry protected the woman against the worst economic effects of divorce which was also permissible under Gaelic law. Gradually in the late sixteenth and early seventeenth centuries such customs were replaced by English common law with its jointure system and the merging of a woman's property rights with those of her husband. The common law gave a husband almost total control over his wife and the property which she brought with her on marriage and, therefore, removed the advantages which propertied women enjoyed under Gaelic law. The marriage settlements agreed between landed families, particularly in the eighteenth century, allowed the women's family some control but at lower levels of society such arrangements were rare. If women were disadvantaged by this change, they also benefited from other legal changes. Katharine Simms points to another vital transition in the law relating to marriage. In Gaelic society, the eligibility of bastard sons to inherit their father's land enabled the aristocracy to ignore the Church's decrees and practise not only secular divorce but a form of polygamy. By the beginning of the seventeenth century English common law (with the assistance of the Counter-Reformation) had won a successful battle against both these customs. The common law introduced legitimacy as a qualification for land inheritance and helped to eradicate the practise of polygamy and thus, as Katharine Simms asserts, revolutionised marriage customs in Ireland far more than either the Reformation or the Counter-Reformation had done. As a consequence, women received more protection under the law. Divorce, as practised under Gaelic law, was more popular among men than women who could too easily be cast aside by a husband. English common law offered more marriage security to women than Gaelic law had done as divorce was rare and difficult to procure. Single women and widows also received more legal recognition as a result of the transformation of the law. They were effectively on a legal par with men.

Raymond Gillespie's study of women and crime examines the extent to which changes in the criminal law made an impact on women in Ireland. Unlike in England, women rarely appear in the surviving criminal records. Gillespie's suggestion that social control, and therefore the control of aberrant women, was exercised informally within the community rather than through the formal legal process is worth further investigation. This may possibly reflect the survival of Gaelic law under which a woman's family was responsible for crimes which she committed or, as Gillespie suggests, it may reflect the power of the churches in controlling society, including the social behaviour of women.

One area of life which neither church nor state could adequately control was the establishment of pirate communities in seventeenth century Ireland where women worked as alehouse keepers and prostitutes as well as operating as receivers of pirate booty, as John Appleby's article documents. The lawless nature of society in the pirate colonies gave some women more economic independence but it also allowed others to be exploited and abused.

The transition from Gaelic law to common law did therefore transform the legal position of women but the actual status of women underwent little alteration. In Gaelic society 'a woman held a position of perpetual dependence' to her family while under English common law a married woman was legally dependent on her husband.[5] Single women and widows had more freedom and protection under English common law but they were subjected to other types of restriction such as economic dependence and gender stereotyping as many of the articles published here indicate.

III

The impact of the political changes of early modern Ireland was complex and multi-faceted. Several contributors analyse the political role of women in Gaelic Ireland. Bernadette Cunningham argues that wives of chiefs exercised a certain amount of political influence through the patronage of the official literature of the lordship which was of vital importance for retaining group loyalty to the lord. Kenneth Nicholls's contribution also suggests that women could exercise considerable indirect political influence, while elsewhere, Katharine Simms has written of chiefly wives engaging in negotiations for the release of hostages and even sitting in a council of leading vassals to decide on questions of war and peace.[6] Ciaran Brady also argues that the political framework of early Tudor Ireland bestowed on aristocratic women considerable political importance. Women played a vital role as the media through which dynastic and family networks were established. They were, therefore, essential for the maintenance of order and continuity. Despite their importance, however, Bernadette Cunningham's conclusion that women were not persons of influence in their own right but depended for their status in society on their husbands or their fathers is also paradoxically true.

The introduction of the Tudor reform programme brought a new challenge to aristocratic Irish women, a challenge which only a small number of them appear to have questioned or rejected. It is the latter group, however, who appear in the historical record. The hundreds of women who assisted the anglicising process are rarely documented. Brady also points to what he sees as the failure of the wives of English viceroys to involve themselves in furthering their husband's political aims in Ireland. The absence of a courtly society in Dublin was an obstacle to the smooth establishment of English institutions in Ireland. Nor did access to the court in England compensate for the absence of an Irish equivalent. Under Elizabeth, the privy chamber became a more closed institution than it had been under her father; and consequently personal contact with the monarch was more restricted. With the notable exception of the Earl of Ormond, few Irish visitors to the court actually met the Queen. In his conclusion, Brady raises the question as to how women conformed to the new political world of the seventeenth century. A worthwhile research topic for the future would be to examine women's political role in seventeenth century Ireland and to trace the origins of the social salons and family networks of the eighteenth century, and the development of a courtly society in Dublin Castle.

Women with political influence – however tenuous – in early modern Ireland were from aristocratic or gentry family backgrounds. Lower down the social scale, women's political involvement was limited. O'Dowd's analysis of women's role in the unrest of 1641 suggests, however, that women may have been involved in local popular unrest. This may also be true of other forms of agrarian unrest which erupted in the eighteenth century.

Historically, men are reluctant to acknowledge women's right to engage in political action. Ciaran Brady documents the ambiguity towards women which can be found in sixteenth century literary sources while Nancy Curtin reveals a similar attitude among politically radical men in late eighteenth century Ireland. The United Irishmen was a men-only organisation which believed that republicanism was essentially a manly calling. Women were expected to play a supportive but passive role. The republican beliefs of women like Mary Anne McCracken did not win universal approval in United Irishmen circles, a sentiment which was shared by later Irish republican movements.

If most women's political power was negligible their lives were directly affected by political decisions made by their male relatives. During the war years of the 1640s, as O'Dowd indicates, many women were left alone when their husbands departed to join the armies of the confederates or royalists. Despite some opportunities for more independent action, O'Dowd concludes that women lost more than they gained from the opportunities of war. The nature of the military conflict in Ireland in the 1640s meant that women on both sides were considered legitimate targets for physical attack and abuse.

After the war, thousands of women were left widows or deserted wives as their husbands fled to the continent to avoid prosecution or to seek out more exciting military careers. Jerrold Casway has traced the journeys of women who sometimes reluctantly followed their husbands, fathers or brothers into exile. They faced often an uncertain economic future in a strange country when their male supporters died or left them alone when they travelled to join their regiment. This pattern was repeated in the 1690s when women and children were not provided for in the arrangements to transport Irish soldiers to France.

Both Casway's study of women emigrants and exiles and O'Dowd's study of women who remained in Ireland stress the importance of male 'friends' and connections. In Ireland and on the continent society was controlled by male networks and access to these was crucial for the economic and social prosperity of women. For similar reasons, as Sean Connolly documents, the priority for a rich heiress in eighteenth century Ireland was to find a husband who could manage her estate and protect the political interests of her family. Regardless of her wealth a woman alone lacked the means to do this.

IV

The transition to English law and society also brought changes in religion and education. Historians have been slow to accept the implications of the female-dominated form of Irish catholicism which P.J. Corish outlines in his stimulating essay. The official position of women in the Catholic Church in the seventeenth and eighteenth centuries was one of passive support but the clandestine nature of the Church in Ireland gave women a more significant role than in other Catholic countries where the Church was officially recognised. Many services took place in the home. Wealthy women, particularly in the Pale, offered safe houses and financial protection to priests while at a lower level of society, the absence of a network of parish churches meant that the home was the most frequent venue for most of the services of the Church including those connected with the essential rites of passage of birth, marriage and death. As P.J. Corish points out, this type of 'domestic religion must be a religion very much influenced by women'. The popular Marian devotion and the Irish translation for Mary: *bean an ti* (i.e. woman of the house) also suggests a religion in which the women in the home played a significant role.

Phil Kilroy's study of women in the Roman Catholic Church, however, is a salutary reminder that this form of religion has its negative as well as its positive consequences. She argues that 'no Roman Catholic woman in Ireland was innovative with regard to religious life'. Women in religious orders were 'trapped by the prevailing tendency of the counter-reformation movement: centralisation, regulation and control, a tendency mirrored in clerical and family structures'. Margaret MacCurtain agrees with Kilroy's conclusions. She points to the dispute over the active apostolate for nuns which developed after the council of Trent which she suggests demonstrates the grip which patriarchal attitudes had on Roman Catholicism. The reform programme of the Church ignored women's intellectual information. The innovative vision of Mary Ward was discouraged. The family and the domestic sphere was where wives as well as nuns belonged. Women became the target of catechesis in the home which ensured an unquestioning religious conformity and understanding. For Catholic women, the absence of schools throughout the seventeenth century is overwhelming evidence of how they were rendered silent and invisible. The subordination of women in early modern Ireland was accomplished through lack of proper education and explains the absence of women in the cultural and scientific expansion of the second half of the seventeenth century.

While the Church of Ireland's official attitude to women was similar to that of the Catholic Church – apart from the theoretical approval of married clergy which in practice was slow to be accepted in Ireland – some of the Protestant sects which emerged in the mid-seventeenth century were more radical in their attitude to women. These less formal and more open religious groups seem to have attracted women in large numbers – particularly during the upheavals of the 1640s and 1650s and again in the late eighteenth century. Most of the women involved with such groups in Ireland came from the settler community. There were relatively few converts from catholicism. The Quakers were the first large ecclesiastical group to allow women preachers and, as Phil Kilroy indicates, the first women preachers in Ireland attracted considerable hostility. By 1700 when the church had become established women were no longer encouraged to preach publicly or take a leadership role in the church. Methodism, argue David Hempton and Myrtle Hill, also allowed women considerable freedom in its initial years and consequently attracted large numbers of women. But the phenomenon of women preachers was a transient one in the Methodist Church, as it had been among the Quakers. As Methodism became more institutionalised and accepted, female preaching was frowned upon and ultimately, officially condemned. By the middle of the nineteenth century, women were directed away from areas of influence in the policy making or debates on the doctrine of the Church towards what were considered more female areas of teaching and background supportive work. Women's experiences in Quakerism and Methodism confirm Joan Thirsk's wry comment that it is a 'generally observed fact of life that women frequently play a significant part in the founding of new enterprises, before they become institutionalised and harden their structures. Then rules are devised, or other factors intervene, that effectively exclude them.' It is a fact of life which could usefully be applied to women's involvement in other areas of life in Ireland.

The educational revolution was slow to make a significant impact in Ireland and the question could be asked if it ever made an impact on Irish women. This central theme is dealt with in different ways by the contributions of Simms, Cunningham and MacCurtain. Katharine Simms and Bernadette Cunningham both agree that women rarely feature as authors in the traditional world of Gaelic learning. Women earned admiration by displays of piety and hospitality rather than learning. Women were frequently the subjects of literary composition but as Bernadette Cunningham writes, 'Where women were the subjects of poetry in Irish it was not the image of women, real or imagined but rather the actuality of the male poet, or the male relative of the woman which was central.' Women in Gaelic poetry were not invisible but nevertheless they 'reflected men's glory rather than their own'.

In Scotland, a small group of women authors with aristocratic backgrounds began to emerge in the sixteenth century and the close links between Scotland and Ulster in the late sixteenth century led to women from this circle inter-marrying with Gaelic chiefly families. Simms suggests that their influence combined with the slow infiltration of new ideas about women's education from elsewhere, led to some Irish-born aristocratic women taking a more active role in intellectual matters than their predecessors had done. The implications of her argument raise new questions about life in Gaelic Ulster and should open up new lines of research.

The counterparts of intellectually aware Gaelic women can also be found in the Old and New English communities. Within the Pale, in the late sixteenth and early seventeenth centuries, as

Margaret MacCurtain indicates, daughters as well as sons of Pale gentry were tutored together by a resident chaplain but she also argues that the seventeenth century witnessed a narrowing of the educational training for women. We know little as yet about the education of women in the New English community but Margaret MacCurtain suggests that Calvinism led to more innovative attitudes in relation to the education of women. Godly learning was the climate of the Puritan home which as Nancy Curtin indicates by the eighteenth century had transformed the education of women in middle-class dissenting families. The faithful had to be able to read the Bible and as the woman was seen as the guardian of moral and religious values it was her duty to educate her children in sound Christian doctrine. Women from Presbyterian backgrounds may, therefore, have achieved higher literacy levels than women from other religious denominations. On a more sophisticated level, the emergence of the blue stocking movement in Dublin and London in the eighteenth century is evidence that some women in Protestant circles had by then achieved a high standard of education and intellectual development.

For the majority of women in Ireland, however, education or even basic literacy were luxuries which they did not acquire before the nineteenth century. Women were involved, as Simms and Cunningham indicate, in the oral tradition of balladeers and keeners which begins to emerge in printed form from the late seventeenth century onwards, but as yet we know relatively little about their contribution.

V

Women's position in the economy of early modern Ireland was vital and a number of chapters outline some of the main areas where women's role was significant. Katherine Simms and Kenneth Nicholls document the economic implications for women in the change from Gaelic to English practices in matters relating to marriage settlements and land ownership.

Below the landed family level, economic opportunities for women were limited and usually confined to within the family household. Much of the daily work carried out by women was not financially profitable. Nuala Cullen documents the labour-intensive and time-consuming nature of women's work in the home in pre-industrial Ireland. At all social levels, the preparation of food was a central part of women's daily labour. The simplest task, such as the baking of bread, could take a long time when it began with the grinding of the grain. At a higher social level, the supervision of a household with large numbers of untrained servants was a task which demanded skills of management and domestic economy.

Employment as a domestic servant in the big houses of the gentry which were established in the seventeenth century was a possibility for women seeking financially rewarding work but it was not a particularly lucrative one because wages were low and the work hard. It could, however, bring unexpected rewards such as learning the skills of household management or learning how to prepare more exotic meals, as Nuala Cullen suggests.

For those women anxious to seek more profitable employment, involvement in the black economy of prostitution, ale houses and illicit trade with pirates or smugglers was a possibility, as Gillespie and Appleby document for the seventeenth century. Appleby also points to the informal trade which developed in coastal areas and which women often managed in the absence of their men at sea: a topic which may repay further study for later periods. Seasonal migration or emigration as an indentured servant also, as Casway indicates, provided possible economic opportunities, especially for single women.

Nuala Cullen and W.H. Crawford also contribute to the wider debate about the effect of early capitalism and industrialisation on women's work. Both agree that the growth in the Irish economy of the eighteenth century brought new opportunities for employment and cash rewards for work to women. In Ulster, employment as spinsters in the linen industry provided new employment for women while in other parts of rural Ireland sales of butter, fowl and eggs meant that women's contribution to the national domestic economy greatly increased in the eighteenth century, with much more cash passing through their hands. Women's crucial role in the developments of the eighteenth century Irish economy has scarcely been acknowledged in the standard accounts of the period which do, however, stress that the increase in the provisions trade was an essential factor in the growth of the economy during the century. Both Cullen and Crawford express doubts that this development brought new economic independence to women. The profit went to the household not to the individual woman. Both articles suggest that the position of women in the rural household and the nature of the control which they exercised, particularly in relation to money matters, is worth further consideration.

Undoubtedly, the growth in towns in eighteenth century Ireland provided new opportunities for women. Widows, freed from the legal restraints of marriage, as L.A. Clarkson and E.M. Crawford document, made an important contribution to the economic prosperity of a small market town such as Carrick-on-Suir, although their article warns against the tendency of historians to concentrate on a small number of wealthy widows who inherited and successfully ran their husbands' businesses. The great majority of widows could expect to receive very little from their husbands. In Carrick-on-Suir and, no doubt, in other towns, the majority were employed as charwomen, washer-women and petty traders.

Single women establishing their own businesses must have been exceptional. Mary Anne McCracken and her sister did it in Belfast but they were clearly unusual and even McCracken, as Nancy Curtin indicates, complained about the lack of economic opportunities available to women: 'The sphere of women's indus-try is so confined, and so few roads lie open to her, and those so thorny, it is difficult to fix on any'. Among the thorny obstacles facing women in business were male associations which com-bined in Dublin and elsewhere to exclude women from certain trades – another topic which would merit further investigation.[7]

The consequences of financial dependence and inability to earn an independent living could be traumatic. Unmarried women were frequently exploited as unpaid servants in large households and impoverished women, many of them widows, constituted a large part of the poor and vagrant population. Crawford and Clarkson document for one Irish town the large number of widows who had no independent source of income and were dependent on their families. The placing of a single woman in a convent was one solution to the economic problem which she could represent for her family, as Casway and other contributors to this volume suggest. Elizabeth Malcolm's conclusion that some families registered unwanted or economically burdensome female dependants in lunatic asylums chillingly confirms the vulnerable position of women without financial independence.

VI

Analysis of population statistics in early modern Ireland is hindered by the absence of adequate source material but David Dickson's contribution indicates the way in which surviving documentation – no matter how scanty – can be probed to produce an outline of family size and age at marriage. His article is an innovative and pioneering contribution to a difficult and complex area.

Irish economic historians agree that one of the most important developments of eighteenth century Ireland was the dramatic growth in the Irish population in the last decades of the eight-eenth century. The reasons for the rise in population have been the subject of much scholarly discussion yet very little of the debate has focused on the impact of the population explosion on women's lives. Frequent childbirth and finding the means to feed and clothe large families were problems which dominated the lives of hundreds of thousands of Irish women by the end of the eighteenth century.

The male medical profession's response to the population increase was to assert male authority and expertise in the whole area of childbirth and midwifery, as Jo Murphy-Lawless indicates. Her study reveals fascinating distinctions made by male doctors in relation to childbirth: distinctions which were based more on the class prejudices of the doctors than on sound medical judgement. The establishment of maternity hospitals such as the Rotunda in Dublin asserted male control of midwifery and childbirth of the poor women who were the main victims of the demographic rise of the eighteenth century.

Elizabeth Malcolm's analysis of the portrayal of women in medical textbooks reveals a similar sort of gender stereotyping. Women were assumed to be more prone to madness than men. Both Murphy-Lawless and Malcolm suggest that this type of medical analysis communicates more about men's fears and misconceptions than it does about the health problems facing women. The medical texts echo the misogyny revealed in litera-ture and which was clearly part of common currency by the eighteenth century as the folklore examined by Anne O'Connor reveals.

Male historians might also be accused of gender stereotyping. The rather rigid models used to analyse family history contain their own implicit stereotyping of the woman's role in the family. Sean Connolly's study of family, love and marriage in the eighteenth century argues that such models are of little value for an examination of family life in eighteenth century Ireland. His analysis indicates the potential of a more detailed investigation of the family in the eighteenth century where sufficient family papers exist to make such research possible. Dr Anthony Malcolmson has pioneered this field of study and his archival work in the Public Record Office of Northern Ireland has accumu-lated a large amount of source material which could be examined with profit.[8]

VII

The history of women in Ireland is still at the discovery stage. The articles in this volume indicate some of the areas where women either played a significant role or where research on women's activities is both possible and rewarding. Much more 'discovery'-type research is needed before women's history can or even should be integrated into 'mainstream' Irish history. While the ultimate aim of Irish women's history should always be to challenge and change perceptions and expectations of the reading of all Irish history, it is important that Irish women's history establish itself in its own right. Otherwise the history of women in Ireland risks being confined to an occasional paragraph inserted almost as an afterthought or as a form of light relief after the more serious study of men's activities.

As several contributors to this volume indicate women's historians in Ireland have yet to confront and grapple with several problems of methodology – not the least of which are sources which reveal or, often, conceal considerable prejudice to women. As Jo Murphy-Lawless points out, historians must examine the story behind the sources: their silences and their negative attitude to women. The advantages as well as the problems associated with feminist interpretations of history need also to be analysed from an Irish point of view. The agenda for Irish women's history is a challenging and exciting one. The contributions to this volume should help considerably in deciding the order of business and hopefully will prevent women in Irish history being relegated to 'any other business'.

REFERENCES

1. See R.W. Dudley Edwards and M. O'Dowd, *Sources for Early Modern Irish History 1534–1641* (Cambridge, 1985), pp. 194–5, 202–6; J. Lee, 'Some Aspects of Modern Irish Historiography' in E. Schulin (ed.), *Gedenkschrift Martin Gohring Studien zu Europaischen Geschichte* (Wiesbaden, 1968), pp. 431–443.

2. D. Ó Corráin, 'Women in Early Irish Society' in M. MacCurtain and D. Ó Corráin (eds), *Women in Irish Society. The Historical Dimension* (Dublin, 1978), pp. 1–13.

3. See Mary Cullen (ed.), *Girls Don't Do Honours: Irish Women in Education in the 19th and 20th Centuries* (Dublin, 1987).

4. See bibliography in M. Luddy and C. Murphy (eds), *Women Surviving* (Dublin, 1990), pp. 266–73.

5. K. Simms, 'Women in Norman Ireland' in *Women in Irish Society*, p. 14. See also K. Simms, 'The Legal Position of Irishwomen in the Later Middle Ages' in *Irish Jurist*, new series, 10 (1975), pp. 96–111.

6. Simms, 'Women in Norman Ireland', p. 18.

7. See I. Brophy, 'Women in the Workforce' in D. Dickson (ed.), *The Gorgeous Mask: Dublin 1700–1850* (Dublin, 1987), pp. 51–63.

8. A. Malcolmson, *Pursuit of the Heiress: Aristocratic Marriage in Ireland, 1750–1820* (Belfast, 1982).

SECTION I

Law, Politics and War

1

Irishwomen and Property in the Sixteenth Century

KENNETH NICHOLLS

The 'rules and directions' concerning 'the estates of the Irish' which were issued by the Irish judges, perhaps at the instigation of Sir John Davies, in 1606, and which were afterwards treated as having the force of law, after decreeing the abolition of the customs of partible inheritance and illegitimate succession, conclude with a direction that 'where married women among them claim and hold goods in severalty from their husbands, we think it meet that . . . the property of all their goods shall be adjudged in the husbands, according unto the due course of the common laws'.[1] It would therefore seem that in the purely Gaelic regions of Ireland at least, married women enjoyed the right to hold and administer property independently of their husbands. This was quite contrary, of course, to the rules of the English common law, which vested the wife's moveable property entirely in the husband, or, to put it another way, established a community of goods between spouses of which the husband had absolute use and control at his discretion. In this respect, as in so much else, the common law followed a legal tradition of Germanic origin which was enshrined in the customs of northern France and of Belgium, as well as in the law of Scotland. In less closely approximating forms, it could be found over most of western Europe, until ousted in large part by the revival of Roman law. In later English law, from the seventeenth century onwards, the absolute rights of the husband and the harshness of the rule towards the married woman were evaded by the propertied classes through the development of equitable settlements, by which the wife's assets were secured against the husband's claims by being vested, prior to the marriage, in trustees.

In most of these systems, this rule which vested the property of both spouses entirely in the husband was linked with a system of succession which gave both wife and children an automatic right to a share of his property of his decease, but this right never became accepted as part of the general common law of England. It was, however, the customary law of the north of England until 1692, of Wales until 1696, and of the City of London until 1724, as well as being that of the English colony in Ireland and, of course, the law of Scotland.[2] In addition, in most Germanic systems of law, the widow was entitled to a life interest in a share – normally one-third – of her husband's lands, although as time went on this right came to be replaced by the creation of a jointure (Scots, 'conjunct-fee'), a portion (or sometimes even, indeed, the whole) of the estate settled on the joint names of husband and wife and enjoyed by her by survivorship after his death.[3] In the Irish colony, the rule of succession entitled the wife (if there were children) to a third of the moveable goods on her husband's death, after the payment of debts and of his funeral expenses, while the children were entitled to another third, and only the remaining third could be freely bequeathed by the husband. If there were no children, the wife's share rose to half. This remained the law of Ireland until abolished by statute in 1696.[4] It would appear from a chancery pleading of c. 1577, which speaks of this as 'the custome in the counties of Kildare, Dublin, Meath and in . . . the cittie of Dublin, and the countie of Catherlough tyme out of mynde used and allowed', that the wife's share rose to one-half not only in the absence of children but also when the children had been previously 'preferred', that is to say, dowried or set up in life by their father.[5] Such an automatic right to succession did not necessarily obviate the distribution of the assets by will: rather, it established a norm which the testator was obliged to follow. John Quin, an Elizabethan citizen of Dublin, 'by his last will ordained that his wife and children should have two partes of all his goods and chattels real and personal', while Edmond Grace of Ballywalter, County Carlow, by his will (in Irish) in 1606 left one-third of his goods 'for his soul', another third to his daughter and her husband, and the remaining third to his wife.[6] But it is clear, not only from the chancery pleading quoted above, but from the 'Statute of Distributions' of 1696 which abolished the right, that the rights of the wife and children were absolute ones, if they chose to enforce them, and that, as in Scots law, the testator's freedom to disinherit his immediate family was severely limited.

In the Gaelic and Gaelicised regions, however, a quite different system seems to have prevailed in the sixteenth century. By this, although the wife was required to bring a dowry to her husband on marriage and had no rights of succession beyond the bare repayment of this dowry,[7] she could hold and acquire other property independently of her husband. We do not know to what extent, if at all, the lawyers (and whether we call them 'Brehons' or 'Roman lawyers' is probably, by this date, of little relevance[8]) required the husband's consent to his wife's transactions. In early Irish law women, while having considerable property rights, were subject to a perpetual tutelage which placed them in the juridical status of minors,[9] but I can find no trace of this in the later period, and given the important political and legal roles fulfilled by women, it seems highly unlikely that it survived. Irishwomen were freely accepted as witnesses[10] and we find noblewomen not only acting as political agents for their husbands but also as arbitrators in disputes over property.[11] The remarkable agreement regarding lands of 2 May 1586 between the Countess of Ormond and her sister-in-law 'Lady Giles' Butler, wife of Brian O Kennedy Finn, each binding, apparently, her husband,[12] may be exceptional, but we find other examples of married women engaging in land transactions on their own account. When Awly MacCoghlan, 'having stolen a beefe, wanted money to save himself from the gallows', he sold or mortgaged half the share of Clonoony (County Offaly) which came to him by 'gavelkind' to Mairgread ní Coireacháin, wife of his elder brother Cohogry.[13] Johan fitz John purchased with her husband Tumultagh O Hellye lands in Garrynoe, County Limerick, 'uppon her owne proper goods and his', and in her will, having no issue by Tumultagh, bequeathed her half share in the land, along with half her goods, to her son by her first marriage, Owen O Mullowny.[14] Leases jointly to husband and wife, and mortgages or sales of land to husband and wife, which are common in the Ormond deeds and to be found elsewhere, do not conclusively prove an independent legal capacity in the wife, since their function may be simply to secure her interest by survivorship, but if they were significantly more common – as an impressionistic view suggests they were – in regions of mixed law than in the Pale or the towns, they would suggest that there was at least some recognition of her legal independence. The wife's right to hold property independently of her husband was of considerable interest to the Church, since it invalued not only her right to make bequests for the good of her soul but also the Church's right to take a 'mortuary' – usually the best suit of clothes left by the deceased – and a 'canonical portion' (a kind of death duty levied by the Church) on her decease, a practice repugnant to practitioners of the common law.[15] The taking of mortuaries on the death of married women was forbidden in 1621.[16]

The wives of Irish lords were often entitled to receive certain revenues set aside by custom for their own use, although of course this entitlement would presumably have lapsed when the husband died. The wife of MacCarthy Mór, we are told, had 'a small spending . . . out of divers quarters of the country, called "canebeg"' [*Cáin beag*]. In late sixteenth century Beara, 'the standing rent due to O'Sullivan upon his country was but £40, and that itself was ever allotted to the lady for the time being towards her idle expenses', while in the little Burke lordship of Pobal MacHubert in County Galway 'by a certain custom used from of old . . . the parcel of land called Caherneheni belonged and should belong to the wife of every captain of the said Poble for her maintenance'.[17] In great Anglo-Norman lordships there was sometimes, it seems, a customary endowment assigned to the lady, but this she enjoyed, like an English jointure, for her lifetime. Thus Thomas, Earl of Desmond (1529–34) granted to his second wife Katherine (who has enjoyed a perhaps undeserved reputation as the 'Old Countess' of Desmond), besides 'the manor of Inchiquin, County Cork, an annual rent of 33 marks (£22) in Kerry 'as fully as Evlina Roche (wife of Maurice, earl 1487–1520) and other countesses had been accustomed to receive the same'.[18] Perhaps unique is the remarkable marriage treaty of 1513 between Donal MacCarthy Reagh, 'prince of the Carbrymen', and Eleanor, daughter of the 'Great Earl' of Kildare, by which MacCarthy Reagh conceded to her the manor of Dundaniel and a full half of all his lordship, existing or to be acquired, as well as a veto over his appointment of 'officers and officials' and over his choice of galloglass.[19] 'Lordship' was seen here to refer not to his political property but to his direct ownership of land. The concessions in this agreement no doubt reflected the power of Eleanor's father and his wish to establish her as his representative in the south.

By the sixteenth century the system of marriage through a brideprice (*coibhche*) paid to the family of the bride seems to have finally succumbed, and a marriage system of the typical 'mediterranean' form, involving the payment of a dowry by the bride (or her family) to the husband had become universal. It was to survive in rural Ireland down to the present century.[20] Its triumph, and the disappearance of the older system, seems to have occurred around 1400, and to have been the result of direct ecclesiastical pressure, since the payment of a dowry was prescribed by the canon law.[21] In this change Ireland followed, at the remove of a couple of centuries, the other countries of southern and western Europe,[22] and the lateness of the change is shown by the fact that the Irish language did not evolve a proper term for the dowry (the Scots adapted the Old Irish *tochra*, originally denoting a gift made by the husband, to denote the dowry, in the form 'tochar', the standard Scots term for dowry).

In Ireland it was known simply as *cró nuachair* or *spréidh* (*spré*) *nuachair*, usually shortened into simple *spré*, and corresponding in formation as in meaning to the English term 'marriage goods'. One might query what was the status of the 'wives' of the clergy in pre-Reformation Ireland. It seems hardly likely that they paid a dowry for the doubtful advantages of their precarious position, and one wonders did they continue to receive a *coibhche* from their partners. There is little evidence regarding them, but it may be remarked that in contemporary Scotland Marion Ogilvy, 'wife' of Cardinal David Beaton, was the dowryless daughter of a nobleman, and was amply provided for by the Cardinal.[23] One may wonder whether the clerical wives of late medieval Ireland were not similarly compensated for their irregular status by receiving a financial endowment from their partners, rather than bringing one to them, and whether the denunciation of the man who kept a *bean coibhche*, a woman for whom he had paid a brideprice, to be found in a late religious poem,[24] is not primarily directed at the clergy.

Be that as it may, by the sixteenth century Irish marriage normally involved the payment of a dowry by the wife or her family to the husband, or in certain cases to the husband's father, where the latter was living and in possession of the property, and the son not yet independently established.[25] This pattern of marriage was that prescribed by the canon and civil laws, and had, as I have said, become the norm in southern and western Europe in the course of the later Middle Ages. Its extension to Ireland can be seen as a reflection of the importance of Roman law – comprehending under this term both canon and civil law, the *utrumque jus* – in the late medieval period.[26] Although the payment of a dowry was not an absolute requirement for a valid marriage, the constitution *nullum sine dote fiat conjugium* ('let no marriage be formed without a dowry') followed with the let-out words *iuxta possibilitatem* ('as is possible'), it was nevertheless obligatory unless good reason could be shown for its absence,[27] and a dowryless marriage rapidly became not only economically but socially unacceptable. The bestowing of dowries on poor girls was seen in Ireland, as in southern Europe, as a charitable work. Sir Henry Lynch of Galway, by his will in 1633, left the sum of £500 to establish a charity called 'The Guardians of the poor maidens of Galway', who would endow with 'competent portions' poor girls of Galway birth, in which 'those that shall be of the Lynches shall be first provided, and next them of the Martins'.[28] By the law, if the dowry had been agreed but had not in fact been paid, or not paid in full, the husband was entitled, if he had already taken home his bride, to expel her from his house.[29] On the dissolution of the marriage by annulment or the husband's death the wife was entitled (unless disqualified by her adultery), to the repayment of the dowry she had brought. In such a case, she had no other claim on her husband's property, either outright or in life interest, in contrast to the Germanic systems of community of property described above. This situation for Ireland is expressed in the statement of Gráinne ní Mháille that

> Among the Irishry the custom is, that wives shall have but her first dowry without any increase or allowance for the same, time out of mind it hath been so used, and before any woman so deliver up her marriage [dowry] to her husband she receives sureties for the restitution of the same in manner and form as she hath delivered it, in regard that husbands through their great expenses, especially chieftains, at the time of their deaths have no goods to leave behind them, but are commonly indebted. At other times they are divorced upon proof of precontracts; and the husband now and then without any lawful or due proceeding do put his wife from him, and so bringeth in another so as the wife is to have sureties for her dowry for fear of the worse.[30]

These sureties for repayment of the dowry are authenticated in sixteenth century records. Margaret Tobin brought on her marriage to Thomas fitz Richard (MacThomas Geraldine) a dowry of 80 cows, 24 stud mares, five riding-horses, a pair of backgammon tables and a harp, 'besides household goods'. Four years later MacThomas put her away, 'without divorce, aid or consent of Holy Church', and afterwards married another wife, whereupon Margaret's father sued Lord Power, who had gone surety for MacThomas's performance of the marriage contract.[31] This case, like others, shows how real was the need for the reasons addued by Gráinne, for security for the repayment of the dowry, especially the frequency of annulments ('divorces') and the simple repudiation of wives in Gaelic society. In such an eventuality, the wife might find it very difficult to recover her dowry, and several surviving Elizabethan chancery bills are those of divorced wives seeking redress in such cases. Owny (Úna) Mageoghagan brought her husband, also a Mageoghagan, Feagh, a dowry of 18 cows, five work-horses, 24 swine, 24 sheep, a pan worth 20 shillings and an iron griddle with a 'barnis' (trivet), also worth 20 shillings; after their divorce 'according the laws of the church', Feagh and a certain Hugh Mageoghagan (perhaps his father) who had engaged to repay the dowry on such an eventuality failed to do so, and Una and her new husband (yet another Mageoghagan) were forced to sue them, successfully, in chancery (1592).[32]

However, by the late sixteenth century it seems to have been more usual, at least in the areas for which documentation survives, to mortgage land in security for the dowry. Presumably the husband enjoyed the profit of the land during the marriage, the mortgage only coming into effect in the wife's favour on death or divorce, and the whole transaction approximated to the jointure of common law, with the important difference that the land could be redeemed by the husband or his heirs by the repayment of the dowry. In seventeenth century Ireland we can see the one system passing into the other, the change coming latest in the west. In the earliest example known to me we find both sureties and mortgage. This is a deed of 1546, which records that Ulick Ó Bruadair gave a dowry of 21 cows, a bull and three horses with his daughter to Sean mac Donnchadha (MacNamara) for which the latter not only provided sureties for repayment but mortgaged certain lands as well.[33] Slightly earlier but not preserved in a contemporary document is the record that Reamonn mac Maoilir de Burgo gave the lands of *Diseirt Chleircín* (St Cleran's, County Galway) to his wife Syly ní Huag, in mortgage for her dowry (*spré*), and that she retained possession for 30 years until his brother redeemed them.[34] It would seem that a husband could make such a provision by will, as when Melaghlin MacClancy, lord of Dartry in County Leitrim, who died in 1590, provided by his will that his widow should hold his land 'in pawn of her marriage goods, until his heir should redeem it'. Richard O Reilly left his lands of Omard (County Cavan) in mortgage not only to provide dowries to his daughters but also to pay 32 cows and six work-horses to his wife, presumably her dowry.[35] Similar mortgages in security for dowries, or rather redeemable jointures, since they explicitly reserve the husband's life interest, continue in the west well into the seventeenth century.[36] Teig mac William O Kelly of Mullaghmore, last tanist of the O Kellys, settled much of his lands in 1588 on his (second) marriage to Una Ferrall, with condition of redemption on repayment of her large dowry, 120 cows, 20 (or 30) mares with their colts, 'a good chief horse' and 'a big silver cup'.[37] A few other examples of special interest may also be cited. Hugh O Kelly of Clogher, County Galway, received a dowry of 40 cows, eight work-horses and a hackney (riding-horse) with his wife Fionnuala (also an O Kelly), for which he settled lands, with the condition that 'if Fynnawalla die without children by Hugh then her father is to have the just half. And if there be no son but daughters or weak heirs of her begotten, that then [her father] is to have the whole sum of money and is to keep the daughters or weak heirs'.[38] I cannot explain the term 'weak heirs': does it imply sons of doubtful paternity? The rule implied here that in the eventuality of the wife dying childless before her husband half the dowry was to be repaid to her family is also to be found in the very interesting settlement made by John Boey mac William Burke of Annaghkeen (County Galway) in 1620. In return for a dowry of 38 cows of various kinds, three mares, three work-horses and a hackney, he settled his fifth share of the castle of Annaghkeen and the other lands of his sept on the brothers of his wife Sissely, in trust for the repayment of the dowry if she should outlive John, 'And the said Sissely is to be hereby excluded from demaundinge any further dower, joinctur or marriadge'. If she died childless before her husband, then one-third of the dowry was to pay her funeral expenses, another third to be repaid to her family and 'thother third parte to be for the husband in honnor of his marriadge, accordinge the custom and manner of the countrey'.[39] This contract differs from others only in prescribing a fixed proportion to be expended on the funeral, which would include payment for masses for the deceased's soul. A final example of a redeemable marriage settlement, also from County Galway, is that made by Brian mac Carbery Kelly of Moneyveen on the marriage of his eldest son John to Nell Mannin in January 1648/9. In return for her dowry of 40 cows and six mares, he settled half of his lands in jointure on her and his son, with a condition of redemption on the repayment to her of the dowry. If she died childless, her heirs were to hold the settled lands until repaid half the dowry, after deduction of her 'legacy' (bequests to the Church?) and funeral expenses.[40]

But long before the date of these survivals, the typical (irredeemable) jointure of English type, to be enjoyed by the widow during her life, had become established among the Gaelic Irish; first, as might be expected, among those adjacent to the Pale. Awly Magawly of Ballyloughloe, County Westmeath, chief of his name, granted his lands in 1572 to his wife's father and uncle, William and Walter Tuite, in a typical equitable settlement in trust to provide a jointure for her and to raise dowries of £60 each for his daughters. Tadhg Óg Ó Duinn settled lands in jointure in 1583 on his wife Elizabeth FitzGerald, 'in consideration of such somes of money as I have received of my said wiffe's father and other her friends', with an unusual proviso that she might devise the lands to whichever of their sons she thought fit.[41] In 1594 Hugh mac Tertagh Roe O Connor Roe granted lands to trustees as a jointure for his wife Owny (Úna) nyne Teige Oge during her life, 'in consideration of her third part and jointure of all his lands',[42] although this wording does not explicitly exclude the possibility that she was also entitled to the repayment of her dowry. While the redeemable jointure continued in use, as we have seen, for a considerable period, it was clearly on the way out, to be replaced by the standard English-type jointure or marriage settlement which remained general in Ireland, not only among the landed gentry but among ordinary farmers, into the nineteenth century.[43]

It is clear, from the sizes of dowries known to us, that a very large proportion of the portable wealth of the country must have been tied up in them, and was in fact passing in the female line. An impressionistic view would suggest that the size of dowries was increasing during the period in question – a normal progression in dotal systems elsewhere – but the surviving evidence is too scanty to allow this to be established. It would however seem likely in the case of the lesser landowning class that by 1600 the whole farming stock was being provided by the wife in the form of dowry, the husband contributing only the land. Forty cows would seem to have been a normal amount among lesser gentry, and double or triple this amount among minor chiefly families.[44] Forty pounds and upwards seems usual among urban merchants in the period, while Earl Thomas of Ormond, in a will made in 1582, provided dowries of £100 apiece for his nieces and illegitimate daughters.[45] A Limerick fisherman in the 1590s, Thomas O Heryrie, was promised with his wife a dowry of 'three cows and three heifers, 21 sheep, a brass pan worth 40 shillings, two pairs of sheets (worth 40 shillings), a bushel of beare (winter barley) and 3 shillings in money'.[46] Given the size of the amount required, it is not surprising that it was common for dowries to be raised by a subscription among friends and relations, as we are told happened in the case of Margaret Tobin, mentioned above, and as Sir Henry Piers tells us was the general custom in his time, the late seventeenth century.[47] It was probably by an extension of this custom that the sixteenth century Irish lords solved the problem of raising their daughters' dowries by assessing them on their subjects. This is in fact implied by the words of the 1576 County Cork Presentment which says that this imposition was taken by the lords, 'some by way of petition, which the freeholders dare not deny, and some by compulsion'. The practice was general among the Munster lords, but not confined to them. An inquisition of 1587 found that the MacNamaras 'had always towards the marriage of every of their daughters upon the whole barony [of Bunratty] six score cows', and another inquisition of 1607 that O Flaherty of Connamara received by custom a 2-year-old heifer from every inhabited quarter of land towards the dowry of any of his daughters.[48] This raising of dowries for the lord's daughters by assessing them on the country was also found in the Highlands, where it was practised by the sixteenth century Campbells of Glenorchy.[49] A different form of fiscal exploitation, but also arising from the importance of the dowry in financial terms, was that of the Ulster bishops, who levied a tax upon dowries of 4d for every cow.[50] At the old value of 6s 8d for the 'legal' or notional cow which probably prevailed when it was fixed, this would have represented 5% *ad valorem*, although the proportion would have fallen with the inflation of the late sixteenth century.

By native Irish law and custom a woman could not inherit the hereditary land of her clan, and even in early Ireland, where a daughter was in some cases permitted to inherit, this was only for her lifetime, the land reverting on her death to the agnatic patrilineage instead of passing to her children.[51] I have found no trace of such a practice in late medieval times, although its existence cannot be altogether ruled out. In Elizabethan days the Irish Court of Chancery set itself against the rule which excluded women from inheritance, affirming the right of daughters to inherit in the absence of sons.[52] Presumably as the result of some such intervention the whole inheritance of the O Molloys of Broughal, County Offaly, passed in this period through an heiress to the marcher family of Bermingham.[53] But apart from this changing situation brought about by the introduction of English legal ideas, it is clear that a woman or her husband could be granted lands by her father or kindred in mortgage for the amount required for her dowry. Richard O Reilly of Omard, as we have seen, devised his lands in mortgage by will, not only for the repayment of his wife's dowry but for the provision of dowries for his two daughters – 40 cows and four work-horses apiece. In 1607 the O Doyne inquisition records that 'Sheelie neene Doine and her husband have certain lands in their hands until her marriage goods be paid'. A chancery pleading of 1622, referring to lands in County Galway, says that the owner some 50 years earlier, 'for that he had no other marriage goods to bestow on his daughter Mary ny Madden granted to [her] and her heirs for ever in consideration of her preferment the two acres of land'.[54]

The English common law in force in the Pale enforced the inheritance of daughters in the absence of sons, but in practice this was obviated by the use of entails, and actual instances of its occurrence are few and far between. Two fifteenth and sixteenth century Plunket lords of Killeen, and two sixteenth century St Lawrence lords of Howth left only daughters, but in every case the inheritance passed intact, with the title, to a brother. Only in the case of a weak or declining lineage, or where agnatic heirs had totally failed, would a daughter be permitted to bring the inheritance into another surname. The Rathaldron estate in County Meath passed to Michael Cusack with the heiress of the Dexters in the middle of the century,[55] but here the male line would seem to have totally failed. Siddan, County Meath, passed with an heiress from its ancient lords, the Telings, on the extinction of the immediate male line, although a collateral line, the Telings of Mullagha, survived. One might query whether this would have happened if the heiress had not been married in succession to two members of the family of the overlord, Lord Slane, and it would seem that another potential heiress, her cousin, married to an insignificant husband, had been already passed over.[56] The urge to keep lands in the surname was already strong among the Irish Anglo-Normans in the late thirteenth century,[57] and was manifested in the profusion of entails to agnatic heirs which we find from that period onwards. In early fifteenth century Louth the sonless Sir Bartholomew de Verdon could declare that 'as long as there is anyone bearing the name of the nation of Verdon, no daughter of his should have any of his lands'.[58] Even in the towns we find it said in 1527 that 'according to the custom and ordinance of the nation of Blake' (in Galway and Athenry) a woman could not inherit.[59] But even after the introduction of English rules of succession, when we find even Gaelic property passing to heiresses (as the case with the lands of Tadhg Ó Briain of Smithstown, a son of the first earl of Thomond),[60] it is clear that there could be strong pressure on female heirs to release their claims to the agnatic male heirs. This occurred in the well-known case of the O Callaghans, where Manus O Keefe, heir by English law through his mother, released his rights to the nearest (but illegitimate) male heir, Cahir Modartha O Callaghan.[61] There are many other examples. An interesting case is that of Mary ny Nicholas (FitzGerald) of Kilmurry, County Kerry, who recovered before the Plantation Commissioners in 1592 the lands which had belonged to her father and which, apparently, had gone on his death to the collateral heir male, Thomas fitz David of Ardnagragh, who had been slain in the Desmond rebellion. Mary was successful in her claim, but she had already conveyed the land to Thomas's young grandson, David fitz Thomas Oge, and so this portion of the family inheritance remained with the FitzGeralds.[62]

The Irish townswoman of the period has been rather neglected in this essay. One has the impression that she played a lesser role in public and economic life than her sister in the Gaelic and Gaelicised regions, perhaps a natural reflection of the nature of urban life. The Irish port towns, however (like merchant communities everywhere), had many rich widows, and the surviving evidence shows large quantities of portable wealth in their hands.[63] Again, the role of women as tenants and land exploiters by lease, evident from the surviving evidence, has not been touched on. We have seen that married women acquired land; no doubt widows did the same, but land acquisition could take the form of large-scale tenancy as well as of mortgage and outright purchase. With the warning that this essay has left these and no doubt many other aspects of the relationship between Irishwomen and property in the period unexplored, I will conclude.

REFERENCES

1. F. Bickley (ed.), *Report on the Manuscripts of the Late Reginald Rawdon Hastings . . .* (vols II–IV, Historical Manuscripts Commission, London, 1930–47), Vol. IV, p. 153. For the background to this legislation by judicial pronouncement see H. Pawlisch, *Sir John Davies and the Conquest of Ireland: a study in legal imperialism* (Cambridge, 1985), p. 69.
2. Sir F. Pollock and F.W. Maitland, *The History of English Law Before the Time of Edward I* (2nd edn, Cambridge, 1968), Vol. II, pp. 348–56, and now, especially, Amy Louise Erickson 'Common Law versus common practice: the use of marriage settlements in early modern England', *Econ. Hist. Rev.* 43 (1990), 21–39.
3. *Ibid.*, pp. 420–8. For jointures and marriage settlements see J.P. Cooper, 'Patterns of Inheritance and Settlement by Great Landowners from the Fifteenth to the Eighteenth Centuries' in J. Goody, J. Thirsk and E.P. Thompson (eds), *Family and Inheritance: Rural Society in Western Europe, 1200–1800* (Cambridge, 1976), pp. 192–327; B. English and J. Saville, *Strict Settlement: A Guide for Historians* (Hull, 1983); Erickson, *op. cit.*
4. Ireland 7 William III c. 6. S. 10 of this statute abolished the *legitim* (as it was technically known) of wife and children. For the deduction of debts and funeral expenses see the following reference.
5. Public Record Office of Ireland, Salved Chancery Pleadings (hereafter cited as P.R.O.I., C.P.), C. 72.
6. *Ibid.*, C. 41; *Twenty-ninth Report of the Deputy Keeper of the Public Records in Ireland* (Dublin, 1897), Appendix 49.
7. *Calendar of State Papers, Ireland, 1592–96*, pp. 133, 135. It was 'against the custom of Ireland for the wives to have any more after the death of their husbands than they brought with them'.
8. For the influence of Roman law on native Irish law in this period see the remarks of Sussex (*Calendar of Carew MSS, 1509–74*, p. 331) and of Conall Mageoghagan (D. Murphy (ed.), *The Annals of Clonmacnoise From the Earliest Period to A.D. 1408, Translated into English by Conell Mageoghegan, A.D. 1627* (Dublin, 1896), p. 280), and (for actual practice) *Calendar of Carew MSS, 1603–24*, pp. 30–31).
9. F. Kelly, *A Guide to Early Irish Law* (Dublin, 1988), pp. 75–6.
10. For women as witnesses see e.g. K. Nicholls 'Gaelic Landowner-

ship in Tipperary in the Light of the Surviving Irish Deeds' in W. Nolan (ed.), *Tipperary: History and Society* (Dublin, 1985), p. 94. Women occur commonly as witnesses in surviving notarial instruments recording depositions e.g. those in the Ormond Deeds and in the Power archives (in possession of the Marquis of Waterford).

11. E.g. E. Curtis (ed.), *Calendar of Ormond Deeds, 1172–1603* (6 vols, Irish Manuscripts Commission, Dublin, 1932–43), Vol IV pp. 1509–47, no. 347; G. MacNiocaill (ed.), Archives in *Analecta Hibernica*, Vol. 26 (1970), pp. 62–5.

12. N.L.I.D. 3123= National Library of Ireland *Calendar of Ormond Deeds, 1584–1603*, no. 37. Giles or Sile Butler was a natural daughter of James, Earl of Ormond (Butler genealogy in Lambeth Palace, MS 626). For her and Brian O Kennedy see P.R.O.I., C.P., E. 170.

13. Public Record Office, London (hereafter cited as P.R.O.), S.P. 46/90, f. 33.

14. P.R.O.I., C.P., C. 124.

15. H.F. Hore and J. Graves (eds), *The Social State of the Southern and Eastern Counties of Ireland in the Sixteenth century . . .* (Annuary of the Royal Historical and Archaeological Association of Ireland for 1868–9), pp. 134, 192.

16. Trinity College Dublin, MS F.2.1 (808), f. 36.

17. W.F. Butler, *Gleanings from Irish History* (London, 1925), pp. 21, 34–5; *Calendar of State Papers Ireland 1588–92*, pp. 384–5; Inquisition, 22 March 1591/2 (P.R.O.I., R.C. 9/14).

18. National Library of Ireland 2174= *Calendar of Ormond Deeds, 1509–47*, no. 151. The grant was, however, conditional on her maintaining 'fidelity and friendship' towards his grandson and heir James, a reflection of the forthcoming struggle for the succession which he must have foreseen.

19. National Library of Ireland, D. 1999 (2), very badly calendared in *Calendar of Ormond Deeds, 1509–47*, no. 16 (2).

20. References are given, and conveniently summarised, in D. Fitzpatrick, 'Divorce and Separation in Modern Irish History' in *Past and Present*, 114 (1987), pp. 178–80, though it need hardly be said that not all will be convinced by Dr Fitzpatrick's argument that the dotal system was a principal, if not *the* principal, cause for the rejection of divorce in modern Ireland.

21. See K. Nicholls, 'The introduction of dotal marriage in late medieval Ireland' (forthcoming).

22. See in general D.O. Hughes, 'From Brideprice to Dowry in Mediterranean Europe' in *Journal of Family History*, Vol. 3 (1978), pp. 262–95.

23. M.H.B. Sanderson, *Cardinal of Scotland: David Beaton, c. 1494–1546* (Edinburgh, 1986), pp. 34–91; *Mary Stewart's People* (Edinburgh, 1987), pp. 3–21.

24. M.K. Simms, 'The Legal Position of Irishwomen in the Later Middle Ages' in *Irish Jurist*, Vol. 10 (1975), p. 102.

25. See e.g. M.J. Blake (ed.), *Blake Family Records, 2nd Series, 1600–1700* (London, 1905), p. 23.

26. See note 9 above.

27. The fullest account of the dotal system, from the point of view of a canonist and moral theologian, is that by M. Bonacina in *Opera Omnia* (Antwerp, 1632), Vol. II, pp. 225–8, 418–9, 477–93.

28. K.W. Nicholls (ed.), 'The Lynch Blosse Papers' in *Analecta Hibernica*, Vol. 29 (1980), pp. 29, 143.

29. See on this Thomas Sanchez, S.J., *De Sancto Matrimonii Sacramento Disputationum tomi tres* (Lyons, 1637), Vol. iii, pp. 183–5. Cf. Fitzpatrick, *op. cit.*, p. 178.

30. *Calendar of State Papers Ireland, 1592–96*, p. 135.

31. *Calendar of Patent and Close Rolls of Chancery in Ireland Elizabeth, 19 Year to End of Reign* (Dublin, 1862), pp. 507–8.

32. P.R.O.I., C.P., J. 166; P.R.O.I., R.C. 6/1, p. 222. For similar cases see P.R.O.I., C.P., C. 55; D. 67; G. 10.

33. J. Hardiman (ed.), 'Ancient Irish Deeds and Writings' in *Royal Irish Academy Transactions*, Vol. 15 (1828), pp. 68–9. Hardiman's translation by a *lapsus calami*, in one place has 'John' for 'Ulick'.

34. Royal Irish Academy, MS C iii 3, f. 103v.

35. K.W. Nicholls (ed.), 'Some Documents on Irish Law and Custom in the Sixteenth Century' in *Analecta Hibernica*, Vol. 26 (1970), pp. 122–3. John O'Donovan (ed.) *Miscellany of the Celtic Society* (Dublin, 1849), 85.

36. For further examples see J. Hardiman, 'A Statute . . . Enacted in a Parliament Held at Kilkenny' in *Tracts Relating to Ireland* (Irish Archaeological Society, Dublin, 1843), Vol. II, p. 53n; M.J. Blake, *op. cit.*, pp. 22–3.

37. P.R.O.I., R.C. 10/5, p. 59; Inquisition, 7 January 1615/16 in P.R.O.I., R.C., 9/14.

38. P.R.O.I., R.C. 10/5, p. 41. In the event Hugh and Fionnuala had only five daughters. On his deathbed Hugh granted the lands to his brother John, on condition that he paid over the same sum to Hugh's eldest daughter, Banowan (although Fionnuala was still living) (*ibid.*, p. 46); cf. inquisition, 8 January 1615/16 in P.R.O.I., R.C. 9/14.

39. National Library of Ireland, D. 26,861.

40. P.R.O.I. (Bellew MSS), 1121/1/2, pp. 19–20, 28. The same rule is to be found in a marriage settlement of 1629, in the MacDermot MSS, Coolavin, Co. Sligo.

41. P.R.O.I., R.C. 5/11, p. 237; K.W. Nicholls (ed.), *The O Doyne (O Duinn) Manuscript* (Irish Manuscripts Commission, Dublin, 1983), pp. 25–6.

42. P.R.O., C. 106/153, Box 2 (unsorted collection). A settlement alleged to have been made by Sir Hubert Boy Burke of Glinsk, 'MacDavid', on 15 May 1589 (P.R.O.I., R.C. 10/5, p. 33) included a jointure for his wife, but this deed was afterwards impugned (probably tendentiously) as a forgery (P.R.O.I., C.P., AA.72).

43. For marriage settlements and jointures among the Irish upper classes see A.P.W. Malcomson, *The Pursuit of the Heiress: Aristocratic Marriage in Ireland, 1750–1820* (Belfast, 1982). There is no general study of the strict settlement in Ireland, but I have seen even 21- and 31-year farming leases made the subject of marriage settlements. The fact that marriage settlements and jointures were regarded as 'discoverable' interests under the penal laws against Catholic landholding, and so liable to forfeiture, was perhaps the severest aspect of that legislation.

44. For other examples, besides those quoted or referred to in notes see *Analecta Hibernica*, Vol. 15 (1944), p. 336; *ibid.*, Vol. 20, p. 92. *Calendar of Patent Rolls of Ireland, Elizabeth*, p. 451.

45. *Calendar of Ormond Deeds, 1547–1584*, p. 118; Richard Caulfield (ed.), 'Wills and Inventories, Cork, *temp.* Elizabeth' in *Gentleman's*

Magazine, July 1861, pp. 34–5; September 1861, p. 257; April 1862, pp. 443–4.

46. P.R.O.I., C.P. A. 249. The Limerick bushel was a measure equivalent to three Bristol barrels, or 126 gallons (*ibid.*, B. 309).

47. *Calendar of Patent Rolls of Ireland, Elizabeth*, pp. 507–8; cf. 'An Irish Achivist' (J.T. Gilbert), *On the History, Position and Treatment of the Public Records of Ireland* (2nd edn, London, 1864), p. 53. However, the 'colp' given towards the dowry was certainly a heifer (*colpach*).

48. Hore and Graves, *The Social State of the Southern and Eastern Counties . . .*, pp. 188, 233, 271–2; *Calendar of Ormond Deeds, 1509–47*, p. 215; W.F.T. Butler, *Gleanings From Irish History*, pp. 131, 188, note 70; inquisition, 27 January 1587/8 (P.R.O.I., R.C. 9/14); Hardiman, 'A statute . . .', p. 113n.

49. I owe this information to Dr Martin McGregor.

50. A.F. O'D. Alexander (ed.), 'The O'Kane Papers' in *Analecta Hibernica*, Vol. 12 (1943), p. 81.

51. Kelly, *A Guide to Early Irish Law*, pp. 104–5.

52. Nicholls, 'Some Documents . . .', pp. 107–8, 117–22. The decree given on 25 April 1589 in favour of Anabel Dillon (P.R.O.I., R.C. 6/1, p. 191; her bill is P.R.O.I., C.P., C. 57), must be one of the examples referred to in the quotation there given.

53. *Calendar of Patent Rolls of Ireland, Elizabeth*, p. 452. Cf. P.R.O.I., C.P. B. 20, E. 149, 151.

54. Nicholls, *The O Doyne Manuscript*, p. 20; 'Some Documents . . .', pp. 122–3. There are several other examples known to me.

55. H. Gallwey, 'The Cusack Family of Counties Meath and Dublin' in *Irish Genealogist*, Vol. 6/3 (1982), p. 287.

56. Compare Trinity College, Dublin, MS E. 3.2 (1212), pp. 23, 38 with Lambeth Palace, MS 635, f. 6. The heiress Elizabeth or Beale (Isabel) Teling was married first to Edward Fleming, a grandson of Lord Slane, by whom she was ancestress to the later Flemings of Siddan, and afterwards to Thomas Fleming, who held Siddan for a long period in her right. An attempt to entail the lands on the heir male, Thomas Teling of Mullagha, appears to have failed.

57. A.J. Otway Ruthven, *A History of Medieval Ireland* (London and New York, 1968), pp. 106–17.

58. Public Record Office of Northern Ireland, Armagh Archepiscopal Registers, Reg. Prene, Vol. iii, f. 35.

59. M.J. Blake (ed.), *Blake Family Records: 1300 to 1600* (London, 1902), pp. 63–4.

60. G. MacNiocaill (ed.), 'Seven Irish Documents from the Inchiquin Archives', pp. 52–9.

61. Pawlisch, *Sir John Davies*, p. 83; P.R.O.I., R.C. 5/7, p. 275.

62. P.R.O., S.P., 63/168/10; *Irish Patent Rolls of James I: Facsimile of the Irish Record Commissioners' Calendar Prepared Prior to 1830*, with foreword by M.C. Griffith (Irish Manuscripts Commission, Dublin, 1966), p. 567; genealogy of the Ardnagragh sept in Lambeth Palace, MS 635.

63. Much information on the economic status of townswomen can be found in the surviving Salved Chancery Pleadings in the P.R.O.I. (especially with regard to Dublin); cf. also the 'Wills and Inventories, Cork *temp.* Elizabeth', calendared by Richard Caulfield in the *Gentleman's Magazine*, May 1861 to September 1862.

2

Women in Gaelic Society
during the Age of Transition

KATHARINE SIMMS

I

The three great experiences which transformed Irish society during the sixteenth century, the Renaissance, the Reformation/ Counter-Reformation and the Tudor reconquest brought the same influences to bear on the lives of women as men, but due to their differing circumstances the effects were not always identical. Education is a case in point. Whereas the later Middle Ages saw the emergence of a literate laity, lay scholars were to be the hallmark of the sixteenth century northern European Renaissance. Earlier the overwhelming majority of distinguished writers and thinkers were churchmen, or very occasionally church women like the nun Hrotswitha (c. 935–75), the abbess Héloise (ob. c. 1164), or Mother Julian of Norwich (1342–1416/23), the anchorite and mystic. Gaelic Ireland possessed a further dimension in the wealth of vernacular learning cultivated by the hereditary bardic families of poets, historians, judges and physicians, a class midway between clerics and laymen, a tightly knit group of professionals who were often church tenants, and sometimes themselves ordained.[1] Their schools had no place for female pupils, and the scantily recorded nunneries of Ireland[2] produced no exponents of Latin scholarship. Consequently the spread of learning to members of the lay aristocracy, both men and women, in the early modern period had greater novelty in the case of the women.

There are hints that women had not always been excluded from the upper echelons of the bardic orders: for instance the notice in the Annals of Inisfallen of the death in 934 of Uallaige daughter of Muinechán, 'poetess of Ireland', or allusions in the literature to legendary or fictitious figures such as the poetess Liadán, who abandoned the poet Cuirithir to become a nun[3] and Feidelm the poetess of Connacht who encounters Queen Medb in the Old Irish saga *Táin Bó Cuailnge* while on her way back 'from Albion after learning the art of *filidecht*' (or poetry).[4] However it appears

that from about the eighth century onwards a distinction grew
up in the poetic order between the honoured ranks of the *filid*
who were distinguished by book-learning, and the humbler
bards, who were illiterate.[5] Since the monastic schools had a
monopoly of book-learning in early Ireland, it was inappropriate
for women to receive the more advanced training, and in this
respect the secular schools of post-Norman Ireland seem to have
followed the example of their monastic predecessors. The Middle
Irish retelling of the *Táin Bó Cuailgne* found in the twelfth century
Book of Leinster describes Feidelm as a bondmaid and prophetess
(*banchumal, banfáid*) with no reference to her learning.[6] Similarly
in bardic poetry of the thirteenth and fourteenth centuries there
are derogatory references to women fortune-tellers, *mná mana*,[7]
and to women balladeers, who composed the popular *abhrán*
verse in praise of the Irish nobility in return for food and lodging:

> Their prizes, namely the getting of food by means of their
> doggerel(?), are their very nature; there is a great demand
> for their wares, they seek not gold or kine.[8]

The early sixteenth century Scottish Book of the Dean of Lismore,
among other miscellaneous pieces of medieval Gaelic verse,
contains a poem of 'hates', in which 'a poet-band that includes a
woman' is considered as detestable as 'sadness in a drinking
house' or 'a host that would make no foray'.[9]

The medieval Irish scholars who so heartily despised such
uneducated women entertainers were organised into hereditary
professions and consequently had womenfolk of their own.
There are 44 entries in the post-Norman annals concerning female
members of clerical or bardic families. Seven of these simply
name daughters of important men without reference to their
husbands,[10] but there was a tendency for the daughter of one
learned man to marry another, particularly noticeable with the
poetic family of O hUiginn and the O Duibhgeannáin historians.[11]
The wife – or in the case of a clerical household, the concubine –
of a scholar had an honoured role in Gaelic society, but earned
the annalists' admiration by a display not of learning but of piety
and hospitality, particularly towards the learned classes themselves. In 1437 Gormlaith, daughter of the *ollamh* of history David
O Duibhgeannáin and widow of the *ollamh* of law Brian Mac
Aodhagáin, ended her days as an anchoritess with the Premon-
stratensian Canons on Trinity Island, Lough Key.[12] We find
Sadhbh, wife of the historian Maoilín O Maolchonaire, styled
'lady professor' apparently with the same force as the modern
'lady mayoress': 'Banollamh of Silmuiredhy fitz ffeargus and a
nurse to all guests and strangers and of all the learned men in
Ireland'.[13] Fionnghuala, wife of the historian, poet and erenagh,

Fearghal Muimhneach O Duibhgeannáin, is somewhat enigmati-
cally described as 'the woman who was the best that was in
Ireland in her own sphere [or "profession", *re cerd féin*] as the wife
of a learned man'.[14] This social equality combined with an
absence of intellectual activity is epitomised in a series of
proverbs compiled by some Gaelic man of learning at the end of
the medieval period:

> Marry a wife who is your equal – Silence in woman is an
> excellent thing since it is by not speaking that good manners
> and discretion are recognized in every one; for if a fool kept
> silence it would be a sign that he was clever – Do not keep
> company with a woman unless necessity or folly drive you
> to it – Let your gift be suited to those upon whom you bestow
> it, that is, not useless as a weapon to a woman, or a book to
> a clown and the like.[15]

At least this last saying does not imply that women are of
necessity illiterate, and while no women of the bardic families
were employed as scribes on the medieval manuscripts, it is
possible that some of them could read and write. For instance
in a sixteenth century compilation of brehon law the scribe
Domhnall wrote in the margin one day:

> My curse, and God's into the bargain, I bestow on the
> women that have muddled up together all that I possessed
> in the way of ink, of colours, and of books. God's curse on
> him too that shall read this and fail to curse them (the
> women). My God, this is a wretched business. Ochone for it!

In reply to his criticism, another hand has written on the
following page: 'I'm not the woman, Domhnall'.[16] However since
this exchange took place in the mid-sixteenth century, this
apparent example of female literacy may simply reflect the
improved education of most gentlewomen at this later period
rather than any peculiar advantage attached to membership of a
learned family. Outside Ireland some sixteenth century women
such as the daughters of Sir Thomas More, Lady Jane Grey and
the Princess Elizabeth underwent quite gruelling intellectual
training, but even the less academic Mary Queen of Scots
produced French verses of some merit. In the Gaelic world the
earliest women authors are found in western Scotland where the
great lords enjoyed a closer contact with the royal court at
Edinburgh than the Irish chieftains had with the courts of either
London or even Dublin. The Book of the Dean of Lismore
contains three short poems in Gaelic by the late fifteenth century
Isabella, Countess of Argyle, two of them love poems and the
third an obscene satire on her chaplain's penis.[17] A more striking
piece in the same collection is the elegy composed by Aiffric

McCorqudale for her husband Niall Og MacNeill, Constable of Castle Sween (*fl.* 1455–72). It is in syllabic metre, *óglachas* of *rannaigheacht mhór*, and though simpler and more sincere, resembles the formal elegies of the professional bard rather than the *extempore* lament of the keening woman.[18]

Women from this cultivated circle of Gaelic-speaking aristocrats associated with the earls of Argyle married Irish chieftains and came to live in Ulster, where their superior standard of education attracted some attention. The Lady Agnes Campbell's first husband was James MacDonnell, Lord of the Isles (1545–65), who had been brought up at the Scottish court in his youth and was consequently the only member of his family who knew how to write. When he was defeated and killed by Shane O'Neill, Lady Agnes avoided a threatened marriage with the victor, eventually bestowing her hand on Turlough Luineach, Shane's successor as the Great O'Neill of Tyrone, bringing with her a dowry of some 1200 Scottish mercenary troops. In 1575 the English lord deputy, Sir Henry Sidney, professed himself deeply impressed with Lady Agnes' wisdom and address.[19] The Calbhach O'Donnell (+1566) married the widowed Countess of Argyle, a daughter of MacClean 'noted for her wisdom and sobriety, a good French scholar with a knowledge of Latin and a smattering of Italian', who was to prove more susceptible to the charms of Shane O'Neill than Lady Agnes had been. In 1561 she betrayed her husband into his clutches and subsequently suffered rape and over 2 years imprisonment at O'Neill's hands.[20]

Evidence of an improved standard of education for Irish-born ladies is not plentiful and tends to be later in date. The Maguire chieftains of Fermanagh, Cúchonnacht (+1589) and his son Cúchonnacht Og prided themselves not only on their appreciation of Gaelic literature but on their powers of composition. The father's vanity was pandered to by more than one professional eulogist:

> you explained a line which you had made about visiting poets; you know their art so well that you are not too severe with them.
>
> You excelled the knowledge of every poet when you attempted exegesis . . . It is hard for Ulster to support all the poets you have trained.[21]

The son, Cúchonnacht Og, addressed a conventional love poem to Brigid FitzGerald, daughter of Henry, 12th Earl of Kildare, presumably around the time of her marriage to Rudhraighe O'Donnell, Early of Tyrconnell, *c.* 1604,[22] claiming to speak as a disembodied spirit since he has been slain by the angelic vision of her beauty, and ending with a riddling stanza containing his first name. The poem was in faultless, ornamented *dán díreach* and evoked a verse reply which has been attributed to Bridget herself reproaching Cúchonnacht with dishonesty. If he had addressed her with inept, amateur verse (*dán bog*) like everyone else, he would have made a better impression, but this poem was clearly the work of a professional such as Fearghal Óg Mac an Bhaird or Eochaidh O hEoghusa.[23] Indeed the Book of O'Conor Don was subsequently to cite Eochaidh O hEoghusa as the true author of Cúchonnacht's poem.[24] Brigid's reply is composed in an amateur's metre, *óglachas* of *rannaigheacht mhór*, so that the simple but witty lines could well have been her own work – indeed much of the point of the reproach to Cúchonnacht would have been lost if someone else had ghosted this composition also.

From about the same period we have an indignant poem by Tadhg Mac Dáire, bard to Donnchadh O'Brien, 4th Earl of Thomond, and an eminent though controversial teacher of history,[25] whose account of the Burke pedigree had apparently been criticised by Síle daughter of Eamonn Burke. In a back-handed way his words suggest that Síle had received, or claimed to have received, some education:

> Twas to test or attack or anger me that thou, O gentle face, didst ask me that guileful question – no puzzling one for me
> . . .
> Thou art not to blame for thy ignorance; thy teachers bear the blame, O waving hair, queen of peace in the Breagha's soft Isle.
> Sensible is thy speech, vigorous and frank thy judgement, but thou hast not known learned men, O thick hair and bright brown graceful cheek.[26]

Whatever the real extent of both these ladies' accomplishments, it is clear that they saw themselves and were seen by others as entitled to a more active role in intellectual matters than the medieval one of perfect hostess to the men of art, lavishly rewarding the most indifferent compositions of the professional poets.[27] In the seventeenth and eighteenth centuries the oral tradition of the women balladeers and keeners merged with the improved education of the ladies to produce texts such as the stressed verse compositions of Caitlín Dubh for the O'Briens' circle[28] and the *Caoineadh Airt Uí Laoghaire* of Eibhlín Dubh Ní Chonaill.[29]

II

The changes in institutions and social attitudes brought about by the religious convulsions of the sixteenth century had particular implications for the position of women in Gaelic society. In medieval times the canon law of the church had provided a court of appeal for wives too lightly divorced by their husbands under the secular customs of brehon law.[30] Yet it was not until the religious revival associated with the Franciscan Observantines was fully under way that customary practices of multiple marriages, divorce at will and concubinage were seriously challenged within this society, most notably in the case of Maghnus O'Donnell's alliance with the friars of Donegal against his father's concubine.[31] MacCon O'Clery (+1595), poet and historian to Aodh son of Maghnus O'Donnell, is described in the Annals of the Four Masters as 'pious, devout, religious and charitable', but in a poem composed on his deathbed he expressed confidence that the divorce of his wife was no offence to God – the creator of Eve would still receive him in heaven. The lady had obtained a 'bull' confirming the validity of her marriage from the Protestant Archbishop of Armagh, Adam Loftus, but the poet rejected the moral authority of such a bull, not made in Rome.[32] His startlingly savage vituperation of his ex-wife indicates that the divorce in this case had personal grounds rather than being the outcome of economic or political convenience as often appeared to be the case with the chieftains' marital arrangements.

The confusion and overlap this poem shows between the jurisdiction of the Protestant primate and the Pope in Rome was typical of the Elizabethan period and was redoubled over the question of clerical celibacy. In the fifteenth century the recruitment of diocesan clergy from the hereditary tenants of church land often resulted in the clerical profession itself becoming hereditary, with clerical concubines enjoying a status equivalent to wives as for instance 'Joan, daughter of the bishop MacCathmhail, wife of Maurice Mag Uidhir, that is, of the Great Archdeacon (of Clogher)' who died in 1427.[33] The Protestant Reformation in theory allowed these women to enjoy official marital status, while the Counter-Reformation introduced a new hostility and contempt for them. Miler Magrath, traditionally reputed the handsomest man in Ireland in his day, was a member of a hereditary clerical family in Clogher diocese who began his career as a Franciscan friar and Catholic Bishop of Down and Connor. He changed his allegiance, however, and after becoming Protestant Bishop of Clogher in 1570 and Archbishop of Cashel in 1571, married Ann O'Meara and had a family of five sons and two daughters. A long, stinging satirical poem against him composed by the friar Eoghan or Eugene O'Duffy about 1572 plays on Miler's name 'Maol Mhuire' or 'servant of Mary', to call him 'not servant of Mary but servant of Ann', who deserted the portals of God and Mary for the portal of Ann and the devil. He and his wife will descend side by side into eternal flames. The Catholic historian Dom Philip O'Sullevan Beare makes much of the mental agonies endured by Miler's wife who is otherwise known to have remained Catholic in her sympathies:

> The same woman, asked by Miler why she wept: 'Because,' said she, 'Eugene who was with me to-day, assured me by strong proof and many holy testimonies that I would be condemned to hell if I should die in this state of being your wife, and I am frightened and cannot help crying lest this be true'. 'Indeed' said Miler, 'if you hope otherwise your hope will lead you much astray, and not for the possibility but for the reality, should you fret.'
> Not long after Anna died consumed by grief.

Clearly this is a biased source, but the self-doubting epitaph Miler caused to be carved on his own tomb at Cashel suggests the anecdote may have been true enough in spirit if not in fact.[34]

Miler's earlier vocation as a Franciscan friar left him and his wife particularly exposed to criticism. No such disapproval is expressed by the compiler of the Annals of Loch Cé of his kinswoman, Beanmhumhan Og Ní Dhuibhgheannáin, who in 1599 erected a tomb of carved stone in memory of her husband (*a fir posta*), the vicar Eoghan MacDomhnaill. Here the hereditary church families of the fourteenth and fifteenth centuries seem to have transferred their attitudes intact into the new Protestant establishment.

III

The political conquest of Ireland in the course of the sixteenth and early seventeenth centuries touched the lives of women in two main ways. The customary law of Gaelic Ireland which allowed wives to retain considerable control over their marriage portions meant that those brides whose dowries consisted of troops and ships inevitably took an active role in military and political events: women such as Gráinne, daughter of O'Malley (Granuaile),[35] Lady Agnes Campbell mentioned above and her daughter Fionuala MacDonnell, 'Inghean Dubh' ('Dark Maiden'), described as 'the head of advice and counsel of the Cenél Conaill' with 'the heart of a hero and the mind of a soldier'.[36] The poet Tadhg Dall O hUiginn rather misleadingly characterised her as a peacemaker:

> In any province where that woman is, none dare to talk of strife; the land of Fionntan has shown(?) that she has curbed the race of Conall.
> Until the daughter of James came to us, and until the land

of regia became subdued to her will, we would not keep peace with the rest for the twinkling of an eye.

From the time that she came across the sea the race of Dálach, on account of the queen of Cobha's pure plain, do not remember in their hearts the offences of others.[37]

However Lughaidh O'Clery, the biographer of her son Aodh Ruadh O'Donnell, said of her 'she exhorted in every way each one that she was acquainted with, and her husband especially to avenge his injuries and wrongs on each one according to his deserts'.[38]

The majority of women in Gaelic society were less actively involved in the momentous changes taking place. The conquest affected them most directly with the nationwide imposition of common law relating to landed possessions, as Kenneth Nicholls's contribution to this volume indicates. Also of some importance was the requirement of common law that heirs should be born after the canonically valid marriage of their parents, which revolutionised marriage patterns among the prop-ertied classes of rural Ireland more effectively than either the Reformation or Counter-Reformation. The degree of confusion which reigned during the period of transition is well demon-strated in the objections raised by Charles O'Doyne to the royal fiant drawn up by the Attorney-General in 1608 granting the country of Iregan to be held by his elder brother and chief, Tadhg or Thady O'Doyne, 'his heyres and assignes':

That the said Thadye his eldest sonn Teig Reoghe, sonn to Margarett daughter to Shane O Neyle and mother to Coconnaght oge McGuyer, deade beyond the seas, is not a fitt ruler over so stronge a Contrye and so fitt for rebellion as Iregaine . . . That the said Margarett mother to the said Teig Reoghe and the gentlewoman nowe kept by the said Thadie in his howse and by whome he hath many sones beinge both alive, the issue begotten by the venter of one of them is illegitimate.[39]

Even the highly educated and litigious Charles O'Doyne was not prepared to state which of his brother's unions was the illegitimate one, and the ambiguity was not solved by Thady's reply:

To the 9th the defendant will not denie but that the said Teig Reogh did mightilie forgett himself . . . and withall . . . amended the same then after with good service . . . And whether he shalbe the defendant his heyre or not God knoweth.

To the 10th he saieth that he kepeth his lawfull wife in his house notwithstanding the complainants slanderous speeches. And let not the Complainant take any greate care howe the defendant shall dispose his inheritans but let him assure himselfe that none shall e(n)ioye the same by discent or conveyance from the defendant but the most legitimate and that shalbe most faithful to his Prince.[40]

The uncertainty as to the true position involuntarily shown by both brothers in this dispute matches the self-doubt attributed to Miler Magrath and his wife and the outrage felt by the poet-historian Tadhg Mac Dáire when his monopoly of learning was challenged by Síle Burke. For the whole of Gaelic society the transition from the Middle Ages to the early modern world of western Europe in the seventeenth century was a violent and confusing experience, painful because of the rapidity with which change was in most cases imposed from outside. While this brief glance at the implications the transition held for women confirms the existence of much bewilderment, it also shows, as is further borne out by Kenneth Nicholls's detailed study of Irish women and property, that Gaelic Ireland was experiencing internal change leading in much the same direction, though at a slower pace. However the speed with which the transformation was pushed through at government level made it almost impossible for the ruling classes of Gaelic Ireland to adapt in time to survive, and the interests of the planter class did not lie in encouraging such adaptation. Again the experience of the women in old aristocratic families was rather different. Jointures, settlements and even government pensions might cushion them from the political and economic disasters suffered by their menfolk,[41] and in some cases the widows or daughters of Gaelic landowners married their English successors.[42] Some of them, therefore, survived economically in the new Ireland, but the Gaelic world from which they came had perished.

REFERENCES

1. P. MacCana, 'The Rise of the Later Schools of *filidheacht'* in *Eriu*, Vol. XXV (1974), pp. 128–31.
2. A. Gwynn and R.N. Hadcock, *Medieval Religious Houses: Ireland* (London, 1970), pp. 307–26.
3. G. Murphy (ed.), *Early Irish Lyrics* (Oxford, 1956), pp. 208–9.
4. C. O'Rahilly (ed.), *Táin Bó Cuailgne Recension I* (Dublin, 1976), pp. 2, 126.
5. L. Breatnach (ed.), *Uraicecht na Ríar* (Dublin, 1987), pp. 99–100.
6. C. O'Rahilly (ed.), *Táin Bó Cuailgne from the Book of Leinster* (Dublin, 1970), pp. 6, 143.
7. See K. Simms, *From Kings to Warlords* (Woodbridge, Suffolk, 1987), pp. 26–7.

8. L. McKenna (ed.), *The Book of Magauran* (Dublin, 1947), pp. 379–80.

9. W.J. Watson (ed.), *Scottish Verse from the Book of the Dean of Lismore* (Edinburgh, 1937), pp. 244–5.

10. *AC* (A.M. Freeman (ed.), *Annála Connacht: the Annals of Connacht* (Dublin, 1944)), 1525(7), 1530(9); *AU* (W.M. Hennessy and B. MacCarthy (eds), *The Annals of Ulster* (4 vols, Dublin, 1887–1901)), 1327, 1373 (bis), 1439; *AFM* (J. O'Donovan (ed.), *The Annals of Ireland by the Four Masters* (7 vols, Dublin, 1851)), 1548; *ALC* (W.M. Hennessy (ed.), *The Annals of Loch Cé* (2 vols, London, 1871, reprint Dublin, 1939)), 1599. Annals are cited by the A.D. date of the entry unless otherwise stated.

11. *AC*, 1391(7), 1437(4), 1471(26), 1510(8); *AU*, 1531; *ALC*, 1584, 1599.

12. *AC*, 1437(4).

13. *Ann. MacFirb.* (J. O'Donovan (ed.), 'The Annals of Ireland . . . by Duald MacFirbis' in *Miscellany of the Irish Archaeological Society*, Vol. i, (Dublin, 1846, pp. 198–302), 1447.

14. *AU*, 1347.

15. C. Marstrander (ed.), 'Bídh Crínna' in *Eriu*, Vol. V (1911), pp. 129, 131, 137, 139.

16. S.H. O'Grady (ed.), *Catalogue of Irish Manuscripts in the British Museum* Vol. I (London, 1926), p. 123.

17. *Scottish Verse from the Book of the Dean of Lismore*, pp. 307–8; E.C. Quiggin (ed.), *Poems from the Book of the Dean of Lismore* (Cambridge, 1937), p. 78.

18. *Scottish Verse from the Book of the Dean of Lismore*, pp. 60–5, 271. See A. Partridge, 'Wild Men and Wailing Women' in *Eigse*, Vol. XVIII (1980), pp. 27–33; K. Simms, 'The Poet as Chieftain's Widow: Bardic Elegies' in D. Ó Corráin, L. Breatnach and K. McCone (eds), *Sages, Saints and Storytellers: Celtic Studies in Honour of Professor James Carney* (Maynooth, 1989), pp. 400–11.

19. R. Bagwell, *Ireland under the Tudors* (3 vols, London, 1885–90), Vol. I, pp. 273, 281–2, Vol. II, 90, 92, 150, 304.

20. *Ibid.*, Vol. II, p. 21.

21. D. Greene (ed.), *Duanaire Mhéig Uidhir* (Dublin, 1972), pp. 83, 85; and see *ibid.*, pp. 71, 79, 189.

22. J. Casway, 'Mary Stuart O'Donnell' in the *Donegal Annual*, no. 39 (1987), p. 28.

23. D. Ó Floinn, 'Bríd Iníon Iarla Chille Dara cct (más fíor)' in *Irisleabhar Muighe Nuadhat* (1953), pp. 18–19.

24. O. Bergin, *Irish Bardic Poetry* (Dublin, 1970), p. 133.

25. L. McKenna (ed.), *Iomarbhágh na bhFileadh* (2 vols London, 1918), Vol. I, pp. ix–x, 102–3.

26. L. McKenna (ed.), *Aithdioghluim Dána* (2 vols London, 1940), Vol. II, p. 100.

27. *Ibid.*, p. 3; L. McKenna (ed.), *The Book of Magauran* (Dublin, 1947), pp. 379, 387.

28. P. Ó Fiannachta, *Catalogue of Irish Manuscripts in Maynooth College Library* fasc. 4 (Maynooth, 1967), p. 26.

29. S. Ó Tuama (ed.), *Caoineadh Airt Uí Laoghaire* (Dublin, 1961).

30. K. Simms, 'The Legal Position of Irishwomen in the Later Middle Ages' in *The Irish Jurist*, Vol. X n.s. (1975), pp. 99–101.

31. B. Bradshaw, 'Manus the Magnificent: O'Donnell as Renaissance Prince' in A. Cosgrove and D. MacCartney (eds), *Studies in Irish History Presented to R. Dudley Edwards* (Dublin, 1979), p. 20.

32. *AFM*, 1595; T. Ó Rathile (ed.), *Dánta Grádha* (Cork, 1926 repr. 1976), pp. 129–31.
33. *AU*; see Simms, 'The Legal Position of Irishwomen', pp. 101–2; C. Mooney, *The Church in Gaelic Ireland: thirteenth to fifteenth centuries* (Dublin, 1969, *A History of Irish Catholicism* ed. P.J. Corish, II, fasc, 5), pp. 56–60.
34. E. Ó Muirgheasa (ed.), *Dánta Diadha Uladh* (Dublin, 1936), pp. 284–319; R.W. Jackson, *Archbishop Magrath: the Scoundrel of Cashel* (Dublin, Cork, 1974), pp. 21–5, 39–40, 86–8.
35. See A. Chambers, *Granuaile, the Life and Times of Grace O'Malley, c. 1530–1603* (Dublin, 1979).
36. P. Walsh (ed.), *Beatha Aodha Ruaidh Uí Dhomhnaill* (2 vols, Dublin, 1948, 1957), Vol. I, p. 39, Vol. II, p. 136.
37. E. Knott (ed.), *The Bardic Poems of Tadhg Dall O hUiginn* (2 vols, London, 1922/6), Vol. II, p. 12.
38. Above, note 36.
39. K. W. Nicholls (ed.), *The O'Doyne Manuscript* (Dublin, 1983), pp. 61, 64.
40. *Ibid.*, p. 70.
41. *Calendar of State Papers Ireland 1608–10*, pp. 183, 216, 429, 540, 543–4; P. Breathnach, 'Dánta Bhriain Uí Chorcráin' in *Irisleabhar Muighe Nuadhad* (1929), pp. 47–8.
42. For the cases of Mrs Mary Cooper and Mrs Honora Wingfield see J. Ainsworth (ed.), *The Inchiquin Manuscripts* (Dublin, 1961), pp. 7–8, 313, 329, 351, 358, 368–9, 441, 443–4, 507–9.

3

Women and Crime in Seventeenth-Century Ireland

RAYMOND GILLESPIE

The picture of social change between 1500 and 1700 which is emerging from a growing number of regional studies has revealed very significant variations within the British Isles. In England, and to a lesser extent in Scotland, rapid population growth before the mid-seventeenth century placed increased strain on resources which, together with large inflows of precious metals, generated unprecedented price rises. This and other factors, such as commercialisation, helped to redistribute wealth and increase polarisation within society. One result was increased tension between the various social groups and to many contemporaries it appeared that the social order was dissolving. The unruly woman, for instance, who refuses to obey her husband and insists on making her own decisions is a familiar subject in seventeenth century English literature. Some groups, such as women and the poor, became increasingly marginalised. They came to be seen as a threat to social stability and increased efforts were made to ensure that they were controlled; and in the case of women prosecution in the manor courts for antisocial activities, such as 'scolding', increased significantly.[1]

In Ireland population was also rising rapidly, mainly as a result of immigration. But this rise was from a much lower base than in contemporary England and so resources, such as land, were never placed under the same sort of strain as in parts of England or Scotland.[2] Monetary factors also kept price rises in Ireland negligible. In the early seventeenth century, land and wealth in Ireland were not usually transferred within an existing social structure but were redistributed from native Irish to settler newcomers either as part of formal plantation schemes or mortgages and sales between natives and newcomers. Tensions within the social order were correspondingly less although those between native and newcomer often spilled over into open conflict as in 1641. It is hardly surprising, therefore, that in the

1640s and 1650s Ireland did not usually experience the social
radicalism of many English sects such as the Fifth Monarchy Men
or the various forms of Levellers generated by the social tensions
of contemporary England. The result of this different social
experience was that those pushed to the margins of society in
Ireland were not the economically disadvantaged poor but the
ethnically disadvantaged native Irish. The social divisions which
were formulated in Ireland in the course of the seventeenth
century differed fundamentally from those emerging in England
and Scotland. The environment in which women were perceived
as a threat to an existing social order was absent in Ireland. One
result of this situation was that women did not suffer the
attempts to use the law to control what were seen as socially
disruptive activities which occurred in parts of England. Undoubtedly the idea of the social role of women as adjuncts to their
husbands was as prominent among the settlers in Ireland as it
was in England. As the town book of the corporation of Belfast
put it in 1615 when setting fines for all those absent from church,
'the forfeitures before mentioned for the married woman, servants and children to be likewise levied out of the goods of the
husbands, fathers, mothers and masters of the said offenders
respectively as aforesaid'.[3] Unlike England, however, there does
not seem to have been any real concern that women were
attempting to break free of this subservient role. Unfortunately
few records of the manor courts in Ireland have survived which
would enable a comparison to be made with England as to the
extent of prosecutions for antisocial activities associated with
women, such as gossip or 'scolding'. In the manor court rolls of
the Archbishop of Armagh's lands, the only early seventeenth
century rolls to have survived, prosecutions of this kind are rare.
Of 225 cases coming before the court leet between 1625 and 1628
only two involved women as scolds. Again in the Presbyterian
session books of Templepatrick in County Antrim for 1646–7 only
two cases accusing women of slander or scolding occur.[4] This
was probably not untypical throughout the country. Most Irish
towns did not see the need for a ducking stool which was used
to punish scolds by ducking them in the river. The maps made
by Thomas Raven of towns in Counties Londonderry and Down
in the 1620s show that only one town, Comber, saw the need for
a stool. In Youghal, for instance, it was 1653 before the corporation erected a ducking stool and a cage for the punishment of
scolds and then only under pressure from the Cromwellian
regime anxious for a reformation of manners. At New Ross no
stool was set up before 1710.[5]

It seems therefore that economic conditions and the social

structure of seventeenth century Ireland did not promote the criminalisation of women in the way that that of England did. As gender tensions mounted in England so did prosecutions of women for criminal and antisocial activities which previously had been ignored. Perhaps the most dramatic example was the increase in prosecutions in early modern England and Scotland for the crime most closely identified with women, witchcraft. The ideological framework which underlay the belief in witchcraft had existed in England from before the Reformation, but it was only in the mid-sixteenth century that social and political conditions were right for magical beliefs to be linked with those who had become socially undesirable: the old, poor and, especially, women.[6] In Ireland, by contrast, there were almost no witch trials in the seventeenth century. Only one full scale trial, that of Florence Newtown at Youghal in 1661, is known of. This case has many of the features typical of English trials of the period. Florence appears to have been a poor woman who asked Mary Longdon, a servant of John Pyne, for a piece of beef. Mary refused and within a fortnight fell ill, blaming Florence for bewitching her. The outcome of the trial is not known. It seems that at least part of the reason for the similarity with English cases was due to the presence of the English healer or 'white witch' Valentine Greatrix who played a leading part in the trial since 'he had read of a way to discover a witch which he would practice'. Occasionally there are incidental references to other Irish witch-craft trials. In 1678, for instance, a woman called Bessie Weir was burnt at Paisley in Scotland as a witch. She had been tried and convicted in Ireland before but had reputedly been freed by the devil before she could be executed.[7] Even taking account of all these fragments it is clear that there was never in Ireland anything which even vaguely approached the witch hunts which characterised most of early modern Europe.

This does not, of course, mean that there was no belief in witchcraft in Ireland either among the settlers or native Irish. As one observer in County Kildare reported in 1683 the Irish 'are much given to charms, spells, incantations, divinations and attribute all diseases . . . to fascination or witchcraft' yet 'of witches there are very rarely heard of any detected and convicted amongst them'.[8] The Presbyterian Church had felt it necessary to condemn sorcery in the 1670s and in 1699 the Presbyterian minister at Enniskillen asked the Laggan presbytery for 'advice what he should do with persons that used charmers and charms in curing the sick'.[9] Even earlier James Ware recorded the case of John Cave of Dublin who died in October 1630 because he believed that he could not drink. Cave's explanation for his mal-

ady was 'that he was bewitched by a woman at Powerscourt'.[10]
This belief in the reality of witchcraft was reflected in provision
for the prosecution of witches. An Irish statute of 1586 had made
witchcraft a felony and had set down the appropriate death
penalty although it did not prescribe burning alive. The terms of
this statute were recorded in Richard Bolton's *Justice of the Peace
for Ireland* published in 1638. Bolton also set down standards by
which a J.P. could recognise witches, standards which had been
adopted in the infamous English trial of the Lancashire witches
in 1612.[11]

The question, therefore, is not why there was no witchcraft
practised in Ireland, which there clearly was, but why this was
not translated, through the legal system, into prosecutions. The
reasons leading to accusation and prosecution in English witchcraft trials are clearly complex and not amenable to any single
interpretation. However, two factors may be useful in understanding this phenomenon. First, at a national level there was a
concern in early modern England about a potential breakdown of
the social order and the need to control any deviations from the
norm and eradicate evil influences within the community. High
on this list of priorities came the devil and his agents in the form
of witches. Certainly in Scotland the Presbyterian revolution had
placed this purging of the nation high on its agenda. The targeted
groups were those most likely to disturb the social order and so
be associated with evil: masterless men and women who were
not behaving according to their perceived social roles. In Ireland
however those most likely to disturb the new society being
fostered by the authorities were recusants. Many of the witchcraft
accusations which survive from the seventeenth century occur in
the context of religious difficulties. In the depositions taken after
the 1641 rising it was alleged by one Armagh native, for example,
that all Protestants served the devil and from the other side of
the religious divide the theology of the Church of Ireland had
associated the Pope with antichrist and hence his followers were
allies of Satan.[12] Perhaps the best instance of this type of
accusation arose during the trial of Stephen Browne, a Carmelite
friar, in 1631. A girl who was a witness against him alleged that
Browne's mother bewitched her by crossing her in the street on
her way from the house of the Attorney-General, Sir William
Ryves, where she had been giving evidence against Browne. As
a result sorcery was added to the charges against Browne.[13]

The second, and more immediate, cause for accusation and
prosecution were the tensions which erupted from time to time
within specific communities. Witchcraft trials were almost always
confined to easily defined localities. There are examples of this

type of witchcraft accusation to be found in an Irish context. In 1627 in the course of a dispute between James Spottiswood, the Bishop of Clogher, and a Fermanagh landlord, Lord Balfour, Spottiswood denounced the wife of one of the parties as a witch but the matter was never pursued further.[14] At least part of the explanation of this lies in the fact that in Ireland the internal cohesion of the community seems to have been much greater than in contemporary England or Scotland despite the fact that society as a whole was much less well integrated. Economic reasons played a part here. Much greater availability of cheap land and a labour shortage in Ireland certainly seem to have reduced the economic tensions within the community. There was also a tendency within Ireland to resolve disputes within the community rather than allow outsiders in the form of the central courts to become involved. In the Ulster gaol delivery rolls for 1613–15 disputes between individuals from within one community are rare. Social control was exercised by informal rather than formal means. Landlords, for example, were often unwilling to allow the Dublin authorities any pretext for investigating their tenants or their rights to landholding, which were often dubious. They preferred to resolve disputes within the estate system rather than have them go to law. Richard Boyle, Earl of Cork, for instance, was not beyond exercising summary justice without any court to assist him. The position of settlers as a dominant minority within Ireland as a whole may also have created more cohesive bonds than might otherwise have existed.[15] The courts which were most effective were those which were coterminous with the local community. In particular the Presbyterian session which operated from within the community served to deal with a large volume of complaints which might otherwise have given rise to violence or other felonies.[16] Less formal control was exercised by the Catholic clergy who frequently acted as arbiters in disputes. Thus the very distinctive social structure which emerged in seventeenth century Ireland prevented in large measure local economic and gender tensions spilling over into witchcraft accusation and prosecution.

Many of the features which reduced the importance of witchcraft trials in seventeenth century Ireland can also be used to understand the incidence of other female crime. Writing the history of these other types of criminal activity for seventeenth century Ireland is not an easy task. The records of the main criminal courts, the quarter sessions, assize and King's Bench, either did not survive the seventeenth century or perished in the Public Record Office fires of 1711 or 1922. It is not possible to construct the sort of statistics which historians of crime in

England and Scotland have been able to do. The pattern of Irish crime before the nineteenth century must be constructed from fragments and hence must remain impressionistic. Fortunately the assize books for the Tipperary assizes held at Clonmel in 1633, 1665–7, 1669, 1674–5, 1683 and 1685 have survived although we do not have complete records of all the assize visits for any one year.[17] From these books it is possible to understand something of female participation in crime in that region. Of almost 1500 people brought before the assize in the years for which records survive only 84, or 5.6 per cent, were women. The Tipperary evidence does not seem to be untypical within Ireland as a whole. The gaol delivery rolls for Ulster for 1613–15, for instance, record only one woman being tried out of over 120 cases. The same pattern is demonstrated in the 1614 Grand Jury presentments preserved in the corporation book of Youghal. Out of 63 cases women featured in only two – one woman for keeping 'misrule' in her tavern and two women presented for being scolds. Again in the mayor's court at Youghal in 1646 of 62 persons appearing four were women, a scold and thief, a forestaller, an unmarried mother and a stopper of watercourses.[18] It seems that female prosecution for criminal activity in the British Isles was generally low in the early modern period. The home circuit indictments for the reigns of Elizabeth and James I, for example, show that only 14 per cent of persons indicted were female.[19] In Ireland, however, the prosecution of women was unusually low.

Not only were Irish women rarely seen in court but when they appeared the range and types of offences which they committed were usually well defined. Of the 84 women who appeared before the assizes at Clonmel, 51 (61 per cent) were charged with theft, 11 (13 per cent) with being accessories to other crimes, eight (10 per cent) with assault and seven (8 per cent) with murder, the rest being miscellaneous indictments such as keeping ale-houses without a licence. Yet further distinctions can be made. In the area of theft for example women tended to steal smaller, less valuable items than their male counterparts. The average value of an item stolen by a woman was 3s. 6d. whereas the average value of an item stolen by a man was 18s. 6d. although women tended to steal larger amounts of cash than males: an average of almost £10 as against £8 9s. 0d. Part of the explanation for these differences lies in the nature of the goods stolen. The items most commonly stolen by men were cattle, horses and sheep which had relatively high values. Women on the other hand tended to steal smaller items. Joan Mearae was charged in April 1663 with the theft of one pound of salt beef, five pottles of meal, one knife and two pieces of pork, each item being valued at 1s.

Clothes were also prominent among the items stolen by women, Ellis Barry was charged in 1685 with stealing two petticoats, one waistcoat and one apron and Catherine Russell with theft of a linen hood, two pinafores, another hood and a gold ring valued at 8s.[20] This may explain why women stole more cash than men since it was small in volume, easy to conceal and readily accessible to those living in towns. Most of this type of theft was simple opportunism and it was rare for women to be charged with burglary unless they were accompanied by male companions. It may be that the opportunity for women to engage in criminal activity was limited by their social role and their position in the home rather than in the fields and markets where more opportunities for theft or violence presented themselves. In the case of assaults women were usually, though not always, part of a larger group which included a number of men, often their husbands. This pattern of theft may explain, in part, why women do not appear as frequently as men in the assize records. Their crimes were small and possibly not worth pursuing. Perhaps the goods were returned if the woman was caught and the victim may have been reluctant to pursue a woman through the courts.

While it is relatively easy to analyse women's role in readily recognisable criminal activities, such as felonies, it is much more difficult to chart their role in the activities at the margins of the criminal world or those activities which were anti-social. Women, for example, seem to have acted as receivers of stolen goods and as fences while men did the actual theft. In 1582, for instance, the Dublin corporation complained of apprentices who stole goods which were fenced by their concubines. Ralph Turner of County Westmeath deposed in 1642 'the women of the septs were rebels and very foreward actors in the rebellion and did take, sell or otherwise dispose of all the robbed or stolen goods that came into their hands'.[21] With this sort of activity much depended on the perception of contemporaries as to what was criminal and what was not. The keeping of alehouses without a licence was, for example, technically a crime and also in the eyes of many contemporaries anti-social since it was in alehouses that many of the undesirables of early modern society congregated.[22] However unlicensed alehouses were frequently ignored except for occasional purges. In the Tipperary assizes, for instance, of the 72 individuals presented for keeping alehouses without licence 50 were presented in the years 1666 and 1667. This type of socially undesirable conduct is best seen in the records of the more local courts where community difficulties were aired. In the Presbyterian session records for Templepatrick in County Antrim drunkenness is a commonly recorded fault and in the 11 cases which give the source of the alcohol reported in 1646–7 all the suppliers were women.[23] The keeping of alehouses was a logical extension of other female activities as an alehouse could be run in the dwelling where they lived and where brewing was done as a matter of course.

The extent to which women became involved in this under-world of socially undesirable activities clearly depended on their economic status and their access to alternative sources of income. Women were driven to the margins of society and criminal activity, in its widest sense, where the competition for resources was greatest and the existing social hierarchy most rigid. In Ireland this occurred mainly in the larger towns. In seventeenth century Dublin, for example, women seem to have been at their most vulnerable. Women outnumbered men in Dublin by about 1.17 to 1 according to a survey of 1644 and this ratio had risen to 1.37 to 1 (excluding servants and children) by 1696. By contrast in late seventeenth century London men outnumbered women by 1.03 to 1. The reason for the Dublin situation is unclear. In the case of children in 1696 males outnumbered females by 1.25 to 1 so it would appear that the female surplus was caused by immigration to the city. Women seem to have been proportion-ately most predominant in the poorer parishes of the city, the highest female/male ratios being in the three poorest parishes of St Audeons, St Andrews and St Michans.[24] Given the rapid expansion of the city during the seventeenth century it is hardly surprising that many women found themselves pushed out into the margins of the social and economic order. In 1659 the corporation demanded 'the supressing of the great number of idle women and maidens that sit in most streets of this city selling of apples, oranges, lemons and others regrating of eggs, hens and several other commodities to the great prejudice of the inhabi-tants of this city'. It was ordered that a 'large cage [be] set in the corn market . . . to imprison all beggars, idle women and maids selling apples and oranges'.[25] Not surprisingly such women were prominent in such activities as the keeping of alehouses, which required almost no capital investment and could yield significant profits. As Barnaby Rich commented of Dublin in 1610 'they have a number of young idle housewives that are both very loathsome, filthy and abominable, both in life and manners and these they call tavern keepers, the most of them known harlots'. Such alehouses he concluded were 'the very nurseries of drunkeness, of all manner of idleness, of whoredom and many other vile abominations'.[26] Rich is not known as a sympathetic commentator on Ireland but his views were echoed a few years later by the more sober corporation of Dublin. In 1616 the commons petitioned the corporation about those 'who harbour multitudes of wicked harlots under colour of tapping ale and beer, whose ungodliness of life can do no less than procure the indignation of God against this honourable city'.[27]

In some ways the experience of seventeenth century Dublin was untypical of the country as a whole. There, because of the economic and social pressures generated by rapid growth in a confined region, practices of which little notice was taken in other parts of the country became regarded as criminal activities. In Ireland as a whole women were not pushed to the margins of society as in parts of England and Scotland. Greater community cohesion, achieved through informal social control, together with the availability of cheap land, curtailed social tensions. This worked to prevent the criminalisation of women, and reduced the risk of a belief in witchcraft developing into witch trials as found in England and lowland Scotland.

Some of the reasons for the distinctive characteristics of the Irish society in the context of women and crime have been outlined in this essay but others surely existed. Much more detail is required on the details of everyday life in Irish local society, before more firm conclusions can be reached as to why women seem to have been less involved in the Irish criminal world than elsewhere.

REFERENCES

1. For example D.E. Underdown, 'The Taming of the Scold: the Enforcement of Patriarchial Authority in Early Modern England' and S. Amussen, 'Gender, Family and the Social Order 1560–1725' in A. Fletcher and J. Stevenson (eds), *Order and Disorder in Early Modern England* (Cambridge, 1985), pp. 116–36, 196–217.
2. L.M. Cullen, T.C. Smout and A. Gibson, 'Wages and Comparative Development in Ireland and Scotland 1565–1780' in R. Mitchison and P. Roebuck (eds), *Economy and Society in Scotland and Ireland* (Edinburgh, 1988), pp. 105–16.
3. R.M. Young (ed.), *The Town Book of the Corporation of Belfast* (Belfast, 1892), p. 4.
4. W.T. Latimer (ed.) 'The Old Session Book of Templepatrick Presbyterian Church' in *Royal Society of Antiquaries of Ireland Journal*, Vol. 31 (1901), pp. 162–75, 259–72; Public Record Office of Northern Ireland (hereafter cited as P.R.O.N.I.), T. 475.
5. P.R.O.N.I., T. 870, T. 510; Richard Caulfield (ed.), *The Council Book of the Corporation of Youghal* (Guildford, 1878), p. 229; P.D. Vigors (ed.), 'Extracts From the Old Corporation Books of New Ross' in *Royal Society of Antiquaries of Ireland Journal*, Vol. 31 (1901), p. 50.
6. Witchcraft in England has been studied from a number of perspectives including K. Thomas, *Religion and the Decline of Magic* (London, 1971) esp. Chs 14–18; A. Macfarlane, *Witchcraft in Tudor and Stuart England* (London, 1970) and C. Larner, *Enemies of God* (London, 1981). For the importance of witchcraft in a wider

criminal context see C. Larner, 'Crimen Exceptum' in B. Lenman, G. Parker and V. Gatrell (eds), *Crime and the Law* (London, 1980), pp. 49–60.

7. Much of the available material is gathered in St John D. Seymour, *Irish Witchcraft and Demonology* (Dublin, 1913). The depositions in the Newtown case are printed on pp. 105–31.

8. Trinity College, Dublin, MS 883/1, f. 297.

9. P.R.O.N.I., D1759/1A/2, p. 72, D1759/1E/2.

10. Dublin City Libraries, Pearse St, Gilbert MS 169, f. 204.

11. Richard Bolton, *A Justice of the Peace for Ireland* (Dublin, 1638), Bk I, pp. 97–8.

12. Trinity College, Dublin, MS 836, f. 49; Alan Ford, *The Protestant Reformation in Ireland* (Frankfurt, 1985), pp. 193–242.

13. Dublin City Libraries, Pearse St, Gilbert MS 169, ff. 200, 205, 214.

14. Raymond Gillespie, 'The Trials of Bishop Spottiswood 1620–40' in *Clogher Record*, Vol. xii, no. 3 (1987), pp. 323–4.

15. Raymond Gillespie, *Colonial Ulster* (Cork, 1985), pp. 89–93, 157–61, 206–10; for Boyle see A. B. Grossart (ed.), *Lismore Papers*, 1st ser. 2 (London, 1886), p. 124.

16. Raymond Gillespie, 'The Presbyterian Revolution in Ulster 1660–90' in W.J. Shiels and D. Woods (eds), *The Churches, Ireland and the Irish: Studies in Church History*, Vol. xxv (Oxford, 1989), pp. 161–4.

17. National Library of Ireland, MSS 4908, 4909.

18. Caulfield, *Youghal*, pp. 30–3, 258–60; J.F. Ferguson (ed.), 'The Ulster Roll of Gaol Delivery 1613–18' in *Ulster Journal of Archaeology*, 1st ser vol. 1 (1853), pp. 261–70, Vol. 2 (1854), pp. 24–8.

19. J.S. Cockburn (ed.), *Calendar of Assize Records. Home Circuit Indictments*, introduction (London, 1985), app. V, VI; Carol Z. Weiner, 'Sex Roles and Crime in Late Elizabethan Hertfordshire' in *Journal of Social History*, Vol. 8 (1975), pp. 18–37; J.M. Beattie, 'The Criminality of Women in Eighteenth Century England' in *Journal of Social History*, Vol. 8 (1975), pp. 80–136.

20. National Library of Ireland, MS 4908, ff. 1v, 2; MS 4909, f. 31v.

21. Dublin City Library, Pearse St, Gilbert MS 42, f. 16; Trinity College, Dublin (hereafter cited as T.C.D.) MS 817, f. 8v.

22. Raymond Gillespie, *Conspiracy: Ulster Plots and Plotters in 1615* (Belfast, 1987), pp. 17–18; Peter Clark, 'The Alehouse and the Alternative Society' in D. Pennington and K. Thomas (eds), *Puritans and Revolutionaries* (Oxford, 1978), pp. 47–72.

23. Latimer, 'Old Session Book'.

24. J.T. Gilbert and Lady Gilbert (eds), *Calendar of the Ancient Records of Dublin*, Vol. 3, (Dublin, 1889), p. xxxi; T.C.D., MS 883/1, f. 83; R.A. Butlin, 'The Population of Dublin in the Late Seventeenth Century' in *Irish Geography*, Vol. V, no. 2 (1965), pp. 58–64. The London material is from Gaunt's analysis of the bills of mortality (see C.H. Hull (ed.), *The Economic Writings of Sir William Petty*, Vol. 2 (Cambridge, 1899), pp. 374, 604).

25. Gilbert, *Cal. Anc. Records*, Vol. 4, pp. 156–7.

26. Barnaby Rich, *New Description of Ireland* (London, 1610), pp. 70–2.

27. Gilbert, *Cal. Anc. Records*, Vol. 3, p. 69.

4

Women and Piracy in Ireland: from Gráinne O'Malley to Anne Bonny

JOHN C. APPLEBY

There can be little doubt that piracy was one of the most male-dominated activities in former times. Maritime plunder was a violent, ruthless enterprise, apparently drenched in masculinity, which seemed to hold out little attraction or opportunity for the participation of women. The nature of life and work at sea, among a community of men living in cramped conditions, cheek by jowl with each other for days or weeks on end, inhibited the participation of women in maritime occupations either aboard pirate or other ships. The exigencies of shipboard life created an environment that was pervaded by male values. The notable profanity of many mariners, their heavy drinking, and the thinly veiled brutality and violence were part of a life-style which few women seemed to share or even feel comfortable with. Practical considerations alone suggested that the presence of women aboard ships could be a disturbing and disruptive element among other male crew members. And while there were no legal constraints preventing women from going to sea, folklore and popular superstition created informal barriers which were very difficult to break.[1]

But this portrait of a maritime world dominated by men, and pervaded by a masculine ethos, needs modification at several points. The seaborne activities of mariners, fishermen and pirates cannot be divorced from the lives of those who remained ashore. At many points these activities continued to intersect with the lives of family and kin. The very structure of life and work within the maritime community left a deep impression on the daily lives of many women. The prolonged absence of men, engaged on voyages lasting weeks, months or longer had complex consequences for the position of women, as well as for the family and household in general. Whether the increased burdens facing such women were offset by a greater degree of independence remains obscured by the paucity of evidence, at least for the period before 1800.

Of course women within the maritime community were more than a conventionalised 'help-meet' or a silent surrogate for an absent spouse. There is plenty of scattered evidence to indicate that at certain times and in certain places women were able to play an active role in the life of the maritime community. Some engaged in inshore fishing when men were pressed for naval service; others controlled the marketing and retail of fish brought home by their husbands, as occurred at Claddagh, near Galway, during the eighteenth century and possibly earlier. Many widows seem to have continued the commercial ventures of deceased spouses in trade, shipowning or retailing. Where these ventures were organised in partnership with others, however, some widows may have been left in the position of a 'silent partner' whose control over business decisions was rather limited. Nevertheless there is evidence of women playing a more direct role in trade and retailing. Thus by the eighteenth century the participation of women in trade in Dublin seems to have been widely accepted. Further research among customs accounts and trade directories might reveal a similar situation in other Irish ports. In addition the role of women as alehouse-keepers is now fairly well documented. Within the maritime community, where the tavern or alehouse was a vital centre for the drifting population of single men who served in the merchant marine, such women could easily come to play an important part in the lives of many seamen. Mariners who were between voyages no doubt relied heavily on women tavern-keepers for the provision of board and lodgings, and occasionally loans or pawnbroking facilities. Although the broad impact of this on women's position in society remains unclear, in some areas the alehouse or tavern became the focus of a subculture of crime based on prostitution, theft or receiving stolen goods. Thus in the late sixteenth century complaints were voiced in Dublin against women in the city for keeping taverns and enticing apprentices and others to whoredom and theft. In addition the wives of mariners were active in organising wage protests and demonstrations on behalf of absent husbands.[2]

Women also played an active role in the business of piracy for much of this period. In part this was a reflection of the nature of piracy in the sixteenth and early seventeenth centuries. At this time the business of plunder, in both Ireland and England, was deeply rooted within the maritime community. Mariners, fishermen and even landsmen usually turned to piracy as a means of supplementing work and wages. Such men tended to retain close connections with communities ashore, seeking aid and assistance from women when need arose. As 'aiders and abettors', indeed, many women played a varied role in the business of piracy, acting as receivers of stolen plunder or harbouring pirates from the authorities. In some places piracy fed off the hidden support of women. But by the same process it could easily turn women into victims: wherever piracy flourished so did the business of prostitution. The relationship between the two is clearly revealed by the spread of prostitution into the remote coastal communities of south-west Munster in the early seventeenth century, when large numbers of English pirates were regularly visiting the coast.[3] At times when piracy became an endemic problem it could affect the lives of a large number of women in a variety of ways. The effect might only be short and superficial; but occasionally it could be deeper and more enduring.

Women from diverse backgrounds were connected with piracy during this period. Moreover, in the later sixteenth and early eighteenth centuries two women of Irish background were directly involved in piratical activity. Gráinne O'Malley, the so-called 'pirate queen of Connacht', is the more celebrated of the two. Her life of piracy and plunder along the west coast of Ireland during the 1580s and 1590s has assumed legendary proportions, and inspired several romantically inclined modern novels. By contrast Anne Bonny, whose career during the 1720s was subsequently recounted by Daniel Defoe, has left little trace in Irish history. Her life at sea, serving aboard a pirate ship in male disguise, along with that of Mary Read, has also found a modern echo in dramatic form.[4] Steve Gooch's play on *The Women Pirates*, for example, portrays two rebel women escaping from female stereotypes in 'a small "alternative" society of anti-colonial' rebel pirates. From this perspective Read and Bonny were not just breaking with conventional life ashore, they were also trying to construct a new way of life at sea. These later interpretations, in literature or drama, testify to the almost unparalleled lives of both women. A detailed survey of the lives of such isolated individuals, however, would inflate the importance of women's role in piracy and piratical activity. Instead, this paper will examine their activities within the broader context of Irish piracy as it developed during the period from the sixteenth to the eighteenth centuries.

I

Piracy was a persistent problem in Ireland throughout the sixteenth and early seventeenth centuries. It was an activity involving all social groups, including Gaelic lords, old English merchants and new English planters. In the west families such as the O'Malleys and O'Flahertys of Connacht maintained a tradition of opportunistic piracy which helped supplement the local economy in various ways. Much of this activity was relatively unsophisticated in character. It usually involved short-distance raids along the coast, to nearby islands, or upon isolated and vulnerable merchant shipping. There was nothing glamorous about these ventures; they were merely part of a broader struggle to survive in a difficult, sometimes inhospitable, environment. In an area where the opportunities for profitable farming were restricted by bog and rock, piracy was but one way of reaping an alternative harvest from the wealth of the sea.

This type of localised piracy was based upon a broadly defined lordship of the sea claimed by families like the O'Malleys, which included levying tolls or selling fishing rights within certain coastal areas. Its most visible expression, still to be seen today, were the castles and tower houses built by the O'Malleys in and around Clew Bay. Castles at Rockfleet, or on the islands of Achill, Clare and Inishbofin were powerful structures that dominated the coastal waters of the region, providing a network of safe havens and bases for the O'Malley fleets.[5]

It was within this context that Gráinne O'Malley's career unfolded during the second half of the sixteenth century. This was a time of protracted crisis within Gaelic society in the west of Ireland, marked by rebellion and internecine conflict whose complexity defies simple analysis. Hostility towards the encroaching power of the English was overlaid by the survival of traditional rivalries amongst the Irish. The combination of these elements was to affect the activities of the O'Malleys, on land as well as at sea, in complex and sometimes contradictory ways. In the case of the latter it brought them face to face with an English concept of the law and custom of the sea whose application in Ireland clearly implied an end to the independent maritime rights and customs exercised by Gaelic lords. Indeed the tension between these two different systems ran like a thread through Gráinne O'Malley's own career.

Despite the burden of legend much of Gráinne O'Malley's maritime activities remain shrouded in obscurity. The limited evidence, which is mainly from the perspective of hostile English administrators in Ireland, has only fed the imagination of poets and historians who have portrayed O'Malley as an Irish Amazon, a 'Diana of the Atlantic', or as a candidate for nationalist sainthood.[6] None is a particularly fitting description for a woman who found herself in the rare position of acting out the traditional role of a petty leader within the O'Malley septs, from a small power base in Clew Bay. As the daughter of a chieftain of the O'Malleys, and then as the wife successively of Donal O'Flaherty and Richard Burke, she enjoyed a position of some privilege and power within Gaelic society. Other contributors to this volume have pointed to the indirect influence and power which wives of Gaelic chiefs could exercise. Grainne O'Malley was in this tradition. After marriage she retained control over her family's maritime interests. In 1575, for example, when Sir Henry Sidney marched west to deal with the rebellion of the Earl of Clanrickard's sons, she was able to offer the lord deputy the assistance of three of her galleys and 200 fighting men. Sidney did not take up the offer; subsequently he condemned O'Malley as a 'terror to all merchantmen that sailed the Atlantic'.[7] In 1578 the president of Munster also complained that O'Malley was the 'chief commander and director of thieves and murderers at sea' who were then spoiling the province.[8]

This type of coastal raiding was a traditional pursuit of the O'Malleys. But its scale under Gráinne O'Malley is difficult to gauge. At most it probably involved about 20 vessels; often the number may have been less than a handful.[9] Most were small vessels, bearing sails and oars, and carrying ordnance of some kind. These vessels, or galleys as the English confusingly described them, were well suited to coastal enterprise of this nature: they were fast, manoeuvrable, and easy to run ashore. But they were ill suited to long-distance piracy and would have been a poor match for a well-armed Elizabethan merchantman or naval vessel in open water. They enjoyed such local advantages in the west of Ireland, however, that the English were forced either to buy or build similar ships to deal with the growing menace of O'Malley and O'Flaherty piracy.[10]

Although O'Malley's maritime activities retained their customary character, they were increasingly affected by the changing political situation in the west. In 1589 most of Mayo burst into rebellion, partly as a reaction to the harsh rule of the English president of Connacht, Sir Richard Bingham. The extent of Gráinne O'Malley's involvement in the rebellion remains unclear. However, it must have been very difficult for her to remain aloof from a rebellion which affected most of west Connacht: according to the annals 'there was not one of note from the western point of Erris [in Mayo] . . . to the Plain of Connaught [in Roscommon], that did not unite in opposition to the governor' or president of the province. Indeed in 1593 Bingham informed the privy council in London that O'Malley was a 'notable traitoress and nurse to all rebellions in the province', and had been so for the past 40 years. But the only evidence that Grainne O'Malley played any direct role in the disturbances in the west occurs towards the end of the rebellion, in 1590, when she raided the Isle of Aran with

'2 or 3 baggage boats full of knaves', apparently at the instigation of Sir Morrogh Ne Doe O'Flaherty who bitterly resented the island's grant to Sir Thomas le Strange, an English adminstrator and adventurer.[11]

In the aftermath of the rebellion Bingham seized the opportunity to deal with recalcitrant Gaelic elements in the west once and for all. Grainne O'Malley was one of several Gaelic leaders whom he was determined to cow into submission. By 1592 he was in Clew Bay, clearing the islands of rebel groups. This impressive display of power forced O'Malley to try and reach some accommodation with the English regime in Ireland, even though this was probably unpopular with other members of the O'Malley septs. At the same time she apparently forsook 'her former trade of maintenance by land and sea'. By 1593 she was living a poor farmer's life in west Connacht, impoverished by the increasing burdens of cess.[12]

The imposition of fresh burdens such as cess only served to exacerbate the social and economic dislocation in the west which the outbreak of the Nine Years' War brought in its train. One result of this was a resurgence of piratical activity by the O'Malleys and others which easily became entangled with the war against the English. Although Gráinne O'Malley avoided taking sides in the conflict, she too was involved in this activity. In 1601, shortly before her death, she set out in a galley to plunder the lands and islands of MacSweeney Fanad and MacSweeney Ne Doe in Ulster.[13] On the way north, however, the galley was forced ashore by an English naval vessel under the command of Captain Charles Plessington. The skirmish between the two vessels was brief, but it underlined the fragility of Gaelic maritime enterprise as the naval reach of England penetrated these remote western and northern waters.

Following her death, *c.* 1603, the exploits of Gráinne O'Malley passed into local legend in the west. Later, with the subsequent accretion of myth, she became identified as a symbol of Ireland's struggle for freedom against 'all the might of England'. This image of a proud, undaunted woman, a patriot who would one day return from exile, was embroidered thereafter in varying guises, in popular songs, poetry and print; at times she became almost the embodiment of Erin and her people, part of a tradition of 'self-possessed and masterful women' which inspired a later generation of radical nationalists.[14] Interesting as these subsequent interpretations are, they bear little relation to the reality of Gráinne O'Malley's life and career. She was no defiant rebel engaged in a life or death struggle with the English but a petty leader who struggled to survive in an environment which was undergoing profound transformation. And within this changing situation piracy became one of the arts of survival.

II

Alongside coastal plunder of the type organised by the O'Malleys, the waters about Ireland were also visited by increasing numbers of English pirates in search of safe bases and markets. The coastal settlements of south-west Munster were especially attractive as secure bases for long-distance raids on shipping in the Atlantic. In May 1589 Sir William Herbert complained that the province was becoming a 'receptacle of Pirats' because of the hospitality and favour they received ashore in Kerry. Among those whom Herbert accused of being involved in the business of receiving pirate plunder were Sir Edward Denny, vice-president of the province, and his wife Lady Elizabeth. From their residence in Tralee the Dennys provided a safe haven for pirates which propped up an 'elaborate system of piracy' with links across the Irish Sea in south-west England and Wales.[15]

This illicit trade flourished after 1604 with the increasing presence of English pirates in Ireland. During the early seventeenth century as many as 20 pirate ships were regularly visiting the coastal communities of the south and west. And many of these pirates, perhaps 1000 in number, developed close connections with the community ashore. Most of the victuallers of pirates in Baltimore at this time were either the wives or mistresses of pirates, who pretended to be engaged in the trade of fishing. In August 1610 the council of Munster complained of the number of desperate and dishonest men joining the pirates, as well as 'such shameles and adulterus women as daylie repaired unto them . . . [in] divers Taverns, Alehouses, and victualling houses' in Baltimore, Inisharkin and other places along the coast.[16] According to Captain Henry Mainwaring, an ex-pirate subsequently pardoned and knighted by James I, one of the reasons why pirates frequented Ireland was 'the good store of English, Scottish, and Irish wenches which resort unto them'. When the naval captain William Monson sailed into Broadhaven in 1614, pretending to be Mainwaring, he was entertained by a local gentleman, one Cormac, who apparently 'spared not his own daughters to bid them welcome'. Monson later alleged that all the people of the region 'in their hearts were piratically affected'; and this clearly included women as well as men.[17]

The structure of piracy in the early seventeenth century promoted close connections ashore in Ireland, especially in the 'new English' settlements of the south-west, which affected the lives of women in a variety of ways. As most of the surviving evidence is from a predominantly male perspective, and is more concerned with the activities of pirates at sea, most of these women tend to remain nameless or faceless characters who make only fleeting appearances in the pirate life-cycle. It is clear, however, that the nature of the connection ranged from the formal and regular to the informal and intermittent; and this was obviously an important factor in the way in which piracy influenced the lives of women ashore.

These connections are illuminated by the depositions of pirates who were caught by Admiralty officials in Ireland, and subsequently tried by the High Court of Admiralty for their offences. During 1609 John Walter escaped ashore from the company of the pirate, Captain Finche, as the ship lay moored in the River Shannon. Walter, a Gloucester man, later admitted that he had also sailed with Captain Richard Bishop, who was 'admiral' of the English pirate community for a time, but claimed that on both occasions he had been pressed to serve against his will. After escaping from Finche's company Walter settled at Bandon with his wife and family.[18] Other pirates also had spouses ashore in Ireland. The wife of one pirate captain, Mistress Suxbridge, ran a lodging house near Dublin with her daughters. The wife of another pirate lived on Sir William Hull's land near Leamcon. In October 1618 Hull complained that this woman had warned her husband and his fellow pirates, who were then at Schull, of the recent arrival on the coast of the naval captain, Sir Thomas Button, 'by which meanes they escapt'.[19]

Informal liaisons also flourished between pirates and women ashore. Baptist Ingle, one of Captain Robert Stephenson's company who came into Whiddy Island in 1612, often went ashore 'to make merry with a young woman that lay at Ballygubbin'. According to some of his crewmates Ingle planned to marry the young woman, but the courtship was interrupted when he ran off with £100 stolen from one of the company's chests.[20] As in many other maritime communities prostitution thrived in the small ports and havens visited by pirates. The comments of Captain Mainwaring, and the complaints of the council of Munster, indicate that the increase in prostitution and alehouses, especially in the south-west, was closely related to the problem of piracy. For a time prostitution was a significant element in the social profile of settlements like Baltimore and the nearby islands, although it remained a marginal, insecure and often dangerous activity. On one occasion in 1609 a merchant ship, engaged in trading with pirates at Baltimore, 'hoysed sayle and went away . . . with . . . two of the pyratts and some of their whores, about fyve in number' still aboard, in order to evade the local Admiralty officials. And prostitution also existed in more remote ports further north. In May 1627 the crew of a Dutch pirate ship were apparently always drunk ashore with the 'Queanes' of Killybegs. Sir Basil Brooke informed the Lord Deputy that the pirates were very rich, 'for such as Come on shoare are full of Spanish Silver & Ducketts'. Indeed, Brooke complained this 'wealth (was) too much for such hoores'. Others who had 'runne straunge courses' since the arrival of the pirates included James and William Hamilton, high constable and minister respectively of Killybegs. Indeed the pirates apparently 'glutted' themselves with 'drink-eing and whoreing' daily at the house of the latter.[21]

Some women no doubt benefited from their relationship with pirates, or from the pirate trade in plundered cargoes. Once ashore many pirates could be generous with their plunder. The wife of Henry Skipwith, captain of the fort at Kinsale, received gifts of silverware, linen and canvas from Captain William Baugh, partly because Baugh hoped to marry her daughter. In 1610 John Bedlake sent a kinswoman a parcel of striped canvas and blue starch which was used to make a waistcoat.[22] Other women were involved in the business of piracy as 'traders, truckers or vitelers'. At Leamcon the wife of Thomas Barlowe was engaged in the retail trade of beer to pirates who visited that lonely haven. On nearby Long Island 'blacke dermond' and his wife supplied victuals to pirates in exchange for goods such as wine, canvas, broadcloth, steel, and other commodities. Three women were also accused of receiving various amounts of sugar out of a Dutch rover which came into Bantry Bay during 1625 to re-victual. Mrs Ashdowne, a widow from Ballygubbin, had about 50lb; one 'Bruer's wife of the Bridge' (i.e. Bandon) received two barrels of sucketts; and the wife of Nicholas Calfe had some sugar which she subsequently sold in Bandon.[23] While the amounts were admittedly small, it is clear that this was a commercialised traffic involving a wide range of local society, although the number of women who were able to participate in the trade was obviously limited by lack of resources or opportunity.

Women also provided support and assistance for spouses or kinsmen when need arose. The wife of Thibault Suxbridge seems to have run a safe house near Dublin to harbour friends and relatives from the authorities. In July 1612 she provided safe accommodation for a brother, Henry Orange, for six or seven nights until he could get a ship to England. Orange had recently served with Captain William Baugh but fled the pirate's company after stealing a bag of jewels and diamonds. Edmund Flinte, a Chester yeoman who shared a room with Orange, later declared that the pirate recounted his story before his sister and her daughters, revealing that the diamonds were 'quilled up in the plates of his hose'. Orange subsequently managed to get safely aboard a Chester-bound vessel, where he tried to sell some of the stolen jewels to a fellow passenger, Lady Cooke.[24]

In these various ways the lives of many women became enmeshed with the lives of those pirates who haunted the coasts of the south-west during the early seventeenth century. But the way in which this contact affected the day-to-day lives of women, or their broader social and economic position, is difficult to determine. Piracy was a dangerous and risky activity, the dangers of which must have been shared by a wider circle of family and kin. Unfortunately the emotional cost, the pain of loss or the fear of desertion, cannot be recaptured from the written record. Nor is it possible to balance lengthy male absence from home against the potential independence for women ashore. Thibault Suxbridge, for example, was at sea almost without break from 1607 to 1610, when he was killed during a bitter conflict with a French vessel at Newfoundland. Although some pirates managed to send money home to their spouses this was poor compensation for the widows or abandoned wives who struggled to survive in a difficult environment. A small number of women, especially widows or women acting with husbands, were able to benefit from the illicit pirate trade. But many more swelled the ranks of the prostitutes who inhabited the unlicensed taverns and ale-houses which sprang up along the coast of south-west Munster. Above all, there was always the danger that women would become the victims of pirate violence. Thus in May 1623 more than a dozen women 'were ravished by the . . . company' of Captain John Nutt, who was cruising just outside Dungarvan harbour.[25] Rather different in nature was the attack on Baltimore, by Turkish pirates, in 1631 when more than 100 men, women and children were carried off into slavery in Barbary. Two of the victims, Joan Brodbrooke and Ellen Hawkins, were ransomed and brought home in 1646. The attack on Baltimore came at the end of a decade of mounting depredation by the Turks in northern waters, whose main purpose seems to have been the capture of human victims to sustain the economies of their city bases in north Africa. According to a report in 1625 there were more than 1500 such captives in the port of Sallee, including English, Scottish and Irish men and women. The personal consequences and costs of this wave of depredation are suggested by the issue of a licence to Ellen Daniel, in August 1618, authorising her to beg for two years to support herself and five children, and accumulate sufficient funds to redeem her husband, Richard, who had been seized by pirates in 1614 and later sold into slavery.[25]

The problem of piracy in Ireland in the early seventeenth century cannot be divorced from the broader social context. In south-west Munster the areas regularly frequented by pirates, the coastal communities beyond the official plantation, attracted a shifting population of men and women, both English and Irish, who lived in a casual and improvising way. And in such areas where respect for the law was tempered by the harsh realities of survival, piracy, like smuggling later, was an activity that flourished with the connivance of the community ashore.

III

Piracy continued to be a problem in the waters about Ireland for the rest of the seventeenth century. But with the exception of the 1640s and 1650s, when there was a resurgence of privateering and piracy, it remained more of an intermittent irritant than a large-scale organised activity. As the local waters about Ireland and Britain became too dangerous because of regular naval patrols, piracy became an increasingly marginal activity which continued only on the 'peripheries of empire', in the Caribbean or along the eastern seaboard of the north American colonies. Even here the state's relentless war against pirates continued, reaching a climax during the 1720s when the English Navy ruthlessly hunted down pirate ships.

Unlike their predecessors in south-west Munster in the early seventeenth century most of the Anglo-American pirate community in the early eighteenth century seem to have had few familial ties to land and home. Among those who did, however, was Captain John Criss from Larne who died leaving three wives surviving him. Multiple marriages such as this were probably encouraged by the common law marital arrangements that prevailed within many maritime communities. Under these arrangements women might establish a temporary relationship with a mariner, 'drawing his half-pay while he was at sea and looking after him in port'. When times were hard such 'wives' might resort to part-time prostitution to survive. As Criss's case suggests relationships of this nature were undoubtedly exploited by some members of the pirate community, although their extent and significance are impossible to gauge.[26]

The lives and experiences of many English pirate captains and companies of this period were recaptured by Daniel Defoe in his celebrated *History of the Pyrates*. This unprecedented collection of pirate biographies, which was adorned with a number of splendid illustrations, soon became something of a bestseller, going through four different editions within three years of its publication in 1724.[27] The book's popularity was partly due to the evocation of a world which was passing; its sympathetic portrayal of many pirates may also have struck a chord among readers fascinated by a way of life beyond the pale of respectable society.

Alongside accounts of well-known English pirate captains like William Teach or Bartholomew Roberts, Defoe included short life histories of Anne Bonny and Mary Read, both of whom served with Captain John Rackham until their capture in 1720.

According to Defoe's account Anne Bonny was an illegitimate child, born near Cork, who was brought up as a boy to conceal her background and identity. She subsequently emigrated to Carolina with her father and mother and married a seaman who 'was not worth a Groat'. After being 'turned . . . out of Doors' by her father she moved to the island of Providence in search of employment. It was here that she became acquainted with Rackham, a pirate with whom she eloped. Thereafter she sailed with Rackham's company disguised in male attire, as B. Cole's engraving from the first edition of the *History* convincingly portrays. Rackham's crew also contained Mary Read who was similarly disguised. 'In all these Expeditions', Defoe recounted, '*Anne Bonny* bore him Company, and when any Business was to be done in their Way, no Body was more forward or couragious than she, and particularly when they were taken, she and *Mary Read*, with one more, were all the Persons that durst keep the Deck.'

After the capture of Rackham and his company, however, both women were imprisoned and later convicted of piracy at a court of vice-admiralty held in Jamaica on 28 November 1720. Bonny was reprieved on the grounds that she was pregnant; her career thereafter remains unknown.[28]

The careers of Bonny and Read seemed so strange that Defoe was unusually defensive about including them in his *History*. Some, he admitted, 'may be tempted to think the whole Story no better than a Novel or a Romance' but, he continued, 'since it is supported by many thousand Witnesses, I mean the people of *Jamaica*, who were present at their Tryals, and heard the Story of their Lives, upon the first Discovery of their Sex; the Truth of it can be no more contested, than that there were such Men in the World, as *Roberts* and *Black-beard*, who were Pyrates.' The defence was perhaps needed all the more given Defoe's occasional tendency to mix fact with fiction.

Defoe's account of Bonny and Read can be supported by the printed account of their trial which was published in Jamaica in 1721. According to this account both women began their piratical careers on 1 September 1720 when they agreed to sail with Rackham 'to commit acts of piracy'. Both were accused of taking part in the seizure of seven fishing boats on 3 September, and in the subsequent plunder of four merchant vessels about Jamaica or Hispaniola. In all the value of these captures came to £1330. Although Read and Bonny pleaded not guilty the evidence of the witnesses at the trial was incontrovertible. Dorothy Thomas, who was taken by Rackham's company off the north coast of Jamaica, declared

> That the Two Women, Prisoners at the Bar, were then on Board the said Sloop, and wore Mens Jackets, and long Trouzers, and Handkerchiefs tied about their Heads; and that each of them had a Machet and Pistol in their Hands, and cursed and swore at the Men, to murther the Deponent; and that they should kill her, to prevent her coming against them, and the Deponent further said, That the Reason of her knowing and believing them to be Women then was, by the largeness of their Breasts.

Likewise two French witnesses, Jean Besneck and Pierre Cornelian, claimed that Bonny and Read were

> very active on Board, and willing to do any Thing; That *Ann Bonny*, one of the Prisoners at the Bar, handed Gun-powder to the Men, That when they saw any Vessel, gave Chase, or Attacked, they wore Men's Cloaths; and, at other Times, they wore Women's Cloaths; That they did not seem to be kept, or detain'd by Force, but of their own Free-Will Consent.

This testimony is particularly revealing about the use of male disguise by Read and Bonny.[29]

Yet the lives of Anne Bonny and Mary Read were only remarkable for the paths they chose to follow into piracy. During the eighteenth century a growing number of women disguised themselves as males in order to follow an unconventional career. Those women who served aboard naval vessels or in the army reflected an obsession with disguise and cross-dressing, which figured so prominently in broadsides and ballads. Anne Bonny's life at sea, in particular, seems to follow the career of the archetypal female warrior as a 'high-mettled heroine who disguises herself as a soldier or sailor and goes to war for her beloved'.[30] Disguise was a form of protection and a means through which women were able to break out of the constraints of customary life; it also gave some women the opportunity to flout conventional morality, as Defoe's account of Anne Bonny makes clear.

At sea of course piracy remained a male-dominated activity. Anne Bonny, like Gráinne O'Malley, was a rare exception whose seaborne career was almost unmatched in the history of piracy. This undoubtedly reflects the broader lack of female involvement in violent criminal activity during this period, as well as the special circumstances of piratical enterprise.[31] On land, however, it is clear that a larger number of women were engaged in the business of piracy, especially as the receivers of stolen goods. And the lives of even more women were affected by the rhythms of piratical activity, as is indicated by the experiences of women in south-west Munster in the early seventeenth century. While the documentary sources remain sparse and fragmentary they may well repay further study, not only to provide a more rounded view of women's activities but also to create a better balanced survey of piracy in past society.

REFERENCES

1. There is an ever-growing literature on piracy. P. Gosse, *The History of Piracy* (London, 1934) retains its value as a single volume survey. Recent valuable contributions include C. Senior, *A Nation of Pirates* (Newton Abbot, 1976), and M. Rediker, *Between the Devil and the Deep Blue Sea: Merchant Seamen, Pirates, and the Anglo-American Maritime World, 1700–1760* (Cambridge, New York, 1987). On superstitions see also, D. Vickers, 'Work and Life on the Fishing Periphery of Essex County, Massachusetts, 1630–1675' in D. D. Hall and D. Grayson Allen (eds), *Seventeenth-Century New England* (Boston, 1984), pp. 112–4; P. Thompson with T. Wailey and T. Lummis, *Living the Fishing* (London, 1983), pp. 167–81; J. Fingard, *Jack in Port; Sailor Towns of Eastern Canada* (Toronto, 1982), pp. 57–60.

2. J. Hardiman, *The History of the Town and County of Galway* (Galway, 1926), pp. 300–7; M.M. Oppenheim, *The Maritime History of Devon* (Exeter, 1968), pp. 26–7. For Dublin women see pp. 49–51 above. Linda Levy Peck, *Northampton: Patronage and Policy at the Court of James I* (London, 1982), pp. 165–6.

3. On the general context see Senior, *A Nation of Pirates*, pp. 53–7, and M. MacCarthy-Morrogh, *The Munster Plantation: English Migration to Southern Ireland 1583–1641* (Oxford, 1986), pp. 215–21.

4. See, for example, M. Llywelyn, *Grania, She-King of the Irish Seas* (New York, 1986) and E. Fairburn, *The White Seahorse* (Dublin, 1964); S. Gooch, *The Women Pirates: Ann Bonney and Mary Read* (London, 1978).

5. A. Chambers, *Granuaile. The life and times of Grace O'Malley c. 1530–1603* (Dublin, 1979), pp. 26–30; *The Western Islands, and the Antiquities of Galway, Athenry, Roscommon, &c.* Royal Society of Antiquaries of Ireland, Antiquarian Handbook Series, II (1897), p. 9; *Illustrated Guide to the Northern, Western, and Southern Islands, and Coast of Ireland* Ibid., Antiquarian Handbook Series, Vol. VI (1905), pp. 37–8, 43.

6. R. O'Flaherty, *A Chorographical Description of West or H-lar Connaught* (Dublin, 1846); B. Fuller and R. Leslie-Melville, *Pirate Harbours and their Secrets* (London, 1935), p. 189; T.H. Mason, *The Islands of Ireland* (3rd edn, London, 1950), p. 36. For a good example of earlier nationalist rhetoric, which argued that O'Malley encouraged early marriages and the 'rearing of healthy

children who would be a bulwark against the enemies of faith and fatherland', see J.F. Cassidy, *The Women of the Gael* (Boston, Mass., 1922), pp. 97–9, 117.

7. Chambers, *Granuaile*, pp. 56–7, 77–8, 84–6; Cassidy, *Women of the Gael*, p. 98; *Dictionary of National Biography*. Katherine Simms has placed O'Malley firmly in 'a long tradition of masterful Irish chieftain's wives', in M. MacCurtain and D. O'Corrain (eds), *Women in Irish Society: The Historical Dimension* (Dublin, 1978), p. 18.

8. Chambers, *Granuaile*, p. 93.

9. *Calendar of State Papers Ireland 1588–92*, pp. 333, 397. (hereafter cited as *C.S.P.I.*); A. MacDermott, 'Grainne O'Malley' in *Mariner's Mirror*, Vol. 46 (1960), pp. 133–41.

10. On one occasion Bingham boasted that a vessel of 30 tons would be able to deal with O'Malley and all the boats of Mayo (Chambers, *Granuaile*, p. 142). But the type of vessels employed by O'Malley were part of a northern tradition of shipbuilding which was connected with Viking 'long boat' precedents (see *C.S.P.I. 1600*, pp. 446–7; *C.S.P.I. 1600–1*, pp. 258–9, 421, 436–7, for descriptions of galleys and ways of dealing with them).

11. *C.S.P.I. 1588–92*, pp. 223, 333; *C.S.P.I. 1592–96*, p. 141; Chambers, *Granuaile*, pp. 98–102, 109–10, 123; Mona L. Schwind, 'Nurse to all Rebellions: Grace O'Malley and Sixteenth Century Connacht' in *Eire-Ireland*, Vol. 13 (1978), pp. 40–61.

12. *C.S.P.I. 1588–92*, p. 579; *C.S.P.I. 1592–96*, pp. 133–6, 312.

13. Chambers, *Granuaile*, pp. 166–7; P.R.O., S.P., 63/208 part 3/81.

14. Chambers, *Granuaile*, pp. 169–77 and 180–99 for a collection of songs and poetry. On O'Malley see also H.T. Knox, *The History of the County of Mayo* (Dublin, 1908), pp. 186–7, 196, 245, 253–4, 278–9. And Declan Kiberd, 'Irish Literature and History' in R.F. Foster (ed.), *The Oxford Illustrated History of Ireland* (Oxford, 1989), pp. 285–6. See also p. 79 below.

15. P.R.O., S.P. 63/144/56; D. Mathew, *The Celtic Peoples and Renaissance Europe. A Study of the Celtic and Spanish Influences on Elizabethan History* (London, 1933), Ch. XV.

16. *C.S.P.I. 1608–10*, pp. 277–8; R. Dudley Edwards (ed.), 'Letter-Book of Sir Arthur Chichester 1612–1614' in *Analecta Hibernica*, Vol. 8 (1938), pp. 43, 47; British Library, Cotton MS Otho E VIII, f. 368; Harley MS 697, f. 36.

17. G.E. Manwaring and W.E. Perrin (eds), *The Life and Works of Sir Henry Mainwaring* (2 vols, Navy Records Society, 1922), Vol. II, pp. 39–40; M. Oppenheim (ed.), *The Naval Tracts of Sir William Monson* (4 vols Navy Records Society, 1912), Vol. III, pp. 58–69; Gosse, *History of Piracy*, pp. 124–7.

18. Public Record Office (London), High Court of Admiralty, Examinations, 13/226, unnumbered (hereafter cited as P.R.O., H.C.A.). And for a fuller discussion see John C. Appleby, 'A Nursery of Pirates: The English Pirate Community in Ireland in the Early Seventeenth Century' in *International Journal of Maritime History*, II (1990), 1–27.

19. P.R.O., H.C.A. 13/42, ff. 223v–4; Chatsworth House, Lismore Papers, Vol. 9, f. 115. Hull had also been involved in piratical activity in the Mediterranean but had settled at Leamcon, marrying Sir Richard Boyle's widowed sister-in-law. He was also deeply involved in the pirate trade (J.C. Appleby, 'Settlers and Pirates in

Early Seventeenth Century Ireland: A Profile of Sir William Hull'
in *Studia Hibernica* (forthcoming)).

20. P.R.O., H.C.A. 13/42, ff. 139v–41v, 156v–8.
21. Senior, *A Nation of Pirates*, p. 57; P.R.O., S.P. 63/244/659, b and
    678, b.
22. P.R.O., H.C.A. 13/42, ff. 192–3v, 213v–4; Lambeth Palace, Carew
    MS 619, ff. 119, 133.
23. P.R.O., H.C.A. 13/226, 228; Chatsworth House, Lismore Papers,
    Vol. 11, f. 65.
24. P.R.O., H.C.A. 13/42, ff. 223v–4.
25. Senior, *A Nation of Pirates*, pp. 38–9, 64–7. In August 1615 a pirate
    captain left a 'negro wenche' in Bearhaven as a 'gift' for a local
    admiralty officer (P.R.O., H.C.A. 1/48/104–4v); *C.S.P.I., 1615–2* p.
    209.
26. Rediker, *Between the Devil and the Deep Blue Sea*; Robert C. Ritchie,
    Captain Kidd and the War Against the Pirates (Cambridge, Mass.,
    1986), for the general context. On marriages see also John R. Gillis,
    For Better, For Worse. British Marriages, 1600 to the Present (Oxford
    and New York, 1985), pp. 201, 234; Philip Gosse, *The Pirates Who's
    Who* (London, 1924), p. 94.
27. Daniel Defoe, *A General History of the Pyrates*, ed. M. Schonhorn
    (Columbia, South Carolina, 1972); *Piracy and Privateering*, National
    Maritime Museum, Catalogue of the Library, Vol. IV (London,
    1972), pp. 83–97.
28. Defoe, *A General History*, pp. 159–65.
29. Ibid., pp. 148–65; Pat Rogers, *Robinson Crusoe* (London, 1979), p.
    34. For the trial account see P.R.O., Colonial Office 137/14, ff. 9–
    28v.
30. Dianne Dugaw, 'Balladry's Female Warriors: Women, Warfare,
    and Disguise in the Eighteenth Century' in *Eighteenth Century Life*,
    IX (1985), pp. 1–20. Most surveys of piracy usually include some
    reference to Anne Bonny based on Defoe's account. See also
    N.A.M. Rodger, *The Wooden World: An Anatomy of the Georgian
    Navy* (London, 1986), pp. 75–9; Gomer Williams, *History of the
    Liverpool Privateers and Letters of Marque with an Account of the
    Liverpool Slave Trade* (London, 1897), pp. 118–9.
31. Olwen Hufton, 'Women in History: 1 Early Modern Europe' in
    Past and Present, 101(1983), p. 139; J.A. Sharpe, *Crime in Early
    Modern England 1550–1750* (London, 1984), pp. 108–10.

5

Political Women and Reform in Tudor Ireland

CIARAN BRADY

> Women have been the cause of many troubles, have done great harm to those that govern cities, and have caused in them many divisions . . . absolute princes and governors of republics are to take no small account of such matters.
>
> Machiavelli, *The Discourses*, Book III, Ch. 26

I

Until recently a reading of the standard historical accounts would have suggested the simple conclusion that the relationship of women to politics in sixteenth century Ireland was not unlike that once posited by an English tabloid between Prince Philip and the Profumo affair: that is no relationship whatsoever. A few isolated individuals, to be sure, continued to hold their place in the folk memory. There were the viragos, most notably Gráinne O'Malley (Granuaile), whose stories of derring-do continue to exert a grip over the popular imagination, despite their dubious historical foundations.[1] There were the crones, like the old Countess of Desmond who presided over the ruin of her family and lived for almost 140 years before succumbing to injuries received in a fall from a tree.[2] And there were the tragic heroines, like Rose O'Toole, forced by the evil English governor to choose between the life of her son and the life of her husband.[3] But beyond such obvious stereotypes the role of women as a group in the political history of sixteenth century Ireland has received scant consideration.

The old women deliberately singled out for especially harsh treatment by Humphrey Gilbert during his campaign in Munster in the late 1560s have been represented only as examples of Gilbert's abominable cruelty. Likewise the Scottish women slaughtered by Essex in the 1570s and the Mayo women massacred by Bingham in the 1580s have been remembered only as instances of the Elizabethans' increasing ruthlessness, while the women of Carlingford raped and murdered by Shane O'Neill and his men during one of their raids on the Pale in the 1560s have not been remembered at all.[4]

The relative absence of women from Tudor Ireland's political register can be explained in a number of obvious ways. It may be said, for instance, that women make little appearance in the history books because they feature little in the sources themselves; for apart from some idealised portraits in Gaelic love poetry, brief and formulaic entries in the Gaelic annals and some colourful observations or anecdotes in English descriptions, the surviving evidence has little to reveal about the role or the conduct of women in political life. From this it may be concluded that the records do not lie, and that women have not been noted simply because they played but a minor or a passive role in the distinctly masculine series of conflicts, rebellions and wars of conquest that constituted the central theme of Irish political history in the sixteenth century.

Arguments of this kind are not without some point. The major sources have little indeed to say of women, and often what they say is formal and unremarkable. Again it is clear that the vast majority of women, like the vast majority of men in the same period, had little share in the political processes that governed their lives. But such a readily reached conclusion is uncritical both of the sources upon which it rests and of those very political processes which it assumes they describe.

However conventional and repetitive they may be, the very frequency of the annalistic obituaries – the deaths of the wives of even the most minor lords are respectfully recorded – testifies to the recognised status of noble women within the Gaelic political elite. The obituaries, moreover, are not without individual variation: as in the case of the chieftains, some women are singled out for exceptionally detailed praise, like Sadhbh, daughter of MacWilliam and wife to Mac Dermott who merits half a page in the *Annals of Loch Cé*.[5] Even the highly formalised idiom of most of the eulogies, however, should not be too easily dismissed. 'A most humane, generous and hospitable woman', the epithets most commonly attributed to the chieftain's wife, are intended to suggest the qualities of moderation, tolerance and munificence with which the ideal noble lady should complement the strength, determination and good husbandry of the ideal chieftain. Similar attitudes can be discerned in regard to the political role of women in the praise poems of bardic verse where separate stanzas in praise of the chieftain's wife are frequently appended which laud the lady in the formal manner of the annals. The occasional exceptions are themselves significant: Eochaidh O'hEoghusa once addressed a poem directly to Rois O Tuaithail (Rose O'Toole); but, as James Carney has suggested, there is more than a hint of irony in the poet's claim that he himself might make a suitable husband for this noble woman fallen from grace.[6] Once again the modern reader may perceive in another guise that ambivalence which characterises so much contemporary commentary on women in politics: a clear recognition of the importance and necessity of their role coupled with an attempt to delimit and subordinate it.

The surviving English and Anglo-Irish sources require less subtleties of interpretation. Here again the appearance of women in the public documents of the period is infrequent and irregular. Prominent figures such as the last Countess of Desmond are characterised, sometimes at length, in the correspondence of the Dublin administrators; and in pardons for felony issued by the Dublin chancery the wives of the principal nominees are often (but not always) included.[7]

Evidence of this kind allows of little more than the most obvious interpretation. But it is from the literary sources that more interesting patterns emerge. There is for instance a curious internal tension in several late Elizabethan descriptions of native women. The women Thomas Churchyard describes are all dismissed as 'calliackes', but they are politically influential and subversive; and he wholly approves of their summary despatch by men like Gilbert and his crew.[8] For Fynes Moryson the chieftains' wives are especially savage. Devoid of all courtliness, they were lazy, dirty and sometimes drank so much that they urinated openly in front of their husbands. More seriously they renounced all the normal familial responsibilities. Sexually promiscuous themselves, they refused to exercise discipline over their children, retained their maiden names throughout their marriage and most scandalously of all (Moryson returns to the subject twice) retained the right to declare the true paternity of their children only upon their deathbed.[9] To Moryson the chieftains' wives were a dangerously subversive group; wild and irresponsible, they none the less exerted a terrible influence over the central dynastic affairs of their countries. A similar blend of cultural contempt and political fear can be found in the writings of that inveterate misogynist Barnaby Rich. For Rich also Irish noble women were sluttish, vain and idle, yet they exercised an inordinate influence over their families and that influence was employed always in the interests of disorder.[10]

A somewhat more subtle variation of the same unresolved tensions can be found in the writings of a Palesmen with whom Rich and Moryson had little else in common. Richard Stanihurst's treatment of women in his *Chronicle of Ireland* is odd and rarely sympathetic. The persecution of Dame Alice Kytler is noted, but the allegations of witchcraft made against her are simply reported as fact. He recounts the 'humourous' tale of Margaret, Countess of Ossory, who in the midst of all her husband's troubles in the 1520s demanded to be supplied with wine regularly throughout her pregnancy. He dwells at length and with little sympathy on the sad case of Genet Delahide who died under interrogation in the aftermath of the Kildare rebellion and whose body was left to rot in the open, noting that she was after all the principal influence behind the real leader of the rising, her son James.[11] Even when Stanihurst adduces stories that reflect favourably upon women his treatment is carefully qualified. Thus in the *Description of Ireland* which serves as a prologue to his history he introduces the tale of Rose of Ross, the legendary 'Dido' of New Ross whose determination forced the men of the town to build the fortified walls that saved them from many incursions. But to this edificatory story, he adds the following epilogue. One of Rose's three sons had the misfortune to marry a 'pretty popelet' who during his absence overseas indulged in an affair with one of the town's friars. On his return the cuckold had the adulterous cleric murdered. But in revenge the friars set about sowing dissension among the townsmen, engineered the drowning of Rose's sons and secured the excommunication of the town:

> so that there was such cursing and banning of all hands and such discentious hurly burly raised between themselves as the estate of that flourishing town was turned arsey versey, topside totherway and from abundance of prosperity quite exchanged to extreme penury.[12]

Stanihurst's deeply ambivalent attitude toward women in public life is echoed in another Anglo-Irish literary product of the 1570s, 'The Book of Howth'. Again women feature only occasionally in this long compilation of Anglo-Irish history and myth, but their appearance is usually significant. In a mythical account of ancient Irish history, the following story is told. A great queen came to Ireland disguised as a man to challenge the king of Connacht's son and seven lords. In their first encounter the queen unhorsed the king's son and might have killed him but that she had fallen in love with him; but in a later meeting the prince charged at the queen and 'ran her through the shoulder' with a strong spear that one of the queen's ladies had given him. In 'the fall the queen brake her leg and could do no more', her true identity was revealed, the prince took her prisoner, 'and after she was whole married her and continued to their deaths'.[13] The obvious symbolism of the tale needs no labouring; but the story gains in significance when it is juxtaposed to two other occasions when anecdotes concerning women are allowed to interrupt the general narrative.

The first concerns Dervogilla, the wife of O'Rourke whose abscondment with Diarmait Mac Murrough was to lead to the coming of the Normans. By way of introduction to this, the central event of Anglo-Irish history, the Book proffers the following story as an account of Dervogilla's unfortunate marriage. Enraged by the impotence of her lord whose folly led him like many old men to think 'that goodwill may please whereas their power may not', the lady offered her lord some apples. The king greatly enjoyed them and enquired from whence they came; to which 'the queen answered merrily . . . "these apples were where you hath most delight and pleasure, wherof I marvel not that this same doth please you" . . . and at length did tell him that the apples were that morning in her tail'. In revenge the king seized two of his lady's foster-brethren, castrated them, 'had their stones baken' and presented to the queen in a pie. 'And from that day forward as evil as she was contented before, worse did she like him after till that king of Leinster being a young man and a young prince came to O'Rourke . . .'.[14]

This cautionary tale of irreparable marital breakdown is balanced later on in the Book by another anecdote concerning women which interrupts an account of the contemporary cess controversy in the Pale. The story recounts how the wife of the fifteenth century justiciar, Sir Stephen Scroope, whose 'violent extortions' and futile campaigning was the cause of much impoverishment and 'outcry to the poor people damned', interceded on their behalf and at length persuaded her husband to relent, change his strategy and work more closely with the local lords, after which he not only ceased to be a burden to the loyal subjects but won many victories against the King's Irish enemies. Here indeed was the ideal public woman in the ideal public marriage; one who, in contrast to the unfortunate Dervogilla and her foolish malignant old king, had apprehended the true relationship of noble lady to noble lord which the ancient myth had enunciated. A perfect complement to her husband, she was humane, generous and hospitable, as the Gaelic annalists would have said.[15]

II

To seek to abstract some deep underlying unity from such diverse and complex sources would be a foolish exercise. Yet while sustained comparative analysis is impossible, each in their very different ways can be seen to reveal a common ambivalence concerning the role of women in political life. Each, that is, clearly recognises the importance of women's role in the maintenance of political order, each is ready to acknowledge the especial status which that role conveys, but each also displays a deep anxiety concerning the way in which women have actually discharged that role in the past. For each, in other words, the realisation that certain women were of central political importance was suffused with the fear that women as a sex were perennially, irremediably and fatally dangerous. This nervously vacillating attitude toward women in politics – the open acknowledgement of their role combined with an impulse to subordinate and at times to negate it – is by no means historically unique and arises from forces far deeper than the conditions prevailing in sixteenth century Ireland.[16] Yet as has often been noted, it recurred most frequently and in its most intense forms in periods of great social and political change. It was, as is now well known, a marked feature of several renaissance and early modern literary cultures, and became a preoccupation not simply of alarmist propagandists and polemicists but of serious political thinkers, like Machiavelli, who sought a deeper understanding of the nature of political instability and change.[17]

The peculiarly Irish form of this tendency is worthy of attention for the light it may throw not only on the condition of Ireland's women, but upon the nature of the larger processes of historical change. It seems useful to enquire, in other words, as to what underlying changes in sixteenth century Irish society gave rise to these tensions and as to why, given the obvious and accessible sources in which they are to be found, such tensions have for so long been disregarded by historians.

The second of these questions is perhaps the least important; but it provides a useful avenue of approach toward the more formidable problems raised by the first. The neglect of women in sixteenth century political history has doubtless been due in part to the male domination of the intellectual discipline. But it is more than that. A deeper reason is to be found in the influence exerted by a single interpretative concept over almost everything written about the century until recent years. For long, that is, the political history of sixteenth century Ireland has been perceived and summarised under the aegis of one stark and simple event, that long drawn out series of wars and confiscations known in the history books as 'the Tudor conquest'.

Within this war-torn interpretative framework, military historians and historians of high politics have prevailed and women as a group have had little share in their accounts. Moreover the compelling authority of an indisputable historical outcome – the completion of the conquest – imprisoned their history within a narrow chronological narrative that largely precluded an analytic approach through which the political role of women along with any number of other subjects might have been considered. Indeed when women featured at all in such traditional accounts they did so only as part of highly schematic introductory surveys designed to show that the two cultures in sixteenth century Ireland were wholly incompatible with one another and that one was determined to triumph (politically, at least) over its rival.[18]

In recent years this determinist view of sixteenth century political history has been subjected to searching criticism. Historians of late medieval Ireland have demolished the view that Gaelic society was in some way primitive or totally resistant to change from without, and have shown it to be a sophisticated system, then in the midst of complex political and social change. Similarly students of the Tudor intervention in Ireland have demonstrated that far from seeking direct military confrontation, successive English administrations sought to exploit the tendencies toward change displayed by the native lordships in the interests of the gradual transformation of Irish society into a replica of the English constitution.[19]

This long-term objective of internal reform was an extremely ambitious undertaking. The acceptance of English law and social customs promised considerable benefits in the long term not only to ruling families, but to freeholders and tenants who were promised relief from the arbitrary extortions of the great private armies of traditional Gaelic politics. It was however from these armed forces and from those members of the ruling dynasty who felt that they were being denied a legitimate aspiration of succession to the chieftaincy that the most dangerous resistance to reform arose. In the short term, therefore, reform placed a considerable strain on the internal politics of the lordships within which it was introduced by intensifying existing dynastic and political rivalries. The stresses it imposed, moreover, were greatly increased by the chronic failure of the Dublin administration to sustain the impetus of the various projects which it launched to advance the progress of reform over any reasonable period of time. As a result the reform policy gradually failed: many of the native lords became convinced of the weakness or the disingenuousness of English government and many more, who had already compromised themselves by their initial reception of the project, reacted against it in order to reassert their authority. It is now evident that several of the central events of the old Tudor conquest, such as the Desmond rebellion of 1579 and the Ulster rebellion in the 1590s, were the result not of deliberate conflict, but of an abortive experiment in peaceful cultural change.[20]

This new perspective has deepened our understanding of the complex nature of sixteenth century politics in general. But in the present context it suggests a number of questions concerning the role of aristocratic women in such rapidly changing times. For from within this alternative framework women can no longer be seen merely as the marginal accessories to or victims of a great military confrontation; they appear rather as crucial elements within the existing Irish political system, central to the maintenance of its stability, and central therefore in determining its response to the highly charged propositions now being placed before it.

III

The political order within which women played such an influential role was neither as primitive nor as anarchic as disillusioned late Elizabethan commentators like Spenser and Rich sought for their own propagandist purposes to depict. Rather the system which the Tudors confronted at the beginning of their reform initiative in the 1520s and 1530s was a complex and delicately balanced organism which had evolved gradually over the previous hundred years. By the beginning of the sixteenth century the old frontier war between the Gaelic Irish and the descendants of the Anglo-Norman conquerors had disappeared and the politics of Ireland was being reshaped by the emergence of a complicated network of alliances which transcended the old divisions of Gael and Gaill and joined old opponents in union with one another in rivalry against former friends and ethnic compatriots. By then too the ascendancy of the Anglo-Irish Geraldines over these local and regional alliances was clear. Between them, the Houses of Kildare and Desmond now exerted a political influence that extended beyond their own territories into every province of the island and even into the heart of Gaelic Ulster. The Geraldines' claims to hegemony, of course, had never gone undisputed, and their chief rivals, the Butlers of Ormond, had gradually established a smaller but hardly less extensive web of counter-alliances which sought to challenge the Geraldine influence where ever it was exerted.[21]

But the manner in which they had evolved, allegiance within these national networks was conditional and highly uncertain: the maintenance of authority was at all times dependent upon the regular demonstration of strength, wider political influence, liberality and patronage. Amidst these pressures certain structures served to maintain a basic stability. The employment of large private armies and of large households, the collection and distribution of protection payments, the confiscation and dispersal of properties were all employed toward this end. But above all of these, the establishment of personal relationships through marriage, concubinage and fosterage provided the central pillars for each alliance.

The role of women in this process of balance and control is obvious. The daughters of leading families among the Fitzgeralds, the Butlers, the Burkes, the O'Neills, O'Donnells, O'Connors and MacCarthys, as the labyrinthine genealogies of each of these great dynasties reveal, provided the essential means through which their ramifying alliances were sustained and extended from generation to generation; and a similar function was doubtless being discharged by the women of countless lesser families whose marriages and affinities are carefully but laconically recorded in the annalistic entries. The political importance and diplomatic influence of these women accounts in good part for their remarkable legal privileges and high social status which have often been noted by scholars and which were such a scandal to hostile commentators like Moryson. The point needs no further elaboration here.[22] But what must be stressed is that it was precisely this vital, intermediate role which was placed under particular pressure by the complex forces unleashed within the family networks by the Tudor policy of reform.

The response of Ireland's political women to the prospects of reform allows no easy generalisation. It is possible to suggest that in the long term the displacement of dynastic and familial politics by the standardised methods of legal process would have led to a diminution of these women's public role and eventually to their de-politicisation and domestication. Such an argument has been plausibly advanced concerning the fate of women at the time of the emergence of the classical Greek polis and again on the stabilisation of European feudalism in the high Middle Ages, and its relevance to sixteenth century Ireland where equally profound changes were at work cannot be denied.[23] Yet in the absence of any significant body of evidence it is impossible to generalise as to how the prospect of fundamental changes in their political and social roles actually influenced the attitude of Irish political women in practice.

For those noble women who successfully embraced political change with all its implications for their own traditional role their has of necessity been little left to record. Concerning Honora Burke, first wife of the 3rd Earl of Clanrickard and Una O'Brien, second wife of the 3rd Earl of Thomond little is known simply because they acquiesced in the abandonment of an overtly active political life which their husbands' acceptance of reform entailed. Margaret Cusacke, daughter of the Pale reformer Sir Thomas Cusacke, who was married to the 3rd Baron of Inchiquin in order to tie him more closely with the Dublin government, appears in the records only because the sudden and early death of her husband in 1573 compelled her to fight a long and ultimately successful struggle in Thomond to preserve her son's inheritance under English law.[24]

For others, conversely, the implications of reform may have been so immediately clear that their decision to resist it was easily made. Such was the case, for example, with Margaret O'Carroll, second wife of Brian Mac GillaPatrick and stepmother of Sir Barnaby Fitzpatrick whose wholehearted support of the government's reform proposals threatened to dislodge her and her relatives from the position of influence in Upper Ossory which she had carefully constructed.[25]

A similar and better known response was that of Fionnuala MacDonnell (Inion Dubh), third wife of Aodh Dubh O'Donnell, chieftain of Tirconnell between 1566 and 1594. A latecomer to Tirconnell's dynastic politics whose influence in the lordship was sustained only by the large contingent of galloglass which she brought as her dowry to Aodh, Inion Dubh was deeply threatened by Sir John Perrot's reform plans which envisaged the demilitarisation of the territory and the recognition of the tenurial claims and liberties of ancient freeholders. Recognising her inevitable hostility, Perrot moved to forestall her by seizing her eldest son by the chieftain, Aodh Ruadh, and holding him in Dublin Castle until the reforms had begun to take root. In her son's absence, however, Inion Dubh and her soldiers waged a veritable campaign of terror in Tirconnell, assassinating the leading supporters of Perrot's plan among the O'Donnells and intimidating others into silence. Within five years Tirconnell had been reduced into such a state of turmoil that Perrot's successor as viceroy, Sir William Fitzwilliam, was willing to tolerate or even to connive at Aodh Ruadh's escape from Dublin and his usurpation of the chieftainship.[26]

Agnes Campell, the Scottish wife of the contemporaneous chieftain of the O'Neills, Turlough Luineach, initially displayed a similar attitude toward the proffer of reform. In the 1570s her control over a large number of Scottish mercenaries was a major factor in fuelling Turlough's increasingly hostile attitude toward the Dublin government in general and in particular toward Sir Henry Sidney's efforts to establish a provincial council in Ulster. By the mid-1580s, however, when Perrot had guaranteed a secure inheritance both to her children by O'Neill and to her relatives in the north-east, her views had changed considerably. A principal influence in persuading O'Neill to accept the division of Tyrone between himself and the Baron of Dungannon as proposed by Perrot, she worked also to reach a final agreement between the Dublin administration and the Antrim Scots, and most ambitiously of all she sought to attain a permanent settlement of relations between the Highland clans and the Edinburgh and London governments which had exercised such a chronically disruptive effect on Ulster and Irish politics in the past.[27]

An even more ambivalent attitude may be discerned in the conduct of Gráinne O'Malley, the legendary Granuaile. Though it is difficult to disentangle the real historical circumstances from the body of tradition which has surrounded her, Grace's erratic responses to crown policy between the 1570s and the 1590s can be seen to have been determined by her perception of her own immediate interests within the highly unstable dynastic politics of west Connacht. Thus in the early 1570s, while married to the chief of the O'Flaherties whose principal source of income was supplied by the exaction of semi-feudal rights and by piracy along the western seaboard, Grace showed little interest in making overtures toward the English provincial president. Her marriage to Richard 'an Iarainn', a claimant to the lordship of the Mayo Burkes later in the decade, however, prompted her to take a rather more conciliatory approach to Sir Henry Sidney in an effort to secure his support for her husband's ambitions.[28]

Her practical dealings with Sir Nicholas Malby and Sir Richard Bingham, the two provincial presidents charged with the enforcement of the policy of composition in Connacht, followed a similar pattern.[29] After intermittent confrontations and reconciliations with both Gráinne succeeded in persuading the Dublin government of the justice of her claims to acquire legal title to lands withheld from her by the Burkes and was allowed safe passage to present her case at court. Whether she succeeded in making a peaceful transformation to English ways in her final years remains uncertain, but that Tibbot, her eldest son by Richard Burke, should have become one of the principal supporters and beneficiaries of the composition in Connacht was due in no small part to her determination to ensure that her own political interests would be served rather than subverted by the policy of reform.

Considerably more information has survived concerning another noble woman who made similarly strenuous efforts to reconcile the interests of her family with the requirements of reform: Eleanor Butler, the Countess of the last Earl of Desmond. The daughter of the Lord of Dunboyne, her marriage to the 14th Earl of Desmond in 1565 was intended, as so many others of its kind, to serve as a bridge of alliance between two great Munster families. Yet the Countess soon had wider obligations to meet, for she soon found herself enmeshed in a fierce struggle to persuade her husband to concede to the Dublin government's increasing demands for reform while defending his authority against the hostility which such concessions inevitably provoked among his own followers.[30]

Upon Desmond's arrest and despatch to the Tower in 1567, however, this diplomatic strategy seemed doomed to fail. Yet by her outright opposition to the rebellion immediately raised in Munster by James Fitzmaurice Fitzgerald and by her refusal to countenance the intrigues subsequently begun by her brother-in-law, Sir John of Desmond, to unseat the Earl, the Countess acquired a reputation for steadfastness which was to be of central importance in determining the English Privy Council's decision to restore the Earl to full authority within his lordship in 1573. And throughout the remainder of the 1570s this modern 'Abigail', as the English provincial president Sir William Drury called her, maintained her campaign to persuade Desmond to dispense with his armed followers and to accept the terms of 'composition' being offered to him by the government. By 1578 with the completion of a new agreement between the Earl and the Dublin government, she seemed to have made remarkable progress toward this goal. But with the return of Fitzmaurice from exile in the following year and the outbreak of a massive revolt of the swordsmen of the province, whatever hopes the Countess may have had of controlling affairs in the earldom were wrecked. She remained with the Earl even after he had (unwillingly) joined in the rebellion, conducting secret negotiations with the English commanders and with their cousin the Earl of Ormond, and hoping to salvage something from the debacle as she had done in the early 1570s. In the summer of 1582, however, as it became clear that Desmond himself would never be pardoned, she fled the rebellion, throwing herself on the mercy of the government and abandoning the earldom to its inevitable fate.[31]

The destruction of the House of Desmond did not mark the end of Eleanor Butler's remarkable career. After some years of personal danger and more of real hardship spent in attempting to secure a partial restoration of her livings, the Countess found herself propelled once again into her old diplomatic role through her second marriage, sanctioned and probably arranged by the great Lord Burghley, to Donough O'Connor Sligo in 1596. The circumstances of north Connacht in the later 1590s, where wholly irreconcilable swordsmen confronted equally uncompromising government agents, seemed to replicate in an even more acute manner those which had frustrated the Countess's attempts to salvage the Desmond earldom more than a decade before. But on his occasion, partly because of the O'Connors' ambivalent relations with the O'Donnells, partly because of the stable personality of her new husband, and in part also through sheer luck, the Countess's endeavours to act as mediator between the government and her lord proved to be remarkably successful. Thus O'Connor survived; and his lordship was, in the decades immediately following the war, to undergo a gradual transformation into shire government.[32]

Eleanor Butler's career is extraordinary not only because so much evidence concerning her political life has survived, but because she had a second chance. Few of her contemporaries enjoyed such good fortune; for in the years after 1580 most of the native lordships chose to follow Desmond's way rather than O'Connor Sligo's and the lordships' women who refused or who failed to discharge the mediating role assigned to them amidst the reform process have for the most part been lost to history. The reasons behind this sharp deterioration in relations between the native lordships and the Dublin government have been strenuously debated by historians in recent years; but while opinion has varied over the origin of this process, there has been a general agreement that the abandonment of hope in the possibility of peaceful assimilation and the adoption of increasingly confrontational attitudes on the part of English administrators in Ireland was the immediate cause of the great conflagration which occurred at the close of the century. There has been silent agreement also on the assumption that women from either side had little direct responsibility for this unfortunate outcome. Yet there remains a select group of women and one woman in particular whose actions or, more precisely, whose lack of activity may be seen to have contributed in no small measure to the gradual estrangement of Irish lords and English administrators.

IV

Central to the Tudor strategy of gradually replacing Ireland's existing political structures with conventional English institutions had been the act of 1541 which established Ireland as a kingdom in its own right. At the time of its passage this 'constitutional revolution' amounted to little more than a declaration of intent, an attempt to establish a framework within which practical reforms could take place. There was always an inherent fiction in this formulation, as the Irish monarch never existed outside of the person of the far more important English sovereign. But this intrinsic flaw was greatly exacerbated in practice by the failure of the Irish monarch's proxies, the viceroys, to establish an Irish court within the new kingdom which might have served both as a symbol and a practical instrument of the reformist intent of government. Early suggestions that special viceregal palaces should be established as centre points in each of the provinces were not pursued, and throughout the century the viceroys' residences at Kilmainham and at Dublin Castle continued to serve only the most basic functions of providing board and lodging for the governors' household and retinue.[33]

The viceroys' unwillingness to serve overlong in Ireland was doubtless largely responsible for their failure to develop an Irish court; but an additional responsibility must also be attributed to their wives who despite their high social standing and an often remarkable political influence rarely assumed any active part in the tortuous diplomatic process that was essential to the reform policy. Nothing is known of Lady St Leger whose husband has been credited with launching the greatest reform initiative of the century. Scattered evidence reveals that the Countess of Sussex resided in Ireland at some period during her husband's tenure of office, and remarkably she seems to have established some personal relations with Sean Maguire, the Lord of Fermanagh. But this association was exceptional, for the Countess had no further contacts in Irish political and social life. When indeed Shane O'Neill once suggested that relations between himself and the governor could be cemented by a marriage with one of Sussex's sisters, the idea was not merely dismissed out of hand, but interpreted as a deliberate gesture of contumacy.[34]

A woman of even greater potential influence was the wife of Sussex's successor as viceroy, Sir Henry Sidney. As the sister of Lord Robert Dudley, and a principal lady-in-waiting to Queen Elizabeth herself, Lady Mary Sidney was frequently involved in political and courtly intrigues at the highest levels in Whitehall. Yet she seems never to have exploited her especially favoured position in the interest of drawing the Queen and her Irish subjects closer to each other. Again there is evidence that she sometimes resided with her husband during his periods of service in Ireland; and even on one occasion in his absence: Campion reports her spirited participation in the defence of Drogheda in 1567. But, if Sir William Fitzwilliam is to be believed, her visits to Ireland were insufficiently long to prevent Sir Henry from taking comfort in the arms of one of his captains' wives.[35]

Fitzwilliam's own wife, Anne, was also a woman with powerful connections. A sister of Sir Henry Sidney, she acquired an unsavoury reputation among her detractors for using family connections to advance her own and her husband's interests. Lady Fitzwilliam clearly attempted to exert an influence during her husband's terms of office, exonerating the viceroy from criticisms made against him at court and urging Burghley to respond favourably to requests for money, men and munitions. But she maintained a narrow and rather defensive attitude toward her political role. A committed Protestant, she deliberately distanced herself from the religiously suspect or openly recusant society of the Pale, and seems to have cultivated during her time in Dublin only a small circle of English clergy and military men.[36]

The absence of even the semblance of a courtly society in Dublin was undoubtedly a major obstacle to the Tudor government's attempt to replicate England's political and social processes in Ireland. But a far more serious blow was dealt to the reform strategy's hopes of reconstructing a model English kingdom in Ireland by the failure of the real court to supply in relation to Irish politics those functions which it discharged so effectively at the centre of the English political scene. And in this regard it was one woman, Queen Elizabeth herself, who may be said to be in large part responsible for such a crucial diplomatic disappointment.

Elizabeth's attitude toward the government of Ireland was not especially distinctive. Financially stringent as she was in all other matters of governance, she was often, and rightly, suspicious of her servants' motives and actions. She was also reasonably consistent in her objectives; for although she was occasionally pleased to allow radical departures from the conventions of politics in times of emergency and rebellion, she continued to profess both in proclamations and in formal addresses to the Irish nobility her continuing commitment to the establishment of a peaceful and amicable settlement within the kingdom of Ireland. Thus far Elizabeth's influence on the course of reform in Ireland may be seen to have been marginal or mildly beneficial. Yet it was the manner in which she shaped and maintained her court that Elizabeth, inadvertently but no less gravely, served to undermine the reform policy's operations and aspirations.

From the beginning the court of the monarch of England and Ireland was understood to occupy a place of central importance in the strategy of the Irish reformers. The elaborate ceremonies of surrender and regrant orchestrated by Sir Anthony St Leger before King Henry were intended not merely as propaganda exercises, to impress the Irish lords with the authority of the English Crown, they were designed also to introduce the lords to a new arena of political bargaining and decision making to which they should look henceforth as their ultimate resort in the defence of their interests and the settlement of their disputes.[37]

Henry VIII's attitude toward the Irish chieftains was erratic; but up to the end of his reign he continued to be receptive to suggestions that further lords should visit court, that the newly created peers be given the opportunity to acquire lands in England, and most importantly that their heirs be sent to England to enjoy the benefits of a courtly education. Such Henrician aspirations survived under Edward, though little was actually done, apart from the pardon and rehabilitation of the exiled Earl of Kildare, to advance them in practice. Under Mary and Elizabeth, however, they gradually faded from view. The court of Queen Mary was itself too ridden by political and religious tensions to function effectively as an instrument of communication and arbitration. But the removal of such strains in the following reign allowed no significant improvement.

Under Elizabeth the privy chamber which had developed steadily throughout the first half of the century as an influential centre of political and administrative business, suddenly contracted and assumed once again the character of a household department in the narrowest sense. Dominated by the Queen's chosen ladies-in-waiting and by a select group of her closest relations, it was, as Pam Wright has shown, an 'essentially female' institution, whose principal purpose was the entertainment of the Queen and her protection from the unwanted attention of suitors and political intriguers. Occasionally a royal favourite, notably Robert Dudley, Earl of Leicester, succeeded in penetrating this *cordon sanitaire*; but the number of individuals granted such a privilege was so few and the influence which they could exert over the Queen in matters of high policy so unpredictable that they were never to succeed in reconverting the privy chamber into an arena of political rivalry and debate. This neutralisation of the innermost circle of court was doubtless beneficial in some respects; but its effect in relation to the Irish reform policy was further to distance the Irish lords from their supposed sovereign and to deepen the conviction that the establishment of the Irish kingdom was no more than a once convenient and now irrelevant piece of rhetoric.[38]

The high formality of Elizabeth's court and the gradual restriction of access to the Queen herself entailed several difficulties for the prospects of the Irish reform strategy. First, although the Irish governors continued to recommend important Irish lords for presentation at court, few were actually invited to attend. Under the viceroyalties of the Earl of Sussex and, more notably,

Sir Henry Sidney, representatives of the Mac Carthys, the O'Donnells, the O'Reilly's and the O'Connor Sligo were actually despatched with the aim of conducting a ceremony of surrender and regrant in the manner established under King Henry. But the reception accorded to them was in each case modest: no record of their entertainment has survived, there is no evidence that they were received in person by Elizabeth, and most importantly no formal agreement of surrender was completed during their time at court. The career of young Hugh O'Neill, the Baron of Dungannon, is illustrative of this aloofness. Though much has been written concerning the influence which his exposure to Elizabethan courtly life had on his subsequent career, there is little to indicate that he spent any significant time at the court. Resident in Dublin until 1562 at least, he may then have travelled to England, but it is more likely that he went there in the company of Sir Henry Sidney only in 1567. Whether he ever enjoyed an audience with Elizabeth herself remains a matter of speculation.[39]

Two apparent exceptions to these observations tend merely to confirm them. The early years of Elizabeth did indeed witness the quite spectacular visit of one Irish potentate to court. In 1562 Shane O'Neill spent over four months in its environs, was personally received by Elizabeth, and negotiated while there the foundations of a major agreement concerning the government of Ulster. Yet O'Neill's visit was from the beginning shrouded in controversy. Unlike his father he came to court against the express will of the viceroy, Sussex, rather than on his recommendation. His arrival was, instead, the result of a complicated intrigue by the royal favourite, Lord Robert Dudley, who planned to use Shane as a means of discomfiting his principal aristocratic enemies, the Duke of Norfolk and his ally the Earl of Sussex. During his time at court Shane was then regarded as little more than another, somewhat exotic protégé of the favourite. He failed to establish any wider connections within court society, and, when he departed, discovered to his dismay that the agreement he believed he had completed was simply negated as soon as Dudley had lost interest in him. By these means one of the most crucial and most delicate of Irish political issues was catapulted into prominence and then abandoned simply as the caprices of erratic and ephemeral court politics dictated.[40]

The second apparent exception also concerns a favourite, and remarkably, an Irish one. From early on in the reign Thomas Butler, the Earl of Ormond, established a close personal tie with Elizabeth which was to prove less intense but more enduring than Dudley's. Though he cautiously refrained from involving himself in overtly political matters, it was an advantage which he skilfully exploited to advance and defend the interests of his family and dependants. Ormond's remarkable career at court provides an indication as to how that institution might have served to cultivate a genuine confidence among the ranks of the Irish nobility as to the practical reality of the Anglo-Irish dual monarchy – were it not for the fact that it was indeed exceptional. No other Irish lord enjoyed anything like Ormond's access to Elizabeth, and when their interests rivalled Ormond's, it was invariably his which prevailed. In the 1560s and 1570s some of the most important figures in Irish politics underwent this dis- illusioning experience. Some, like the Earl of Desmond, were eventually driven into open rebellion by their courtly defeats; others, like the Earl of Kildare, aimed at more subtle but equally futile intrigues, while others again, like the Baron of Upper- Ossory – King Edward's boy companion from whom so much had been expected – simply withdrew from all involvement in government. But each in their way had come to recognise that Ormond's unique influence with Elizabeth had rendered the court unresponsive if not overtly hostile to their own needs.[41]

This experience of an unequal competition for the Queen's attentions was not confined to Ormond's Irish rivals. For as the plans of the reforming English governors came into conflict with Ormond's own concerns, so the Irish favourite moved to cur- tail their activity by appeal to the Queen. Every Elizabethan viceroy was conscious of this powerful influence at work behind their backs, and some, like the Earl of Sussex and Sir William Fitzwilliam, sought simply to accommodate themselves to it. But the most ambitious of the Elizabethan reformers, Sir Henry Sidney and Sir John Perrot, who were determined to establish their personal authority in Ireland, inevitably came into open conflict with the Earl; and when they did the result in both cases was the same. Each was the recipient of highly critical letters from Elizabeth herself, each was ordered to desist, and their refusal was to contribute significantly to their recall. Though he himself was, ironically, no enemy to the political transformation of Ireland, the cumulative effect of Ormond's unique personal influence with Elizabeth was merely to undermine further any prospect that the Dublin administration would continue its com- mitment to a sustained campaign of reform in Ireland.[42]

V

To attribute the gradual failure of the reform policy in Ireland to the political deficiencies of Elizabeth and her court is, of course, as pointless as to blame Fionnuala Mac Domhnall, Eleanor Butler

or Anne Fitzwilliam for their failure to rise to the challenges
which the reform strategy placed before them. The demands
placed upon each of these women were in very different ways so
onerous and so complex that none could have been expected to
meet them in any persistent manner. Given the extraordinary
strains which it imposed on all parties, it is surprising not that
women failed to discharge their political roles successfully, but
that so many should have struggled for so long to do so. It was
indeed only in the circumstances of extreme duress such as those
which the ambitious Tudor reform scheme imposed on Anglo-
Irish political relations that the importance of aristocratic
women's place in the maintenance of order and continuity in
politics, so often presumed and so often denied in the ambivalent
literary sources discussed at the beginning of this essay, becomes
so evident.

Yet it is not surprising also, in the years following the onset of
that series of confrontations known as the Tudor conquest, that
women should have withdrawn from the active political and
diplomatic engagement which the policy of Tudor reform had
demanded of them and returned, until the crisis years of the
1640s at least, to rather less overt and more indirect ways of
deploying influence. Such a subtle process of resignation and
reorientation has by its very nature left little for the historian to
record. But it may be traced, however dimly, in a remarkable
literary exchange that took place between Brigid Fitzgerald,
daughter of the Earl of Kildare and Countess of Tyrconnell, and
Cuchonnacht Og Maguire sometime around 1607. On the surface
the exchange of poems in which Cuchonnacht claims that he will
die if the lady refuses him her love and the lady politely demurs
seems quite conventional. Yet there are, as Cathal O'Hainle has
pointed out, a number of unusual features in the encounter
which gesture towards a larger and less personal issue.
Cuchonnacht's preoccupation with death and a more general
desolation is remarkably intense; while Brigid's response is
cold and unmoved, for in a clever reply (which was itself
commissioned) she denies the sincerity of Cuchonnacht's claims
by questioning the veracity of his authorship (the poem, O'Hainle
suggests, was probably composed by Eochaidh Ó Eoghusa).[43]

An explanation for such curious attitudes may be found at least
in part in the immediate circumstances within which the dialogue
took place. At the time that he addressed Lady Tyrconnell,
Maguire was in fairly desperate straits. Financially ruined by the
redivision of Fermanagh, he was openly hostile to the new
settlers in his old lordship and was contemplating exile or rebellion. In this disillusion with post-Mellifont Ireland he was joined
by Rory O'Donnell, Brigid's husband, who when confronted by

a similar combination of financial and political pressures had
already chosen exile. When he finally left in September of 160?
Brigid was in the Pale expecting their child. Interrogated by the
government, she denied all knowledge of her husband's actions
and intentions, publicly condemned them and affirmed her
intention to remain in Ireland and have no further contact with
him. The administrators remained unconvinced and it was only
after Rory's death and Brigid's subsequent marriage to a gentle
man of the Pale that their doubts were assuaged. But unbeknown
to them Brigid had already made her intentions clear in the poetic
dispute with Cuchonnacht. Rejecting the Gaelic lords' pleas as
false and illusory, this daughter of Kildare and wife of O'Donnel
renounced also the central mediating role assumed by so many
other women in the previous century, and concluded:

No one will hear my surname until yesterday returns . . . .[44]

REFERENCES

1. For a modern account, see A. Chambers, *Granuaile: the Life and
   Times of Grace O'Malley, c. 1530–1603* (Dublin, 1979).
2. A.B. Rowan, *The Olde Countesse of Desmond* (Dublin, 1860), esp.
   pp. 20–1.
3. B.G. Mac Carthy, 'The Riddle of Rose O'Toole' in Seamus Pender
   (ed.), *Feilschribhinn Torna* (Cork, 1947), pp. 171–82.
4. On Gilbert see, D.B. Quinn (ed.), *The Voyages and Colonising
   Enterprises of Sir Humphrey Gilbert* (2 vols, London, 1940), Vol. I,
   pp. 15–18; T. Churchyard, *A Generall Rehearsall of the Warres*
   (London, 1579); on Essex, W.B. Devereux, *Lives and Letters of the
   Devereux Earls of Essex* (2 vols, London, 1863), Vol. I, pp. 113–19;
   Proclamation against Shane O'Neill, 8 June 1561 (P.R.O., S.P. 63/
   4/1); Bingham's 'Discourse of services', October 1586 (*ibid.*, 126/53,
   enclosure (i)).
5. W.M. Hennessey (ed.), *The Annals of Loch Cé* (2 vols, London,
   1856), Vol. II, p. 333.
6. S. Mac Airt (ed.), *Leabhar Branach* (Dublin, 1944), poems 60, 61,
   pp. 226–38; James Carney, *The Irish Bardic Poet* (Dublin, 1967),
   p. 34.
7. See for example *Deputy Keeper Public Records of Ireland Reports*,
   16–17, Fiants nos 4510, 4853, 5445, 5476.
8. Churchyard, *A Generall Rehearsall*, Sig Q1–R1.
9. F. Moryson *An Itinerary* . . . (4 vols, Glasgow, 1907), Vol. IV,
   pp. 198–9, 237; and in Charles Hughes (ed.), *Shakespeare's Europe*,
   pp. 196–7, 235.
10. For an overview of Rich's attitude toward women see, P.A.
    Jorgensen, 'Rich: soldier, suitor and honest critic of women' in
    Shakespeare Quarterly, Vol. VII (1956), pp. 23–37.
11. L. Miller and E. Power (eds), *Holinshed's Irish Chronicle 1577*
    (Dublin, 1979), pp. 220–1, 326, 281–2.
12. *Ibid.*, pp. 56–7.

13. J.S. Brewer and W. Bullen (eds) 'The Book of Howth', *Cal Carew Mss*, Vol. V, pp. 15–16.
14. *Ibid.*, pp. 42–3.
15. *Ibid.*, p.212.
16. See *inter alia*, B. Carroll *et al.* (eds), *Liberating Women's History: Theoretical and Critical Essays* (Chicago and London, 1976); R. Bridenthal and C. Koonz (eds), *Becoming Visible: Women in European History* (Boston, 1977).
17. See L.B. Wright, *Middle Class Culture in Elizabethan England* (Durham, North Carolina, 1935), Ch. XIII, and in particular, H.F. Pitkin, *Fortune is a Woman: Gender and Politics in the Thought of Niccolo Machiavelli* (Berkeley, 1984).
18. See for instance the introductory comments in Cyril Falls, *Elizabeth's Irish Wars* (London, 1950), pp. 24–34.
19. Useful syntheses of recent work are Steven Ellis, *Tudor Ireland: Crown, Conflict and Community, 1470–1603* (London, 1987) and N.P. Canny, *Reformation to Restoration: Ireland 1534–1660* (Dublin, 1988).
20. I have discussed these points more fully in 'Sixteenth Century Ulster and the Failure of Tudor Reform' in C. Brady, M. O'Dowd and B. Walker (eds), *Ulster: An Illustrated History* (London, 1989), pp. 77–103.
21. A valuable political gazetteer of Ireland at the beginning of the century is provided by D.B. Quinn and K.W. Nicholls in T.W. Moody, F.X. Martin, F.J. Byrne (eds), *A New History of Ireland. III 1634–1690* (Oxford, 1976), Ch. 1.
22. Donncha O Corrain, 'Women in Early Irish Society' in M. MacCurtain and D. O Corrain (eds), in *Women in Irish Society: the Historical Dimension* (Dublin, 1978), pp. 10–11; K.W. Nicholls, *Gaelic and Gaelicised Ireland* (Dublin, 1972) pp. 73–77; M. MacCurtain, 'Marriage in Tudor Ireland' in A. Cosgrove (ed.), *Marriage in Ireland* (Dublin, 1985), pp. 56–58.
23. See the essays by Marylin Arthur on classical Greece and Joan Kelley-Gadol on the early renaissance in Bridenthal and Koonz, *Becoming Visible, op. cit.*, pp. 60–89, 139–64.
24. *A.F.M.* s.a. 1597, 1598.
25. Fitzpatrick to Sir Henry Sidney, 6 May 1573 (P.R.O., S.P. 63/40/27); Instructions to Edmund Tremayne, 9 July, 1573 (*ibid.*, 41/13).
26. P. Walsh (ed.), *Beatha Aodha Ruaidh O'Dhomhnaill* (2 vols, Dublin 1948), Vol. II, pp. 24–5; *A.F.M.*, s.a. 1588, 1590; Sir Nicholas Bagenal to Burghley, 9 June 1586 (P.R.O., S.P. 63/124/70); Perrot to Burghley, 2 May 1587 (*ibid.*, 129/64); Bingham to Burghley, 15 May 1588 (*ibid.*, 135/26); Patrick Foxe to Walsingham, 12 February 1589 (*ibid.*, 141/22).
27. Nicholas Malby to Cecil, 8 April 1570 (P.R.O., S.P. 63/30/37); Sidney to Privy Council, 17 March, 1577 (*ibid.*, 57/39); Archbishop Loftus to Burghley, 12 May 1586 (*ibid.*, 124/14); Perrot to Privy Council, 1 July 1587 (*ibid.*, 130/27); Lady Agnes to Robert Bowes, 25 April 1590 (*Cal State Papers Scotland, 1588–90*, p. 54).
28. A. Chambers, *Granuaile, op. cit.*
29. See pp. 55–9 above.
30. For a good modern biography see A. Chambers, *Eleanor, Countess of Desmond, c. 1545–1638* (Dublin, 1986).
31. C. Brady, 'Faction and the Origins of the Desmond Rebellion of 1579' in *Irish Historical Studies*, Vol. XXII (1981), pp. 289–312.

32. For the general context of the Countess's later years in Sligo see M. O'Dowd, 'Landownership in the Sligo Area' (Ph.D thesis, National University of Ireland, 1980).

33. See B. Bradshaw, *The Irish Constitutional Revolution of the Sixteenth Century* (Cambridge, 1979), and C. Brady, 'Court, Castle and Country: the Framework of Government in Tudor Ireland' in C. Brady and R. Gillespie (eds), *Natives and Newcomers: essays on the making of Irish Colonial Society* (Dublin, 1986), pp. 22–49; for the proposal to establish viceregal residences, Privy Council to Bellingham, 6 January, 1549 (P.R.O., S.P. 61/2/3).

34. Shane Maguire to the Earl of Sussex, August 1562 (British Library, Cotton MSS, Vespasian F XII, no. 46); also Shane O'Neill to Elizabeth, 18 November 1563 (P.R.O., S.P. 63/9/62) and to Sussex, 23 May 1564 (*ibid.*, 10/65).

35. For an account of Lady Sidney's relations with Elizabeth see P. Wright, 'A Change in direction: the Ramifications of a Female Household' in D. Starkey *et al.*, *The English Court from the Wars of the Roses to the Civil War* (London, 1987), pp. 147–172; also N. Williams, *All the Queen's Men: Elizabeth I and her Courtiers* (London, 1972), pp. 79–80; A.F. Vossen (ed.), *Two Bokes of the Histories of Ireland compiled by Edmund Campion* (Assen, Netherlands, 1963), p. 140; on the gossip concerning Mrs Issham see Fitzwilliam to Cecil, 8 June 1565 (P.R.O., S.P. 62/13/57).

36. Fitzwilliam to Burghley, 14 November 1589 (P.R.O., S.P. 63/148/10); Baron Castle Connell to Burghley, 31 January 1593 (*ibid.*, 168/12); Robert Legge's 'Book of accusations', April 1593 (*ibid.*, 169/3).

37. Bradshaw, *Constitutional Revolution, op. cit.*, esp. part III.

38. P. Wright, 'A Change of Direction: the Privy Chamber in the Reign of Elizabeth' in D. Starkey *et al.*, *The English Court, op. cit.*; also D. Loades, *The Tudor Court* (London, 1986), pp. 51–6, 156–9, 199–202.

39. See H. Morgan, 'The Outbreak of the Nine Years War' (Ph.D thesis, University of Cambridge, 1987), pp. 76–77.

40. J. Hogan, 'Shane O'Neill comes to the Court of Elizabeth' in S. Pender (ed.), *Feilschribhinn Torna* (Cork, 1947), pp. 154–70.

41. C. Brady, 'Thomas Tenth Earl of Ormond and the Kingdom of Ireland' in C. Brady (ed.), *Worsted in the Game: Losers in Irish History* (Dublin, 1989), pp. 49–59.

42. See H.F. Hore (ed.) 'Sir Henry Sidney's "Memoir" of service in Ireland' in *Ulster Journal of Archaeology*, series 1, Vol. III (1855), pp. 37–44, 91–9, 346–53; Vol. V (1857), pp. 305–15; Vol. VI (1858), pp. 179–95.

43. C. O'Hainle, 'Flattery Rejected: Two Seventeenth Century Irish Poems' in *Hermathena*, Vol. CXXXVIII (1985), pp. 5–27. See pp. 35–6 above for a different interpretation.

44. *Ibid.*, p. 19. Moshloinneadh nt chluinfe cách uaimsi-go dtille an la inne.

* I should like to express my thanks to Dr Jeffrey Kallen and Prof. Cathal O Hainle for their advice in the preparation of this paper.

6

Women and War in Ireland in the 1640s

MARY O'DOWD

Much has been written in recent years on the impact of war on the status of women in society. War, it is argued, can open up new opportunities for women for independent action and responsibility as women take over work and services normally monopolised by men.[1]

Most of the historiography on women and war has focused on the First and Second World Wars but the research of Patricia Higgins, Keith Thomas, Antonia Fraser and others has examined the impact of the English Civil Wars on the status of women. Their conclusions suggest that these wars also brought new opportunities to some women in seventeenth century England. Women, for example, managed and defended family estates, engaged in military service and acted as war couriers and diplomatic go-betweens. Most importantly, they petitioned the government for help and assistance in large numbers and thus participated more publicly in the political process than was normal in times of peace. New political ideas about the equality of men and women emerged in England in the 1640s and religious sects which encouraged a more active role for women, including that of preaching, became popular.[2] Although, as David Underdown has rightly argued, it 'would be absurd to depict the war as a milestone in the liberation of women', yet, as he acknowledges, 'the war did allow more independence for a few of them, especially in London'.[3]

The purpose of this article is to analyse the experience of women in Ireland during the same period and to examine the extent to which the Irish wars of the mid-seventeenth century brought benefits or changes to women's lives.

I

Women's direct involvement in the military conflict of the 1640s took a variety of forms, depending on the class and economic background of the women concerned. At the highest social level, women from landed backgrounds could find themselves as heads of households under siege from enemy fire. There are many examples of women heads of households under attack. Some quickly accepted offers of safe convoy for themselves and members of their household but others decided to defend their homes and resist the besiegers. The most well-documented example of resistance is Lady Offaly's defence of Geashill Castle in County Offaly. The castle was besieged several times and on each occasion Lady Offaly, a widow since 1618, refused safe convoy claiming that there was 'no place safer than my own house', a claim which eventually proved to be true when the besieging forces were obliged to withdraw.[4] Other women proved equally difficult to frighten out of their homes. Lady Offaly's neighbour, Lady Forbes defended Castle Forbes under siege for nine months. At the beginning of the rebellion she furnished the castle with arms, ammunition and victuals and assembled in the castle the British tenants from the estate in order to defend the house. She also offered refuge to over 200 Protestants from the neighbouring area. At the end of nine months, supplies had run out and the residents of Castle Forbes were reduced to eating dried cow hides. As a result, Lady Forbes felt obliged to accept an offer of safe convoy for all the occupants to leave the castle.[5] In Westmeath, later in the war, Sir Luke Fitzgerald's wife won the grudging respect of an English writer for her defence of the castle of Trecroghan, although he could not resist describing her men's sally from the castle on one occasion as 'desperate as men usually do when they are commanded by a woman'.[6]

It is difficult to assess the extent to which women who defended their homes in this manner were thereby engaging actively in the military conflict. Lady Offaly argued that she was simply defending her home. When she finally abandoned her home she retired to England and took no further part in the war in Ireland.[7] On the other hand, some women who withstood a siege of their homes clearly did have strong political views. The evidence of the depositions, taken after the rebellion began in late 1641, contain accounts of women hiring soldiers to attack settlers or actively encouraging male relatives to participate in the rebellion.[8]

Another woman who manifestly was politically committed was Lady Elizabeth Dowdall. She appears to have relished the opportunity to command a group of men to defend her castle at Kilfenny in County Limerick. She subsequently wrote her own account of her military achievements in which she described how at the beginning of the rebellion she hired a soldier to train 80 men and then sent them out to attack the Irish troops.[9] Her narrative suggests she was proud of her achievements which she felt had protected the area from being overrun by the Irish forces:

> The ninth of January, [1642] the High Sheriff of the county, and all the power of the county, came with three thousand men to besiege me. They brought two sows and thirty scaling-ladders against me. They wrote many attempting letters to me to yield to them which I answered with contempt and scorn. They were three weeks and four days besieging me before they could bring these sows to me, being building of them all that time upon my own land, yet every day and night in fight with me. The Thursday before Ash Wednesday, High-Sheriff, Richard Stephenson, came up in the front of the army, with his drums and pipers, but I sent him a shot in the head that made him bid the world good-night, and routed the whole army, we shot so hot. . . . On Thursday, they drew their sows nearer, and Friday, they came on, at night with a full career and a great acclamation of joy, even hard to the castle. But I sent such a free welcome to them, that turned their mirth into moaning. I shot iron bullets that pierced through their sows, though they were lined with iron gridds and flock-beds, and bolsters, so that I killed their pigs, and by the enemy's confession that night two hundred of their men.[10]

Lady Dowdall's account of her activities is interesting not only because it provides a rare insight into a woman's involvement in the war but also because she refers in passing to the fact that her husband, Lord Dowdall, was in the castle when she was commanding her force of 80 men. In other words, Lady Dowdall was clearly a woman with a strong personality who was probably accustomed to taking charge of the household prior to the outbreak of war. The status or control which Irish women exercised in the early modern household has not yet been examined by historians but many at the highest levels of society such as the women noted here must have been familiar with long periods of time when their husbands were absent. Even more so than in England, involvement in official business entailed a considerable amount of travel to Dublin or London. Wives of officials as well as widows would have been accustomed to acting as heads of household in their husbands' absence. For such women, military defence of the household was in many respects a logical extension of managing household affairs in peacetime. Their military activities may therefore reveal more about their position before the war than indicate new opportunities presented by wartime conditions.[11]

Another means of participation in the conflict for women was to act as messengers or diplomatic go-betweens in negotiations. The myriad of marriage connections between leaders of the royalist and confederate forces meant that wives or sisters could easily mediate or negotiate between men on both sides. Women from this type of privileged and politically influential background were also in a position to exert indirect pressure on male relatives. And examples can be found of women doing just that but again it is doubtful if this can be identified as a new role for women. Women from politically important families were always in a position to exercise a certain amount of political influence. Their negotiating importance may have assumed a new significance as a result of wartime circumstances but it was not a totally new concept.

The more covert activities of some aristocratic women did present a fresher challenge. The unsuspecting trust given to women from aristocratic and gentry families by military leaders could be used and exploited. Sir John Burke's wife, for example, was found with two bags of gunpowder and other ammunition in her coach which she was trying surreptitiously to transport from Dublin to the midlands. Lady Alice Moore plotted unsuccessfully to help the Scots from Ulster to seize Drogheda from the crown forces, providing them with 'false keys' to the town. In another castle siege women were used to lure the besiegers into a trap. Later in the war, Lady Costello and Lady Dillon were involved in a similar and also unsuccessful attempt to take Athlone Castle. Other women were suspected of more covert activities, passing intelligence to the other side. Lady Bellew of Castletown was accused of this by one deponent while the widow of Edward May (described as a 'meere Irish woman whom the gentleman long kept for his fancy, and thereafter married out of conscience') was said to have regularly passed information to Phelim O'Neill from Dublin where she lived. But overall this type of secret activity involved only a small number of women and is not, therefore, significant in the more general context of the experience of women during the war.[12]

Further down the social scale women were also active in the rising. A small number participated directly in the military conflict. Ireland, like England at the same time, had its 'she-soldiers'. An account of a skirmish between Irish and parliamentary troops in Connacht describes how when a montero was pulled from the head of one of the Irish soldiers 'there fell down long tresses of flaxen hair, who being further searched was found to be a woman'.[13] Irish women who accompanied their husbands who served in the royalist army in England were recorded as

having been involved in physical conflict and they earned an
almost mythical reputation for their ferocity. A report of a group
of Irish women captured after the battle of Nantwich described
how they carried long knives 'which are such bloody instruments, that the eye of man never beheld before, being about halfe
a yard in length, with a hook and point at the end of them made
not only to stab, but to teare the flesh from the very bones'.[14]
Such reports, perhaps, however, reveal more about the prejudices of the narrator than the military skills of Irish women.

The reasons why women chose to accompany the army in any
war either in disguise or otherwise are difficult to pinpoint. They
could vary from a concern to stay with their husbands for reasons
of economic necessity or affection to a desire to join the army as
a 'she-soldier', as they were dubbed in England. Despite the wild
stories about their ferocity, it is likely that most of the women
who accompanied Irish soldiers to England did so for economic
reasons.

Of more significance in terms of the opportunities which the
war presented to women, is the participation of women in the
rising in local areas. There has been little research done on the
outbreak of the 1641 rising at local level but it does seem possible
to distinguish between areas where the rising manifested itself
first as a popular rising which was spontaneous and lacked
organisation and counties where it was pre-planned and led by
a group of local gentlemen who concentrated on seizing selected
military targets. In the latter areas, the resulting military conflict
tended to be male dominated. In other parts of the country where
the rising had more popular support, women as well as children
became involved. The rising often initially took the form of an
assembly of a large crowd which then attacked and looted the
homes of local Protestant settlers. Women could play a prominent
role in such assemblies which lacked formal or traditional structures or clear methods of procedure.

In this type of popular rising women were given unusual
opportunities to influence public affairs and there are descriptions in the depositions of mobs either led by women or in which
women played an important role. In Armagh a woman, Jane
Hamskin, was alleged to have led a mob which set fire to a
cottage in which a group of settlers had taken refuge. In Athlone
a woman carrying a message for the president of Connacht was
reported to have been stoned to death by a group of women from
the town.[15] In Galway, according to an eye witness, a similar
crowd of about 300 gathered and marched through the streets
and women were in the forefront encouraging attacks on any
Protestant who could be found. For example when John Fox, a

chandler, was beheaded by some of the crowd, his head was seized and thrown up in the air by 'a great lustie Irish woman'. The crowd subsequently attacked two women in a house and, later, one of the occupants of the house described how he was discovered in hiding by the word of the daughter of the provost of the town, Martin Lynch. He claimed that Lynch's daughter was going around the town searching for him 'saying in Irish where is the English dog'.[16]

The deposition evidence also contains some intriguing references to women taking on male roles. Henry Ayliffe of King's County, for example, described how in the town of Mullingar, the portriefe was attacked by a large crowd when he tried to read the proclamation denouncing the rebels and subsequently he was seized and tried for his life by a jury of women, the forewoman of which threatened him with his life.[17] Robert Aldrick of Monaghan described how a woman was hanged and was 'guarded to the place of execution' by Margaret MacMahon, wife of Rory McGillapatrick MacMahon who went before her 'with a white rod in hand and a skine by her side saying she would be sheriff for that turn and so stood by, till the poor woman was hanged'.[18]

These references are tantalising and open to at least two interpretations: either the women and the local society were mocking the English legal system in a charivari sense of a world turned upside down in which the women took on men's roles, or the breakdown of formal law and order structures allowed women to play a more prominent public role. Women are recorded as playing a leading role in eighteenth century food riots so that the assumption by women of a leading role in local risings in the 1640s in Ireland may not be that unusual.[19]

The participation of women in popular protests helps to explain the accusation of many deponents that Irish women were as violent as the men in the attacks on settlers. In a conflict where the main issue was male political control the participation of women at any level must have surprised and shocked many observers. It also led to women being described in subhuman terms as 'amazons' or 'devilish viragoes', emphasising their departure from the normal feminine role.[20]

Inevitably perhaps, popular protests often spilled over into uncontrolled looting and women were often prominent in the seizure and distribution of looted goods. Several deponents accused women of wearing their clothes or using their household goods. Sergeant Major William Burley's description of the looting of his house by a crowd of men and women is both graphic and convincing:

And further sayth that this deponent and his wiffe and children being gone away to shun the danger of that great multitude, severall of his servants confidently told him that after he was gone away, and that the Rebells had entered his howse, the wife of the said Hugh O'Lory, taking upon her to order and dispose of the household [goods], furniture, apparrell and provision, went up into this deponent's wiffe's chamber, and seasing on the deponent's wiffes apparell, attired and dressed herself in the best of that apparell, and that [done] coame down into the parlor, called for strong beare, and made her servants fetch it and drunck a confusion to the English doggs; and being sett at the upper end of the table, in a chaire, asked the people whether that choice apparell did not become her as well as Mrs. Burley [meaning the deponent's wife]; and she and her base crew contynued their rebelly carousing and drincking untill all or most of them were drunck.[21]

As Raymond Gillespie suggests elsewhere in this volume women also acted as receivers and sellers of looted goods. On a slightly more formal level, Turlough Oge O'Neill was reported to have made the shopkeepers in Armagh and Lough Gall 'accountable to his wife for all the wares they sold out of their shops', although what exactly this entailed is not clear.[22]

On a more positive note, women were often also the only source of help for the victims of violence. Nursing and hospital services did not exist in most parts of the country and in many cases women provided the only available help. Lady Elizabeth Preston, the Earl of Ormond's wife, was reported to have provided considerable material help and sanctuary for many refugees in Kilkenny and Tipperary as well as in Dublin. Sir Phelim O'Neill's mother, Katherine Hovenden, provided a similar service in the north for English and Scottish families. In other parts of the country women secretly provided food for besieged castles and the poor in the neighbourhood, as well as giving blankets to clothe families stripped of their clothes and generally doing what they could to help the victims of the war.[23]

Women were, therefore, involved in the action of the rebellion in a number of different ways. Women from landed backgrounds took on the defence of their homes, hired men to defend them and encouraged and assisted their male relatives. They also acted as couriers and diplomatic go-betweens as well as undertaking more covert activities. But it is difficult to argue that the war opened up new opportunities for this category of women. Defence of a household may have been simply an indication of the dominant role which women exercised in domestic affairs while women from politically important families were always in a position to influence political events and developments either through indirect pressure on male relatives or as diplomatic go-betweens in different family networks. The war possibly heightened this role but it did not create it.

The popular risings, on the other hand, may have provided some women with genuinely new opportunities for public leadership. The informal structures of the popular movements allowed women to play a leading public role.

It would, however, be misleading to suggest that the war was overall a positive experience for women allowing them participation in public affairs which they would not have had during peacetime. The small number of women involved in such activities does not reflect the more general experience of women in Ireland during the war years. There is overwhelming evidence to suggest that for the majority of women, the war was a miserable and often harrowing experience.

II

The way in which the conflict first manifested itself in the winter of 1641 determined that from the beginning of the war women on both sides were considered legitimate targets for physical attack and abuse. The attacks on Protestant settlers in late 1641 did not distinguish between men and women. The most graphic evidence for what happened is to be found in the depositions where there are horrific accounts by women from the Protestant community of their wartime experiences. Many recounted how they were physically abused, stripped of their clothes and robbed of other possessions. Others were widowed during the war: their husbands killed as serving soldiers, or as a result of the attacks on settlers which took place in the winter of 1641/2. Hundreds of women found themselves homeless and abandoned, wandering the countryside in search of sanctuary. For those living in isolated areas, this could be a long and harrowing search.[24] The depositions contain numerous descriptions of women, often with young children, who were forced out of their homes in the winter of 1641 with little or no clothing and with no means of subsistence. They tended, where possible, to travel, usually on foot, to the larger towns and cities. Large numbers of women found their way to Dublin which by 1642 was inundated with Protestant settlers, many of them women and children, seeking refuge and material help. The number of women looking to the government for assistance was further increased by the hundreds of soldiers' wives whose husbands had been pressed or had volunteered for service in the army. As the lord justices and council explained in March 1642, many of the 4000 poor in Dublin were women whose 'husbands have put themselves into companies to serve as common soldiers thereby to maintain their own persons, but not able to . . . relieve wives or children'.[25] The women were in effect deserted wives responsible for their own subsistence and that of their children.

Another category of women looking for help in Dublin was a group of 'distressed ladies and gentlewomen' which consisted of 22 women of 'honourable condition' or 'of the better rank of gentlewomen' from Protestant families who had fled to Dublin from various parts of the country leaving behind estates, houses and belongings. In imitation of women in England, they pet-itioned the House of Commons in England for relief as a separate group who did not feel they could avail of the charity designated for the poor of Dublin because of their higher social rank. Their names are indicative of the destructive nature of the war for women regardless of their class or economic background. They included the wives and sisters of well-known Irish administrators such as Anne Docwra, widow of Sir Henry Docwra who had died in 1631, Anne Blayney, widow of Edward and Jane, daughter of Garret Moore and husband of Henry Moore who died in 1646.[26]

The large number of women looking for relief from the state forced the Dublin government to devise a policy to deal with this unexpected 'woman' problem. They appealed for funds to be sent speedily from England where every parish had been ordered to collect money for the relief of Irish Protestants. Some of this money was used to buy materials to employ wives and children of soldiers' families to make shirts for the soldiers but the finance for the scheme did not last long and most of the clothing for soldiers in Ireland continued to be sent from England. A separate sum of £600 was allotted to the 'distressed gentlewomen' but this seems also to have been inadequate and several of the petitioners were later reported to be in great want.[27]

As the resources of the government were exhausted and as more and more familes flooded into Dublin, the city felt unable to cope. In September 1642, attempts to reduce the population in the city were made by purging it of the wives and children of men suspected as rebels.[28] Efforts were also begun to encourage those without financial means to return to their native parishes in England or Scotland. Alice Stonier, for example, from Leek in Staffordshire, described how her husband had been pressed as a soldier and was killed at Drogheda. She was left in Dublin with five children to care for. 'By reason of the multitude of poor' in Dublin, the city was not able to relieve them and so she was sent back with other women in a similar position to her home parish in Staffordshire.[29] Scottish parishes also witnessed the return of native women from Ireland, widowed and often with children to support. London, not surprisingly, attracted large numbers of Irish families. Irish women, for example, were noted among those who petitioned parliament for peace and help in 1642 and 1643.[30]

The fate of women without financial means after they left Ireland is difficult to trace. Some of the 'distressed gentlewomen' retired to family homes in England and continued to petition the government for assistance. Local parish records enable us to document the fate of others. Alice Stonier, for example, received assistance from Leek parish and her daughters were put into service. Scottish widows were also assisted by their home parishes but many women, particularly those who went to London, must have been reduced permanently to the status of beggars or vagrants. One writer attributed the women's parliamentary petition of 1643 to 'whores, bawdes, oyster-women, kitchenstuffe women, beggar women and the very scum of the suburbs, besides abundance of Irish women', suggesting that most of the Irish women were in the same economic category as beggars and other poor women.[31]

On the confederate side in the war, the situation for women was little better. As in any military conflict the behaviour of the soldiers towards the civilian population was criticised but the attacks on the settler community at the beginning of the war and the belief that women had encouraged and had been involved in the attacks meant that military violence against women and children received official sanction from the army authorities. The normal rules of war which gave women and children immunity from attack were not observed. As the lord justices explained in June 1642:

> We have hitherto where we came against the rebels, their adherents, relievers and abettors, proceeded with fire and sword, the soldiers sometimes not sparing the women, and sometimes not children, many women being manifestly very deep in the guilt of this rebellion, and as we are informed, very forward to stir up their husbands, friends and kindred to side therein, and exciting them to cruelty against the English acting therein, and in their spoils even with rage and fury with their own hands.[32]

In other words, the unusual nature of the conflict in Ireland, and particularly the way in which it began, meant that attacks on women were officially sanctioned by the royalist and later by the parliamentary forces.

This situation was compounded by the chronic shortage of food and pay for soldiers on both sides which also exposed women to pillaging and rampaging soldiers. The lord justices and army commanders actively encouraged soldiers 'for mere want to rob and pillage some good subjects' in Dublin and elsewhere.[33] There were also complaints about the pillaging and bad behaviour of the Scottish troops in Ulster and Connacht. The creaghts of Owen Roe O'Neill's soldiers expected to be fed and lodged by local people and their arrival in a district was often a source of much hardship on the country inhabitants in general and the women in particular. Rinuccini described in 1647 the devastation and atrocities caused by O'Neill's forces in Kilkenny. To Rinuccini's horror, Viscount Mountgarret whose lands had been plundered gathered a party of women from the devastated areas and brought them to the door of the council room in Kilkenny and later to Rinuccini's house in order to protest against the behaviour of the Ulstermen. Mountgarret's tactic was designed to embarrass both O'Neill and Rinuccini but it was also an indication that women were the main victims of the army.[34]

Rape and other violent attacks on women must have been an element in the women's complaints but documented evidence for rape is curiously small. There are many accounts in the depositions relating to the stripping of women but very few references to rape. On the other hand, the petition presented to the House of Commons by women in London referred to the 'savage and unheard of rapes exercised upon our sex in Ireland'.[35] The women's petition registered their reluctance to speak of such matters and it is likely that a similar reticence was exercised by the deponents, particularly if the victim was still alive or of a high social standing. The small number of rape cases that are noted in the depositions usually relate to servant girls. One such case reported that the woman was sick for days afterwards and 'thought she would never be well nor in her right mind again the fact was so foul and grievous unto her'.[36] This suggests that the shame attached to rape prevented more cases from being publicly reported, particularly if the victim was socially respected.

For the vast majority of women in Ireland, therefore, the war years were not years of opportunity and independence. For most they were a time of great misfortune and family tragedy as thousands of women were widowed, left homeless and without financial income. Nor did their troubles cease when the conflict ended in the early 1650s. For women on both sides of the war, the legacy of the war was a permanent and impoverishing one.

III

If the way in which the war began exposed women to attack so

too the way in which the war ended brought hardship and
poverty to many women. The ending of the war led to a mass
exodus from Ireland of supporters of the confederates and the
King. On the confederate side, Petty estimated that about 40,000
people opted to leave Ireland at the end of the war and of that
number only 15 per cent were women. Most of the men who
left were soldiers anxious to pursue a military career on the
continent. Some undoubtedly were single men with no family
commitments in Ireland. Others, however, must have left behind
wives, sisters, mothers and children. Women and other family
dependants may not have been intentionally deserted or abandoned. Plans to reunite the family on the continent once a
position and permanent residence had been secured were
probably made by many men. In the surrender agreements which
were made at the end of the war, clauses allowing the women of
the castle to remain in residence and permitting husbands to
return to transport their wives overseas were sometimes
included.[37]

Despite such hopes and plans for the future, the reality was
that in the 1650s in Ireland there were a substantial number of
women who had willingly or unwillingly been deserted by their
male supporters. Other women without male heads of household
included large numbers of women who had been widowed
during the war or whose father or brothers had died in the
conflict, and women from royalist families whose men also went
into exile after the execution of Charles I.

It is very difficult, if not impossible, to calculate the number of
women who found themselves in this position. But from government policy and legislation which specifically focused on women
we can get some idea of the scale and nature of the problem
presented to the administration by large numbers of women
without male heads of households. It is arguable, indeed, that
more legislation and government action was focused specifically
on women during the 1650s than at any other time in the
sixteenth and seventeenth centuries.

In the land settlement legislation, the problem of women arose
in several different ways. There was firstly the plight of widows
and orphans of soldiers who were owed arrears. The widows
were divided into the young and the old. Under the act of
settlement, the latter were initially granted land in Dublin and
Cork along with maimed soldiers and orphans but this was
subsequently deemed impractical because the arrears due to them
were so small and the women were too old to work the land. It
was decided, instead, to make them cash payments for their
husbands' arrears.[38]

Younger widows were, in theory, entitled to claim their husbands' arrears in the same way as surviving soldiers in the form of land debentures but in practice many encountered difficulties doing so. In the scramble for land in the 1650s, serving soldiers were in a better position to have their debentures recognised than the widows of dead soldiers. Women experienced delays while their claims were processed, during which time they had little or no means of support for themselves and their children. J.P. Prendergast who examined the commonwealth records before their destruction in 1922 noted that many widows found themselves in financial difficulties as a result of such delays and for those living some distance from Dublin, their 'distress was increased by the great cost of coming to Dublin in hopes of possession of their lands, and long attendance there about taking out their husband's debentures'.[39]

Women from royalist families whose husbands had gone into exile with Charles I also presented the government with a problem. In general, as in England, they were usually allowed a portion of their husband's estate (from a third to a fifth). Cromwell had a reputation of treating such women liberally declaring, for example, in the case of Lady Elizabeth Preston, wife of the Earl of Ormond, that she should not want 'bread' for the bad luck of having a delinquent husband.[40] It should be acknowledged, however, that Lady Preston's success in petitioning the government was largely due not to Cromwell's clemency but to the fact that she had considerable support and advice from influential male patrons in Ireland and in England. Even some of her husband's most bitter enemies such as Sir Robert King supported her claims. Lord Inchiquin's wife lacked access to this male network and consequently her husband complained in 1659 that his estate had been given away and that his wife had been denied any subsistence out of it 'on pretence that she has not made her claim in time'.[41] As in the case of soldiers' widows, unattached women from royalist backgrounds often lacked the influence and connections to establish their claims to their land. Access to influential male circles was essential for success, regardless of the women's theoretical right to land grants or debentures.

The transplantation scheme formed an essential corollary to the payment of soldiers' arrears with Irish land. Women played an important part in the transplantation process in two ways; first as wives of transplanted proprietors, and second as landowners deemed eligible for transplantation in their own right.

As wives of transplanted proprietors, women were essential. The usual procedure involved in the transplantation process was that the men went to Connacht to receive their lands from the

Athlone commissioners and prepare the new territories for the arrival of their families. In the meantime, the wives were given permission to remain on the forfeited estate; and then to lead the household group, which usually included servants as well as children, with the cattle, sheep and other stock cross country to the west of Ireland. On the women, therefore, was to fall the main task of the actual transplantation.[42]

Given the size of the enterprise involved in the transplantation scheme, delays were inevitable. For several years after the initial orders were issued, wives, left behind while their husbands went to Connacht, petitioned for and secured dispensations to remain for another short time on their estates until the crops for that year were reaped or until their cows and stock were in fit condition to make the long journey.[43] Life cannot have been easy for women left behind in such circumstances. They lived under the constant threat of eviction and often had to deal with the anger and frustration of soldiers who had been allotted their estates. The soldiers were instructed to allow the women to reap the crops which they had sown but inevitably friction arose and there were reports of women and children being evicted by soldiers eager to take full possession of their new lands.[44] Women in such circumstances may have been given unprecedented opportunities for independence in managing an estate, petitioning the government and fending off the hostility of the new landowners, but the circumstances in which these opportunities became available were hardly those in which women could develop or assert their independent authority.

Another group of women who were given even more opportunities to act independently were those who were deemed eligible for transplantation in their own right rather than that of their husbands. These included widows of Catholic landlords entitled to a widow's jointure on their husband's estate. For the purpose of the transplantation scheme, they were deemed to be proprietors of their widow's portion and accordingly deemed transplantable. The wives and daughters of swordsmen who had gone to Spain were also treated as landowners in their husband's absence and therefore also eligible for transplantation.

The legal status of these women was therefore changed by the authorities. Under English common law, they were not the owners of their family estates. All property was vested in their husbands or their husbands' families but for the purpose of the land settlement in the 1650s they were elevated to the status of landowners in their own right. It was a legal fiction, designed to get around the problem that these women represented for the administration. The government was conscious that women from landowning backgrounds had legal claims as widows, wives, sisters or daughters to landed estates throughout the country which included large parts of the land to be distributed to the soldiers and adventurers. The legal claims of the women could have undermined the whole land settlement. Elevating them to the status of Catholic landowners overcame this problem.[45]

A total of about 470 women unaccompanied by a man are listed as recipients of transplantation decrees which amounted to almost one-quarter of all those given decrees in the west. Thirty per cent were named as widows; 27 per cent were women on their own who were not specifically identified as widows and may have been widows or wives of proprietors who had gone to the continent; two per cent were women accompanied by daughters who must also have been widows or deserted wives; nine per cent consisted of 15 groups of women, most of whom seem to have been sisters and were probably daughters of proprietors who had either died or gone abroad. Finally fourteen percent of the women without husbands were listed as being accompanied by their sons. The age of the sons is not noted but most were clearly minors and their mother was taken as the head of the household and must therefore also be included in the widow or deserted wife category. The women came from landed families throughout Ireland although the government did pay special attention to widows of 'English extraction' i.e. from Old English families who would have had legal claims to some of the most profitable land in the country in the Pale and adjoining areas.[46]

Despite government efforts to deal with the problem of women from Old English backgrounds, some were able to make use of political influence and connections to have their position reviewed by the government and effectively prevented their transplantation. Ormond's mother, Viscountess Thurles, for example, had her transplantation delayed time and again right through the 1650s. She still had not moved in 1660 when she was restored to her estates. Depositions taken in the early 1650s often, however, stressed the active role of women from landed families in the war in an attempt to prevent the granting of an exemption from transplantation.[47]

Aged widows were allowed exemption. As in the case of aged widows of soldiers, special treatment was given to older widows with claims to Catholic landownership. They could be spared the upheavals involved in the transplantation process and were entitled to enjoy a portion of the profit of their estates during their lives.[48]

A woman could also claim exemption from transplantation if she married an English Protestant, renounced popery and professed the Protestant religion. That some women opted for this exemption is evidenced by the frequent orders forbidding English soldiers from marrying 'Irish women that are papists or have lately been papists whose change of religion is not or can be judged to flow from a real work of God upon their hearts'.[49] Special tests were introduced to test the authenticity of women's conversions to Protestantism. The most famous example of such a conversion is Maire Rua O'Brien from Leamaneh Castle in County Clare who was alleged to have refused to receive the dead remains of her husband Connor in 1651. Instead, she rode immediately to Limerick where she married Colonel John Cooper and thus retained the family property intact.[50]

The women who did participate in the transplantation scheme either as wives or as landowners in their own right, were usually responsible for organising the actual move by gathering together the household goods and personnel and making arrangements for the journey to Connacht (or, in the case of those already resident in the west, to their new estates in other parts of the province). Some of the surviving certificates give some indication of what was involved. Women from gentry families could be responsible for quite a large entourage. Dame Katherine Morris of Lathragh, County Tipperary, had a proposed household group of 35 followers as well as stock which included 10 cows, 16 garrans, 19 goats, and two swine. Lady Mary Hamilton of Roscrea listed 45 persons in her entourage along with 40 cows, 30 garrans, 46 sheep and two goats. Lady Dowager of Castleconnell who was 70 years of age at the time of her transplantation had 29 people to accompany her, most of whom were household servants. They took with them 20 cows, 20 sheep, 10 mares and garrans, and two horses as well as four sows. Other women from less wealthy backgrounds listed smaller entourages. Margaret Healy of Limerick, a widow of 30 years of age, had a modest household consisting of two male servants and one female servant and her young daughter. Her stock consisted of two cows and three ploughs of garrans.[51]

The fate of unaccompanied women after they arrived in Connacht is difficult to trace. As with their male counterparts, they would have had to join the queue in Athlone to get certificates to land and when alloted a portion of land to find the means to work it and settle on it. Many of the unaccompanied women were allotted very small portions of land and would, therefore, have encountered difficulties making a living from it for themselves, their families and servants. This must have been particularly the case with those who had brought only a small household and small quantity of agricultural stock with them.[52]

The Restoration of Charles II in 1660 gave hope to the transplanted landowners that their western exile was only a temporary matter and most attempted to return and reclaim their former lands. But the land settlement of the Restoration made it difficult if not impossible for many transplantees to recover their estates and inevitably given that patronage and influence were an important factor in reclaiming land women claiming on their own often lacked the necessary influence.[53] According to J.P. Prendergast, widows and orphans found so many difficulties in having their claims heard that they appealed for a certain day to be set aside for investigation of their claims. They complained that they 'were almost consumed . . . with long attendance, without subsistence in that city as well as their helpless families in the county'.[54]

Few succeeded in having their claims to land heard or granted and many women from former landed families were reduced to permanent poverty. The petitions of those who appealed to the government for help give some indication of their reduced status. Three daughters of Jordan Roche from Limerick, for example, were said to be reduced from the affluence of a landed estate of £2000 a year to living off what 'they could earn by their needles, and by washing and wringing'.[55] Joan Archer, widow of Captain Thomas Archer of Corbettstown, County Kilkenny, reported that she and her daughter had wandered from place to place in a miserable and starving condition having been unable to have their claim heard before the dissolution of the court of claims.[56] Lady Dunboyne also failed to have her claim to innocence heard in time. She left Connacht at the time of the Restoration but was not restored to her land. She settled on a mountain farm on the estate of the Duchess of Ormond, claiming that without the charity of the Duchess she 'must have died'.[57] Terence Coughlan's wife was left behind in Ireland when her husband and son went to Flanders where they later died. Mrs Coughlan was transplanted to land in Galway and Mayo in 1656. The restoration of the Coughlans was ordered by the King but was delayed and in the meantime Mrs Coughlan lost most of her property in the west through the restoration of the Marchioness of Clanricard.[58]

Of course, it is important to note that women entitled to land either in the transplantation or as soldiers' widows formed only a small proportion of the thousands of widows and deserted wives in Ireland in the 1650s. Their experiences can at least be partially documented. The experiences of the landless remain undiscovered and perhaps incapable of discovery. As Jerrold Casway's contribution to this volume indicates, some women faced the threat of transportation to the colonies; others opted for emigration but we know almost nothing about the lives of the majority of women in Ireland in the 1650s and 1660s.

IV

In conclusion it can be argued that women lost more than they gained from the war in Ireland in the 1640s. The aftermath of the war revealed the devastation which the war had wrought on the lives of hundreds of women as the government faced the problem of a society with a large number of widows and deserted wives. The war created a 'woman' problem for the administration and forced it to legislate specifically for women. This was particularly the case in relation to the land settlement where widows and deserted wives of prominent Catholic landowners threatened to undermine the transfer of land to the new owners. The government solution to the problem was to declare women in this category landowners in their own right. Thus the status of these women was raised in the eyes of the law. Uniquely, married women were recognised as owners of their husbands' property and widows as owners of their widows' jointures but this new status can hardly have been welcomed by many of the women concerned.

The experience of women in the land settlement reveals a basic problem which confronted all women in early modern society and exposes a crucial weakness to the argument that war opened up new opportunities for women. Early modern society was one in which political action and influence was determined by male patronage and connections. If a woman lacked access to the appropriate male networks then she was powerless in practice to achieve any meaningful independence. This emerged clearly in the land settlement where unattached women from all sections of society had difficulties having their claims and rights to property confirmed. In short, opportunities for independent action for women in a society dominated by a male patronage system were very limited without the support of male 'friends' or patrons.

If this study can only contribute a negative view on the wider debate about the opportunities which war presented to women, it can contribute something more positive to the general intepretation of Irish history in the seventeenth century. Women clearly played an important part in the 1641 rising, particularly at popular and local level. Equally, the transplantation of Connacht and the departure of the wild geese take on a new perspective when seen from the women's point of view. Women to a certain extent emerge as the unsung heroines of the transplantation process and the unwilling victims of their husbands' departure to the continent which has so often been depicted in romantic and dramatic terms of men forced into exile. The women they left behind them are rarely considered.

REFERENCES

1. For a review of recent literature on women and war see R. Roach Pierson, 'Beautiful Soul or Just Warrior: Gender and War' in *Gender and History*, Vol. I (1989), pp. 77–86.
2. P. Higgins, 'Women in the English Civil War' (M.A. thesis, University of Manchester, 1965); 'The Reactions of Women, with Special Reference to Women Petitioners' In B. Manning (ed.), *Politics, Religion and the English Civil War* (Manchester, 1973), pp. 177–221; K. Thomas, 'Women and the Civil War Sects' in T. Aston (ed.), *Crisis in Europe 1560–1660* (London, 1965), pp. 317–40; A. Fraser, *The Weaker Vessel* (London, 1984).
3. D. Underdown, *Revel, Riot and Rebellion. Popular Politics in England 1603–1660* (Oxford, 1985), p. 211.
4. Trinity College Dublin (hereafter cited as TCD), MS 814, ff. 70–4, 91; Lord Frederick Hamilton, 'Lettice Baroness of Offaly, and the Siege of the Castle of Geashill, 1642' in *County Kildare Archaeological Journal*, Vol. 3 (1899–1902), pp. 419–34.
5. TCD MS 817, ff. 177–80.
6. *The English Revolution III Newsbook 5 Volume 1 Mercurius Politicus 1650* (facsimile, London, 1971), pp. 5, 25, 44, 63.
7. Lord Frederick Hamilton, *op. cit.*, p. 423.
8. See for example, TCD MSS 809, ff. 5–6; 813, f. 356; 814, f. 112; 815, ff. 65, 92; 829, f. 74; 832, ff. 125, 126; 837, f. 4; 838, ff. 68–9; M. A. Hickson, *Ireland in the Seventeenth Century or The Irish Massacres of 1641-2* (2 vols, London, 1884), Vol. I, p. 307. Some of these accusations should, however, be seen in the context of the land settlement of the 1650s (see below).
9. Printed in J.T. Gilbert (ed.), *The History of the Irish Confederation and the War in Ireland (1641–9)* (7 vols, Dublin, 1882–91), Vol. II, pp. 69–73.
10. *Ibid.*, p. 71.
11. For a brief discussion see N. Canny, *The Upstart Earl* (Cambridge, 1982), pp. 116–17.
12. TCD MS 813, ff. 35–6; Gilbert, *History of Irish Confederation . . .*, Vol. IV, pp. 131–3; *Irelands True Diurnall, or a Continued Relation of the Cheife Passages That Have Happened There Since 11th of January unto this Present* (London, 1641), pp. 6–7; Robert Dunlop (ed.), *Ireland Under the Commonwealth and Protectorate. 1649–56* (2 vols, Manchester, 1913), Vol. I, pp. 52–4; TCD MS 809, f. 8.
13. Gilbert, *History of Irish Confederation . . .*, Vol. I, p. xlvii.
14. A. Fraser, *The Weaker Vessel*, pp. 197–9.
15. M.A. Hickson, *Ireland in the Seventeenth Century or The Irish Masacres of 1641-2*, Vol. I, pp. 292–3; TCD MS 817, f. 39. See also Hickson, *op. cit.*, Vol. I, p. 313.
16. TCD MS 830, f. 226. See also fs. 1346, 142, 147, 151, 158, 166.
17. TCD MS 814, f. 60.
18. TCD MS 834, f. 62. This woman was also a letter carrier.
19. E.P. Thompson, 'The Moral Economy of the English Crowd in the

Eighteenth Century' in *Past and Present*, Vol. 50 (1971), pp. 115–6.

20. For example Hickson, *op. cit.*, pp. 292, 307; TCD MS 814, ff. 59, 63, 112; 815, f. 66; 818, ff. 21, 22, 24; 832, f. 61; 836, ff. 35, 87.

21. Quoted in T. Fitzpatrick, *The Bloody Bridge and Other Papers Relating to the Insurrection of 1641* (Dublin, 1903, reprinted 1970), pp. 247–8.

22. TCD MS 834, f. 183. See also TCD MSS 813, ff. 331, 356; 814, ff. 63, 67, 81; 815, ff. 63–4, 68; 817, f. 7.

23. See, for example, *Calendar of the Manuscripts of the Marquess of Ormonde* (new series, 7 vols, London, 1902–12), Vol. II, pp. 367–75; TCD MS 809. f. 9; 813, f. 71; 821, f. 31; Hickson, *op. cit.*, Vol. I, p. 336.

24. The extracts from the depositions printed in Hickson, *op. cit.*, include many examples.

25. *Calendar of the Manuscripts of the Marquess of Ormonde*, Vol. II, pp. 75–6, 91–2, 168. See also Hickson, *Ireland in the Seventeenth Century*, Vol. I, pp. 202–3.

26. TCD MS 840, f. 27.

27. TCD MS 840, f. 54; *Calendar of Manuscripts of the Marquess of Ormonde*, Vol. II, pp. 183–4, 189–90. For fate of 'distressed gentlewomen' see family entries in *G.E.C.*

28. *Calendar of Manuscripts of the Marquess of Ormonde*, Vol. II, pp. 199–200.

29. D.A. Johnson and D.G. Vaisey (eds), *Staffordshire and the Great Rebellion* (Staffordshire, 1964), pp. 6–7, 44; A. Frazer, *The Weaker Vessel*, p. 191.

30. J. Kirk (ed.), *The Records of the Synod of Lothian and Tweedale, 1589–1596, 1640–1649* (Edinburgh, 1977), pp. xxviii, 121, 143–4, 144, 149, 150–1, 166–7, 243, 292; A.R. Bayley, *The Great Civil War in Dorset 1642–1660* (Taunton, 1910), p. 327n; Higgins, 'The Reactions of Women, with Special Reference to Women Petitioners', p. 192.

31. *Ibid.*

32. *Calendar of the Manuscripts of the Marquess of Ormonde*, Vol. II, p. 128.

33. *Ibid.*, pp. 86–7.

34. A. Hutton (ed.), *The Embassy in Ireland of Monsignor G.B. Rinuccini, Archbishop of Fermo In The Years 1645–1649* (Dublin, 1873), pp. 283–4.

35. Printed in *The Harleian Miscellany*, Vol. VII (London, 1811), pp. 605–8.

36. TCD MS 830, f. 172. See also TCD MS 839, f. 7; 814, ff. 107–8; 817, f. 204. I am grateful to Professor Michael Maxwell for most of these references. See also the deposition of Robert Maxwell for an example of almost incredible restraint (Hickson, *Ireland in the Seventeenth Century*, Vol. I, p. 335).

37. For Petty's figures see p. 113 below; for examples of surrender agreements see Dunlop, *Ireland Under the Commonwealth and Protectorate, 1649–56*, Vol. II, pp. 222, 319–20.

38. *Ibid.*, pp. 453–4, 519–20, 536.

39. J.P. Prendergast, *The Cromwellian Settlement of Ireland* (Dublin, 1922), pp. 195n, 223–4.

40. A. Fraser, *The Weaker Vessel*, pp. 206–7; Dunlop, *Ireland Under the Commonwealth*, Vol. I, pp. 71–2; *Calendar of the Manuscripts of the Marquesse of Ormonde*, Vol. II, pp. 266, 324–6, 366–75.

41. *Ibid.*, pp. 326–7.

42. Prendergast, *The Cromwellian Settlement of Ireland*, pp. 103–6, 127–8, 179–86.
43. *Ibid.*, pp. 110–14; Dunlop, *Ireland Under the Commonwealth*, Vol. II, pp. 422, 568–9, 619–20.
44. Prendergast, *The Cromwellian Settlement of Ireland*, p. 109.
45. *Ibid.*, pp. 130–1, 163; Dunlop, *Ireland Under the Commonwealth*, Vol. II, pp. 423, 494–5.
46. See list in *Report on the Manuscripts of the Marquis of Ormonde* (2 vols, London, 1895–99), Vol. II, pp. 114–76.
47. Prendergast, *The Cromwellian Settlement of Ireland*, pp. 254–5. See also p. 119; Dunlop, *Ireland Under the Commonwealth*, Vol. II, pp. 606–7.
48. *Ibid.*, pp. 498, 574–5; Prendergast, *The Cromwellian Settlement of Ireland*, p. 379.
49. Dunlop, *Ireland Under the Commonwealth*, Vol. II, pp. 356–7, 363; Prendergast, *The Cromwellian Settlement of Ireland*, pp. 231–5, 261–6.
50. R. Ua Croinin and M. Breen, 'Interesting Remains at Lemaneagh' in *The Other Clare*, Vol. XI (1987), pp. 46–8.
51. Prendergast, *The Cromwellian Settlement of Ireland*, pp. 105, 369–70. See also p. 376 and pp. 228–9 below.
52. The list in *Report on Manuscripts of the Marquis of Ormonde*, Vol. II, 114–76 notes the acreage granted in the decrees.
53. L.J. Arnold, 'The Irish Court of Claims of 1663' in *Irish Historical Studies*, Vol. XXIV, 96 (1985), pp. 421–2 describes the legal process involved in the court of claims. The success rate of women claimants who were not transplantees is worthy of further study.
54. J.P. Prendergast, *Ireland From the Restoration to the Revolution, 1660–1690* (London, 1887), p. 34.
55. Prendergast, *The Cromwellian Settlement of Ireland*, pp. 339–40.
56. Prendergast, *Ireland From the Restoration to the Revolution*, pp. 35–6.
57. *Ibid.*, pp. 19–20.
58. Prendergast, *The Cromwellian Settlement of Ireland*, pp. 252–4.

7

Irish Women Overseas, 1500–1800

JERROLD CASWAY

The literary metaphor 'wild geese' has been popularly associated with pre-nineteenth century Irish refugees. The general assumption is that most people leaving Ireland before 1800 were involuntary exiles compelled by political-inspired circumstances to seek careers – primarily in the military in Catholic Europe. Although the romantic nationalism of a later era exaggerated the intentions, numbers and identities of these émigrés, it overlooked Irish women. If the term 'geese' is genderless, then the 'goose', not just the 'gander' deserves our attention.

Like the multitude of ordinary Irish exiles, women rarely attracted the illumination of centre stage. Much of their story can only be pieced together from disjointed fragments and educated deductions that must take into account the relationship of gender to the variations of the emigration phenomenon. People leave a homeland for a variety of reasons. Some of them aspire to establish a new mode of existence (innovative migration), others seek a new home for the preservation of a traditional way of life (conservative migration), while still others view exile as transitional, with assimilation restrained by expectations of returning home to restored premigration conditions.

Irish emigration for the period 1500–1800 also contrasts greatly with the larger and better known emigrations of the last two centuries. From 1500 to 1691 the overwhelming number of emigrants were Catholics, people involuntarily 'pushed' or impelled to leave Ireland because of their political–religious loyalties and lifestyle circumstances. Although many exiles retained some choice about their decision to leave, others were victims of forced relocation. The majority of the former sought refuge in Catholic Europe, while many of the latter were resettled in the New World. Most of the exiles who were pulled to the continent were conservative and transitional emigrants. The involuntary nature of the New World exiles provided them with little choice about their innovative predicament.

Irish emigration during the period 1691–1800 differed from its predecessor by its numbers, intentions and destinations. The largest number of these migrants were Protestant Scotch–Irish, who were 'pushed' by economic/religious conditions to the eastern coast of the North American continent. Catholic emigration, primarily native Irish, was not as significant in comparison, stunted by a provincial–traditionalism that resisted irrevocable emigration. Not until the post-famine decades of the nineteenth century would Catholic emigration become the kind of voluntary mass exodus that marked the Scotch–Irish migrations of the eighteenth century. But if economic conditions were compelling, voluntary-seasonal cross-channel movement for the labouring classes was preferable to migration to the continent, or to the finality of transoceanic relocation. Those Irish seeking career/ sustenance changes on the continent after 1691 were generally Catholic Irish of English descent who were responding to the 'Protestant ascendency' of Ireland. These people were conservative and, to a degree, transitional migrants.

Determining the input, role and proportion of women who participated in these original exile experiences is difficult at best. Scholars constantly are hard-pressed without precise calculations or inventories to say how many people actually left Ireland, let alone estimate gender percentages. Sex ratios often are disputable because of faulty and insufficient data. However, if a particular migration was family orientated, like the dominant eighteenth century Scotch–Irish exodus, it might easily assume sex ratio proportions exceeding 40 per cent. Trying to calculate the wives and female relatives of the next largest emigrating group – soldier/pensioner/labourer – is more hazardous. No normal patterns or ratios exist, and without detailed lists, variation is great and conjecture abounds. For example, the coerced levies to the Baltic in 1609–10, totalling about 6000 men, involved few if any women. But evidence indicates that higher proportions of women accompanied their menfolk abroad when exiles had some input into the emigrating decision. The large and better documented levies of the Commonwealth and Williamite periods testify to varying sex ratios. According to William Petty's projections, less than 15 per cent of the approximated 40,000 people who left Ireland under Cromwell's regime were women, compared with an estimated 7 per cent who accompanied the post-Limerick levies. Servitude/labour migrations for these centuries were generally individually orientated with average sex ratios approximating 18 per cent.[1] It is, therefore, conceivable from estimated calculations and percentages that about 30 per cent of the guess-timated 602,000 pre-nineteenth century emigrants from Ireland were women.

At some point during the last decade of the sixteenth century, a character from Thomas Dekker's pen lamented that the Irish in England swarmed 'like crickets to the crevise of a brewhouse'.[2] These sentiments reflected conditions that predated Dekker by centuries. To the Irish migrant, England embodied the 'pull' of sustenance and the attraction of opportunity. Many of the original Irish who crossed the channel were little more than vagabonds, tempted by more prosperous conditions and the need for seasonal field labour. The decision of labourers to remain in England prompted the enactment of statutes which lamented how 'wandering' and 'idle' persons 'haunt and repair' the coun-try. One solution for the authorities was to arrest and confine these undeserving vagrants before shipping them back to Ireland.

The overwhelming number of Irish that generated this vagrant image were drawn to England by the harvest/haymaking labour cycles. These migrants were usually Irish-speaking peasants or low-paid seasonally employed weavers, attracted by the higher pay of field work. 'Pulled' by these opportunities, many saw the benefit of remaining between work cycles in the port towns and early industrial cities of England. London in particular drew many of these labourers and their families into the inner city parishes. From these urban settings Irish migrants struggled to sustain themselves until the next agricultural season.

Operating outside the organised guilds many Irish resorted to begging or to adopting the unskilled 'mean trades' of street vending, portering, and heavy day labouring. The wives of these workers often became costermongers – sellers of fruits and vegetables. Among the tolerable Irish emigrants were skilled craftsmen/labourers, Protestant clerics, and Irish attendants of returning officials and cross-channel merchants; in fact a 1594 proclamation exempted Irish householders, servants and officials from arrest or expulsion.

The numbers and problems of the Irish drawn to England expanded sharply over the next century because of economic slumps and agricultural famines. Since most Catholics still resisted the 'pull' of migration, especially to the New World, they found appealing the self-recruiting advantages of seasonal labour to England. Inevitably a resident alien population, extolling cross-channel opportunities, attracted more labourers to stay and to bring over their families. The decision to remain, however, depended on personal and economic circumstances. Often the 'chain migration' of bringing over relatives, generally wives and children, was accomplished by the accumulation of 'half-penny after half-penny . . . for years'.[3]

Poor and often solitary, the Irish congregated in urban enclaves near tavern lodging houses and market places. But not all remained sedentary, for casual and restless labourers survived as vagabonds. Ineligible for local relief, these people followed the harvest cycle and practised odd piecework and gang-rate jobs like market gardening, dairying, weeding, and haymaking. It was not uncommon to find families of such workers sleeping in barns and outhouses, subsisting on the garden produce of their employers. An alternative and supplement to this existence was the use of women and children as beggars. Surviving by their guile without licences and claiming ignorance of the language, these people relied on counterfeit permits and competed with 'pass-masters' who sought to confine them in receiving houses for transportation back to Ireland.

The more sedentary female that remained in England between work cycles either had no prospects in Ireland or was economically dependent on marriage or co-habitation. These women generally resided with their families and fellow-countrymen in the cellars and garrets of the alleys, courtyards and back-streets of England's Irish ghettos. Densely inhabited, these enclaves were poorly constructed, unsanitary, crime-ridden, and immensely overcrowded before the harvest cycles. Cramped together, the eighteenth century urban Irish popularised the practice of subleasing. A room, bed or corner was sublet to individuals or families on a nightly, weekly or monthly basis. It was not uncommon to find three or four families subleasing one room. An 1816 survey reported that one Irish section of London had 700 Irish living in 24 small houses, many without windows, chimneys or floors.[4] Some of these places were converted into common 'two pence a night' lodging houses. Operated by Irish landladies, these premises served drinks and gained a notoriety from their clientele that affected the moral reputation of Irish women.

The 'rowdy', 'fallen' and 'virtueless' Irish female was a popular exaggeration of nineteenth century English commentators, who misread the pauperism–prostitution phenomena of early industrial cities. The whores of Charing Cross were not a peculiarly Irish condition or monopoly, for all young immigrant country girls were vulnerable to the wiles and overtures of the urban underworld. Modern research actually describes eighteenth century prostitution as voluntary and gradual; a rational, albeit fluid decision by unskilled–unemployed girls – the laundress, domestic, and seasonally unemployed woman in the 'needle trades'. The cycle of prostitution was only broken when a job or mate altered the woman's circumstance.[5]

While the illicit side of urban life can be documented by use of court records, knowledge of female domestic activities is deficient and overlooked because of its ordinary routines. Most Irish women migrated to English cities at younger ages than their male counterparts. Studies also suggest that industrialisation did not increase women's work outside of the home. Research of Irish women in Victorian London does indicate that only 22 per cent of all married women, and 75 per cent of Irish female heads of families, worked outside of the house. The so-called hidden and supplementary in-house work was dependent on the household's needs and economic opportunities. Generally the wife admitted and cared for boarders, did laundry/mending work, watched other people's children, or did contracted 'needle' work. On occasion an elderly or adolescent female would assume domestic responsibilities that permitted a housewife to work outside of the home. It was only after the children were grown that a wife, if physically able, returned to the workplace. Their most frequented jobs were street vending, domestic work, 'needle' trades, and sifting/sorting work at mines. Of course, there were the opportunities from the harvest cycles, which for women declined by the end of the eighteenth century.

The numbers and personal lives of Irish females are equally obscure. Living in their ethnic ghettos, Irish women married or co-habited with Irish men of their own class. The women consummated these relationships at an earlier age than their male counterparts, for they were younger, more sedentary and in greater numbers initially than the men in this environment. Without specific data it is also hard to dispute the presumption that the overwhelming number of Irish city dwellers were Catholic. The supposition regarding sex ratios is another matter for educated speculation. Only after a settled urban population was established and normal patterns of birth took place could the previously explained 40 per cent plus sex ratio cycles become applicable. Therefore, by applying this ratio to a reliable early nineteenth century survey on mendicity, some figures on the female population can be conjectured. The calculated 14,000 total for the Irish in London is deemed to be less than half the actual number.[6] If accurate, the resident Irish population for England at the turn of the century may have approached 40,000, to which the 40 per cent plus sex ratio is applied.

These cross-channel migrations are poorly recorded. They were primarily lower class, native Catholic and voluntary seasonal labourers. By contrast, many continental migrants tended to be upper class, Catholic, transitional migrants preferring involuntary residence. These continental migrations also possessed two of the three 'push' categories: political/religious and economic/ commercial. The 'pull' factors were pensions, careers, and economic opportunities not possible in Ireland.

Men discovered that the career (educational and training) opportunities were more plentiful in Catholic Europe. Medical, legal, military, educational and clerical were the most sought after professions. Associated women were less career orientated than their menfolk. Females generally migrated to the continent as a wife or part of a family unit. Often the most advantageous refuge for individual Irish females was a continental convent. In this cloistered life many females secured an identity and security that insulated them from deteriorating circumstances in Ireland and collapsed continental expectations.

Irish nuns appeared on the continent towards the end of the sixteenth century. But not until 1626 was an Irish convent founded in Europe – the Poor Clares in Dunkirk. Little is known about them except they eventually returned to Dublin in 1629. Ten years later, an Irish Dominican convent of Bon Sucesso, housing 40 sisters, was established in Portugal. Only after the Cromwellian persecutions did nuns from the Poor Clares and Dominican houses in Galway go to Spain. With the exception of Mother Catherine Bernard Browne's followers, who founded a new house in Dieppe, most nuns found solace in non-Irish sister houses such as those of the Poor Clares of Nantes, Gravelines, St Omer, Rome and Naples, the French Ursulines, or the convents of the Capuchins at Maestricht and Charleville. These residential associations continued well into the eighteenth century, with two notable exceptions: the Irish Benedictine convents at Ypres and the Franciscan house at Louvain. On occasion a few bold sisters chanced a return to Ireland. In 1681 Benedictine nuns from Ypres ventured home looking for novices and aid, and a century later Judith Wogan Browne, educated at Ypres, returned to her native land, and founded a little motherhouse convent of Brigidines in Tullow.

What little information is extant about Irish nuns on the continent often details their efforts to survive. Among the most common and revealing continental sources are their petitions for commendation and maintenance. In a revealing series of letters, Dermot O'Mallun, a knight of Calatrava, wrote in 1618 how his loss of pension affected his ability to support and oversee his several daughters. For his eldest daughter, Marie, he sought admittance to the Benedictine house at Avesnes, near Arras. Six months later the archduke instructed the abbess, a kinswomen of O'Mallun, to educate her in 'religion and virtue'. Also extant are institutional appeals soliciting secular relief or grants to subsidize seminaries and convents. Occasionally the condition of these houses and their nuns is disclosed in documents contesting individual wills or bequests of property. In a 1743 episode two Irish nuns in a French convent, daughters of John Power, a former colonel in the French army, sought to settle their late father's Dublin estate through two Parisian bankers.[7] Information may be gleaned also from intelligence summaries reciting the relationships between Irish political refugees and religious houses, like the Jacobites and the Benedictines of Ypres. All of these sources expose the vulnerability of an Irish female community whose numbers rarely exceeded more than a few hundred at any one time. The closing of many of these continental houses during the French Revolution prompted Irish nuns to turn their attention again to Ireland.

Another 'push–pull' factor influencing Irish immigration to the continent was economic/commercial opportunity. Irish trade with the continent had for centuries concentrated itself in certain European regions and ports. The merchants from south-eastern Irish centres traded and settled primarily in Brittany in north-west France. Operating from the cities of Nantes, St Malo, Le Havre and Rouen, they imported beef, hides and tallow from Ireland. The merchants of Galway and Munster had long-established ties to the west coast of southern France and the Iberian peninsula. Bordeaux, the ports of Galicia, the coastal cities of Bilbao, Lisbon, Cadiz, and the market centres of Barcelona and Malaga witnessed an expansion of the wine trade. Not to be overlooked are the channel ports in the Spanish Lowlands, and the trading centres on the Italian peninsula. These market places by the eighteenth century were swelled by the self-recruiting dynamics of emigrant societies that lured other Irish to these prospering sanctuaries. Building upon pre-existing nuclei, European cities and ports developed Irish enclaves that attracted indigent Irish vagabonds, pilgrims, displaced political/religious refugees, and struggling pensioners.

The greater distance and complexity involved in emigrating to European cities *vis-à-vis* England prevented the Irish communities in Europe from approaching the eighteenth century figures for cross-channel Irish settlements. The majority of these commercially minded Irish emigrants came from Old English Catholic merchant families, who expanded voluntary–seasonal excursions into more permanent residences in Europe. Unlike expelled political/military refugees, merchants relocated without much commotion or notice. They were also better suited to be accompanied by their womenfolk. What is known about females of this emigrant category concerns mainly post-Williamite merchants in France. Often the first-generation girls married within the Irish communities, in some cases continuing the merchant family bonds begun in Ireland. But the longer a family resided in exile the greater the likelihood of marrying outside the community. John O'Byrne of Dublin, for example, settled in Bordeaux in 1750, and prospered in the wine trade. Typically he married the daughter of Richard Gernon of County Louth, a merchant in Bordeaux. But the O'Byrne's sisters reflected a broader range of options. Emily O'Byrne married Andrew Kirwan of Galway, a newspaper editor living in Bordeaux; her sister Lucinda took Benjamin Bloomfield of Dublin, residing in Bordeaux, as her husband, while a third sister married a French army colonel. In many cases female Irish military dependants resided in these Irish centres and married into the business community. The sister of James Louis Rice, who served in Austria, lived in Nantes and married Count John Waters, an Irish banker from Paris.[8] For single or widowed women, places were found in the family household, business, or an affiliated convent. Unfortunately, until research is completed on other merchant communities, it must be surmised that similar conditions existed for Portugal and Spain.

These deficiencies pose less of a problem for Irish political/ religious refugees, because their activities and resettlement attracted a disproportionate share of attention and controversy. Sex ratio levels are also different. As émigrés, females more likely accompanied their menfolk abroad when 'push' conditions were less acute. Cases of coerced levies, political flights, and military disbandments provided neither the time nor circumstances appropriate for women. In these situations the female decision to emigrate was more a matter of compliance than choice. Their input was generally passive, or involuntary, constrained by the extremity of the moment, the intention for exile, depreciated post-exodus prospects, and the capacity of the ship. Much of a woman's relocation ordeal was associated with cultural patriarchal traditions. Bound by legal and material dependencies to male kin, a woman might expect better opportunities and conditions in exile with her menfolk than in Ireland without them.

In one of the best documented migrations, the 1607 flight of the earls, Nuala O'Donnell, older sister to the Earl of Tyrconnell, exerted her independent nature and decided to test her fortunes abroad. Estranged from her husband, O'Donnell perceived that her prospects were better as a political refugee in Catholic

Europe. Her sister-in-law, Bridget Fitzgerald, did not accompan
Tyrconnell. Pregnant and living apart from the Earl, Fitzgeral
profited from her mother's caution and her grandfather's politica
ties. The daughter she was carrying when her husband fle
would later seek refuge on the continent after failing to follov
her mother's more temperate example. Finally there is the Ea
of Tyrone's young third wife, Catherine Magennis, who afte
nine years of marriage and three children, was not anxious t
leave her homeland, family and friends. An English account o
her husband's hurried departure recounts how she 'being exceed
ingly weary slipped down from her horse, and weeping said sh
could go no further'. Tyrone responded with little compassion
He threatened her with his sword 'if she would not pass on witl
him, and put on a more cheerful countenance'. Once in Europ
the relationship further deteriorated to the point where the Ear
stipulated in his will that if his wife could not 'maintain hersel
honorably', she was not to receive 'a penny'.[9] After Tyrone'
death in 1616, his widow's share of his pension was contested b
his clients and relatives. Although her stipend was officiall
reconfirmed, it was always in arrears. In 1619 this 'afflicted an
unprotected widow', a casualty of her husband's decision t
emigrate, died in Naples.

More than four decades later, the Cromwellian occupation lef
émigrés with little room to manoeuvre. Leonor O'More, th
daughter of Rory O'More, eluded soldiers by hiding out for eigh
days with her fugitive future husband, Arthur O'Neill, th
grandson of Sir Turlough MacHenry O'Neill of the Fews. Th
urgency and danger of their flight gave the couple little time t
save anything besides their lives. Provided with refuge in Spain
they married and had six children. Before his death in Septembe
1663, O'Neill became the colonel of the regiment of Tyrone an
a knight of Calatrava. His wife focused her attention on th
advancement of the children, and on her inconstant widow'
pension.[10] But the quality of her exile and her decision to migrat
were more than most Irish women could expect.

In a reverse circumstance, the willing wives of Irish soldier
were denied transport to France in 1691. Some 11,000 of Patrick
Sarsfield's men agreed to enter the French service after the
surrender of Limerick. Sarsfield, recognising that these soldier
were leaving 'all that is most dear in life for a strange land'
promised that their wives and children could accompany then
abroad. But when these soldiers and their families assembled or
the docks at Cork, there were not enough transports. As the mer
were rowed out to their ships, 'Loud cries and lamentations brok
from the wives and children', many of whom 'dashed' into the

water and drowned, while others clung to the oared boats. Equally distressing were the doomed efforts of men who plunged into the water, only to lose their lives trying to reach the shore.[11] The exact number of women who lost their lives or who later followed their menfolk to France remains unknown.

Determining what percentage of females went abroad with any particular exodus is difficult. Fragmentary data suggest that most women who were political/religious immigrants went to Europe after the initial relocation. Only estranged relationships, unsatisfactory prospects, or death would discourage women from reuniting themselves with their menfolk. For the majority of women who reached the continent, life was harsh, insecure and disappointing. Sustenance often revolved around the status and success of their men, whose deaths, disabilities or discreditings exposed female vulnerabilities. Denied their accustomed family-support system, women depended, as in the dominions of Spain, on pensions, allowances (*ventajas*), or grants-in-aid (*ayuda da costas*). These subsidies were quite unreliable, for financial cut-backs, bureaucratic red tape and loss of favour often jeopardised the well-being of those Irish women who were fortunate or significant enough to enjoy a form of monetary support. The controversy between Caecilla O'Gallagher and Anna ny Madden was not unique. O'Gallagher was the wet nurse and foster mother to Hugh O'Donnell, son of the Earl of Tyrconnell. She lost her position to an impoverished pre-'flight' exile, Anna ny Madden, when she could no longer nurse the child. Madden welcomed this opportunity in order to support her unemployed spouse and her young child. Bereft of compensation, O'Gallagher and her husband responded with petitions for relief. They complained that they had 'no other consolation except this child, or means of support or income', because as clients of Tyrconnell they had 'lost all . . . possessions' by coming to Flanders. There is no evidence that the O'Gallaghers were compensated, but Anna ny Madden wrenched as many benefits as possible – from a laundry allowance to meals – at the Dame Blanches convent where the child was kept.[12] Pettiness and bickering of this kind also deterred potential benefactors, but whereas relief for a fortunate few might encompass the full range of benefits, many were sustained by humiliating begging licences.

A typical case involved Daniel O'Farrell, an officer in the Irish regiment in Flanders, who complained that he lost everything after he left Ireland for the Spanish service. The reduction of his monthly pension by two-thirds forced his wife and three children in Brussels to sell their clothing to survive. 'Without hope', he applied for a licence for his wife and children 'to go about the countryside begging' until his reformed pension was reviewed. The widow of Neal O'Neill, a captain in the Irish regiments of France, reminded her benefactors in 1720 that her husband's death had resulted from wounds suffered during his 28 years of service. She lamented her current 'miserable state' as a poor widow with three young orphaned children, and asked only for a sustaining pension which was ultimately granted. In another episode, the daughter of Henry O'Neill, captain of the Irish regiment of Galmoy, asked in 1746 for her deceased mother's widow pension. She spoke of her 'deplorable situation' and 'pitiful state' whereby she lacked both 'the bare necessities of life' and 'the means to avoid shameful want'. Ultimately she received half of her mother's pension. These cases contrast sharply with the account of Marianna MacCarthy and her husband, Thadec O'Mouroghu. Pregnant when she accompanied her husband to Portugal in 1622, MacCarthy gave birth to a son. Impoverished, the couple and their child made their way to Madrid, where they were granted a royal audience. The young Spanish queen, grieving over her lost first child, was moved by the sight of the couple's beautiful baby, who was consequently taken into the royal household and raised in great favour at court. The parents were well cared for by life allowances.[13]

Unlike the lists of grants or reconsidered payments for widows and orphans, the petitions that were denied or ignored generally have not survived. From many extant petitions the connivances forced by desperation are disclosed. Orphaned as a young girl, Leonore Ryan was brought to Spain where she was sustained by her uncle, the exiled Bishop of Killaloe. His death in Portugal left Ryan 'more orphaned and unprotected than ever'. Dissatisfied by her current allowance, she returned to Spain where she appealed on three occasions for an increased stipend. Her persistence led to an inquiry that uncovered her marriage to a pensioner living in Lisbon. Provided with expenses back to Portugal, she was to 'content herself . . . and refrain from sending any more useless memorials'.[14]

A critical factor, even for upper class women with pensions, was to find well-connected men. Many Irish men in fact recognised the advantages of European rather than Irish marriages. The precious pensions and token allowances of Irish women could not compensate for their archaic titles and dissipated kinship ties. Nor was beauty, character or love always a sufficient catalyst for relationships destined for debt, struggle and anonymity. Leading political–military figures such as Thomas Preston, Gerald O'Connor, John O'Neill, Hugh O'Donnell, Gerald Lally, Ambrosio O'Higgins and Maximillan von Browne were involved or married to well-connected non-Irish women. These lessons were not lost on Irish females.

The prominent and attractive Nora Bourke, Patrick Sarsfield's widow, avoided the bondage of poverty by marrying the Duke of Berwick, the illegitimate son of James II. Teresa O'Byrne, whose father was an officer in Crofton's regiment of Spanish dragoons, became a much admired maid of honour to the Queen; at court she met the recently widowed and dissolute English Duke of Wharton. Reputed to be a great landowner, Wharton, although considered a 'fawning toady', courted and married the young O'Byrne. After Wharton's death, the widow and her grandmother in 1747 posed as Spanish subjects in London where they unsuccessfully claimed the deceased Duke's forfeited estates. Male relationships better served Marie-Louise Murphy. The daughter of an Irish soldier in the French service turned Rouen shoemaker, Murphy was taken along with her sisters to Paris by their mother, Margaret Hickey, after their father's death. Supported by her mother's successful business in selling old clothes, Murphy became a model at the Academy of Painting where she attracted Louis XV's attention. She became one of his mistresses and bore him a daughter; in 1785 she married her first husband, a major in the French army. Her dowry, provided by the King, could have sustained hundreds of pensioned Irish women, and her network of important connections was reinforced when her sister, Bridgette, followed her in the Royal suite. Consequently, Murphy survived the rigours of the revolution and died of old age before the end of 1814.[15]

Another method to combat the uncertainties of a future in exile lay in the reconfirmation of identity and status. As in the case of Leonor O'More and Arthur O'Neill, documents and licences of all kinds were lost or destroyed during the ordeal of emigration. Marriage and baptismal certificates, as well as proof of bequests and lineage, necessary for continental recognition and preferments were usually lacking. Women in particular were susceptible to such shortfalls. Relatives and clients often had to swear to or vouch for each other's legitimacy, nobility and marital status. To re-establish identity and claims also required an association with a community, garrison or parish familiar with the applicant. The ultimate recourse for many exiles was confirmation from Ireland. Catherine Fox, the wife of Christopher Dillon, a lieutenant in Lee's Irish regiment in France, wrote an anxiety-filled letter in March 1717 about her concern over the accuracy of her confirmed lineage and the amount of money her sister, the Countess of Cavan, or the Dublin Herald of Arms, might charge her for the information.[16]

Women also had limited freedom of movement, insulated as they often were in alien circumstances they had not chosen. The widowed Rosa Geoghegan wanted to leave Galicia to join her sons and brothers in Flanders. Nuala O'Donnell and Rosa O'Doherty, refugees from the 1607 flight, sought to escape confinement in Italy to care for young children in Louvain.[17] Most women, however, sought to rectify displacement caused by regimental reorganisations. Subsequent requests to follow their menfolk or to relocate during widowhood illustrate the presence and suffering of Irish females. But the greatest problem with relocation was the difficulty in receiving continued payment of pensions or allowances. Both the permission to resettle and to receive sustenance required official consent which was ineffectively administered and dispensed.

These mundane struggles for survival often were overshadowed by exploits of extraordinary individuals. There were Rosa O'Doherty's logistical efforts on behalf of her second husband, Owen Roe O'Neill, and his confederate war effort, the Jacobite machinations of Lady Lismore (Maria Josepha O'Brien), and the heroic behaviour of Lucy Fitzgerald during the Napoleonic siege of Gerona. Normally, however, the overwhelming majority of Irish women in this political/religious category lived as struggling army wives.

Although most Irish soldiers never had the opportunity or desire to wed, those that did marry or co-habit would generally select females outside of the Irish community. The problem was the dearth of Irish females available or suitable for the regular regimental recruit. No description of the soldier's wife can exceed Henrietta 'Lucy' Dillon's depiction of her mother, who 'married at seventeen to a boy only a year older than herself, who had been brought up with her and owned nothing in the world but his Regiment'.[18] This dependence on the inward-looking self-contained world of the military garrison was a reflection of a social hierarchy that mirrored the regiment. The officers' women undoubtedly enjoyed advantages not anticipated by the ladies of common soldiers, but each group was exposed to similar and proportional economic pressures. All women and their families lived on credit and developed working networks with local tradesmen. Often females of the lower rank supplemented the family income as seamstresses, cooks or laundresses. Some of the more desperate women even became seasonal *femmes publiques* until family accounts were settled. Many of the wives of senior officers also maintained urban residences, and did not accompany the regiment in the field. It was the womenfolk of the rank and file who became part of the regiment's host, that small army

)f camp followers and families. Preliminary work on the wills and
egisters in the Spanish army also suggest that the offspring of
he regimental rank and file frequently intermarried.

The greatest threat to women of the regiment was disbandment
)f companies, and the death or incapacity of their menfolk.
Destitute widows, or wives of invalid husbands, perhaps with
small children, who begged for sustenance were not unique.
From Stanley's Elizabethan levies, the Irish serving in the Baltic,
:o the regiments of Irish in France, Spain and Austria, each
soldier and his spouse experienced a powerlessness over their
ate. Their despair and impotence often was proportional to the
ndependence of the emigrating decision and the capability of
eturning home. Documentation of women from this category
also testifies to the anguish, loneliness and futility of exile. These
women and their male kin were transitional figures, who never
really assimilated until their expectation of 'return' abated. These
émigrés recreated instead an imagined sense of community that
for a time resisted full assimilation. This defensive insulation
perpetuated an ambivalence and despairing fatalism common to
modern female political refugees.

This sense of desolation also affected the involuntary exiles of
the servitude/maintenance group. Exile for the enforced-
servitude emigrants was intended as a punishment for their
actions, beliefs, or ways of life. These undesirables were generally
relocated like their voluntary indentured counterparts under
varying degrees of 'indenture' – contracts guaranteeing passage
for service to be rendered. The difference between the two forms
of labour migrants involved the duration of servitude, the working conditions and the discretionary powers of the merchant and
colonial masters. The original Irish settlements for servitude
evolved during the early seventeenth century in the Atlantic
tobacco-growing colonies and the Caribbean sugar islands.
Actual numbers of emigrants cannot be accurately determined,
but women probably never made up more than one-quarter of
the original involuntary, and less than one-half of the voluntary
servitude migrant populations.

Most involuntary pre-1800 labour emigrants were Catholic,
predominantly impoverished native Irish. Young and unskilled,
their resettlement was promoted as a remedy for the so-called
'vagrant' problem, and as a labour source for early New World
agricultural plantations. Initially, unmarried women were not
plentiful, despite a 1636 boast that young 'lusty and strong
bodied' Irish colleens were 'Readier to go [to the Indies] than
men'.[19] This alleged predisposition is not supported by evidence.
Most relocated women labourers were probably impressed young

widows or orphans girls. Unlike their indentured/voluntary counterparts, these females rarely migrated in family units. The testimonies of the Cromwellian period chronicle the circumstances of female deportation. Although most of these resettlement schemes were never actualised, Irish women were lowly regarded and were exclusively considered for propagation purposes – like the infamous 1655 Jamaican settlement plan to relocate 1000 young Irish girls with Irish lads. These solutions stemmed from an Elizabethan statute (39 Eliz. c. 4) against populations of idle and 'dangerous rogues', which actually encouraged a form of licensed kidnapping among shipping merchants. The actual number of transportees was never very large, but sufficient instances exist of quotas of 'weeping' Irish women 'stolen' or 'collected' by press gangs. Money and the promise of apparel were occasionally used as inducements. Merchants viewed the trade in labourers, voluntary or involuntary, as part of a transoceanic barter system involving sugar, tobacco and humans. Late in the century, the trade in vagrants and incorrigibles was condemned. The underlying cause of that condemnation was not the unscrupulous methods of licensed merchants, but rather the growing demand for African labourers and the general unsuitability of unskilled Irish Catholic servants. Nevertheless, the commerce in forced labourers continued into the next century as a fragment of the total servant trade. The scant surviving data for one quantifiable eight-year period (1735–1743) shows an average of 240 convicts, or 6.8 per cent of the lowest yearly estimate for eighteenth century indentured colonial immigration.[20]

Regardless of century, or the character of servitude, all forms of 'passengers', especially women, suffered during the eight to ten week Atlantic crossing. Rough weather, cramped berth space, inadequate ventilation, malnourishment and disease took their expected toll. In the initial decades, as many as one-third of the human cargo died in transit; young children and pregnant women suffered the highest mortality. Often expectant females, when identified, were put ashore before the ship embarked. A fortunate few were provided with money and a travelling pass. But the greatest percentage of women, especially females making it to the Caribbean, succumbed to disease, the alien climate and overwork in their tropical destinations. Data for white women in the Indies also indicate that the number of miscarriages and birth deaths were the highest in the hemisphere. As a result, Irish gender ratios and the number of children born by the original female population were quite low. Figures from the northern colonies indicate that the mainland achieved earlier balanced sex ratios, longer marriages and more surviving children than the tropical islands.[21]

Women did some field work, but were generally engaged in heavy domestic chores. For the discharged involuntary labourer of either gender, economic prospects, particularly in the Caribbean, were poor. Many labourers found their way to the mainland as indentured/contracted servants. Those who remained joined the growing number of men and women who lacked a 'constant or settled . . . abode', and thereby resumed an 'idle and wandering . . . slothful kind of life'.[22] By the end of the century estimates of the Irish population for the Caribbean region were as high as 12,000, with Barbados, Antigua, Jamaica and Montserrat containing the largest proportions. Recent studies of white women in the early eighteenth century Caribbean indicate that those over the age of 40 ultimately outnumbered their menfolk, but unlike males who sought out black women for sexual release, white women did not generally couple with black men during periods of unbalanced gender ratios.[23]

Although involuntary servitude continued into the eighteenth century, Irish emigration patterns to the western hemisphere changed. Slave labour dominated the Caribbean as mainland colonies absorbed large numbers of voluntary/indentured migrants from Ireland. Voluntary servants greatly outnumbered the combined totals for all types of pre-1800 Irish refugees. The dominant type was the 'passenger' who paid his/her way to the New World as a conservative emigrant. Those migrants that could not afford passage sailed as indentured/contracted labourers. These servants, to compensate for their fare, food and apparel, agreed to work off their debt through contracted labour. If the debt was not settled at disembarkation, the service of the redemptioner was reassigned by the merchant/captain to the highest local bidder. The people of both subgroups in the eighteenth century were largely Protestant and Scotch–Irish. These refugees represented the full range of contracted services, and involved more family units than their seventeenth century predecessors.

The resettlement of the Scotch–Irish to the New World began in the early seventeenth century in the Chesapeake tidewater region. It was not until the eighteenth century that restrictive religious and commercial policies, bad weather and the lure of cheap land and employment opportunities drew as many as 260,000 from Ireland through to the end of the Napoleonic wars. The remaining non-Catholic emigrants of this epoch, less than 50,000, were composed of Irish Quakers, Anglicans and Wesleyan Methodists. A large majority of these non-Catholic migrants were farmers, tradesmen or artisans, who came over as paying 'passengers'. Data suggest that a great many of them arrived in family units during the peak migration periods of the eighteenth century – 1717 to 1776 and 1783 to 1814. The percentage of women in this 'passenger' subgroup was substantially higher than in the contracted/indentured emigrant subgroup, the latter coming generally as individuals. But the migration decision remained primarily male kin orientated with strong community and congregational input, particularly among the Scotch–Irish.

The determining of gender identification and familial association is hindered by the lack of consistent distinctions between such terms as children, adults and servants. Nor is the researcher helped by the lack of female notoriety that distinguished the lives of some women on the continent. Instead, the exploits of females in the New World are obscured by the multitude of settlers, rapid assimilation, frontier environment and the ordinary domesticity that dominated women's lives. Colonial legal and business records may yet provide for females the kind of information disclosed by official continental petitions.

Women were fewer in number and fared the worse among the indentured/contracted emigrants. Slightly more than 42 per cent of all eighteenth century and post-colonial migrants qualified as contracted servants. All labourers, regardless of faith or region, contracted for their passage and worked off their debt as 'indenting' servants. Viewed as merchandise, Catholics and Protestants alike were sold at American ports into 'temporary bondage'. A recent study of immigrants to the Delaware Valley indicates that a great proportion of young unskilled indentured males arrived during non-peak crisis years. Documentation of individual voyages and extant seasonal port figures also reveal that the number of women among these servants ranged from 10 per cent to 15 per cent. But the market demand for women did not always provide merchants with satisfactory profits. An analysis of Delaware Valley immigration suggests that 'men sold better than women, skilled artisans better than laborers, German better than Irish'[24] and Protestants were preferred to Catholics.

A pivotal difference between women 'passengers' and 'servants' was the ability of the former to marry while young and to establish their own households. Those women who had to pay their contracted passages by working could marry only after their debt was settled. This condition was accomplished after multiple years of domestic service, or the willingness of a prospective husband to pay off her indenture. As a result, these women married late; often in their mid to late twenties. It has been estimated that servant women on the colonial mainland lost up to 10 years from their childbearing life. If colonial women survived the hazards of childbirth, they could expect to be widowed before their tenth anniversary, and then to remarry. The greatest plight of the indentured female was pregnancy. Although some girls were sexually exploited by their masters, they were primarily valued as an economic investment. Disrupting their work or compounding their expenses with pregnancy was not financially sound. Unless the responsible male was willing to compensate the master, a woman could be assessed with an additional debt which, in turn, prompted more contracted service for the 'trouble' the pregnancy created. Only after the indenture was settled, with a small separation fee in hand, could Irish females continue with their lives.

It is difficult to estimate the number of former servant females who remained unmarried, but a colonial woman inclined to marriage might have an unaccustomed advantage because of gender ratios of ten men to one woman that decreased to four to one and later to two to one. This imbalance provided females with their best opportunities and choices. Some of the advertisements and promotions in Ireland actually appealed to this disparity.

Notwithstanding their marital status, post-indentured female work was reminiscent of their contracted servant careers. Field labour rarely was a major feminine task, because of the time-consuming nature of food preparation and domestic chores. In their respective households, women cooked, baked, washed, made clothes, milked cows, kept gardens and cared for young children. Wealthier families might even seek relief from the services of a newly indentured female. In urban and commercial families, wives often assumed a greater share in the domestic side of the family business. In the absence of their husbands they represented and managed the businesses and oversaw the daily maintenance of the premises. Women also enjoyed greater property, guardian and economic rights, and in some colonies were endowed with powers of attorney after their spouses died. But these rights had little effect on poor domestic females or property-less women.

In spite of the uncertain fate and hardships awaiting Irish women in the New World their burdens could not obscure their advantages over sisters who sought refuge in other parts of the world. Colonial disfavour toward the Scotch–Irish, or the anti-Catholic legislation against Irish labourers, did not equate with the unsatisfactory and vulnerable life of exile that greeted most Irish female emigrants in Europe.

On the continent, the success of the few cannot detract from the misery and want of the many. Neither can the expanding experiences of these environments, Europe included, be discounted, for migrant communities and households hardly mirrored the world they had left. New places and situations eroded traditional habits and bonds with the successive generations of females born outside of Ireland. Responding initially as passive dependents, few pre-nineteenth century females had great expectations about emigration. But if post-migration communication with Ireland existed, did women gain a greater appreciation for the benefits and options outside of Ireland? This speculation raises the question of whether the 'optimism' and 'willingness' evident in post-famine female refugees began a century earlier;[25] that 'female chains' of endorsement or networking unfettered a woman's migrating decision.

The anguish and despair of exile for both sexes expressed by the lament 'While awake I am in France; in Ireland when I'm sleeping'[26] may be appropriate for those forced out of their homeland, but the pace of assimilation is directly proportional to the distance and 'pull' of the destination and the opportunities it afforded. To fully appreciate migration, researchers should reconsider gender in these movements. Such examination might disclose that the rigours and anxieties of female emigration are excluded from the traditional male 'exile motif'. Even the bardic *aisling* poetry, portraying mournful females grieving over a life without Ireland, may be simply another masculine expression of failed results.

Irishmen may have denigrated exile because of what they had foresaken, but did women react with the same emotional attachment? America and Britain, in particular, became more than a refuge and work place for women. The societal dynamics of these destinations provided females with alternatives and broadening life experiences not anticipated in their homeland. The accuracy of these assessments, however, can only be determined when all the geese and their destinations, after they left their Irish nest, are considered.

REFERENCES

1. W. Petty, 'The Political Anatomy of Ireland, 1672' in *A Collection of Irish Tracts* (Dublin, 1861), Vol. II, p. 25. A 1656 Jesuit report put the figure at 60,000. A. Gwynn (ed.), 'Documents Relating to the Irish in the West Indies' in *Analecta Hibernica* Vol. 4 (Oct. 1932), p. 230. For West Indian population data consult: R.V. Wells, *The Population of the British Colonies* (Princeton, 1975), pp. 212–13, 260–96.
2. T. Dekker, 'The Honest Whore' in R.H. Sheppard (ed.), *The Dramatic Works of Thomas Dekker* (London, 1873), Vol. II, p. 96.

3. H. Mayhew, *London Labour and the London Poor* (New York, 1967), Vol. I, p. 115; D.M. George, *London Life in the Eighteenth Century* (Chicago, 1984), p. 31; E.P. Thompson, *The Making of the English Working Class* (New York, 1966), p. 437. A similar statement was made in a 1697 Board of Trade report cited by George, *London Life*, p. 359, No. 128.

4. *Ibid.*, pp. 122, 128, 252–4.

5. E.P. Thompson and E. Yeo (eds), *The Unknown Mayhew* (New York, 1971), p. 176; J. Rule, *The Labouring Classes in Early Industrial England 1750–1850* (New York, 1986), p. 200; George, *London Life*, pp. 130–1, 348f No. 15; Rule, *Labouring Classes*, pp. 13–4, 200–1; J.R. Walkowitz, *Prostitution and Victorian Society: Women, Class and the State* (Cambridge, 1980), pp. 13–31.

6. Report on Mendicity in the Metropolis, 1814–15, cited by L.H. Lees, *Exiles of Erin: Irish Migrants in Victorian London* (Ithaca, 1979), p. 45.

7. B. Jennings (ed.), *Wild Geese in Spanish Flanders 1582–1700* (Dublin, 1964), pp. 163, 165–6. R. Hayes, 'Biographical Dictionary of Irishmen in France,' in *Studies*, vol. XXXV (June 1946), p. 256.

8. *Ibid.*, Vol. XXXIV (March 1945), p. 115; *ibid.*, Vol. XXXV (Sept. 1946), p. 357.

9. Sir John Davies to the Earl of Salisbury, 12 September 1607. *Calendar of State Papers, Ireland 1606–1608*, p. 270. P. Walsh, *Will and Family of Hugh O'Neill, Earl of Tyrone* (Dublin, 1930), p. 11. For the story of Bridget Fitzgerald and her daughter Mary Stuart O'Donnell consult, J. Casway, 'Mary Stuart O'Donnell' in *Donegal Annual*, Vol. 39 (1987), pp. 28–38.

10. M. Walsh, 'The Womenfolk of the Wild Geese' in *Irish Sword*, Vol. V (1962), pp. 135–6; T. O'Fiaich, 'The O'Neills of the Fews' in *Seanchas Ardmhacha*, Vol VII, No. 2 (1974) p. 282.

11. W. O'Connor Morris, *Memoirs of Gerald O'Connor* (London, 1903), pp. 80–1. M. Hennessy, *The Wild Geese, The Irish Soldier in Exile* (Old Greenwich, 1973), p. 18.

12. Petition of H. and C. O'Gallagher (*c*. June 1610), Jennings, *Wild Geese*, pp. 124–7; Prioress to L. Verreyken, 9 March 1610, *ibid*, pp. 123–4; B. Jennings, 'Career of Hugh, Son of Rory O'Donnell, Earl of Tyrconnell'; in *Studies*, Vol. XXX (1941), pp. 221–5.

13. Petition, 30 January 1614, Jennings, *Wild Geese*, p. 142; *Dossiers Personnels, Ancien Regime* in Archives du Ministere de la Guerre, Paris. For English transcripts see M. Walsh, 'O'Neills in Exile' in *Seanchas Ardmhacha*, Vol. VIII (1975–6), pp. 62–3; *Archivo Historica Nacional*, Madrid Calatrava, Expediente, 1830. See also M. Walsh, 'Womenfolk' in *Irish Sword*, Vol. V (1962) pp. 134–5 and Hennessy, *Wild Geese*, pp. 121–2.

14. *Archivo General Simancas*, legajos 1758 and 2251. See also M. Walsh, 'Womenfolk,' *Irish Sword*, Vol. V (1962), pp. 133–4 and Hennessy, *Wild Geese*, pp. 121–2.

15. M. Walsh, 'Womenfolk' in *Irish Sword*, Vol. V (1961), pp. 100–1; Vol. VI (1962), pp. 137–9; Hennessy, *Wild Geese*, pp. 35, 81, 118–19, 123–4.

16. Walsh, 'O'Neills Exile' in *Seanchas Ardmhacha*, Vol. VIII (1975–6), p. 62.

17. Their exploits are examined in J. Casway, 'Rosa O'Dogherty: A

Gaelic Woman', in *Seanchas Ardmhacha*, Vol. X (1980–1), pp. 48–53 and *Working Papers in Irish Studies*, Vol. 85–6, pp. 8–15.

18. F. Harcourt (ed. and trans.), *Memoirs of Madame de la Tour du Pin* (London, 1969), p. 15; Hennessy, *Wild Geese*, p. 28.

19. A.E. Smith, *Colonists in Bondage: White Servitude and Convict Labor in America 1607–1776* (Chapel Hill, 1947), p. 65; C. Bridenbaugh, *Vexed and Troubled Englishmen 1590–1642* (New York, 1980), p. 420; J. Silke, 'The Irish Abroad' in T.W. Moody, F. X. Martin and F.J. Byrne (eds), *A New History of Ireland, Early Modern Ireland 1534– 1691* (Oxford, 1976), Vol. III, p. 601.

20. *Commons Journal, Ireland*, Vol. IV, pp. cciii–v discussed by J.L. McCracken, 'The Social Structure and Social Life 1714–1760' in T.W. Moody and W.E. Vaughan (eds), *New History: Eighteenth Century 1691–1800* (Oxford 1985), Vol. IV, p. 33. The indentured estimate of 3500/year comes from J.G. Leyburn's analysis of the lowest Scotch Irish migration figure (200 000) for a 58-year period J.G. Leyburn, *Scotch–Irish* (Chapel Hill, 1978), p. 180.

21. The most detailed study of this kind was concluded by R.V. Wells, *The Population of the British Colonies* (Princeton, 1975), pp. 212–13, 261–96.

22. A 1657 Barbados Proclamation spoke of this problem. See A. Gwynn (ed.), 'Documents Relating to the Irish in the West Indies' in *Analecta Hibernica*, Vol. 4 (1932), pp. 236–7.

23. H. Moeler, 'Sex Composition and Correlative Cultural patterns of Colonial America', *William and Mary Quarterly*, 2 (1945), pp. 131–53; P. Molen 'Population and Social patterns in the Barbadoes in the Early Seventeenth Century', *ibid.*, p. 28 (1971), pp. 293–8; Wells, *Population*, pp. 294–5; R. Thompson, 'Seventeenth Century, English and Colonial Sex Ratios: A Postscript', *Population Studies*, 28 (1974), pp. 153–65.

24. The author is appreciative to Dr Maryann Woreck for sharing her paper and thoughts on this subject (M.S. Woreck, 'Irish Immigration to the Delaware Valley Before the American Revolution', a paper presented to the Philadelphia Center for Early American Studies, October 1988, p. 42).

25. H. Diner, *Erin's Daughters in America: Irish Immigrant Women in the Nineteenth Century* (Baltimore, 1985), pp. 12–42.

26. A. de Blacam, *Gaelic Literature Surveyed* (Dublin, 1929), p. 274.

8

Women and Eighteenth-Century Irish Republicanism

NANCY J. CURTIN

The republicanism espoused by the United Irishmen in the 1790s was at once an inclusive and an exclusive ideology. On the one hand these late eighteenth-century radicals imagined a democratic, secular republic which would confer the obligations and privileges of citizenship on all Irishmen, Catholic and Protestant, rich and poor, native or settler. But on the other hand, the United Irishmen refused to entertain the notion that women should be active members of the civic polity. This did not mean that women had no contribution to make to the republican campaign. Indeed, they served as activists within the United Irish organisation, as symbols of an oppressed nation, and as models of republican probity. But women's participation was limited by a gender-based division of labour which, as we shall see, was implicit in the republican tradition. At the same time, however, the political egalitarianism of early Irish republicanism provided a rational justification for the extension of full civic rights to women.

A republican reading of history confirmed for the United Irishmen the necessity for first radical reform and then revolution. The great republican states of the past had fallen because civic virtue was eroded by moral and political corruption. The private interests of citizens, obsessed with wealth and luxury, had taken precedence over the public good. And now this bleak historical record was threatening to repeat itself. Ireland was teetering dangerously on the precipice of despotism. Corruption in government was rampant, and corruption, in classical republican terms, was the cancer which invaded the body politic and brought it to the death agonies of tyranny. The years after the so-called constitutional revolution of 1782 saw only the acceleration and intensification of this disease. The only cure for this affliction was a strong dose of civic virtue, the subordination of private interest to the public good, injected by the needle of radical reform.

When the United Irishmen sat down in 1793 to the serious business of proposing a constructive plan of reform to replace the corrupt, British-controlled, Anglo-Irish parliament, no consideration whatsoever was given to the political rights of women. The rights of men were indeed lustily proclaimed. In one of the most radical reform programmes of the eighteenth century, the United Irishmen called for the enfranchisement of all adult males. But then, to be fair, there were very few voices raised to promote women's suffrage at this time.

The United Irishmen never entertained seriously the notion that women might enjoy the same political rights as men. In one of their very rare observations about the role of women in the state, Irish radicals came close to ridiculing women's active participation in politics. In an article in the United Irish newspaper, the *Northern Star*, the editors decried the extent to which certain wealthy, landed widows could nominate representatives to the Irish parliament. 'Mrs Tighe and Mrs Walcot have as many representatives in the Irish Senate as the city and county of Dublin. So far does the actual absurdity of our practice soar beyond the wildest dreams of French visionaries' who proposed the extension of the franchise to women.[1] The ironic tone actually implied that the notion of equal political rights for women was far less absurd than women exerting power in a corrupt political system. But the *Northern Star* certainly did not take the opportunity to champion the female cause.

But the rights of Irishmen to equal representation and a democratic Republican government of their own choosing was well supported by a number of Irishwomen, even if they were not invited to participate actively in this government. Certainly the wives and mothers and sisters of many of the radicals strongly adhered to the cause of democratic republicanism, offering to serve the movement in whatever way was required of them. Women assisted the United Irish cause in a variety of ways. First, they participated in oath-bound societies of United Irishwomen, a kind of female auxiliary which attended to fund raising and providing amenities for imprisoned United Irishmen and their families. These women might also undertake the dangerous business of gathering information and carrying secret messages within the vast network of local United Irish societies.[2] Women as well as children were certainly required to take the United Irish oath of secrecy, forbidding the swearer to reveal the secrets of the organisation and the identity of its members. Such an oath was also a prerequisite for membership in the organisation.

A second and more specific service performed by women in the republican cause was that of recruitment. Colonel John Bagwell of the Tipperary Militia stationed in Derry complained in 1797 that his men were rapidly coming under the influence of the United Irishmen. The task of the republicans was made all the easier because the 400 militiamen quartered in Derry were billeted throughout the town and its suburbs. United Irish agents would often befriend the militiamen, lonely as they were and chafing under the perennial discontents of soldiers. One of the principal means used to 'entrap' his soldiers, Bagwell lamented, was 'a practice of having an intrigue with a girl and swearing the man as a friend to secrecy when the matter [the aims and goals of the United Irishmen] should be divulged in confidence'.[3]

While the United Irishmen were exploiting these women to seduce the soldiers from their loyalty, they also raised the cry of an endangered Irish womanhood to attract recruits to the cause. When the United Irishmen were feeling the full force of the government's counter-revolutionary campaign in 1797 and 1798, radical propagandists recounted only too many examples of the savagery and cruelty of loyalist forces in Ireland. Favoured targets of these republican pens were the Orange Order and the government-sponsored and gentry-led yeomanry corps, both zealous supporters of the Protestant ascendancy. Orangemen and yeomen figured prominently in the government's repressive campaign against the United Irishmen, all too frequently giving credence to the republican propagandists' claim that these loyalists were waging war against the people. In this propaganda the radicals emphasised the dangers posed to Irish womanhood by the marauding and barbarous Orangemen or yeomen. The *Press*, the United Irish organ in Dublin, recounted an Orange rampage near Dungannon, County Tyrone, in March 1798. The loyalists burned down two Catholic chapels before they attacked the house of one Ruddy, a comfortable, peaceful farmer. The Orangemen raped Ruddy's daughter; when he attempted to stop them they killed him with a hatchet. And when they had satisfied their 'brutal lust', the Orangemen set fire to Ruddy's farm.[4] The yeomanry corps, with their loyalist Protestant exclusivity, became a haven for Orangemen and so enjoyed the enmity of United Irish propagandists. One illustrated handbill designed to discredit the yeomen presented the loyalist as a Turk, an eighteenth-century euphemism for military outrage, brandishing his scimitar and proclaiming 'Damnation! – only in destroying I find ease to my relentless thoughts'. In addition to a lust for 'carnage, devastation, and universal slaughter', this yeoman also professed his preference for rape and his contempt for women – 'to hold women in common . . . [is] ever my most sincere wish'.[5]

Republican propagandists especially urged Irish soldiers and

militiamen to turn against a government which sanctioned such
beastly assaults against the honour of their wives, mothers, and
sisters. One handbill cited the contradiction between an Irishman
serving his majesty 'perhaps at the same moment when his aged
mother lived to see her daughter violated by a horrid soldiery,
who had mingled the ashes of her husband with those of her
humble habitation'.[6] Indeed, the United Irishmen seem to imply
that the victims of the crime of rape were less the women
assaulted and more their male protectors or relatives. 'Irish blood
freezes', proclaimed one handbill, 'at the scenes of persecution
carried on against our countrymen, against our families and
friends'. And so the United Irishmen exploited the incidence of
rape to exhort Irish soldiers to 'awaken every noble and generous
sentiment in your breasts, [and] never to turn your arms against
your fellow men, whose crimes are hatred to tyranny and
oppression and love of liberty'.[7]

This notion of Irish women as victims of an unbridled and
vengeful loyalism enjoyed a recognisable affinity with feminine
allegorical representations of Ireland which figured so prominently in United Irish songs and ballads. Ireland in turns was
presented as an old woman, Granu or the Shan van Vocht,
summoning her sons to protect and defend her homestead, or as
Hibernia, the graceful, dignified Roman matron whose honour
and reputation needed to be asserted by her gallant admirers.
This appeal to filial devotion or manly exertions fed also upon
the central theme of rape. Ireland, the sister kingdom, had
experienced on a national scale a violation of her honour. Actual
women were the victims of real rape, but rape also provided the
metaphor to describe British policy in Ireland. The political
subordination of Ireland to Britain constituted a rape of sorts, as
did the confiscations of the seventeenth-century. Furthermore, as
metaphor or reality, the assault on Irish women posed an even
graver threat, in the eyes of the republican men, for her sexuality
was entrusted to the custodianship of a woman's male protector
– her husband or father or brother. To violate a woman was to
insult and, indeed, emasculate her male protector. Republican
rhetoric abounded with calls to Irishmen to assert their manhood.
The violation of their women was the price Irishmen paid for
suppressing their own patriotism and their civic duty. Conversely, a woman's regard was the reward for patriotic exertion.
Furthermore, to enlist gallantly and boldly in the cause of Ireland
was to honour her.

Women were not only assigned a role as victim in United Irish
propaganda efforts. They could also exert themselves as heroines
in the cause of republican virtue. The role of woman as patriot

had a long heritage in the Roman tradition which inspired much of the late eighteenth-century republicanism not just in Ireland but in America and France as well. Indeed, the Roman tradition of civic virtue and patriotism intersected with this theme of rape in the story of the violation of Lucretia and the consequent abolition of the monarchy. Since the fundamental core of republicanism was the subordination of private interest to the public good, Roman women were expected to display their civic virtue by freely giving up their men to the affairs of state and the defence of the country, to ease the choice which men must often make between happy domesticity and public duty. This proscribed role for women in the state was echoed by Montesquieu as well as Rousseau, who were both concerned that women could seduce men from their civic obligations. Virtuous women must be prepared to sacrifice their sons, their husbands and their brothers to the public good. Women must breed, nurture, and finally relinquish good republican men. The United Irishman Charles Hamilton Teeling rejoiced that in terms of 'national feeling' the 'enthusiasm of the females even exceeded the ardour of the men; in many of the higher circles and in the rustic activities, *that* youth met a cold and forbidding reception from the partner of his choice, who either from apathy or timidity had not yet subscribed to the test of the union [or United Irishmen]'.[8] And so the radicals urged women to demonstrate their support for the United Irishmen by donning an array of republican symbols and emblems – cockades, medals, and of course green articles of clothing and accessories. One unfortunate woman in Newry 'bragged about her green garters'. She was overheard by soldiers of the notoriously anti-republican Ancient Britons (a Welsh fencible corps) who 'tied her garters around her neck and sent her home showing her garters'.[9]

Republicanism was a manly calling. Ireland's bold defenders were called upon to protect her honour, to assert themselves in a just and righteous cause, to render filial devotion and husbandly care to their country. The role of women was to urge men to their patriotic, republican duty. The United Irishmen wished to confer active citizenship on all adult males, but the women of the republic also had their own duties to perform as passive citizens of the republic – to favour republican heroes and to raise republican sons, to be the patriot mother or wife who would permit and encourage her menfolk to meet their civic obligations. In a ballad of the period, 'The Patriot Mother', a young man faces execution unless he betrays the United Irish movement. His mother, fulfilling her republican role by selflessly championing the public cause, urges her boy to choose death with honour. She will not love a traitor, even if he is her own son. 'Dearer, far dearer than ever to me/My darling you'd be on the brave gallows tree'.[10] The same theme is to be found in the poems and ballads celebrating the republicans of 1867 and 1916, affirming the historic, gender-based division of labour which would advance the cause of patriotism.

Ideal republican women nurtured and encouraged republican citizen–soldiers and trusted their men to advance the public good. But real republican women chafed under the constraints imposed on their participation in the cause. The disparity between the ideal of women's involvement and reality of women's lives is clearly evidenced in the case of at least one republican woman in Belfast – Mary Ann McCracken.[11] The devoted sister of Henry Joy McCracken, United Irish activist and general of the insurgent forces in County Antrim in June 1798, Mary Ann was an ardent republican. In her unstinted approval of her brother's revolutionary activities she did, indeed, play the role of nurturing, patriotic woman. But McCracken took the radicals' notion of the natural rights of men to self-government to its logical inclusion – the extension of those rights to women. As she wrote to her incarcerated brother in March 1797, 'If we suppose woman was created for a companion for man, she must of course be his equal in understanding, as without equality of mind, there can be no friendship, and without friendship, there can be no happiness in society.' Certainly women, as rational creatures, were entitled to realise their full abilities and contribute to the public good under the enlightened government proposed by the United Irishmen. Indeed, as McCracken asserts, women were perhaps more rational than men, 'their bodies being more delicately framed and less fit for labour than that of man, does it not naturally follow that they were more peculiarly intended for study'. Her brother need only look at the diminutive Theobald Wolfe Tone, acknowledged by both Harry and Mary Ann as a man of genius, for a demonstration of this particular thesis relating size inversely with intelligence. But more seriously, she asked her brother,

> Is it not almost time for the clouds of error and prejudice to disperse and that the female part of the Creation as well as the male should throw off the fetters with which they have been so long mentally bound? . . . There can be no argument produced in favour of the slavery of women that has not been used in favour of general slavery . . . I therefore hope that it is reserved for the Irish nation to strike out something new and to shew an example of candour, generosity, and justice superior to any that have gone before them.[12]

McCracken had read her Mary Wollstonecraft with keen enthusiasm, and indeed urged her brother to do the same. 'Could you
not find more amusement in reading than drinking?' she asked
her brother and then recommended several titles from the
Godwin–Wollstonecraft circle.[13]

The McCrackens were a prominent family in Belfast. Mary's
maternal grandfather, Francis Joy, noted for his many entrepre-
neurial and charitable activities, founded the *Belfast News-Letter*.
Her father, John McCracken, was a sea captain, greatly respected
by the town's merchants and tradesmen, but also an active
entrepreneur. He established a rope works, built the first factory
in Belfast for the manufacture of sail cloth and canvas, and was
a pioneer in the developing Belfast cotton industry. Captain
McCracken was also noted as a patron of the arts and a sponsor
of several charitable enterprises. Mary Ann, born in 1770, was the
sixth of his seven children. She inherited from her mother and
father a sense of industry as well as social responsibility, an ethos
underscored by the sturdy Presbyterianism of eighteenth-century
Belfast.

It is no coincidence that these values instilled in the burgeoning
feminist Mary Ann McCracken were the same ones which
inspired the Presbyterian merchants and tradesmen of Belfast to
found the Society of United Irishmen there in October 1791.
There had, of course, been an historic affinity in the British Isles
between religious dissent and advanced political ideas. There is
an inherent democratic strain in Calvinist theology, with its
priesthood of all believers which was easily accommodated to the
early Irish republican ideology as well as the radical reform
tradition in Britain. Mary Wollstonecraft, William Godwin and
Tom Paine, so admired by Mary Ann McCracken, were, like
herself, products of this legacy. Strict deference to scriptural
authority also demanded that attention be given to education.
The faithful must be able to read the Bible. In middle-class
dissenting families especially, woman's role tended to shift from
that of producer to guardian of moral and religious values. It was
a mother's calling to educate her children in sound Christian
doctrine. The principle that men and women were equal before
God, therefore, did not preclude a gender-based division of
labour. Women tended to the domestic sphere, in which Christian
values and teachings would be instilled into their children, while
men attended to worldly affairs. Such a division of labour was
also reflected in the classical republican tradition, which merely
substituted civic virtue for Christian values. This domestic sphere
was narrowly confined, yet to the extent that it generated more
respect and even tenderness towards its inhabitants, it may well

have been an improvement. And by placing such emphasis on women's obligation to educate their children, it required that the educators must themselves be educated. The question in the eighteenth century was not whether or not women should be educated, but how they should be educated. Was women's capacity for reasoning equal to or different from that of men? Should the emphasis in women's education be on cultivating their sense or their sensibility?[14]

Clearly, Mary Ann McCracken recognised no gender-based differences in the intellectual capability of men and women, a position confirmed for her by reason, religion, and her own experience. She was fortunate in her own formal education, attending along with her brothers a rather progressive school in Belfast run by David Manson, a firm believer in co-education. In the letter referred to above, McCracken seems quite comfortable lecturing her elder brother on the subject of politics. Indeed, she seems to have been far better read in the classic republican and radical texts than her brother.

Mary Ann thus regarded as nonsense the argument that women could not participate equally with men in politics because of their inferior intellect. But a more prevailing argument against women's political activity was their state of dependence. Radicals and republicans did not agree as to how far the franchise should be extended. Those who favoured limiting the franchise advocated the notion that economic dependency should bar a man from the privilege of voting. Only those with a propertied stake in the country could be relied on to vote independently and in the interests of the general good. Even those like the United Irishmen, the London Corresponding Society, the Jacobins in France, or the Jeffersonian Democrats in America who championed universal male suffrage envisaged a nation of independent producers. A popularly accountable government would hasten this development where it did not already exist, and maintain it where it did. The difference between those who advocated universal male suffrage and those who pushed for a more limited, property-based franchise, was really not that great. In a well-run republican state, an equality of opportunity would prevail, and those who were economically dependent today would be independent tomorrow. To grant women the vote, on the other hand, would be an exercise in political redundancy. Economically dependent married women, so the argument goes, would vote as their husbands did. Since more women were married than not, these arguments conveniently ignored as irrelevant the fact that some women were financially independent, either as unmarried producers themselves or widows, many of them carrying on their husbands' businesses.

Classical republicanism and the radical dissenting tradition equated industry or work with virtue. The former glorified the independent producer, the latter emphasised the Calvinist 'calling' which required the faithful to conduct their worldly affairs with a thoroughness and zest that would honour their Creator. Corruption was equated with unearned wealth and luxury, particularly associated in the minds of eighteenth-century radicals with a self-interested hereditary landed class. The industrious classes of society – merchants, tradesmen, farmers and manufacturers – created the nation's wealth and must have their full share in the nation's governance. Moreover these groups, imbued with republican and dissenting principles concerning social responsibility, were alone capable of advancing the public good. Industry was thus a religious, moral and civic obligation. It also belonged to that sphere in the gender-based division of labour which belonged to men. Once again McCracken defied the male exclusivity of the work ethic by including women. If industry in the world was a virtue, how could it be any less so if undertaken by a woman? And therefore women had an obligation to work, particularly single women like herself.

The barriers to middle-class women's work outside the home were not formidable in the eighteenth century. Widows frequently assumed full direction of their deceased husbands' concerns. They were fortunate in the sense that the opportunity for work was clearly presented to them. Single women, unless economically independent, had to work unless they were to remain an unwanted burden on their families. Their problem was what to do. As McCracken herself complained, 'The sphere of women's industry is so confined, and so few roads lie open to her, and those so thorny, it is difficult to fix on any.'[15] But she is here speaking of a general problem facing women who want or need to work. Mary Ann was fortunate in having an example of female industry in her mother, Ann Joy McCracken. The daughter of Francis Joy, the sister of Robert and Henry Joy, two active Belfast entrepreneurs, and the wife of the industrious Captain McCracken, Ann McCracken was not one to while away her days in leisure awaiting the return of her husband from one of his many voyages. She started her own muslin manufacturing enterprise. At a time when the industrial base of Belfast was characterised by numerous small firms based on the 'putting-out' system, Ann McCracken's business thrived. When she died in 1814, her daughters continued the independent spirit which had been instilled in them by their parents. When barely out of her teens, sometime in the late 1780s, Mary Ann McCracken followed in her mother's footsteps by starting, with her elder sister Margaret, their own business – Margaret McCracken and Co.,

Muslin Manufacturers. Mary Ann, with a special aptitude for figures, was in charge of the books. The sisters started out on a small scale, employing weavers who worked in their own homes, but by 1809 they moved into factory production. Unfortunately, this increase in production coincided with a serious depression in the industry which contributed to widespread backruptcies. The firm survived until 1815 when the McCrackens, faced with threat of ruin, decided to retire. Their chief concern during these troubled times, however, was for their employees. 'I could not think of dismissing our workers', Mary Ann later recalled, 'because nobody would give them employment.'[16] This was no mere hobby. It was, after all, a largely successful enterprise which lasted for over 25 years under astute, capable, and clearly humane direction. Mary Ann's investment in the firm was not solely financial; she saw the business as providing employment and so was socially useful. It was also a proud testament to her industry and independence, those virtues so prized by republicans.

Mary Ann McCracken lived well into her nineties, dying in 1866. No longer a businesswoman and fortunate in possessing a sufficient income to support her, she spent her many remaining years pursuing the kind of charitable activities sanctioned by prevailing notions about women's role. She became a tireless committee woman championing causes such as improvements in the poor house, rehabilitation of female prisoners, and her clearly favourite project, education of the neglected daughters of the poor. The tragic rebellion and the execution of her dear brother Harry in 1798, followed in 1803 by the execution of Thomas Russell, to whom she gave her unrequited love, had considerably dampened the confident revolutionary enthusiasm of her earlier letters. In 1797 she could write: 'I think the reign of prejudice is nearly at an end.' Yet after 1798 she no longer anticipated that age when women would throw off the fetters of 'their abject and dependent situation, degraded by custom and education beneath the rank in society in which they were originally placed'.[17] But while she marked with approval the moral force campaigns of Daniel O'Connell and enthusiastically applauded the temperance efforts of Father Theobald Mathew, she was horrified by the persistence of slavery in the world and the callous treatment accorded to the poor.

Did McCracken retreat from the ardent republicanism which inspired her emerging feminism? Or did she merely accommodate herself to a new age which saw economic individualism and liberalism replacing a more socially responsible republicanism and an increasing confinement of women to a narrowly defined domestic sphere? The answer is perhaps a bit of both. Her republicanism, based on the notion that true civic virtue required public service, compelled her to engage in one of the few public activities left to a middle-class woman in the nineteenth century – philanthropy. 'It is my very peculiar duty to endeavour to be useful while I can . . . this world affords no enjoyment equal to that of promoting the happiness of others.' Whatever talents and abilities she possessed must be applied to promoting the public good, whether providing employment to Belfast weavers as she did in her youth, or attending to the needs of distressed women and children as she did in her charitable activities in her mature years. This dedication to public service is the bedrock of republicanism.

Citizenship, according to republican theory, is more of an obligation than a privilege, a responsibility to promote good government. The exercise of the rights and obligations of citizenship is also a process of self-realization by which republican man can develop and nurture his own true and benevolent nature. Individual happiness cannot be achieved at the expense of the community. Corruption of the body politic was the more pernicious and therefore intolerable because it could spread through society and end up corrupting man's nature. 'The crime, as well as the misery, of our civil society', wrote Dr William Drennan, one of the founders of the Society of United Irishmen,

> are clearly traceable to the corruptions of our political constitution – for it appears to me a truth that the full and free enjoyment of our rights is absolutely necessary to the performance of our duties, and [that] the unequal distribution of the former, preventing the accomplishment of the latter, the freedom of the public must be necessarily connected with their *virtue* as well as their happiness.[18]

Eighteenth-century republicanism denied women the individual happiness and self-realisation which resulted from active political participation. Yet in the long run, the universalism which underscored this republicanism, and of the Enlightenment and the radical dissent tradition which reaffirmed it, contained the seeds for women's political liberation. Not only were all men created equal, but, as McCracken among others asserted, all women were created equal to men, and therefore entitled to all the rights and responsibilities implicit in their fundamental and universal humanity.

REFERENCES

1. *Northern Star*, 13 June 1792.
2. S. McSkimmin, *Annals of Ulster from 1790 to 1798* (Belfast, 1906), p. 38.

3. Col. John Bagwell to Dublin Castle, 28 June 1797 (State Paper Office of Ireland (hereafter cited as S.P.O.I.), Rebellion papers, 620/31/167.
4. *Press*, 3 March 1798.
5. 'Portrait of a soldier yeoman' (S.P.O.I., Rebellion papers, 620/28/249).
6. S.P.O.I., Rebellion papers, 620/53/14.
7. *The Report of the Secret Committee of the Irish House of Commons, with an Appendix*, (Dublin, 1798), pp. 301–2.
8. C. Hamilton Teeling, *History of the Irish Rebellion of 1798 and Sequel to the History of the Irish Rebellion of 1798* (first published, 1876; Shannon, Ireland, 1972), p. 11.
9. Thomas Pelham to [William Pitt], 1 November 1797 (British Library, Pelham papers, Additional MS 33105/188–91).
10. R.R. Madden, *The United Irishmen, Their Lives and Times* (first published 1842–5, 12 vols, New York, 1916), Vol. 10, pp. ix–x.
11. See M. McNeill, *The Life and Times of Mary Ann McCracken, 1770–1866: a Belfast Panorama* (Dublin, 1960).
12. Mary Ann McCracken to Henry Joy McCracken, 16 March 1797 (P.R.O.N.I., McCracken papers, T.1210/7).
13. Mary Ann McCracken to Henry Joy McCracken, 10 August 1797 (*ibid.*, T.1210/26).
14. See A. Browne, *The Eighteenth-Century Feminist Mind* (Detroit, 1987).
15. Quoted in McNeill, *Mary Ann McCracken*, p. 246.
16. Quoted in *ibid.*, p. 244.
17. Mary Ann McCracken to Henry Joy McCracken, 16 March 1797 (P.R.O.N.I., McCracken papers, T. 1210/7).
18. W. Drennan, *A Letter to His Excellency Earl Fitzwilliam, Lord Lieutenant, etc., of Ireland* (Dublin, 1795), p. 18.

Illustrations

1. A sixteenth century sheela-na-gig from Ballylarkin, Co. Kilkenny. These stone images of women were reputed to ward off evil and are often found on the exterior wall of a tower house or in a church.

2. Images of the Madonna and child were popular in late medieval Ireland. This one from Askeaton, County Limerick is one of the best surviving examples.

3. Cross commissioned in 1601 by Janet Dowdall in memory of her first husband, William Bathe, Justice of the Common Pleas in County Meath. Janet also commissioned three other crosses: another for William and two for her second husband, Oliver Plunket, fourth Baron of Louth.

4. Carved stone erected by Beanmhumhan Og Ni Dhuibhgheannain in memory of her husband, the Vicar Eoghan MacDomhnaill in the 1590s in Skreen, Co. Sligo.

5. Domestic interior of Bunratty towerhouse. The internal planning and decoration of the tower house was probably the concern of the women in the family.

6. Wall decoration in Ballinacarriga Castle, Co. Cork, depicting Catherine O'Cullinane, wife of the founder of the castle. Later folklore told stories about Catherine and her children, allegedly represented here by the roses.

7. A portrait of old age: allegedly the old countess of Desmond who was reputed to have lived to be 140 years of age.

8. Monument erected by Eleanor, Countess of Desmond in Sligo Abbey in 1624. Eleanor chose to commemorate herself and her husband in fashionable Stuart costume.

9. Three of Richard Boyle, Earl of Cork's daughters as represented on their father's monument in Saint Patrick's Cathedral, Dublin.

10. Facsimile of letter written at Louvain, 16 September 1642 by Rose O'Doherty, wife of Owen Roe O'Neill. Her scribe was probably the Franciscan scholar, John Colgan.

11. Lady Lettice Offaly who defended Castle Geashil, Co. Offaly in 1642.

Irish Woman

12. Irish woman of the 1680s, dressed in typical fashion of the time: red wool gown, green apron, brown waistcoat and a linen neckerchief and handkerchief.

BUYE the large black Cockle, fine
large black Cockle;—Here's fresh
boil'd Crabs dr Lobsters, here.

OISTERS! curious Oisters:—Here's
the fresh Carlingford Oisters.—
Who wants the fine Oisters?

13. Extracts from handbill illustrating street criers in Dublin in the
eighteenth century. This rather romanticised view of the working Irish
woman contrasts with the more realistic drawings of S.T. Roche in 1831,
depicting women selling milk and eggs.

14. The contrasting frontages of Castle Ward. Lady Ann Ward chose the Gothick. Her husband preferred the more conventional classical idiom. The separation of Castle Ward was followed by the separation of its owners.

15. Katherine Connolly and her niece, c. 1734. Katherine's black band and lack of adornment indicates her widow's status.

Success to the
INDEPENDENT VOLUNTEER
SOCIETIES
of the Kingdom of
IRELAND.

16. The portrayal of Hibernia as a woman became a popular image in the second half of the eighteenth century. The image first appears on coins in the reign of Charles II.

17. A cartoon from *Hibernia Magazine* (1810) summarises many of the common perceptions of women throughout the early modern period. The words in the balloon read: 'Ladies, I shall endeavour by my example, to animate you to exertion on the day of Battle. Use no weapons but your tongues which will be sufficient to harrass any moderate army whatever. In all human probability, the enemy will charge in the van, – I have therefore placed in the front ranks Widows, and Ladies who have been more than once married, having superior knowledge of the Tacticks – Virgins of eighteen, and young married Ladies form the center, and Old Maids bring up the rear, under the appellation of the Forlorn Hope Battalion!'

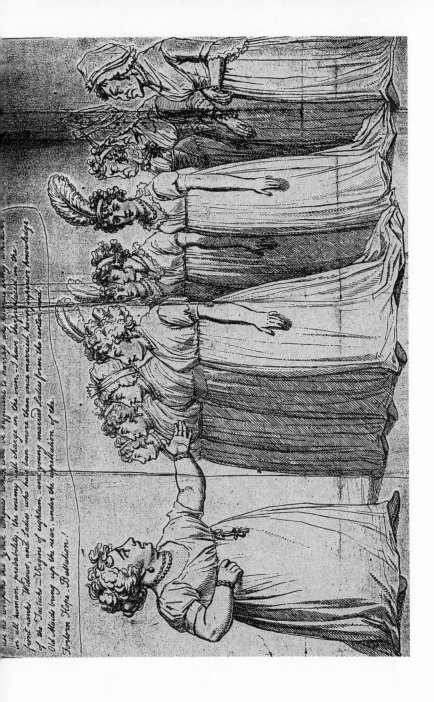

SECTION II

Religion and Education

9

Women and Gaelic Literature, 1500–1800

BERNADETTE CUNNINGHAM

Literature forms a significant element in the historical jigsaw of the early modern world because the literature a society produces is determined by the way society functions. The portrayal of women in Gaelic literature and their involvement in literary pursuits whether as authors or patrons are reflections of the values of Gaelic society and the status of women therein. What members of society will become authors is partly determined by levels of literacy and education. What members of society will be patrons is largely determined by wealth and status. How closely literature reflects the society from which it emanates is a matter of debate, and it is difficult to be conclusive, particularly when so much of it was derivative of other sources. And early modern literature was rarely original. As in Celtic art, so in Gaelic literature the artist aimed at fineness of technique rather than originality of design.[1]

Thus the bardic poetry composed in Ireland down to the early seventeenth century was closely connected with the politics and political propaganda of Gaelic lordship society. The historical annals were likewise the product of a localised monastic structure coupled with the localised lordship structure. A less elitist, more diverse tradition more open to external influences emerged in the poetry and prose which has survived from the late seventeenth century in Ireland. Much of the Irish prose literature of the post-bardic age was adapted for Irish audiences from continental sources. There was perhaps more human interest in the folk poetry, which had a spontaneity lacking in the structured formality of bardic poetry produced for court society. Even then, of course, literature has a tendency to universalise, and so to gloss over the particularities of an age. Yet, despite the drawbacks, the view of Gaelic society obtained from the literature is not without merit. In investigating the role of women in Gaelic society through the literature there are three strands worthy of attention:

women as patrons, women as authors, and women as subjects
of literature.

I

Long before we have evidence of women as authors of Gaelic
literature, either poetry or prose, numerous women acted as
literary patrons. This was an important and not unusual role. In
bardic poetry the female patron was frequently alluded to in the
poem itself, and so the evidence of that literature gives some
indication of the role of noble women in Gaelic lordship society.
The evidence of the poetry can be substantiated by contemporary
evidence from prose literature. In the annals compiled down to
the end of the sixteenth century, obituaries of the elite of society
were a core element. In each of three contemporary annals, the
Annals of Ulster, the Annals of Loch Cé, and the Annals of
Connacht, about 10 per cent of sixteenth century obituaries relate
to women.[2] The following range of attributes emerge: eminent,
humane, charitable, merciful, industrious, religious, noble, virtuous, witty, patient, worthy, beautiful, wealthy, generous, patron. (The main attributes frequently assigned to men but not to
women are those specifically political ones of warrior, leader,
protector, etc., and those concerned with influence in the church
and education.)

It was of course an indication of high standing in lordship
society to merit a mention in the annals at all. One would have
had to be a locally prominent personality who had made a
signficant contribution to lordship society for one's death to be
noted by the annalists. For example, Margaret, daughter of Conor
O'Brien, wife of O'Rourke who died in 1513 was according to the
Annals of Loch Cé 'religious and hospitable', according to the
Annals of Ulster she was 'hospitable and wealthy', and according
to the Annals of Connacht (and of course she was a native of
Connacht), she was a

> radiant paragon of the Gaels, to whom God gave prosperity
> and royal state and great wealth. Hearth of hospitality and
> maintenance, humanity and charitable entertainment for
> scholars and ollaves, the weak and wretched and all whether
> mighty or outcast, who stood in need thereof . . . [and she
> died] after unction and penance and was buried in the
> monastery which she had herself built to the honour of God
> and St Francis, namely the monastery of Creevlea.[3]

Fionnuala O'Brien who died in 1528 was described in the two
Connacht-based annals, Loch Cé and Connacht, as the daughter
of Conor O'Brien, and was religious, hospitable, and charitable.
The Annals of Ulster described her not as O'Brien's daughter but

rather as Queen of Tir Conaill and added 'eminence'.[4] The provincial bias of the annals noted here illustrates the local rather than national approach of the Gaelic annals of the sixteenth century. It was only exceptional people who were accorded a mention in the annals not compiled in their own province.

The qualifications for inclusion in the obituaries in the annals were wide ranging. In 1532, the daughter of Mac Craith, wife of Dubhtach Mac Domhnaill (her own forename was not given) was accorded an obituary where she was described as 'an excellent, virtuous and witty woman'.[5] In 1535 Siobhan O'Neill, wife of Manus O'Donnell, was described as wealthy.[6] In 1580 the daughter of Cuchonnacht Mor Mac Cuchonnacht Maguire was described as 'religious, hospitable, charitable, and a patron'.[7] In 1587 a different type of attribute, which had no connotations for her position in the society in which she had lived, was accorded Mary Queen of Scots. She was simply described as beautiful.[8] This type of attribute accorded Mary Queen of Scots may be an indication that the attributes accorded the other women mentioned were not merely empty flattery without foundation, but were reasonably valid assessments of the women concerned, which made those obituaries credible for the audience for whom they were written. These attributes can therefore be used to create a picture of the role of elite women within Gaelic lordship society.

Women who were the wives or daughters of prominent men had an important position in lordship society. Their role as patrons of poets and scholars was one aspect of their functions as the wife of a lord. However, although women in Gaelic society did not adopt their husband's surname, women mentioned in the annals were invariably described in terms of their father or husband. It is evident that women who acted as patrons, as many did, owed their status and presumably the wealth which allowed them to be patrons principally to their husbands. In turn, their selection as suitable partners for their husbands would have depended on their father's status. Rather than being persons of influence in their own right they owed their status to their role as one element of a marriage partnership which, in the patriarchal world of the lordship, was primarily a political alliance.

That the generosity and hospitality attributed to wives of lords in the annal obituaries were real tangible qualities is amply borne out by the poetry. Women who acted as patrons to the poets were frequently mentioned in the poems themselves, usually in the closing stanzas. Examples from the poembook of the Maguires include a poem entitled 'Cia re bhfuil Éire ar anmhuin', where the main theme of the poem – that of Ireland portrayed as a woman and looking for her rightful husband – is cast aside in

lines 201–216 and the poet's attention turns instead to the wife c
Cuchonnacht Maguire.

> The daughter of Sean surpasses the young women of Irelan
> in generosity, a slender tipped hand which gives what I ask
> she is a friend of giving . . .[9]

The only obvious reason why the poet should interrupt the unit
of the poem to mention the chief's wife is that he felt the nee
to adhere to the custom of acknowledging the patron of th
poem.

Women's role in patronage of the arts was nothing new i
either an Irish or European context in the early modern period
Women patrons were common in medieval court society through
out Europe. Such a phenomenon was likely to emerge strongl
in any war-based society where the elite male element of th
community was occupied at war.[10] In such circumstances, th
women's central role in running the affairs of the household an
the lordship should come as no surprise. Two successive wive
of Cathal O'Hara, the leading figure in the poembook of th
O'Haras, are regularly praised by the poets for their patronage
Some poems address the praise to Cathal directly but sti
attribute the role of patron to his wife.

> Thou hast a spouse like thyself, she does not feel partin
> from wealth, 'tis right to imitate her qualities.[11]

Elsewhere, the poet attributes the role of patron to Corma
himself.

> A common saying of this smooth-haired hero, is that 'ti
> wrong to hoard God's gifts, his lavishness is the mor
> justified as it does not prevent him from supporting poets.[1]

Tadhg Dall Ó hUiginn praises Máire, daughter of Maol Muire
in another poem addressed to Cormac O'Hara:

> Mary daughter of Maol Muire, regal in aspect, chaste i
> mind, a woman excelling those of Bregia's dewy castle th
> favourite of all her kindred.
> Cormac son of Cian has got, if she be estimated in ever
> particular – our choice of all her stock – the best of mates t
> love.[13]

Tadhg Dall frequently praised the wife of the subject of hi
compositions.

> A choice of all the royal ladies of Ulster hast thou made, thou
> dark-lashed eye, happy the man who hath first taken her
> happy he who made that choice.
> A gentle eye, bright as crystal, hath the daughter of the kin
> of Banagh, lips to which the hue of the berry might b
> likened, a glowing cheek that never was made to blush.
> Not every woman of Ulster would suit the husband o
> Gráinne as a companion, none but a generous man woul

suit her, happy he of whom she is the mate.[14]

One traditional poetic motif for praising a woman was to say she was a good prize for a man to win. This subordinate role was emphasised by another poet Irial Ó hUiginn who wanted Cathal O'Hara's wife to intercede with her husband on his behalf.

> May Toirdhealbhach's daughter, that comely girl, give me her earnest help, to her shall speed my song of sweet praise. When a queen conveys a request to a king its result is greatly strengthened, Caitlin's wish is Cormac's, splendid the union of those two kindred desires.[15]

There may be overtones of devotional poems to Our Lady here in the idea of the queen interceding with her lord on behalf the requester.

There is evidence that women's contribution to the lordship may have extended beyond patronage. Manus Ó hUiginn in a poem on Cormac O'Hara praises Caitilin, wife of Cormac, because while Cormac has been active as a warrior and a conqueror of land (a subject on which the poet seems somewhat ambivalent) Caitilin 'has made the land prosperous by her management'. 'She offers reward even when the poets are critical, and thus she need not doubt the poet's good will, her glory grows apace like a plant of good stock',[16] and has a more realistic understanding of how to promote the welfare of the lordship. The women who acted as patrons may have owed their wealth and status to their husbands, but these same women who were eulogised in the closing lines of many bardic poems in the sixteenth century obviously had a significant, if subordinate, role within the formal structure of the lordship.

Where patronage of poetry continued in the early seventeenth century one of the women praised in a number of Ulster poems – Martha Stafford – was an Englishwoman.[17] And at the end of the seventeenth century the Munster poet Daibhi Ó Bruadair, one of the great poets of the first generation of the post-bardic age, also had a female patron, on occasion. In a poem attacking another poet who had praised the Duke of Ormonde above Ireland's ancient heroes, Ó Bruadair intervened to defend Ireland's past glories. But ironically, and he was probably himself aware of the irony, Ó Bruadair notes in the final stanza that an English woman as patron has come to his rescue:

> Had not a maid of British blood and gentle Scottic race relieved the dangerous disease which had unreasonably seized me, at the sour offensive savour of that silly song of thine, loathsome writhings would have racked me at the threshold of the door.[18]

Ó Bruadair lived and worked in a world where poetry was no longer the propagandist product of the traditional lordship society. Yet, the patronage offered him by an English woman provides evidence that women's function as patrons was retained in the new social order. Even where patronage was directed into alternative spheres ranging from scribal activities to musical performance, following the disintegration of lordship society, women's role as patrons did not disappear. Mrs McDermott Roe, who numbered among the patrons of the harper Turlough Carolan, is an example of those who kept the tradition alive.[19]

II

The circumstances which led women to be patrons of Gaelic literature in early modern Ireland, and which gave them recog- nised status as patrons within that society, were not circum- stances necessarily conducive to the emergence of women as authors. As Katharine Simms has noted elsewhere, women were apparently excluded from the bardic schools of the poetic elite, and little poetry has been preserved from the bardic era except the products of the bardic schools. The changes of the seven- teenth century which saw the disintegration of the lordship system and the consequent disappearance of the traditional propagandist functions of the bardic poets, marked a social revolution which was inevitably reflected in the literature of the age. The extant literature in Irish from the late seventeenth century bears little relation to that which had emanated from Gaelic lordship society in earlier generations. The folk poetry which began to be preserved in manuscripts from the late seventeenth century no longer excluded women authors. This folk tradition was no new creation of the late seventeenth century; the innovation of the age was that popular poetry began to be recorded in manuscripts. We must assume that there had been many women poets from this folk tradition in earlier generations whose work has not survived.

One example who can actually be identified was the mother of Padraig Mac a Liondain, an early eighteenth-century south Ulster poet. Padraig records that he learned his craft from his mother, who was herself a poet although none of her work survives.[20] The trait obviously ran in the family and in the mid-eighteenth century we find Padraig's daughter, Molly Lindon, composing poetry in Irish.[21] It should not be assumed that the poetic tradition of this family only started in the mid-seventeenth century with Padraig's mother, it may have gone back many generations before. But it was only in the eighteenth century in places like south Ulster where vibrant scribal activity in Irish survived, that such compositions began to be recorded.

However, even in the early eighteenth century the number of women whose literary compositions have been preserved in Gaelic manuscripts is very small indeed.

The work of women folk poets of eighteenth century Ireland was essentially an extension of the genre produced by men rather than a distinct phenomenon. There was some religious poetry, perhaps not composed with a public audience in mind.[22] There was public poetry concerned with the life and death of ordinary people but not with formal themes like ancestry or heroism, reflecting the strata of society to which these women belonged. Individuality and natural talent were obviously prerequisites for women to earn social acceptability as poets. A reasonable level of education would also have been necessary. But such women were still a minority, and were deemed inferior. A poetic contention between the schoolteacher poet, Peadar Ó Doirnín, and the farmer's daughter, Molly Lindon, in south Ulster in the early eighteenth century is revealing of contemporary attitudes towards women. The introduction to this poetic contention in the manuscripts set the scene where a girl (an insignificant person of course) happened to be playing the harp one evening and singing songs for the entertainment of the assembled crowd, when an unidentified (but of course very eminent) man entered, played a few tunes and then they had a competition to see who could compose the best verses. No verdict was given on the winner but the clear assumption was that the woman's verses should be expected to be inferior. If the woman should prove equal to the man in the contest, this would be a cause of great merriment for all present.[23]

Molly Lindon may have been regarded as something of a freak, being a superior poet to her brother Padraig Óg. The scribal tradition is rather confused. Some manuscripts attribute poems to her saying she used her brother's name as a pseudonym.[24] Perhaps the scribes were still somewhat uncomfortable with the idea of women poets, even though they were members of a family who had for generations maintained an informal school of poetry, as the Mac a Liondains apparently did. Women poets continued to be a small minority, even in south Ulster in the eighteenth century, and those whose work we know of, though still only in manuscript, usually did no more than extend the tradition role of women as 'keeners' into the world of literature.

In general, Irish women writers, like their Scottish counterparts, were disappointing in their choice of subject. The poems composed by women which have survived from early eighteenth century Ireland are mainly laments on male relations of the poets.[25] In Scotland, women poets had attained literary prominence earlier than in Ireland. One of the best known of the seventeenth century Scottish women poets was Mary Mac Leod. A recent assessment of her work shows that many of her poems are formal pieces dealing with well-worn themes of heroism and ancestry.[26] She gained a considerable reputation in the last century by being credited with having invented the three-line stanza in strophic meter which was popular in seventeenth century Scotland. It has long since been shown that such meters were in fact in use as early as 1550, and a recent critic has suggested that 'she wears the strait jacket of the bardic panygerist without his learning . . . wit . . . and metrical virtuosity'. The poetry of another of these women poets of late seventeenth-century Scotland, Catherine Mac Lean, is in a style strongly influenced by folksong. They are transitional poets, typical of the seventeenth century, poets not trained professionally in the bardic schools, but having an appreciation of the ideology which had informed the bardic tradition.[27] No compositions by comparable women poets survive from seventeenth-century Ireland. The reasons for this should probably be looked for in a broader social context than standards of education and levels of literacy alone.

III

When looking at women as subjects of literature in the early modern era, women's involvement is a passive one. We can usually only look at women through the eyes of literature created by men. There are several major subdivisions. First, there are works which deal with individual women. The author's relationship with them is the most usual theme, though the range of relationships is wide. Love poetry is plentiful, dealing with the universal themes of love rewarded, love unrequited, love abandoned. Yet women are hardly ever named specifically, and the real subject of the poem may well be the author himself. It has been argued that the *amour courtois* poetry of France and the similar love poetry produced in Ireland were invariably couched in terms of male/female hostility. The male poet, a real figure, always triumphs over the female subject, a mere abstraction, a figment of the male imagination. It is suggested that this competitive attitude was inspired by the intrigues of the court life from which this kind of poetry emanated, and that it contrasts with the gentle love poetry from the folk tradition where competition was a less important feature of people's daily lives.[28]

In the political poems from the bardic era, as we have seen, noble women usually featured as the relatives of men who were the main subjects of the poems, rather than being the main subject themselves. Numerous poems were addressed to women, but frequently to women who have lost a husband, and the poem concentrated on eulogising the deceased.[29]

The second major category of works with women as subject matter are those in which women appear as personifications of abstract ideas. Abstract male and female symbolism is found in literatures of all ages. In Ireland the symbolism of the lord being married to the lordship, and alternatively of the poet being the spouse of the lord, apparently used to symbolise the closeness and interdependence of the relationship, were very common motifs indeed. The personification of Ireland as a woman was equally commonplace, but such hackneyed abstractions had little contemporary relevance to the workings of society or women's role therein by the early modern period.[30]

A more useful, if only because less stylised, guide may be the image of women in the prose literature. The most obvious text is *Párliament na mBan*, a tract written in 1697 on an imaginary parliament of women.[31] It is borrowed from the vast literary tradition of tracts on women in early modern Europe. These conventional literary defences and attacks on women in the early modern period are set pieces not directly linked to the daily lives of the authors who composed them.[32] The translator and compiler of *Párliament na mBan*, Donal Ó Colmáin, did not use his Parliament of Women to portray his views on women in the Ireland of his day and indeed it scarcely counts as a tract on women at all. Despite its format, for the most part it is not concerned with women in particular, but rather with society in general, and especially with religious and moral values. It was partly comprised of a translation (with certain liberties) of one of the colloquies of Erasmus, entitled a 'Parliament of Ladies', composed almost 200 years earlier. There had been English and French translations of Erasmus's work in circulation in the seventeenth century but Ó Colmáin's Irish text appears to have been taken directly from the Latin.[33] The compiler was a continentally educated clergyman, and although names and places were changed to make it appear to have been located in Cork, the depiction of the role of and attitudes to women is at best second hand. Originality was not a usual quality in any seventeenth century literary composition; translations and adaptations of European texts, both religious and secular, were the norm rather than the exception in Ireland. Yet the divergence between text and translation reveals the translator's prejudices and suggests something of contemporary Irish attitudes. The inversion of the social order implied in a parliament of women' is underplayed by Ó Colmáin. Much of Erasmus's cynical banter is also lost in the translation and O Colmáin's main concern is with protocol and status in the social hierarchy. Irish audiences must have found it enlightening or entertaining, to judge by the frequency with which it was transcribed through the eighteenth century.[34]

The Irish text, in the earliest extant copy of 1733, consists of 33 speeches by women at a parliament. The first nine speeches are more or less direct translations from the text by Erasmus. Sections which were alien to the translator, such as the debate about voting procedures to be adopted in the parliament, were omitted. In the section on the hierarchical order of women, most of Erasmus's framework was retained in the Irish text: women's status was to be determined by their marital status and the number of their children. The Irish translator omitted all references to mistresses and to wives of priests and monks. Another minor variation between the two texts is the fine to be imposed for those who breached confidentiality and spoke about the parliament outside. Erasmus's women decided on a penalty of 3 days' silence. The parliament of Irish women decided on 3 months' silence and a fine of £5. Did Ó Colmáin assume that Irish women needed a greater enticement to confidentiality? (And perhaps the five pound fine of the penal days was not so serious a matter that it could not be joked about.)

Erasmus's text ends with the close of the first day's proceedings, with the phrase: 'And let this meeting be an example of what may be expected hereafter.' Thus the framework of a parliament is established in which the author can present whatever themes are dear to his heart in further sessions of the parliament. If the choice of items included in the subsequent sections was made by Ó Colmáin himself, then these also represent the concerns of a Counter-Reformation clergyman in Munster at the end of the seventeenth century. The contents are very predictable indeed. The themes are didactic and moral, and though the words are presented as though spoken by women, they are actually sermons of universal application and women are not necessarily the intended audience. There are sections on prayer; the seven deadly sins; the four cardinal virtues; on humility, gossip, thieving, idleness; on the Virgin Mary. Presumably this was simply ready-made sermon material for the clergy. There was a rendering of an old story which considered which was more powerful, wine, woman, a king, or truth – the answer, truth of course. There was a section on the evils of dancing – especially dancing women. This argument about the evils of dancing was continental also, found in such tracts as St Francis de Sales' *Introduction to the Devout Life*.[35]

There was little particularly Irish either about the section on the education of women. The argument presented was that men in Ireland had neglected learning. The families of the nobility preferred any sort of amusement rather than devote attention to books. The nation was poor and continuously at war because the nobility would not educate their families although it was greatly to the strength of any kingdom for its nobility to be learned also. The women decided to take responsibility for their daughters and send all their daughters to school until the age of 12. Then the best would advance to the seven liberal arts and later to theology, law and medicine. By this means women would in time come to have public authority, for when men saw women triumphing over them in learning and knowledge, they would be gripped by envy and shame. Men would have power for another 10 years until their daughters were educated. Then they would see on which side the women's coat of arms should be placed, the right or the left, and they would see who best should wear trousers, men or women.[36] In the context of a tract which presented an inversion of the social order this suggested that women were naturally inferior, and not just because of their inadequate education. This echoes the sentiments already illustrated in the poetry in the juxtaposition of a mere woman, Molly Lindon, with an eminent scholar, Peadar Ó Doirnín, in the poetic contention already mentioned.

IV

Women were patrons of the bardic poetry which supported and was supported by the elite of Gaelic society from the late Middle Ages and through to the mid-seventeenth century, such patronage was a standard function of the wife of a Gaelic lord. Where these women were described or praised this was done in terms of their appeal to men, their suitability as wives or their generosity to male poets. From the late seventeenth century the Gaelic literary evidence we have is quite different, no longer the literature of an elite society. The odds against folk poetry being recorded in manuscripts at all must have been considerable and yet in areas of lively scribal activity such as south-east Ulster occasional works by women have survived. The literature produced by these women was not marginalised. Rather it was preserved as part of the mainstream folk literature of the eighteenth century. It reflected a society in which women were less well educated than men and where women poets were considered the exception rather than the norm, abnormal almost, and some may have used male pseudonyms on occasion.

This almost incidental involvement of women as creators and

sponsors of Gaelic literature while they are never considered to be themselves part of the academic or intellectual elite, is reflected in the ways women were portrayed when they were the subjects of literary compositions. Where women were the subjects of poetry in Irish it was not the image of the woman, real or imagined, but rather the actuality of the male poet, or the male relative of the woman which was central. Ultimately too, it may not have been the woman accorded an obituary in the annals who was important but rather the husband or father whose reputation she had enhanced. Women were not invisible in the world of Gaelic literature but they were sometimes transparent figures whom the audience, presumably male, were supposed to look through. They may have been little more than literary devices, used to illuminate the moral world looked for by the clergyman compiler of *Párliament na mBan*, or the patriarchal power structure of the Gaelic lordship perpetuated through the annals and bardic poetry in earlier days.

REFERENCES

1. W.J. Watson, *Bardachd Ghaidhlig: Gaelic Poetry 1550–1900*, 3rd edn (Inverness, 1959), p. xxvii.
2. B. McCarthy (ed.), *Annals of Ulster*, Vol. 3, 1379–1541 (hereafter cited as *AU*; A.M. Freeman (ed.), Annala Connacht: the Annals of Connacht A.D. 1224–1544 (hereafter cited as *AC*); W.M. Hennessy (ed.), *The Annals of Loch Cé: a chronicle of Irish affairs from A.D. 1014–1590*, Vol. 2 (hereafter cited as *ALC*).
3. *AC*, p. 621; *AU*, p. 501; *ALC*, p. 215.
4. *AC*, p. 667; *AU*, p. 571; *ALC*, p. 265.
5. *AU*, p. 585.
6. *AC*, p. 687.
7. *AU*, p. 635.
8. *ALC*, p. 477.
9. D. Greene (ed.), *Duanaire Mheig Uidhir* (Dublin, 1972), pp. 28–31; for another example, *ibid.*, pp. 86–9; the Irish text of poems quoted in English is available in the cited edition.
10. A.M. Lucas, *Women in the Middle Ages: Religion, Marriage and Letters* (Brighton, 1983), pp. 170–9.
11. L. McKenna (ed.), *The Book of O'Hara: Leabhar I Eadhra* (Dublin, 1951), poem 21, verse 22.
12. *Ibid.* poem 16, verses 33, 39–42.
13. E. Knott (ed.), *The Bardic Poems of Tadhg Dall Ó hUiginn* (2 vols, London, Irish Texts Society, 1926), poem 32, verses 82–3.
14. *Ibid.*, poem 27, verses 41–3.
15. *Book of O'Hara*, poem 15, verses 18–19.
16. *Ibid.*, poem 18, verses 36–8.
17. B. Cunningham and R. Gillespie, 'The East Ulster Bardic Family of Ó Gnimh' in *Éigse*, Vol. xx (1984), pp. 106–14.
18. J.C. MacErlean (ed.) *Duanaire Dháibhidh Uí Bhruadair* (3 vols, London, Irish Texts society, 1913), Vol. I, p. 207.
19. On the changing direction of patronage see B. Cunningham and

R. Gillespie, 'The Purpose of Patronage: Brian Maguire of Knock-ninny and his Manuscripts' in *Clogher Record*, Vol. XII, no. 4 (1988), pp. 38–49.

20. Seosamh Mag Uidhir, *Pádraig Mac a Liondáin, Dánta* (Éigse Oirialla, 1977), p. 4.

21. Royal Irish Academy (hereafter cited as R.I.A.) MS 24 L 25, ff. 25–30; MS 24 L 31, ff. 202–12.

22. Maire Ni Dhonnabháin, 'Mo fhaoisidín glan go pras don chléir chirt' (R.I.A., MS 12 E 24, ff. 153–55).

23. Mary (Molly) Lindon, Peadar Ó Doirnín, 'Ba chiuín an tráth, bhí tulca i mbláth' (R.I.A., MS 24, L 25, f. 26).

24. Molly Lindon, 'Mo láimh dhuit a chailín, dá triallfá liom chun bealaigh' (R.I.A., MS 23 B 19, f. 89).

25. Bean Uí Shuilleabháin, 'Osna go cruaidh le guas an scéal so a rith' (R.I.A., MS 23 D 42, f. 51); Nuala Ní Néill, 'Is aoibhinn tír Aodh na nEach' (R.I.A., MS 3 B 38, ff. 102–5); Máire Nic Reachtagáin, 'Is mise chaill an plannta dílis' (R.I.A., Ms 23 I 23, f. 66). On this phenomenon see Gerard Murphy, 'Notes on aisling poetry' in *Éigse*, Vol. I, (1939), esp. p. 48. There are also poems by male poets lamenting female relatives, for example, 'Och gan mé chion na lin dearadh' on the death of Máire Nic Reachtagain (R.I.A., MS 23 I 23, f. 71v), but this was on a female poet, the wife of a well-known poet Tadhg Ó Neachtain, and may have been untypical.

26. D. Thomson, *An Introduction to Gaelic Poetry* (London, 1974), p. 132–7.

27. Watson, *Bardachd Ghaidhlig*, p. 35; Thomson, *Gaelic Poetry*, p. 137.

28. G. Neville, 'Medieval Irish Courtly Love Poetry: An Exercise in Power Struggle' in *Études Irlandais* (Dec. 1982), pp. 19–30; Thomas F. O'Rahilly, *Dánta Grádha: an Anthology of Irish Love Poetry (A.D. 1350–1750)* (Cork, 1926).

29. For example, 'A bhean fuair feall ar an bheart', edited in E. Knott, 'Mac an Bhaird's Elegy on the Ulster Lords' in *Celtica*, Vol. V (1960), pp. 161–71.

30. On Ireland as a woman see for example, *Book of O'Hara*, poem 25; *Duanaire Mhic Uidhir*, poem 2; On the male poet as a woman see *Duanaire Mhic Uidhir*, poem 13.

31. B. Ó Cuív (ed.), *Párliament na mBan* (Dublin, 1977).

32. A.W. Ward and A.R. Waller, *Cambridge History of English Literature, III* (Cambridge, 1908), pp. 485–7; Linda Woodbridge, *Women in the English Renaissance*, (Brighton, 1981), passim.

33. J. Stewart, 'Parliament na mBan' in *Celtica*, Vol. VII (1966), pp. 135–41; Desiderius Erasmus, *The Whole Familiar Colloquies of Desiderius Erasmus of Rotterdam*, (London, 1877), pp. 340–4.

34. Ó Cúiv, *Párliament*, Intro.

35. Saint Francis de Sales, *Introduction to the Devout Life* (New York, 1955), Part 3, cap. 33–4, pp. 204–6; Ó Cúiv, *Párliament*, lines 1647–1723.

36. Ó Cúiv, *Párliament*, lines 621–679.

10

Women, Education and Learning in Early Modern Ireland

MARGARET MACCURTAIN

The educational experience of men and women in sixteenth-century Europe was dominated by the effects of the Reformation. Educational attitudes and pedagogic theory which predated the Reformation certainly influenced the reformers but the revolt against priestly office, religious life and traditional forms of liturgical worship at the time of the Reformation outstripped the aspirations of the Christian humanists, such as Desiderius Erasmus and Thomas More in making the new learning the basis for lay piety. Thomas More was convinced that humanistic studies, as the new learning signified, must be accessible to women as well as to men. In a letter to William Gunnel, tutor to his daughters, More wrote[1]

> Nor do I think that it affects the harvest, that a man or a woman has sown the seed. If they are worthy of being ranked with the human race, if they are distinguished by reason from beasts; that learning, by which the reason is cultivated, is equally suitable to both. Both of them, if the seed of good principles be sown in them, equally produce the germs of virtue.

All Thomas More's children, three daughters and a son, learnt Latin, Greek, logic, theology, philosophy, mathematics and astronomy from an early age. Margaret, his eldest daughter, became a recognised scholar. Apart from her fine classical training, she responded to her father's meditation on death, *The Four Last Things*, by writing her own. Her translation of Erasmus's treatise on the Lord's Prayer, printed about 1526, was of high quality and gained wide circulation.

Christian humanism as it developed in England, France and the Low Countries contained a commitment to religious reform as an inherent part of its content. 'I would', wrote Erasmus, 'that even the lowliest women read the gospels and the Pauline Epistles . . .'. Erasmus connected the life of scholarship with the daily life of a Christian and he regarded his works on spirituality as guidelines for practical piety. This humanistic outlook was held by many reformers and contributed to giving women new educational possibilities as the Reformation progressed.[2]

At the highest level of society the new learning with its orientation towards reform distinguished the conversations and writings of the female monarchs and women of the aristocracy in sixteenth-century Europe. Marguerite of Navarre, sister of King Francis I of France, was a celebrated humanist and wrote devotional treatises, the characteristic of a Christian humanist. Her daughter Jeanne d'Albret, whose education she supervised actively, led the Huguenot movement in France as Queen of Bearn and Navarre. Catherine de Médici and her confidante Jacqueline de Longwy shared humanistic scholarship. Jacqueline's daughter, Charlotte de Bourbon, left her convent in 1571 to take up the Huguenot cause, became a skilled polemicist and married William of Orange. Vittorina Colonna was steeped in Erasmian humanism and in her writings sought to establish a path into mysticism through the study and knowledge of the sacred writings. Catherine of Aragon, Henry VIII's first queen, possessed great erudition. Queen Anne Boleyn, her successor, grasped the essence of the English Reformation intelligently and supported Cromwell in his efforts to push the Reform legislation through parliament. Henry's last wife Queen Catherine Parr was educated in the spirit of Christian humanism and wrote a treatise, *The Lamentation of a Sinner*. Lady Jane Grey was no mean rival in learning to the brilliant Elizabeth Tudor, one of the most intellectual monarchs of the period.

In Ireland women had traditionally esteemed learning; and the endowment of monasteries as places of learning by the wives of princes and Gaelic rulers was a test of nobility, worthy of mention in the annals. In the later Middle Ages and throughout the sixteenth century, women of the upper classes supervised the dwelling-quarters of the elaborate tower-houses, allowing space for a library as in Maynooth Castle and in the Geraldine castles, such as Askeaton and Rathkeale, County Limerick. In the library of the Earl of Kildare were listed 34 Latin books, 36 French, 22 English and over 20 books in Irish.[3]

In the second half of the sixteenth century, as recusancy asserted itself among the laity, secret rooms were built to hide priests. Thus in the spring of 1571, at Turvey House (the country residence of Sir Christopher Barnewall and his wife Marion Bagenal), the distinguished visitor Edmund Campion, according to his own testimony, was furnished with a fine library and an out-of-the-way room. Stowed away there it is reasonable to assume, as Dr Ó Mathúna suggests, that Campion advised on the education of the younger members of the Stanihurst, Barnewall and Bathe families, who were neighbours and close friends. Janet Barnewall, then 11 years old, later married Campion's pupil, Richard Stanihurst, in 1575, and when she died in childbirth in 1579 at the age of 19, Richard wrote a poignant Latin elegy to her memory.[4] Technically the four shires of the Pale were an extension of the English realms. The presence of English wives brought the new learning to the women of the Pale nobility. The family network of the Kildare Geraldines interacted with the St Johns, the Grays and the Zouches in the English court. Elizabeth Zouche, the maternal great grandmother of William Bathe, the pioneer of linguistic studies in Europe, was saluted by his first cousin Christopher Nugent in his address to Queen Elizabeth:[5]

> In profe whereof men yett lyvinge which knew Elizabeth Zouche, daughter to the Lord Zouche, sometime Countess of Kyldare, do affirme that in shorte tyme she learned to reade, write, and perfectly speak the tongue.

The tongue referred to was Irish. She also encouraged her son Silken Thomas to become a skilled harpist and she was a patron of the arts.

The creation of an indigenous reform movement in the Pale received much of its impetus from humanism. Thereafter the same bedrock accommodated the forces of the Counter-Reformation. Margaret Ball supplies the clues as to what women with a humanist education were experiencing in the middle decades of the sixteenth century. Margaret Bermingham (1515–84?) was the widow of Alderman Bartholomew Ball and the mother of two subsequent lord mayors of Dublin. She operated, with her domestic chaplain, a school for 'good scholars and devoted followers' from her home. She catechised her servants and those of other Pale families in an educational network. When her son Walter went over to Protestantism she gathered 'many Catholic bishops, priests and other learned men' to her house to dissuade him. He became instead a committed reformer and as Lord Mayor of Dublin (1580–1) he demonstrated his hostility to recusancy by arresting and imprisoning his mother and her chaplain. She died in prison subsequently. She was described by the contemporary Jesuit Fr John Howlin as a woman 'who trained servants and could read and write'.[6]

When Henry VIII came to the throne of England in 1509, he was an orthodox Catholic who regarded himself as defender of the Faith and supporter of the Pope as head of the Church. Before he died in 1547, he declared himself head of the Church in England and in Ireland; he had abolished monasticism, rejected the supremacy of the Pope, and made significant liturgical changes. Moreover he had constitutionally, by an act of the Irish parliament in 1541, been declared King of Ireland. Thereafter the progress of the Reformation in Ireland was inextricably bound up with the Tudor resolution to subdue the country and bring it under royal writ.

It has been noted by historians that Renaissance, Reformation and Counter-Reformation ran together in Elizabethan Ireland.[7] Education was a critical factor in channelling the direction religious reform took in Ireland. In England the educational revolution was supported by the government and was stimulated by the demand for professional lay administrators. An educated and literate laity emerged from the English Reformation.[8] In Ireland the tardiness of the Tudor government to organise, fund, and control schools allowed the initiative to pass to the Jesuits and other Counter-Reformation activists in the second half of the sixteenth century. Ireland possessed no university. Queen Elizabeth I's foundation of Trinity College Dublin in 1591 came after the pattern of Counter-Reformation schooling and study on the continent had evolved along well-established lines of transportation and acceptance into continental universities such as Louvain, Paris, Salamanca and Coimbra. In Ireland, as in England, the landed classes subscribed to the arguments of the humanists and packed their sons to schools and universities convinced that a gentleman's education required book-learning and enrolment in a European university or at Inns of Court.[9]

In England education was of major concern to government policy. In Ireland education remained a subversive activity, spearheaded by proscribed Counter-Reformation agents: Jesuits, seminary-trained secular priests, laymen from the families of the Gaelic *literati*, and poets who ran bardic schools in remote areas. This was a century when a shift in the perception of family relationships was experienced: children began to be regarded as individuals and the schooling of daughters was included in the new perspective.[10] From Richard Stanihurst's memories it is implicit that the daughters as well as the sons of the Pale gentry were tutored together by a resident chaplain, or priest in hiding. The Barnewall, Bathe and Stanihurst children were schooled together. Increasingly research in convent registers in Europe is bringing to light the presence of young Irish girls as boarders, pursuing the classroom regime introduced by the Ursuline educational reforms which Angela Merici intitiated in 1562. Francis Lavalin Nugent, founder and leader of the Irish Capuchin mission and brother of the Earl of Westmeath, escorted two of his nieces, Mary and Brigid Westmeath, to France to finish their education.

Later he undertook to bring out the younger girls and in true avuncular fashion entertained them in Charleville, the headquarters of the Capuchin mission, before committing them to the care of the Sepulchrine nuns at Charleville.[11]

The dislocation caused by the dissolution of the monasteries affected women more acutely than men. Debarred from university education, schooling in the late Middle Ages for women of the nobility or *haute-bourgeoisie* took place in schools attached to nunneries. Entry into convent life offered to dowered women alternatives to marriage and child-bearing. It provided some professional training in the art of illumination, embroidery and vestment making.[12] With the closing of the convents that accompanied the Reformation many cloistered women were left homeless and though technically in receipt of pensions, an old age of destitution was the lot of those dispossessed inmates of confiscated monasteries. Mary Cusack was one such. The sister of Sir Thomas Cusack, Master of the Rolls and later Chancellor of the Irish Exchequer, she was Abbess of the Augustinian nunnery of Lismullin, County Meath when it was surrendered and dissolved in July 1539. Sir Thomas Cusack, as receiver for the Crown, transacted the negotiations and acquired both the building and its lands. Abbess Mary Cusack was assigned a yearly pension of £16, handsome enough in those times, but decades later she complained bitterly that her brother withheld her pension from her on the subterfuge of 'borrowing' from her.[13] Alison White, Abbess of Grace Dieu, the Benedictine monastery in Fingal which conducted a renowned school for girls, received £6 a year when Grace Dieu was dissolved and purchased by Patrick Barnewall. Undismayed she moved her convent to the rectory in Portrane but had to close the school.[14]

Sixteenth-century noblewomen in Ireland were well educated. Joan Butler, the mature wife of Gerald, Earl of Desmond and mother of his first cousin, Thomas, Earl of Ormond, corresponded frankly with Queen Elizabeth I on the intractable nature of the dispute between her son and her husband. Letters from Gerald's second wife Eleanor Butler to both Queen Elizabeth and to Pope Gregory XIII survive and demonstrate her well-turned phrase and keen grasp of the war situation.[15] Janet Taaffe, née Eustace, bargained successfully with the Queen for the restoration of her late husband's lands, forfeited during the Baltinglass Rising and received back her own lands. Gráinne O'Malley proved her ability to converse with the Queen in Latin when summoned to answer charges of piracy. Her nautical skills as a sea captain and leader of a fleet down the west coast of Ireland raise tantalising queries about her education.[16]

But these were a vanishing group as they desperately rounded on the legal nets that closed around their property. By the end of the sixteenth century, the aristocratic widow-with-daughter in circumstances of poverty was a persistent client in the petitions addressed to the Spanish monarchs. Lady Ellen O'Sullivan, widow of Donal Cam O'Sullivan petitioned and received 100 ducats each month in Madrid from King Philip III. Out of that not inconsiderable pension she was able to maintain a household of dependent women, including two Irish nuns, and two servants, both illiterate.[17] Almost a century later, Anastasia Dillon, widow of Colonel Alexander Barnewall, an officer in Galmoy's Regiment, petitioned King Louis XIV for a pension of 1000 livres, to support herself and the schooling of her two daughters in a French convent. Her petition was granted through the mediation of Madame de Maintenon.[18] The women of the wild geese, from the time of the flight of the earls, 1607, had learned the arts of survival from personalities like Rosa O'Doherty, wife of Eoghan O'Neill,[19] and Catherine Magennis (the fourth wife of Hugh O'Neill, Earl of Tyrone) who displayed the self-confidence and resourcefulness of the educated ruling class as Jerrold Casway indicates above.

By the beginning of the seventeenth century, Reformation concerns dominated the lives of people in their personal aspects of home and family. By then theology in all the major churches was reflected in the use of catechesis for ensuring religious conformity and understanding of Christianity as differentiated within the doctrines of a particular religious denomination or sect. The council of Trent had issued its *Catechism of the Council of Trent*, a basic text of instruction for priests and those engaged in instruction of the faithful. It centred on loyalty to the Roman Church, an appreciation of the mass, and on devotion to Mary, mother of God. International Calvinism established its hold by its doctrinal appeal and its firm logical structure based on the pedagogic methods of the Huguenot, Pierre de la Ramée. The Church of Rome and Calvinism had far more in common in their programmes of evangelisation than the Armenian-influenced Anglicanism of the early Stuart period could handle. The battle for the souls of women was appreciated by the competing sets of protagonists; thus Lady Falkland's conversion to Roman Catholicism was regarded with dismay in court circles in London and in the government set in Dublin, where her husband was lord deputy. James Ussher's mother, Margaret Stanihurst, returned to recusancy but did not live to see her son become Archbishop of Armagh in the established church. Lady Eleanor Douglas, wife of Sir John Davies and daughter of the Munster

settler, the first Earl of Castlehaven, after receiving a learned
education in her youth, became a Puritan non-conformist and in
1625 declared she was 'seized with the spirit of prophecy'.[20]

The seventeenth century paid more attention to literacy than
previous ones. The vernacular languages had stabilised their
grammars, and printing presses of the period ensured a constant
stream of catechetical and devotional writings. The emphasis by
the reformers on the reading of the Bible and on meditation upon
the texts of sacred scripture channelled the drive for literacy.
Calvinism appealed to upper-class women who had leisure and
the education to read the Bible. Calvinism also appealed to the
artisan class and the spread of Scottish Presbyterianism among
the settlers of Ulster in the 1620s is testified by the high number
of non-conformist Presbyterians in east Ulster where tithes to the
established church were a contentious issue.[21] Women and men
were encouraged to acquire literacy to read the contents of the
Bible now appearing in the vernacular. Laurence Stone has
observed that for the first time in early modern Europe basic
literacy made its appearance in English society.[22] In Ireland the
kinds of sources Professor Stone used are not available, but the
flood of books imported into the country in the seventeenth
century has been noted.[23] If letter writing in English, the keeping
of diaries, the financial organisation of household and convent
accounts were an indication of literacy, then seventeenth-century
Ireland abounds in such evidence. The correspondence between
the Earl of Clanrickard and his two sisters, theirs with the wife
of Archbishop James Ussher, the diary of Mary Rich, the writings
of Lady Anne Conway and Lady Eleanor Douglas, the memoirs
of Abbess Cecily Dillon of Bethlehem Convent near Athlone
town, the spirited address of Elizabeth Preston, Lady Ormond,
to Oliver Cromwell on behalf of the Butler estates, all indicate a
level of literacy in the English vernacular at the highest level of
Irish society.[24] The point is not that they wrote but that increasingly in the seventeenth century their writing was becoming
semi-public and worthy of being stored.

One of the striking characteristics of Puritanism was its belief
in the value of education as a weapon against the three great evils
of 'Ignorance, Prophaneness and Idleness'. Godly learning was
the climate of the Puritan home. For the families of English and
Scottish settlers of Puritan persuasion in Ireland the situation was
more volatile as events moved towards the 1640s and the outbreak of war. The early settlers favoured Trinity College Dublin
and in its founding decades the Puritan atmosphere of its
theology was pervasive. For both native and newcomer in Ireland
the laying down of an identity in opposition to each other was

part of the formation of a religious outlook. The theological positions of the religious groupings in the country, Roman Catholic, Presbyterian and Anglican, mirrored their perceptions of 'being different' from each other. It was basic to their sense of identity. Professor Corish notes that Tridentine directives in seminary training for priests emphasised the importance of learning theological treatises rather than the Bible. The development of the 'Controversies' model used by the Jesuits and that of the adversarial theology practised in Trinity College in its first decades contributed to the formation of an identity based on taking up a particular theological position in seventeenth-century Ireland.[25]

This cultivation of an identity in opposition filtered down to the masses by way of catechesis, preaching and reading of devotional as well as biblical texts. The atmosphere of the catechism invaded the classroom and provided a rationale for basic literacy. Women, in the retrenchment that followed the earlier intellectual release of the first phase of the Reformation, were excluded from the highest levels of theological decision making in all the major churches. But they were the target of the catechesis in the home which now became the sphere where the knowledge of God was purified and controlled. Between the ending of the council of Trent, 1563, and the age of enlightenment in the middle of the eighteenth century, the intensification of patriarchialism is noticeable in monarchies, in church government and within the family structures. The increased authority of husbands and fathers was the reality of the seventeenth century domestic life, visible in Puritan households like that of Richard Boyle, Earl of Cork, but apparent also in Old English families who adopted a vigorous Counter-Reformation Catholicism.

In 1610 an edict forbidding the travelling abroad of the children of gentlemen for educational purposes was issued by the Dublin government. The growth of recusancy was widespread in the first decades of the new century. Sir John Davies noted that in the towns, women had withdrawn from attendance at the divine service which was an offence liable to a fine. A determined government policy closed the private Catholic schools of Waterford and Galway in 1615. Yet the suspicion was widespread in government circles that priests were being hidden as chaplains and tutors in the houses of the gentry, and that they were catechising womenfolk and children. The position is summed up in a letter of the bishop of Cork, Cloyne and Ross to Chichester, the Lord Deputy. 'An English minister must needs be beholden to the Irishry; his neighbours love him not, especially his profes-

sion and doctrine, they being compelled to hear him.' Not only
that, the bishop went on wryly, but the conforming lords and
gentlemen of Munster, such as Lord Barry of Buttevant, protected
the priests and friars.

> These priests Sir John countenances openly at his own table
> . . . commending them to the world and applauding their
> profession and manner of life. They be sturdy fellows, well
> fed and warm . . . Besides these friars, every gentleman and
> lord of the country has his priests. Massing is everywhere
> . . .[26]

Nuns, too, made their appearance as a substantial presence
among the forces of recusancy in seventeenth century Ireland.
The dispute over an active apostolate for nuns in the decades
following the council of Trent demonstrates the grip that patriarchal attitudes had on Roman Catholicism as it launched its
revitalised agenda for seminary training and marriage reform. It
was an agenda that ignored women's intellectual formation. The
family and the domestic sphere was where she belonged and
'domestic' religion was the norm of female religious practice.
Innovation in interpreting women's religious vocations had been
attempted by Angela Merici and by Mary Ward, the English
woman, in the sphere of women's education; by Louise de
Marillac and Vincent de Paul in the field of active social charity
outside the convent walls. Angela Merici's Ursuline women and
Mary Ward's group of women helpers hoped to found religious
orders for the education of girls and to teach the poor. The new
nuns wore no religious garb save that of the contemporary
woman in modest circumstances. They did not observe cloister
or bind themselves to the choir recitation of the Divine Office.
From the ending of Trent to the French Revolution most of the
papal decrees and curial directives affecting the religious life of
women pertained to maintaining cloister. In the aftermath of the
great council of Trent church ministry of a semi-official nature for
women such as teaching or nursing was not regarded favourably
by Rome. Pope Urban VIII issued a Bull of Suppression, *Pastoralis
Romani Pontificis*, on 13 January 1630, against Mary Ward's
Institute, she herself being imprisoned in a convent in Munich
the following month. Mary Ward's conviction that the un-
enclosed apostolic religious life should be available to religious
women as it was to men received a severe setback from which
religious life for women did not recover for over a century.[27]

The Counter-Reformation in Ireland was conservative in
character and drew its vitality in part from the massive protest
that recusancy as a movement evoked throughout Ireland.
Though Jesuits spearheaded the evangelisation of the gentry and

became the schoolmasters of their families as part of the process,
it was not part of their mission in Ireland to recruit young women
to follow their apostolic life of teaching and preaching. The
revitalised Franciscans and Dominicans had a similar outlook.
Given the Tridentine prohibitions around uncloistered women
and the Roman decrees which demanded that monasteries of
women always be built or purchased within fortified towns, the
Jesuit resistance to Mary Ward's overtures to develop the Ignatian
Constitutions for women religious is understandable.

Of the several convents which made their appearance in
Ireland throughout the seventeenth century, three (and a
possible fourth) were Franciscan of the Rule of St Clare: one in
Merchant's Quay in Dublin, 1629, a short-lived foundation which
transferred to Waterford from Drogheda in 1642, and the remarkable Bethlehem convent built by the Dillon family on the shores
of Lough Ree five miles from Athlone. It housed over 60 nuns
during its brief life (1632–45). A Franciscan foundation in Galway
was essayed in 1641 but was destroyed during the Cromwellian
occupation of the city. The Franciscan nuns returned in 1672 to
resume a life of enclosed prayer and asceticism. There are records
of one Dominican convent in Galway during the 1640s which
suffered the same fate as the Franciscan nuns during the Cromwellian interlude (1644–52). The Dominican nuns returned to
Galway in 1686, and to a life of enclosure.

Little is known of the brief history of the Benedictine nuns in
Ireland during this century save that a group took ship with
James II's ships shortly after the battle of the Boyne.[28] There are
no instances of teaching within the cloister during this century.
It would appear that seventeenth-century Irish nuns were
oratores, in the medieval sense of being a category or order, and
their presence was a contemplative one, to witness to a people
harried by frequent wars and disruption, an eschatological sign
of a life beyond the grave. Nuns were also part of a family
network in the recusancy movement. Among the names listed in
convent registers were Cheevers, Dillon, Nugent, Dowdall,
Eustace (Franciscan), Blake, French, Kirwan, O'Halloran, Nolan
and Lynch (Dominican).[29]

How educated were the inmates of these Irish convents? We
are fortunate in having records of a convent for Irish Dominican
nuns founded in Lisbon in 1639 by the Dominican friar, Dominic
O'Daly. Continuity with the past rather than bold lines of
innovation mark the constitutions he drew up for those exiled
Irish nuns, fully cloistered in their spacious well-built convent of
Bon Sucesso in Belem, near the mouth of the Tagus. The ability
to read and write, the reading of Latin, and the mastery of plain

chant for liturgical celebration (often attended by members of the royal family of Portugal) were required of the nuns. Three vernaculars, English, Irish and Portuguese, were used, and the impression of a lively, well-educated community emerges from the early annals.[30]

It was the settler element in Irish society as owners and administrators of newly acquired estates who displayed pragmatism and independence in their approach to schooling and matters of learning. For them the planning of schools as part of the new infrastructure of towns was incorporated into their building schemes. Under the Ulster plantation schemes lands were assigned for a free school in every county. Control was exercised by the bishops of the established church and the right to nominate teachers rested with them, the archbishop of Armagh acting as trustee for school lands. With constant warfare, the profile of such schools only begins to emerge towards the last quarter of the century. Officially such schools were monitored by the state; in reality private citizens like Erasmus Smith or individual planters like William Herbert, or a corporate group such as the bishops of the Church of Ireland built and maintained them.[31] In Ulster a number of the schoolmasters were religious dissidents of Scottish and most likely Presbyterian background. Little is known of these plantation schools as yet. For the settler the education of their sons and the marriage alliances of their children were of primary concern for the perpetuation of their property and the upgrading of their social status. In general they yearned for the civility of the gentrified English society at which they gazed eastward constantly. Nothing was more gratifying than an arranged match between a son or daughter with an English aristocratic connection.

Richard Boyle, 1st Earl of Cork, typifies the successful family cycle of the seventeenth century Irish settler. The younger son of a younger son, with enough legal knowledge to make him a sharp practitioner in land speculation, he made his way to Ireland in the late 1580s and picked up Irish land in the mercurial swings of land sales that followed the first Munster plantation. Boyle accumulated his phenomenal wealth in the second wave of settlement that developed after the Treaty of Mellifont, 1603. He became one of the largest landowners and was estimated the wealthiest man in the king's realms. He acquired a knighthood, then a peerage as 1st Earl of Cork. He became a member of the Irish Privy Council and in the interim between the appointment of Deputy Wentworth and the departure of Falkland, he and Loftus held the reins of government as lords chief justice.[32]

A family man of strict Puritan conviction, he had eight daughers and seven sons. He left behind him a detailed *Diary* and his memoirs, *True Remembrances*. His daughter, Mary Rich, Countess of Warwick and his son, Robert both wrote diaries or autobiographies as they named them. Another daughter, Catherine, became an accepted member of the Great Tew circle, which gathered in the Oxfordshire house of Lucius Carey, son of the Irish Lord Deputy Falkland and the formidably intellectual Elizabeth Tarfield.[33] Catherine gained the reputation of being a leading intellectual, praised by John Milton and by Bishop Burnet, esteemed by her brother Robert whose genius she tended for over 40 years as her companion in her widowhood. She retained her own identity as Lady Ranelagh, holding her own gatherings in her Pall Mall residence. The other daughters are recorded for the distinction of their marriages; certainly their letters to their father display a sense of form and at times a witty and wry sense of humour in describing their husbands to him.

From the voluminous correspondence of Richard Boyle and from his *Diary* we learn how the girls in a wealthy noveau riche planter's family in Munster were educated.[34] At the age of two and a half Mary Boyle was removed from her home in Lismore Castle to that of Lady Cleyton near Mallow, County Cork, some 20 miles distant. Lady Cleyton acted as foster-mother for some of the Boyle daughters, beginning with Alice, the eldest. Boyle's second wife was the young Catherine Fenton whose father played a prominent role in the Munster war and had acquired lands in Kerry and Cork in the ensuing plantation schemes. Catherine Fenton appears to have been completely dominated by her husband who even decreed her manner of dressing. She had a succession of pregnancies. It was customary for newborn children of upper-class English families to be put out to a wetnurse and returned home after two years. Lady Cleyton of Mallow was childless and Mary Boyle records that 'she took care to have me soberly educated'. Richard Boyle, a man of high intelligence, encouraged intellectual curiosity in his children. Reading was first taught, followed by writing. Boyle presented each of his daughters with a copy of Sir Philip Sidney's *Arcadia*. There is even a hint in his *Diary* that Mary Boyle may have annotated her copy of *Arcadia*. The Sidney connection and, through it, the humanist tradition of the previous century were strong in Munster circles. Mary, Sidney's sister, had married William Herbert, 2nd Earl of Pembroke whose cousin had received a seignory in Castleisland in County Kerry. He remained close to the Pembrokes. Sir Francis Walsingham's daughter married Philip Sidney (Earl of Leicester); both Walsingham and his cousin Sir Edward Denny played a crucial role in settling the forfeited lands of the late Earl of Desmond in north Kerry. Yet another connection was the marriage between Edmund Spenser and Elizabeth Boyle, a cousin of Richard Boyle. Boyle's son Lewis married the scholarly Elizabeth Fielding, daughter of Lord Denbigh.

Richard Boyle recorded his own reflections and encouraged his children to write. His son Roger wrote plays, a six-volume romance and a treatise on the art of war. Robert became an eminent scientist, equally distinguished in chemistry and physics, the originator of Boyle's Law. All the children wrote moral essays; Francis published his. The education of the Boyle children followed a pattern: wet nursing and fosterage, private tutoring at home under their father's eye. The older boys at the ages of eleven and nine went to Trinity College. Their formal education ended with a continental tour. Francis and Robert, the younger boys, went to Eton. Lewis became a sailor and navigator. Richard Boyle was incessant in his surveillance of his wife and children. Fussy and uxorious, he increasingly supervised their wearing apparel, the household accounts, and arranged both their pocket money and their marriages. The virtues he most admired he enshrined on his wife's memorial: 'religious, virtuous, loving and obedient'. Later he was to build himself an incredibly ostentatious monument to commemorate her (and himself) in the eastern end of St Patrick's Cathedral in Dublin. Archbishop James Ussher who authorised the tomb defended it to Strafford, the Lord Deputy, as a 'very great monument to the Church', presumably a hymn in stone to married life.[35]

Mary Boyle was the rebel in the family. Her *Diary* affords us glimpses of the mind of an upper-class girl educated according to the standards of the time, and on her own admission that education was one which allowed her to read romances. Her mentor was the lively Elizabeth Killigrew who married her brother, Francis, and Elizabeth gave Mary the taste for reading romances. She, too, introduced Mary Boyle to Charles Rich. Mary went against her father's arrangements in order to marry him, refusing her father's choice, James Hamilton, an Ulster settler. Boyle was slightly mollified when Charles Rich fortuitously attained the earldom, but at the beginning he dealt severely with his daughter, cutting off her allowance. It was her father-in-law, the Earl of Warwick, who converted her to Puritanism. She came to revile herself and records in her *Diary* her regret for the 'ill and horribly disobedient answer for a daughter to give her father'. From her *Diary* we receive one of the clearest expositions of the Puritan doctrine of daughterly obedience.[36]

Mary and Catherine Boyle illustrate the almost symmetrical

oscillation between autonomy and dependence that women in Puritan England and Ireland experienced. For Mary her acceptance of the prevailing doctrine of obedient daughter signalled the collapse of her rebellious stage; her desire for parental approval triumphed as she recounts honestly in her *Diary*. Catherine Boyle was the most intelligent and lovable of the Boyle girls. Until her records have been sifted through from the Milton and Ranelagh papers we can form only a general impression of a woman with the capacity of making her mark in the most intellectual elite of the times, the Great Tew circle, and of finding a manner of living which gave her a maximum amount of autonomy over her own life. Her father's intense paternalism was redeemed by the regard in which he held this brilliant daughter and his trust in her ability to advise him in his financial and household affairs.[37] John Leake, the Earl of Cork's most trusted adviser and intimate friend of the household described her thus:

> A more brave wench, nor a braver spirit, you have not met withal. She hath a memory that will hear a sermon and go home and repeat it after dinner, verbatim. I know not how she will appear in England, but she is most accounted of in Dublin.[38]

She accounted well of herself in London. Separated from her husband of whom John Leake remarked 'all that could be said of him is that he seldom went sober to bed', she became the incomparable Lady Ranelagh to Bishop Burnet who declared that she had cut 'the greatest figure in all those revolutions of these kingdoms for above fifty years of any woman of her age'. She arranged for her sons to be tutored by John Milton, who held her in high regard.

The failure of the age to provide an adequate education for the undoubted intelligence of girls like the Boyle daughters, despite the good dispositions of a benevolent father, illustrates the gradual exclusion of women from virtually all spheres of productive work, including intellectual activity. It was an exclusion that accompanied the growth of capitalism, colonialism and the birth of modern slavery in the seventeenth century. The assertion of patriarchy as the dominant governing model in state and family was part of the general movement of approval for authority and order in that period. There was a desire to restore women to their places in the family and to restore stability by returning authority to the head of the household, the father, a doctrine dear to all the major churches. Women were valued because they were perceived to maintain men's domestic privileged role. The differentiated educational development of men and women in such a society, in the age of absolutism, was ensured through the conviction that it was women, not men, who bore and raised children.[39]

This is a *pis aller*, a gloss on women's education towards the end of the century. Happily it affords us a glimpse of the ordinary woman, the woman of the 'lower orders'. *Párliament na mBan* (the parliament of women) was composed towards the end of the century, 1697 its probable date of circulation. Its author was Dr Donal Ó Colmáin, a priest or a learned layman, and his work is cast in the mould of an Erasmian dialogue.[40] The women's parliament is situated in Cork and though the author surrounds the dialogue with moralising sequences on subjects like prayer, women's dress, dancing, thieving, and the seven deadly sins, in quite unexpected ways the framework of the proceedings of this unusual parliament of 500 women is feminist in tone. Fionuala, the first speaker, deprecates the lack of participation of women in public life, 'remaining always at home, attending to our distaffs and spindles, even though many of us are no good about the house' (ll. 295–8). On the second day the education of girls is discussed, and an act passed by which all daughters are to be sent to school till the age of 12 years. Then the more intelligent shall be sent on to learn the seven liberal arts which are listed as grammar, rhetoric, philosophy, arithmetic, astrology, geometry and poetry. A second act decreed that all daughters who are able to should go on to learn divinity, law and medicine as was deemed suitable. Sive, who introduces the enactments, declares: 'I am certain that we will attain public authority as a consequence of these enactments' (ll. 636–50). Ó Colmáin's work reveals a refreshing dimension of the commonalty.

> At a feast or in a public assembly the wife of a rustic or of a churl is so bold that she sits down and moves before a lady who is noble on both her father's and her mother's side, simply because she has a little wealth. Soon there will be no longer any distinguishing marks between one class and another (ll. 592–6).

Satire or humanist tract, *Párliament na mBan* was far from the reality of women at the end of the century.

Early modern Ireland was a major transitional period which culminated in the formation of a transformed countryside and system of government presided over by a powerful socio-political group, the landed ascendancy. The education of women cannot be artificially abstracted from the web of social and economic relationships that developed in Ireland during those centuries. It was not merely a matter of divergent predicaments in which women were placed by religious difference, and by loss of property-owning rights. It was also a predicament of different political traditions, and the manner in which particular groups of women perceived their interests. Religious and political divisions, in part, explain the lack of unified resistance on the part of women to their consignment to a privatised, powerless and subordinate position in the household. Women's ability to question the female destiny in the dominant culture of patriarchy faltered as the growth of the public and private spheres trapped them in domesticity. It also stunted their intellectual growth. At a time when Christian humanism was encouraging the vision of a new society based on plurality and access to educational opportunity for women, the sixteenth century moved into the warring confrontations of dominant religious and political ideologies. So the environment of women's education changed. Anxieties about the erosion of the traditional stability of the family contributed to the authoritarian climate of the seventeenth century and when the massive profile of the dawning scientific revolution became visible after the restoration of King Charles II in 1660, women had not even achieved a toehold on the beckoning peaks of the new sciences. Yet the very consolidation of the public and the private spheres, of gender and home, created moments of doubt among those women who became increasingly controlled and powerless as is evident from women such as the Boyle daughters. For Catholic women the narrowing of their education to catechesis raises another set of questions; the marginalisation of women in Catholic culture in the seventeenth century was reflected in what happened to their education. The sharp lesson that a study of women's education in early modern Ireland teaches is that nothing that happened to women and their intellects during that period is safely past.

REFERENCES

1. Thomas More to William Gunnel, no. 63, 1518 (Elizabeth F. Rogers (ed.) *The Correspondence of Thomas More* (Princeton, 1947), quoted in full in Ruth Kelso, *Doctrine for the Lady of the Renaissance* (Urbana, 1956), p. 62).
2. S. Marshall Wynthjes, 'Women in the Reformation Era' in R. Bridenthal and C. Koonz, *Becoming Visible: Women in European History* (Boston, 1977), pp. 167–91. R. Marius, *Thomas More* (Collins, London edn. 1986), pp. 64–78.
3. For the library of the Earl of Kildare see S.H. O'Grady, *Catalogue of Irish Manuscripts in the British Museum* (London, 1926), Vol. I; A. Stopford Green, *The Making of Ireland and Its Undoing* (London, 1908), p. 251; for Geraldine Castles, M. MacCurtain, 'A Lost Landscape: Geraldine Castles and Towerhouses of the Shannon Estuary' in J. Bradley (ed.), *Settlement and Society in Ireland: Viking and Medieval Times* (Kilkenny, 1990).
4. E. Campion, *Two Bokes of the Histories of Ireland* (Assent, 1963), p. 9; S.P. Ó Mathúna, *William Bathe, S.J., 1564–1614. A Pioneer in*

Linguistics (Amsterdam, 1986), pp. 34–5. For an excellent background to this period, C. Lennon, *Richard Stanihurst, the Dubliner, 1547–1618* (Dublin, 1981).

5. C. Nugent, *Queen Elizabeth's Primer of the Irish Language*, undated, *c.* 1564 for details cf. Ō Mathúna, *op. cit.*, pp. 148, 167.

6. The fullest contemporary account of Margaret Ball is contained in Fr Howlin, S.J., Perbreve Compendium in P.F. Moran (ed.), *Spicilegium Ossoriense: being a collection of original letters and papers illustrative of the Irish church from the reformation to the year 1800* (Dublin, 1874–84), Vol. I, pp. 105–6. For an account of the Ball family, consult C. Lennon, *The Lords of Dublin in the Age of Reformation* (Dublin, 1989), pp. 136, 143, 149, 156, 228.

7. F.X. Martin, O.S.A., 'Ireland, the Renaissance and the Counter-Reformation' in *Topic 13: studies in Irish History* (Washington, 1967); C. Lennon, 'The Counter-Reformation in Ireland, 1542–1641' in C. Brady and R. Gillespie (eds), *Natives and Newcomers: Essays on the Making of Irish Colonial Society, 1534–1641* (Dublin, 1986), pp. 75–92.

8. Laurence Stone, 'The Educational Revolution in England, 1560–1640' in *Past and Present*, Vol. 28 (1964), pp. 41–80; M.H. Curtis, *Oxford and Cambridge in Transition, 1558–1642* (Oxford, 1959).

9. Helga Hammerstein, 'Aspects of the Continental Education of Irish Students in the Reign of Queen Elizabeth I' in *Historical Studies*, Vol. VIII (1971), pp. 137–54; D.F. Cregan, 'Irish Catholic Admissions to the English Inns of Court, 1558–1625' in *Irish Jurist*, Vol. V (1970), pp. 95–114; 'Irish Recusant Lawyers in politics in the Reign of James I' in *ibid.*, Vol. V (1970), pp. 306–20.

10. Thomas More to family, Autumn 1517, in L. Bradner and C.A. Lynch (eds), *The Latin Epigrams of Thomas More* (Chicago, 1953), p. 231; R. Ariès, *Centuries of Childhood* (London, 1962) for changing attitudes to the education and rearing of children in the past.

11. F.X. Martin, O.S.A., *Friar Nugent: a study of Francis Lavalin Nugent, 1569–1635, agent of the Counter-Reformation* (London, 1962), p. 265. For the Nugent girls' expenses at school see Transcript of 11.h.1. (5, ii) in Archives de l'Aube in Irish Capuchin Provincial Archives Dublin.

12. J. Kelly, 'Early Feminist Theory and the Querelle des Femmes, 1400–1789' in *Women, History and Theory, the Essays of Joan Kelly* (Chicago, 1984), pp. 65–109; S. Croag Bell, 'Christine de Pizan: Humanism and the Problems of a Studious Woman' in *Feminist Studies*, Vol. 3–4 (1976), pp. 173–84; S. Shakar, *The Fourth Estate* (London, 1983).

13. H. Gallwey, 'The Cusack family of County Meath and Dublin' in *The Irish Genealogist*, Vol. 5 (1974–9), p. 312. For transcript of Thomas Cusack's letter to his sister apologising for borrowing from her (Public Records Office Ireland: Transcripts of Deeds and Wills from Exchequer, inquisitions County Dublin, Vol. II, p. 443).

14. B. Bradshaw, *The Dissolution of the Religious Orders in Ireland under Henry VIII* (Cambridge, 1974), p. 133.

15. Countess of Desmond to Privy Council, 28 June 1580 (P.R.O., S.P. 63/73/67); for a facsimile of her letter to Sir Robert Cecil, see A. Chambers, *Eleanor Countess of Desmond c. 1545–1638* (Dublin, 1986), p. 216. Eleanor's letter to Pope Gregory XIII, undated, is located in Nunz. d'Inghilterra I, f. 205 in the Vatican Archives Rome. See also pp. 79–80 above and M. MacCurtain, 'Marriage in

Tudor Ireland' in A. Cosgrove (ed.), *Marriage in Ireland* (Dublin, 1985), pp. 57–9.

16. A. Chambers, *Granuaile, the Life and Times of Grace O'Malley. c. 1530–1603* (Dublin, 1979) pp. 25, 55, 62; See facsimile of Grace O'Malley's petition to Queen Elizabeth I in 1593 (*ibid.*, pp. 136–7).

17. M. Kerney Walsh, 'Irishwomen in Exile, 1600–1800, the Eoin O'Mahony Memorial Lecture in Dublin' in *The O'Mahony Journal*, Vol. XI (1981), pp. 35–48.

18. *Ibid.*, pp. 44–5. See also pp. 117–25 above.

19. J. Casway, 'Rosa O'Dogherty: a Gaelic Woman' in *Seanchas ÁrdMhacha*, Vol. X (1980–1), pp. 42–62; 'Mary Stuart O'Donnell' in *Donegal Annual*, no. 39 (1987), pp. 28–36.

20. For Lady Falkland see C.R. Erlington and J.H. Todd (eds), *The Whole Works of James Ussher* (17 vols, Dublin, 1847–64), Vol. XV, p. 356. For Margaret Ussher née Stanihurst see W. Ball Wright (ed.), *The Ussher Memoirs* (London, 1889), pp. 30–42. For Eleanor Douglas, D. Morrissey, 'Never so mad a Ladie: the Life of Lady Eleanor Douglas' in *UCD History Review*, Vol. V (1988), pp. 14–7.

21. R. Gillespie, *Colonial Ulster, The Settlement of East Ulster 1600–1641* (Cork, 1985), p. 77.

22. L. Stone, 'The Educational Revolution in England, 1560–1640', *loc. cit.*, p. 70.

23. The author is indebted to Dr D.F. Cregan, C.M. for drawing her attention to this largely unresearched area, but see T. Flynn, 'The Dominicans of Ireland: 1535–1640' (Ph.D. thesis, Trinity College Dublin, 1988) for references to imports of books into Ireland.

24. Clanricarde to Marchioness of Hertford, 30 January 1644; Marchioness of Winchester to Clanricarde, 4 March 1545; Marchioness of Hertford to Lady Ussher, 20 March 1647 in J. Lowe (ed.), *Letterbook of the Earl of Clanricarde* (Irish Manuscripts Commission, Dublin, 1983), pp. 35, 153–4, 427; T.C. Croker (ed.) *The Autobiography of Mary Rich, Countess of Warwick*, (for Percy Society Journal, London, 1848). The memoirs of Abbess Cecily Dillon form the first section of the *Annals* of the Poor Clare Nuns of Ireland (Archives Nun's Island, Galway). The author is grateful to Sr McCarthy, O.S.F., for supplying a transcript. For Anne Conway consult C. Merchant, *The Breath of Nature, Women, Ecology and the Scientific Revolution* (London, 1980). For Elizabeth Preston, ongoing research by author see *Calendar of the Manuscripts of the Marquess of Ormonde* (Historical Manuscripts Commission, 11 vols, London, 1895–1920).

25. P. Corish, *The Irish Catholic Experience* (Dublin, 1985), p. 105; H. Trevor-Roper, 'James Ussher, Archbishop of Armagh' in *Catholics, Anglicans and Puritans* (London, 1989), pp. 120–65.

26. *Cal. S.P. Ire.*, 1606–08, p. 133.

27. R.P. Liebowitz, 'Virgins in the Service of Christ: The Dispute over an Active Apostolate for Women during the Counter-Reformation' in E. McLaughlin and R. Ruether (eds), *Women of Spirit* (New York, 1979), pp. 131–52.

28. Annals and memoirs of Abbess Cecily Dillon in Archives Poor Clare Nuns of Ireland in Nun's Island, Galway; Irish Dominican Archives (women) in Sion Hill, Blackrock, County Dublin; Archives Benedictine Nuns of Ireland in Kylemore Abbey, Connemara, County Galway.

29. *Loc. cit*, The surnames of the seven founding members of the

Dublin Dominican community of Cabra, 1717 were listed as Bellew, Browne, Keating, Rice, Vaughan, Plunkett, Weever. They opened a boarding school in Channel Row, Dublin in 1719.

30. For constitution of Fr D. O'Daly, O.P. and annals, registers and documents 1639 ff. Archives Bon Sucesso Lisbon. The surnames of the early nuns are Kavanagh of Borris and Pulmonty, County Wicklow, Burke of Brittas, daughter of Sir John Burke, Anne and Cecelia O'Neill, O'Sullivan Beare, O'Mahony and they form a group in the women of the wild geese.

31. J.H. Simms, 'The Restoration, 1660–85' in T.W. Moody, F.X. Martin and F.J. Byrne (eds), *A New History of Ireland, Vol. III, 1534–1691*, (Oxford, 1976), p. 436. Samuel Wilson to Lord Herbert, 21 May 1678 in W.J. Smith (ed.), *Herbert Correspondence* (Irish Manuscripts Commission Dublin, 1963), p. 244. Munster had a head-start on other provinces as planters like R. Boyle established schools in Bandon and Lismore.

32. N. Canny, *The Upstart Earl, a Study of the Social and Mental World of Richard Boyle, first Earl of Cork, 1566–1643* (Cambridge, 1982); A.B. Grosart (ed.), *Lismore Papers, by Richard Boyle, earl of Cork [1566–1643]* (10 vols, London, 1886–8).

33. H. Trevor-Roper, 'The Great Tew Circle' in *Catholics, Anglicans and Puritans*, pp. 171, 173, 179, 209. Lord Dacre refers to her as the 'blue-stocking sister of Robert Boyle'. The 'Bluestockings' was a term first used in the 1750s for men and women of wit and knowledge who frequented houses where the social display of knowledge and advanced opinions was cultivated as a fine art. They wore blue stockings, hence the name. Cf. Dale Spender, *Women of Ideas (and What Men Have Done to Them)* (London, 1983), pp. 101–12.

34. N. Canny, 'The family life of Richard Boyle' in *The Upstart Earl*, pp. 77–123. R. Meehan, 'Boyle's Daughters' (unpublished B.A. dissertation University College, Dublin, 1987); Richard Boyle, 'True Remembrances' in *Lismore Papers*, vol. II, pp. 100–17. For unpublished Boyle material see Canny, *The Upstart Earl*, pp. 151–2.

35. T.C. Croker (ed.), *The Autobiography of Mary Rich* (London, 1848); B.L. Add. MS 27, 351–5; Richard Boyle, 'True Remembrances', *op. cit.*; For Wentworth's remark see *Works of Ussher*, Vol. XV, p. 573.

36. C. Fall-Smith, *Mary Countess of Warwick 1635–1678* (London, 1901). See also note 35 above.

37. N. Canny, *The Upstart Earl*, p. 181. Professor Canny does not refer to Catherine's affectionate relationship with her father.

38. R. Meehan, 'Boyle's Daughters', p. 14; D. Masson, *Life of Milton* (7 vols, London, 1859–80), Vol. V, p. 232.

39. G. Lerner, *The Creation of Patriarchy* (Oxford, 1986), pp. 216–20.

40. B. Ó Cuív (ed.), *Párliament na nBan* (Dublin, 1977), pp. xxxi–xli. For a different perspective see pp. 155–7 above.

11

Women and the Reformation in Seventeenth-Century Ireland

Phil Kilroy

In the seventeenth century the Irish Reformed Church was characterised by a strong independent spirit and, despite divisions and dissent within, it exercised a power and influence beyond its actual numbers. In fact, the division and dissent which grew increasingly in the seventeenth century provided the context and energy for the Reformation Church to root itself in the country. This is not to say that efforts to dispel controversy were not paramount among leaders in the church. Not at all. Indeed, when Charles I, Laud and Wentworth were insisting on conformity and uniformity in the Irish Reformed Church, they were continuing a movement that had grown in strength since at least 1618. It was a search for a *via media* in a world of controversy, a world of great instability and uncertainty. Essentially, it was a backward movement, impossible to sustain in a period of change and crisis. One of the results was to polarise dissenting elements and create further sects and wider movements. The instability caused by the Reformation was a deep source of tension and friction, and there was no guarantee at all that the Reformation had come to stay. Throughout the seventeenth century, men and women were making choices in religious faith for the first time in history, and this is one of the key issues in the Irish Reformed Church at this time.[1]

In 1638 Henry Leslie, Bishop of Down and Connor[2] delivered a sermon at Lisnagarvey which was directed against the Puritan and Scottish covenanters in the diocese. In the sermon Leslie particularly deplored the lack of ceremonies in the church:[3] ceremonies, which of course implied episcopacy, were being overshadowed or pushed aside by the Calvinist stress on the preaching of the word. This was a serious undermining of the stability of the Irish Reformed Church and Leslie tried to stem any diversity of practice. It is quite evident that Leslie received much opposition from those 'preoccupied with prejudice and partiality, and so wedded to their own wills that they were resolved to receive no information'. The people in the diocese had been won by various ways, among them preaching and 'labouring of the lungs, than of the brain';[4] criticism of government and of those in high office; usury was allowed and tithes condemned; and most dangerous of all, some 'boast of the inward testimony of God's spirit assuring their consciences'. However, his final and most damning piece of criticism was reserved for the fact that they 'use women to advance their faction . . . in whom there is the least ability of Judgement'. Moreover, women fell for these preachers 'as they love knowledge and desire liberty'. Indeed, Leslie wished that the law against women misbehaving in religious matters be implemented in Ireland lest this abuse develop and destroy the Church:[5]

> Surely as the Lord taxes the Angel of the Church of Thyatira for suffering the woman Jezabel to teach and deceive God's servants, so may he reprove the governors of our Church, for suffering this feminine heresy so long.

While it is difficult with any great confidence to name the women Leslie refers to in these years, it is certainly true that within a few years the 'feminine heresy' he so dreaded had grown in strength and conviction, although ironically it grew from a different source. George Fox wrote in 1656[6]:

> May not the Spirit of Christ speak in the female as well as in the male? Is he there to be limited? Who is it that dares limit the Holy One of Israel? And you that will not have him reign in the female as well as in the male, are you against Scripture?

Later he developed his thought:[7]

> What, are women priests? Yes Women Priests. And can men and women offer sacrifice without they wear the Holy Garments? NO. What are the Holy Garments men and women must wear? . . . the priest's surplice? Nay, it is the Righteousness of Christ, this is the Royal Garment and the Royal Priesthood, which everyone must put on, Men and Women.

Such a spirit spread quickly to Ireland through the growth of the Quaker movement. Indeed, by 1660 there were at least 30 established meeting places in Ireland.[8]

I

William Edmundson, whose influence was paramount during the early years of Quakerism in Ireland, became convinced by the witness of women preachers in England.[9] When he came over to Ireland the movement grew steadily in strength though not in numbers. It has been estimated that by 1680 there were 780 Quakers in the country, 340 of whom were in the north. Of the

340, 156 were women; in Munster there were 163 Quakers, of whom 61 were women; and of the 295 Quakers in Leinster, 59 were women.[10] Of the names recorded, it seems that only four are truly Irish, the rest being either English or Scottish, and most seem to have come from a mixture of religious backgrounds – Independent, Baptist and Presbyterian.[11] One writer speaking of dissent in Ireland[12] put it thus:

> Most of them are English sects, Atheists, Protestants, Puritans, Presbyterians, Independents, Familists, Anabaptists, Adamites, Quakers, wandering preachers, etc. In addition, these sects are divided among themselves . . .

Certainly women were very much to the fore from the beginning of the movement in Ireland and this is highlighted in Edmundson's journal:[13]

> Then [in 1655] we travelled to Strabane, Clogher, Omagh and Six Miles Cross to Dungannon, so to Kilmore in the county of Armagh. Several honest tender-hearted people lived thereabouts who had a desire to hear friends. We came to a widow woman's house, one Margery Atkinson, a tender, honest woman whose house I had been in before; she was convinced of the truth and received us lovingly. So we had a meeting there.

Which meeting 'was very serviceable and several tender people received the truth at that time in the love of it' and the widow was remembered as: 'a worthy woman, who received the Truth with gladness and lived and died in the Lord, and her memorial is blest'.[14] She remained a fervent Quaker and in 1660 was fined 8s. 4d., and two cows worth £3 10s. were taken because, with others in county Armagh, she refused to pay tithes.[15]

Edmundson also recounts the plight of two women preachers:[16]

> About this time there were two women friends from London, Anne Gould and Julian Westwood, who came to Dublin and travelled to L'derry, having some drawings to that place. They went to Coleraine and so through all the Scotch country . . . all on foot, in winter time wading rivers and dirty miry ways; so that A.G. being a tender woman, was much spent and stayed at Clough [in Antrim].

Up to this point Edmundson knew nothing of their presence, but he was 'drawn to Clough' and:[17]

> took my lodging at an Inn, the country being generally Scotch people and Presbyterian. When I came unto the house I found Anne Gould in despair and Julian Westwood with her, but when they knew who I was, the poor disconsolate women revived in joy and gladness.

Edmundson took them to Carrickfergus and arranged for them to travel to Dublin and from there to England.

In the same year, 1655, two other women preachers arrived in Dublin, Elizabeth Fletcher and Elizabeth Smith.[18] They preached in St Audeon's and at a Baptist meeting. Rejected by the latter, they were imprisoned for the former. However, on their release, they held the first meeting ever held in Dublin, in the house of Richard Fawkes, a tailor. In the same year both travelled to Youghal, and there many families came to be convinced. Nevertheless in Youghal, an independent preacher, John Wood, 'opposed women's preaching' but Elizabeth Fletcher was able to answer him, aided by two other Quaker friends. Her ministry in Limerick was successful and she began to influence a steady number of people. It seems as if she was very much alone at this point, and Edmund Burrough wrote to Margaret Fell:[19]

> Little Elizabeth Fletcher is present here, but I know not how long she stays . . . truly I suffer for her being as it were alone, having no other woman with her in this ruinous nation, where it is very bad travelling every way afoot, and also dangerous . . . If it were the will of the Lord that any woman were moved to come over to her . . .'

Something was done fairly quickly, for two months later, in January 1656, Elizabeth Fletcher joined Francis Howgil in the west.[20]

Another woman was moved to come over to Ireland, though she worked on her own during the time she actually spent in the country. Barbara Blagdon arrived in 1655:[21]

> She came from England in a vessel bound for Cork, but by foul weather carried to Dublin. When the storm was violent, the seamen imputed the course of it to her as being a Quaker, and were conspiring to throw her overboard. She overheard their consultations and told the Master of the Ship that if he did not prevent them, her blood would be required at his hands. So he charged them not to touch her. The storm continuing, and it being the first day of the week, she went upon the deck, finding herself moved to exhort the seamen and also to pray for them, for though they had a priest on board, his fear rendered him incapable of performing his function. Her exhortation and prayer had such an effect on the ship crew that they were very quiet and sedate and acknowledged themselves obliged to her, for her prayers at a time when their chaplain was silenced through fear; at length they came safe to Dublin . . . Barbara going on shore, went directly to the Deputy's house, but was told that she might not speak with him, and that he had just before

banished two others of her persuasion. She applied to the secretary, desiring him to help her to speak with the Deputy. He answered that he did not think he could. She then told him that if he would go up and tell the Deputy that a woman below desired to speak with him, if he refused, she was answered. So the secretary went up and a man came down to fetch her into the with-drawing room.

A substitute had been sent to fob her off, but she recognised the trick:

> When I see your Lord, I shall do my message unto him. Thus they were disappointed and soon after the Deputy himself came forth . . . She then stood up and spoke to him, cautioning him to beware that he was not found fighting against God.

When she was in Dublin, Barbara Blagdon stayed in the house of Stephen and Rebecca Rich, a couple who were well known for their hospitality to the friends.[22] Having done what she could in Dublin, Barbara journeyed to Cork where she had some relations and acquaintances'.[23]

> Great were her sufferings, for she met with bonds of imprisonment, almost everywhere she came, her zeal for the truth exciting her to bear testimony thereto in the public places for worship or concourse. And generally wheresoever she published the truth her preaching was with demonstration, and to the convincement of some of the hearers. Once she was moved to preach in a market place, where a butcher swore he would cleave her head, and lifted up his cleaver to do it; but a woman coming behind him caught hold of his arms and prevented him until soldiers came up and secured him. Divers of her acquaintances, with whom she had been formerly conversant, were now afraid of her, because she sometimes spoke to them in so solemn and awful a manner, that her speech caused them to tremble. Others said she was a witch and avoided her till their servants turned her out of doors.

So in various ways it is easy to see the novelty women preachers were in Ireland, and the several responses their presence evoked. Barbara Blagdon returned to England, to her home in Bristol; yet in the following years she was drawn once again to visit Ireland and crossed the channel. The ship foundered at Dungarvan and again Barbara was almost lost. On arrival in Dublin, she went to the Court of Justice and preached to the judges.[24]

> This good advice was taken so ill, that she was sent to prison, where she lay upon straw on the ground, and when it rained the wet and filth of the house of office ran in under her.

Being arraigned at the bar, she was required to plead guilty
or not guilty . . . but she not answering in that form of
words they required, was sent back to prison, where she
suffered much.

She was released only at the successful pleading of Sir William
King, Colonel Phayre and Lady Brown.[25] Another experience of
jail in Ireland came in Limerick in the same year (1656). She was
arrested on the street, first imprisoned and then banished from
the city, and sent 'towards Cork, as vagabonds . . . from constable to constable, to be banished from the land'.[26] During her
final imprisonment in Cork, Barbara Blagdon was visited by
Suzanne Worth, wife of the future bishop of Killaloe, a significant
gesture at the time. The final irony lay in the journey back to
England, for 'in her passage thither [she] was robbed by a
privateer of all she had on board'.[27]

The influence of these Englishwomen in Ireland was quite
strong, and soon women who ordinarily resided in Ireland began
to exercise a new type of leadership. This came about in several
ways, as for example the case of Deborah Baker:[28]

In the year 1650, Robert Sandham came from England, a
lieutenant in Col. Sanders regiment of foot and arrived in
Youghal. In the year 1652 he took to wife Deborah Baker of
that town, then an Anabaptist, afterwards a faithful friend
of whom hereafter. He [Robert] was convinced in the year
1655 by the ministry of a woman, viz. Elizabeth Fletcher,
who preached in the streets of Youghal.

Another example was the woman preacher from Coleraine,
Katherine McLoughlin. She was 'of Irish parents of account, and
was sent to Londonderry for education'.[29] When she was 16 years
of age a ship sailing to Barbados arrived in Derry, and Katherine
went on it. She married a man called Norton in Barbados, and
when George Fox came to preach there, she was convinced and
in 1678 returned to Ireland as a preacher. She followed the set
pattern of William Edmundson, making visits to houses, holding
meetings in market places all over the north, and, an unusual
feature, preaching in Irish at the Lurgan marketplace.[30] In a letter
to Anthony Sharp, Katherine reported[31]

I have passed through most of the meetings in the North and
hath been very well refreshed and comforted amongst the
Lord's innocent people, for I can say that they are as innocent
a plain people as I have been amongst.

In his turn, Sharp wrote to a friend[32]

K.N. stayed for sometime and was of great service here, and
some were convinced by her and we had very large meetings; while we stayed Justice Simmons wife being convinced

by her, and her husband confirmed and strengthened who was convinced many years since.

At this time Quakers were singled out easily in the community for their refusal to swear, take off their hats, pay tithes, rates, assessments, go to church for public worship, and for consistently withholding fees.[33] Irish Quakers led strict lives and at the meetings insisted on the need for plain dress, plain speech, plain behaviour and plain furniture; this was urged to the extent of indicating the colour of cloth to be worn and width of cuffs in dress.[34] In the earliest minutes of the Cork meetings[35] there are warnings against drunkenness, marriages by a priest, marrying worldly people, wearing fashions (including periwigs) keeping dogs and drinking tea. Just because they were ready to suffer for their convictions, Quakers are listed frequently in the prison and fines lists, and among them are numbers of women. Thus[36]

> [1656] Blanch Holden and Margaret Trotter, two very poor women, for going to the public worship-house [at] Lisnagarvey, alias Lisburn in the county of Antrim, on the day called Christmas Day and saying these or the like words: 'Let them that keep a day, keep it to the Lord', were fined by Judge Kennedy, at the Assizes at Carrickfergus, one hundred marks each and committed to Carrickfergus gaol where they continued prisoner about two years.

Another such example was Lucretia Cooke. She was a real leader in Kinsale and was imprisoned twice.[37] She had learned resistance from her father, Edward Cooke, who in 1655 was a soldier in Cromwell's army, and was called to appear before the General:[38]

> He refused to pull off his hat, spoke in the plain language of Thee and Thou without respect of person, and would not give the customary compliments. For these causes he was dismissed from the army.

He was sent to Newgate prison in Dublin. Nevertheless, the family were noted in 1655 as having 'the most eminent house in town and are of the true seed'.[39] In her day Lucretia became recognised 'as one of the outstanding "Irish" Quaker leaders'.[40]

> She was a baptist and as they cast her out for heresy as they say, a noble woman she is, she declared against the priest in public and was moved to declare against the baptists and one day, the market day, took a load of books of the highest priests in the nation and burnt them in the street.

For such activities and for 'speaking after the priest had quite finished' Lucretia was sent to prison and tried.[41]

Suzanne Mitchel was another Quaker who suffered on many

occasions.[42] In 1669 she was imprisoned in Cork, because she had interrupted a sermon[43]

> On the day of their annual choosing a Mayor for the city of Cork, a priest in his sermon urged the people to take the oaths, urging the lawfulness and expediency of swearing. The said Suzanna Mitchel being present, and grieved to hear the plain precept of Christ so contradicted, in her zeal, with a loud voice, spoke thus: 'Oh! Persuade not the people to swear and to break the command of Christ, who said: Swear not at all.' And to the people, she said: 'Oh People, because of oaths the land mouns, and the Lord is angry because of them, and His judgements are near at hand . . .' For this admonition she was immediately hauled out of that place, carried before a magistrate and committed to prison.

In the same year (1669) she was jailed with several other Quakers for assembling in the meeting place.[44] Suzanne fell ill in jail and the mayor was asked to release her 'but he denied that request and abused her that asked it, calling her Witch of Endor and other approbrious names'.

In 1656, Mary Mallen 'an inhabitant of Bandonbridge' was arrested for speaking after the priest had finished his sermon, and she was brought before the court at Kinsale.[45] Sarah Bennet, a widow whose husband had been in the Cromwellian army, attended a meeting in Limerick in the same year and was jailed for so doing.[46] Indeed, she had travelled with Barbara Blagdon, and like her was ill-used in prison by General Ingoldsby, who

> Ordered that no one should visit her in prison, nor have the necessary supply of food and bedding brought to her by friends, nor yet pen, ink and paper to make known her Wants or the Wants of any other friend there in bonds with her. Then the two women were sent towards Cork [as vagabonds] from Constable to Constable, to be banished from the land.

The Provost of Cork was severe in his treatment of the Quakers. When he arrested Suzanne Worth, 'an aged and sober woman', some of his officers said they would prefer to go to prison themselves than do this deed.[47] Similarly, in Waterford Eleanor Tatlock was arrested 'for testifying against will-worship' and was committed to the Bridewell. Some days later the entire family was banished from Waterford.[48] In the same year, 1660, Margaret Blanch was imprisoned in Waterford for preaching at the funeral of one of her family, and during her six months in jail the Bishop excommunicated both Margaret and her husband. So we see that for their active participation in the movement, these women were singled out for punishment. The anger of the Mayor of Cork was also shown to the 'Widow Bantrim, a poor woman, having seven children', and he took £11 15s. from her in tithe.[49] Indeed widows seem to have suffered particular persecution, all over Ireland. Thus in Wexford county, Suzanna Fisher, a widow[50]

> had her wool and corn taken away, under pretence of tithes, and in a very extravagant manner, by one Walter Bulger, and she was abused by his son with blows. They took away much of her corn and threw her stacks about the fields, making much spoil and havock. When Bulger was told of this inhumanity to a widow, he carelessly answered: 'There's no law for Quakers'.

Another widow in Tipperary, Sarah Davis, suffered: 'A poor widow near Killaloe, having but two lambs, had one of them taken from her for tithe'.[51]

Those who welcomed and harboured the friends were also liable for arrest. Thus in Cork the house of Elizabeth Erbery was known as a centre, and in 1670 she was arrested and kept in jail 'a long time'.[52] The Rich family in Dublin were continuously receiving the friends and seem to have remained undisturbed,[53] while the Greenwoods in Antrim were really active in the movement:[54]

> James being for many years infirm in body was unable to travel much abroad; but Anne being healthy, both in body and mind, was frequently serviceable at the general meetings of friends, where she appeared in such sweetness and evenness of temper so savoury, grave, deliberate and reaching in her expressions, that such as were in the service with her were much strengthened and encouraged by the excellent fruits of the Divine Spirit that appeared through her, both in doctrine, discipline and conversation. Her words in her testimony were but few, and not forwardly expressed, she being careful not to run before her guide, but to observe divine conduct, under which her example was a check to forward and rash appearance; yet she was a nursing mother to the young and tender, a refresher to the weary, an encourager to the distressed, and was so endued with a heavenly wisdom, and a taking way of expression and gesture in conference, that even disorderly and obstinate persons were often times won upon by her. They both died in the same year, in great resignation and assurance of peace with God.

The visit of George Fox to Ireland in 1669 had a stabilising effect. He settled the men and women's meetings, as well as the general half yearly meetings, encouraged discipline, and the keeping of records. This would be needed to help perseverance in times of suffering which were acute and painful. In fact accounts of friends in jail date from the year following George Fox's visitation;[55] indeed William Edmundson was no stranger to imprisonment:[56]

> We had a meeting at Belturbet, and the Lord's power and presence was with us, but the provost of the town was an envious man, who came with some rude people, broke up our meeting and took us to prison, both men and women. We were all night in a very cold place, the women were mightily pinched with the cold, it being frost and snow . . .

Such sturdy growth in the movement, and such courage in face of persecution were bound to cause fear and tensions in society generally. A certain cloud of suspicion hung over the Quakers, new as they were in Ireland at this period. In numerical terms, of course, men suffered a great deal more than women in the movement. Nevertheless, the strong if small body of convinced women in Ireland in the period 1655–70 shows a change in the role and stance of women in Ireland to a degree unthinkable at the turn of the century, or indeed up to 1640. It is evident that women were active and accepted in the Quaker movement and that this was a new profile for women in mid-seventeenth century Ireland. Yet by 1700 the picture changed and Quaker women were generally edged out of the places of influence and decision making, curtailed and controlled. For once the initial stages of Quakerism had been worked through, inevitable institutionalisation came about and modified the role and freedom of women.[57]

II

Another group of women emerged in seventeenth-century Ireland through the Counter-Reformation movement which created the possibility for Roman Catholic women to become religious again. The sixteenth-century Act of Dissolution had effectively ended a structured form of religious life for men and women in Ireland, and for several decades it seemed only a memory fading slowly into the past. Yet gradually women emerged quietly into the open and made their choice in life. Short cryptic references indicate the underground and scattered type of religious commitment.[58] In a letter of 1598 Father Hamill, a secular priest, wrote to the Jesuit Henry Fitzsimon and recorded that Margery Barnewall had received the veil from the bishop. In fact, her manner of life was reported to the Reformed Archbishop of Dublin, Loftus, and Margery was imprisoned and tried. She escaped through the aid of friends and fled to St Malo in Brittany, and eventually made her way to Compostela. After journeying to Rome Margery returned to Ireland, where her example was the means of bringing many others into some form of religious life.[59]

Certainly, by 1598 Father Fitzsimons had begun to guide some ladies who had already taken vows of perpetual virginity and were in Dublin awaiting an opportunity of sailing to join a religious community on the continent. These women perhaps became the Sodality of Our Lady established in Dublin by Father Fitzsimons – 'In it are families of the first rank; it flourishes and increases everyday'.[60]

This group seems to have endured, for in 1607 Father Fitzsimons received a plea while he was in Flanders asking that he continue to support the group of women in Dublin who aspired to religious life.[61] Another group was discovered in Drogheda by Henry Usher, Archbishop of Armagh.[62]

> The Lord Primate one day secretly did go about searching of priests and by chance he broke up a door wherein two or three nuns did dwell [at the back]; there was a little chapel where the friars did say mass . . . he broke the door . . .

This is confirmed in a paper sent to Rome in 1623 which stated that women who had taken simple vows were living at Drogheda under the special care of the Franciscans.[63] However, this was not at all approved by the Roman Catholic authorities in Ireland, and as early as 1614 at the Synod of Dublin held at Kilkenny, it was stated:[64]

> For reasons of prudence we decree that priests shall not have in their houses or as guests at meals any women – even more those who have made a vow of virginity or chastity, or any others, since they might be a cause of scandal: and they are not to undertaken the care of such women, even as a spiritual ministry, without further authorisation.

In other words, the growth of religious life for women was to be organised and controlled by clerical authorities and when this was not possible religious life for women was to be discouraged. Thus in 1624[65]

> We have under consideration the discreet and prudent admission of women to the wearing of the religious habit and to the name and state of religious profession. But enclosed properties which are the normal safeguard for the preservation of religious virtue are not to be found in this country.

In fact the Franciscan men religious in Drogheda were asked for an account of the women religious in the town. When it was understood that the women were admitted to the friary, a directive was given in a softer, more tolerant tone.[66]

> They cannot keep enclosure there, or completely exclude heretics or, indeed, women, so long as the persecution lasts. In France, however, where people are free in religious

matters, women are everywhere allowed into the monasteries of men. It seems, therefore, that this practice must be tolerated, because of the lawlessness of the age, since it is not the cause of scandal there.

Thus there is some body of evidence to show that for some women in Ireland religious life was an option they chose to follow. That it was acceptable and respected as a form of life is shown in some of the wills of the families.[67] Recognition came from another source. In 1629 the Earl of Cork noted[68]

I found by good intelligence that there were by Christmas ten houses of friars, nuns, jesuits, and priests of several orders conventually gotten together in this city and suburbs, each house having a head or governor with mighty resorts unto them. And that in one of the houses erected by the Countess Dowager of Kildare, and by her richly adorned and furnished for the Jesuits, there were many active spirits descended of good houses who held dangerous principles. And that in another of the nunneries there was a governor brought from Dunkirk with one nun, the daughter of the Earl of Westmeath, another of the Earl of Fingal, two of the Lord Viscount Gormanstown, two of the Lord Viscount Dillon, and divers young professed nuns being the daughters of divers prime gentlemen.

With the Countess Dowager of Kildare providing the Jesuits with a chapel, and with some of the oldest, wealthiest families represented in the community of nuns at Dunkirk, it can be seen that religious life was reasserting itself publicly in Ireland. But it was a narrow option for women, for they had to fit into the accepted norms and patterns for them as defined by Roman/clerical authority. At a time when Mary Ward had actually left the Poor Clares at Gravelines because the manner of life was unable to meet her vision, young gentry women from Ireland were travelling there to begin their religious life.[69] It seems that no Roman Catholic woman in Ireland was innovative with regard to religious life and simply conformed to set directives. In other words, they met the expectations of their families and church. They were in fact trapped by the prevailing tendency of the Counter-Reformation Movement: centralisation, regulation and control, a tendency mirrored in clerical and family structures.[70]

Within these constrictions the women who went to Dunkirk, Gravelines and Newport on the continent were making courageous choices and taking real risks.[71] It was equally courageous to decide to return to Ireland, as the Irish women at Newport did in 1629, to Dublin. Soon 12 new members presented themselves for religious life, thus indicating the potential that the little community tapped. The Dillon family were particularly prominent in the Poor Clare community. Cecily Dillon was the abbess; her brother Father Bonaventure Dillon was confessor to the community.[72] Sir Luke Dillon, another brother, was a member of the privy council and could be expected to protect the Poor Clares. Four of Cecily Dillon's nieces subsequently joined the community, all daughters of Elizabeth Fitzgerald of Longford (Ellen, Cecily, Anne and Bridget) as did two other nieces (Elizabeth and Mary), daughters of Sir Christopher Dillon.[73]

However, the years of relative religious freedom were soon over:[74]

> The house of nuns on the Merchant Quay in Dublin was seized on by the Mayor etc. There were 16 of prime noble and gentlemen's daughters therein: 5 of them in their habits were brought before the Lords Justices and council, into the council chamber and there examined and licenced to return into their former place of residence, there to continue for one month, so as in the meantime they did put in good security never to reassemble conventually together in their kingdom and to appear on the Table, if at any time within three months their appearance should be required of any of their sureties.

Certainly, religious houses were suppressed and the possibility of women religious resident in Ireland was once again pushed into the future. The Poor Clares dispersed to Loughrea, to Galway, Athlone, Waterford and Wexford, and there the communities settled and quietly tried to survive suppression. They seem to have had some type of recognition in that they were visited by Lady Wentworth and the Duchess of Buckingham.[75]

Indeed, in 1641 one of the 'Grievances of the Archbishop of Tuam'[76] was that

> A nunnery called Bethlehem wherein are reclused many young gentlewomen, daughters to lords, knights and the best of the country. They pay great sums on entry and are as absolute under the authority of the abbess as the nuns are in that much spoken of nunnery of Lisbon.

Furthermore, and in the same year, it was noted that a 'nunnery [was] erected at Drogheda, which is so spacious that it contains four score windows a side. It is not yet finished but there is great hope for it'.[77] These were in fact Poor Clare nuns whom 60 pious ladies of Drogheda had invited to the city, 'to found the Third Order of St. Francis there'.[78]

Apparently, there were 10 years of relative peace after the expulsion from Dublin, during which time the nuns' rule was translated into Irish and a certain stability was achieved.[79] The war soon broke this and by 1642 Bethlehem had been closed and the community moved to their convent in Galway. In 1653 Cromwell declared that all nuns 'should marry or quit the kingdom', and some decided to go to Spain and France. Others went into hiding and held on quietly throughout the Cromwellian campaign.[80] It is recorded that in 1648 some Irish nuns arrived at Nantes:[81] 'Eight religious of the reformed order of St Elizabeth came by boat from Ireland.' Both their origin and their subsequent history remain obscure, except for the account of their actual arrival in Nantes. However, they do serve to underline the fact that many Irishwomen continued the pattern of going abroad for the purpose of continuing their religious life, or indeed of actually beginning it, in convents where they had received their education, either at Dunkirk, Charleville[82] Pontoise,[83] Liege,[84] Paris,[85] Ghent[86] and finally Cambrai.[87]

It is in these events and hazards that we can see and admire the courage of these women though we know little personal detail about them, nothing of their own personal experience and motivation. This silence tells its own story and begs the question why none of these presumably well-educated women left any significant records behind? Well provided for and protected both on the continent and at home, by family and church, these women seem to have been rendered silent. Yet they were not spared persecution and suppression, seeing the project for which they had given their lives fail: the re-establishment of religious life for women in Ireland.

III

There is no doubt that for a time Quaker women in Ireland were changing roles in society. They were relatively free to the extent that they came from the farming, army and merchant class in England, rather than from aristocratic families. So they emerged into new positions: they were preaching, teaching, travelling, discussing, interrupting sermons; they supported and harboured dissenters; they were fined, imprisoned, persecuted, exiled. And even if the new ground was held only for a while, that such occurred at all is significant in itself. For this came about because Quakerism was new and tentative for some years before it settled down, became institutionalised and reverted to the patriarchal norms and expectations of society.

On the other hand, Roman Catholic nuns, almost extinct since the dissolution of the monasteries under Henry VIII, reappear in the seventeenth century and conform to expectations: the status quo, the controlling power of family and church. Within this constriction no innovative energy was released among seventeenth-century religious women in Ireland, other than the fact of their existence as religious. No doubt many were intelligent, highly educated and had strong personalities, but sadly they made no mark.

It is equally true that women of the established church made no significant public contribution in seventeenth-century Ireland. This points to the fact that women within the established churches, such as the Church of Ireland and the Catholic Church, were unable to move into new places and spaces in their respective traditions; only new movements could accommodate that, and they only for a while. For a paradigm shift alone could have created the possibility for a truly new understanding of the role of men and women in society, and that was not available. Frames of reference at this period were well established and historical evidence has been examined within this constriction. With a growing shift in consciousness today the time is ripe for a wider, more adequate context within which to research. This means that the study of seventeenth-century women has just begun and will in time yield new and significant insights.

REFERENCES

1. P. Kilroy, 'Sermon and Pamphlet Literature in the Irish Reformed Church 1613–34' in *Archivium Hibernicum*, Vol. XXXIII (1975), pp. 110–21. Also, P. Kilroy, 'Bishops and Ministers in Ulster during the Primacy of Ussher 1625–56' in *Seanchas Ard Macha*, Vol. VIII, no. 2 (1977), pp. 284–98; G.A. Ford, *The Protestant Reformation in Ireland 1590–1641* (Frankfurt, 1985).

2. Henry Leslie, born in Scotland, was ordained in 1617 and made prebendary of Down in 1619; in 1627 he became Dean of Down, and in 1635 Bishop of Down and Connor; cf. H. Cotton (ed.), *Fasti Ecclesia Hibernicae* (6 vols, 1848–78), Vol. III p. 205 ff.

3. Henry Leslie, *A Speech delivered at Lisnagarvey, 26 September 1638*, p. 2, in Early Printed Books Library, Trinity College Dublin.

4. Ibid., p. 1.

5. Henry Leslie, *A Treatise on the Authority of the Church, 1636* (Dublin, 1637), p. 86 ff.

6. G. Fox, *The Woman Learning in Silence, 1656* (?London), p. 2 ff., in Friends Library, Dublin.

7. G. Fox, *A Collection of Many and Select Christian Epistles, 1698* (London), Vol. II, p. 244, in Friends Library, Dublin.

8. C.F. Nuttall (ed.), 'Early Quaker Letters from the Swarthmore' (MS (typescript) in Friends Historical Library, London, p. 403).

9. Journal of the Life of William Edmundson, p. 6, in Friends Library, Dublin.

10. J.M. Douglas, 'Early Quakerism in Ireland' in *Journal Friends Historical Society* (hereafter cited as *J.F.H.S.*), vol. 48, no. 1 (1956), pp. 31 ff. These statistics are taken from the Great Book of Tithe, cf. D.E.C. Eversley, 'The Demography of Irish Quakers 1650–1850' in J.M. Goldstrom and L.A. Clarkson (eds), *Irish Population, Economy and Society* (Oxford, 1981), pp. 57–88.

11. J.M. Douglas, *op. cit.*

12. *'Threnodia Hiberno-Catholica 1659'* in *Archivium Hibernicum*, Vol. XIII (1947), p. 84 ff. The author, Maurice Conroy, O.F.M. was a native of Thomond, ordained in Rome, taught in Prague, and worked on the Franciscan mission in England.

13. Edmundson, *op. cit.*, p. 23.

14. J. Rutty, *A History of the Rise and Progress of the People called Quakers in Ireland, 1653–1700* (Dublin, 1751) p. 81.

15. J. Besse, *A Collection of the Sufferings of the People called Quakers* (2 vols, London, 1753), Vol. II, p. 467.

16. Edmundson, p. 23, *op. cit.*

17. *Ibid.*, cf. K.L. Carroll, 'Quakerism and the Cromwellian Army in Ireland' in *J.F.H.S.*, Vol. 54, No. 3 (1978), p. 146.

18. J. Rutty, *The Rise and Progress of the People called Quakers*, p. 81. See also, M.R. Brailsford, *Quaker Women* (London, 1913), pp. 103 ff. Elizabeth Fletcher preached in Oxford in 1654 at 15 years of age and was rejected by the student body – being first whipped and then expelled from the city.

19. O.C. Goodbody, 'Ireland in the Sixteen Fifties' in *J.F.H.S.*, Vol. XLVIII (1956–8), pp. 34 ff. Burrough wrote from Waterford in November 1655.

20. K.L. Carroll, 'Quakerism and the Cromwellian Army in Ireland', pp. 142 ff.

21. J. Besse, *A Collection of the Sufferings of the People called Quakers*, Vol. II, p. 458.

22. Rebecca Rich was imprisoned in 1660 for attending a meeting *cf.* J. Besse, *op. cit.*, p. 446 and for further details consult *J.F.H.S.*, Vol. XLVIII, no. 1 (1956), p. 34; Vol. XLIX, no. 1 (1959), pp. 191 ff.

23. J. Besse, *A Collection of the Sufferings of the People called Quakers*, Vol. II, p. 459.

24. *Ibid.*

25. M.R. Brailsford, *Quaker Women 1650–1690*, p. 194.

26. K.L. Carroll, 'Quakerism and the Cromwellian Army in Ireland', p. 150.

27. J. Besse, *A Collection . . .*, p. 459.

28. J. Rutty, *The Rise and Progress of People called Quakers*, p. 126.

29. *Ibid.* p. 129.

30. *Ibid.*

31. Katherine McLoughlin to Anthony Sharp, 30 March 1678 (Friends Library, Dublin, Sharps Mss, vol. s.5, p. 15).

32. Anthony Sharp to Ralph Fretwell, 30 July 1677 (Sharp Mss, vol. s.4, p. 73).

33. J. Besse, *A Collection . . .*, p. 459.

34. J. Grubb, *Quakers in Ireland, 1655–1900* (London, 1915), p. 81.

35. Records of Minutes in *J.F.H.S.*, Vol. XII, no. 2 (1915), p. 51.

36. J. Rutty, *The Rise and Progress of the People called Quakers*, p. 122.

37. J. Besse, *A Collection . . .*, p. 461.

38. *Ibid.*, p. 459.

39. K.L. Carroll, *op. cit.*, p. 141.

40. *Ibid.* p. 142.

41. J. Besse, *A Collection . . .*, Vol. II, p. 461.

42. J. Rutty, *The Rise and Progress of the People called Quakers*, p. 125.

43. J. Besse, *A Collection . . .*, Vol. II, p. 447.

44. *Ibid.*

45. *Ibid.*, p. 461.

46. *Ibid.*, p. 467.
47. Ibid. Edward Worth was Dean of Cork and later Bishop of Killaloe (1660–9). He founded a hospital in Cork, St Stephen, the Blue Coat Hospital and endowed it with lands cared for by the corporation of Cork, *cf.* J. Ware, *Writers of Ireland* (2 vols, ed. W. Harris, Dublin, 1764), Vol. I, p. 597. His wife became a Quaker and visited B. Blagdon in prison, cf. *J.F.H.S.*, Vol. XLVIII (1956–8), p. 10.
48. J. Besse, *A Collection . . .*, Vol. II, p. 447 (for 1660).
49. *Ibid.*, p. 478 (for 1670).
50. *Ibid.*, p. 480 (for 1672).
51. *Ibid.*, p. 480.
52. *Ibid.*, pp. 476 ff. E. Erbery had been convinced since 1655, *cf.* J. Rutty, *The Rise and Progress of the People called Quakers*, p. 82.
53. Olive Goodbody suggests that they may have died before the persecution of the Quakers became severe, see O.C. Goodbody, 'Irish History and the earliest Irish Friends' in *J.F.H.S.*, Vol. XLIX, no. 1 (1959), p. 191.
54. J. Rutty, *The Rise and Progress of the People called Quakers*, p. 102.
55. J. Besse, *A Collection . . .*, Vol. II, pp. 466–78.
56. J. Rutty, *op. cit.*, p. 102.
57. This subject will be published later as a paper by the author.
58. For further elaboration of this point, consult Franciscan Fathers (eds), *Father Luke Wadding: Commemorative Volume* (Dublin, 1957), p. 82.
59. E. Hogan, *Distinguished Irishmen of the 16th Century* (Dublin, 1894), pp. 34 ff. P.S. Morgan (ed.), *Spicilegium Ossoriense . . .* (2 vols Dublin, 1874–84), Vol. I, pp. 82–109; H. Concannon, *Daughters of Banba* (Dublin, 1922), p. 130.
60. E. Hogan, *Distinguished Irishmen of the 16th Century*, p. 109.
61. *Father Luke Wadding Commemorative Volume*, p. 409.
62. Persecution of Catholics in Drogheda 1606, 1607, 1611, cited in *Archivium Hibernicum*, Vol. VI (1917), p. 17.
63. B. Jennings (ed.), *The Wadding Papers 1614–38* (Irish Manuscripts Commission, Dublin, 1953), pp. 35–6.
64. *Father Luke Wadding Commemorative Volume*, p. 410.
65. C. Giblin (ed.), *Liber Lovaniensis, a collection of Irish Franciscan Documents, 1629–1717* (Dublin, 1956), p. 13.
66. *Ibid.*, p. 35; see 'An Answer to the questions concerning the Regulars in Ireland, 23 August 1623' in *Archivium Hibernicum*, Vol. XII (1946), p. 99.
67. For example, Sir Christopher Cusack, 4th Viscount Gormanston, directed that if any of his daughters became nuns that each should be paid £15 annually. The 5th Viscount Gormanston, Jenico, also left money for those of his daughters who 'take a religious life'. Later on in the century, in 1686, Robert Barnewall, Lord Trimbleston, was less enthusiastic, for he reduced the dowries of his daughters 'if they profess or become religious'. *Cf. Luke Wadding Commemorative Volume*, p. 408.
68. Report of Robert Boyle to Viscount Dorchester 9 January 1930 (*Historical Manuscripts Commission 12th report, appendix, part 1* (London, 1888), pp. 398–9.
69. *Catholic Record Society*, Vol. XIV (1911) Misc. IX, pp. 19, 21, 24, 34; *Archivium Hibernicum*, Vol. XII (1946), pp. 104–5, 133–4.
70. *Archivium Hibernicum*, Vol. XII (1946), pp. 104–5; 133–5; H. Concannon, *The Poor Clares in Ireland* (Dublin, 1929), p. 7.

71. Archivium Hibernicum, Vol. XII (1946), pp. 104–5.
72. *Liber Lovaniensis, op. cit.*, p. 7.
73. H. Concannon, *The Poor Clares in Ireland*, pp. 2 ff.
74. A.M. Grosart (ed.), *Lismore Papers*, 2nd series (10 vols, London, 1886–8), Vol. III, p. 106; A. Clarke, *The Old English in Ireland* (London, 1966), pp. 39 ff.
75. H. Concannon, *op. cit.*, p. 40; B. Jennings, *Poor Clare Tercentenary Record* (Dublin, 1944), p. 41.
76. Grievances of Archbishop of Tuam, 12 June 1641 in *Cal. S.P. Ire., 1633–47*, p. 309.
77. *Op. cit.*, p. 307, dated 30 June 1641.
78. B. Jennings, *Poor Clare Tercentenary Record*, p. 41.
79. *Ibid.*, p. 150 Viscount Dillon built the convent at Athlone for the Poor Clare nuns; *The Mantle* Vol. XXII No. 3 (1969), p. 34 ff.
80. *Ibid.*, p. 36.
81. A.N. Walsh, 'Irish Exiles in Britanny' in *Irish Ecclesiastical Record*, Series 4, Vol. I (1897), p. 318; Canice Mooney, 'The Golden Age of the Irish Franciscans, 1615–50' in Sylvester O'Brien, (ed.), *Measgra i gcuimhne Mhichíl Uí Chléirigh* (Dublin, 1944), p. 106.
82. F.X. Martin, *Friar Nugent, Agent of the Counter-Reformation* (Rome, London, 1962), p. 265.
83. *Catholic Record Society*, Vol. XVIII (1916), Misc. X, p. 275; Vol. VI (1909), Misc. v. p. 45.
84. *Ibid.*, Vol. XVII (1915), Misc. X. p. 2.
85. *Ibid.*, Vol. VIII (1910), p. 403.
86. *Ibid.*, Vol. XIX (1917), Misc. XI p. 53.
87. *Ibid.*, Vol. XIII (1913), Misc. VIII, p. 44 ff.

12

Women and Protestant Minorities in Eighteenth-Century Ireland

DAVID HEMPTON AND MYRTLE HILL

The social and ecclesiastical turbulence of the English civil wars and the more general emergence of pietist communities throughout seventeenth- and eighteenth-century Europe resulted in many new versions of popular Protestantism in both Britain and Ireland. Although they exhibited considerable theological and organisational diversity, it is possible to identify some common attributes. Their concern to separate themselves from the 'ungodly', for example, even if only as a prelude to a renewed assault on Satan's kingdoms, determined many of their most prominent features. Since their very existence was a form of protest against the wider world, both secular and religious, it was imperative that they asserted their distinctiveness. This was most evident in the enforcement of strict discipline in matters of morality, appearance and general behaviour. Moreover, in their forms of worship there was more emphasis on emotion and experience than on tradition and formality. With greater reliance placed on inner truth than on received dogma, the role of a mediatorial clergy was undermined as that of the laity was simultaneously enhanced. New organisational structures and, in the early stages at least, the lack of suitable meeting places outside the home, encouraged a degree of flexibility which gave women easier access to a range of religious activities.

Thus, Keith Thomas states that 'women were numerically extremely prominent among the separatists' of the English civil war period, and that Quakers had 'more women than men among their recognised ministers'.[1] Similarly, Earl Kent Brown states that women were in a majority, 'perhaps a substantial majority', within eighteenth-century Methodism, an assessment confirmed by recent statistical surveys.[2] Surviving class membership lists of the Moravian community in Dublin in the 1740s tell a similar tale.[3] The purpose of this essay then is to offer some preliminary observations on the role of women within these three religious communities, the Methodists, Quakers and Moravians and secondly to show how women achieved a temporary position of influence in the early stages of the evangelical revival which was not sustained into the nineteenth century when male ministers, trustees and administrators regained full control. Equally revealing of social and religious attitudes in the eighteenth century are the boundaries within which women's influence was permitted, and while these were stretched for essentially pragmatic reasons, they were neither redrawn nor discarded.

Without having accurate information on the proportions of men and women within the established Protestant denominations in this period it is impossible to be certain that by comparison women were substantially over-represented within the smaller sects, but their presence was undoubtedly more visible. Various interpretations have been offered to explain the importance of women in such movements. While eighteenth- and nineteenth-century commentators shared the underlying assumptions of Max Weber's statement that women were especially receptive to 'religious movements with orgiastic emotional or hysterical aspects to them',[4] recent studies have drawn attention to more tangible considerations. Some have suggested that women were attracted into the new sects by the wider scope of activity offered to them by the concept of spiritual equality while others have shown how the moral values of the new religious movements, including temperance, frugality, fidelity and self-improvement, had a daily relevance to women who were concerned for the physical and moral welfare of their families.[5] Moreover, the search for motivation must also distinguish between characteristics based on wider cultural patterns and those specific to gender. For example, although accepted notions of what constituted 'natural' female behaviour helped to perpetuate ideal stereotypes, the characteristics upon which they were built, including zealous expressions of piety, excessive spirituality and emotional responses to evangelical sermons, were common to both men and women in this period. In addition, women are no more a cohesive social entity than men, and a shared gender does not in itself produce a common experience. Criteria such as social status, age and personal circumstances shape religious behaviour as they do other areas of life.

At the topmost level of society, aristocratic patronage and benevolence made an important contribution to the support and diffusion of evangelical principles both inside and outside the churches.[6] Wives, widows and heiresses held strong positions of influence in their own locality – an influence frequently exercised on behalf of a strongly held personal faith. Their considerable

inancial and social advantages were frequently employed on
>ehalf of their favourite religious organisations. The will of Lady
5ophia Ward, whose conversion led to conflict with her father,
:he Viscount of Bangor, reflected her religious commitment, with
1early her whole property being left to religious and charitable
purposes.[7] The financing of new churches or chapels of ease was
an equally important outlet for aristocratic piety. Lady Arabella
Denny founded the Magdalene Chapel in Dublin in 1773 which
was frequented by persons of the highest social rank.[8] For some
years this chapel provided an important venue for preachers
connected to Selina, Countess of Huntingdon, one of the most
prominent early patrons of Calvinistic Methodism. Converted
during a serious illness, the Countess joined with a 'select circle
of women of high station' in prayer and scripture-reading meetings, appointed George Whitefield as her chaplain, and utilised her
resources to send 'popular preachers' on evangelistic trips
throughout the country.[9] Determining that 'poor wicked Ireland'
should have 'a Gospel day', she enlisted popular British evangelical preachers in the Irish cause, sending probationers as well as
ministers when the supply outran the demand. She also founded
a chapel in Plunkett Street in Dublin as a centre for evangelical
preaching.[10]

Lady Huntingdon thus played an important part in establishing the links between British evangelicals and their Irish
counterparts which made Dublin an important centre of lively
religious activity in the late eighteenth century.[11] But though the
Calvinist Methodists were dubbed 'the genteel Methodists', and
despite testimonies of 'many of the higher orders' attending these
preachers, some at least did not meet with the approval of high
society.[12] The 'haranguing' to which some over-zealous
preachers subjected their congregations offended the fine sensi-
bilities of aristocratic churchgoers. An important counterbalance
to such difficulties, and a significant factor in the spread of
evangelical Protestantism, was the wide network of personal
relationships which was particularly striking amongst evangelicals. Links between aristocratic evangelical families formed a
compact but powerful unit which utilised its wealth, prestige and
personal influence in the furtherance of a faith which promoted
personal sobriety and social stability. Links between the Rodens
of County Down and the influential Powerscourt family of
Leinster extended over three generations. Lady Harriet Jocelyn
married into the Massereene family at the end of the eighteenth
century, and the Farnhams and the Annesleys were similarly
connected. The Countess of Huntingdon's daughter married the
Earl of Moira, and the couple regularly opened their household

to Calvinistic preachers.[13] The Countess was also related to th
Reverend Walter Shirley, Rector of Loughrea, an Anglican whos
zealous evangelicalism brought him into conflict with his ec
clesiastical superiors.[14] Thus, intermarriage in high societ
operated not only in the interests of wealth and property, bu
resulted in an extensive social and religious influence spannin
the British Isles.

An even tighter set of social relations, based on a commor
ethnic identity, was evident in the Quaker movement. Althougl
these seventeenth-century immigrants interacted widely with th
wider Irish community – particularly in matters of commerce
their cultural assimilation did not extend to intermarriage.[15] Thei
distinctiveness was reinforced by strict rules of dress anc
behaviour, with an emphasis on simplicity often taken to extre
mes. One young Quaker, for example, noted that her mother'
objection to decoration extended to the display of images or
china.[16] Some Quakers did live in humble circumstances,[17] anc
concern for the welfare of their poor was a central and recurrin
theme in monthly meetings, but their emphasis on literacy anc
education, the simplicity of their life style, and their renownec
independence and industry characterised them as an upwardl
mobile community which made 'a profound contribution to every
aspect of commercial life in modern Ireland'.[18] The papers o
Mary Leadbeater, poet, author, and daughter of a Quaker school
master, reveal a social, intellectual and religious network stretch
ing across Britain, and extending to North America.[19] The reli
gious visits of travelling ministers, granted certificates of 'unity
and concurrence' by their local meeting, kept these groups ir
contact with each other. Such ministers could be of either sex
and Quaker women were also given their own separate sphere:
in other areas, with women's meetings at monthly, quarterly anc
provincial level paralleling those of the men.[20] However, while
women dealt with social and disciplinary matters concerning
their own sex including the relief of the poor, widows and
orphans, the good behaviour, marriage plans and dress o
women and girls, the men's meeting alone had executive authority. Nevertheless, interaction between meetings and the idea o
spiritual, if not executive, equality gave women important roles
to play in this distinctive community.

At all levels of society, women, either individually or as part o
a wider network, played a significant part in establishing links
between religious groups and the communities in which they
were situated. In the early days of a new religious movement, for
example, success or failure was often determined by specifically
practical considerations, and this was an area in which respect-

ible, pious and independent women were especially useful. itinerant preachers needed an introduction into the community, and a place to rest and hold meetings on their long and arduous circuits. Crookshank's *History of Methodism* abounds with examples of the support given and initiatives taken by women in introducing Methodism into the towns and villages of Ireland. In Belturbet, in 1782 Mrs Alice Dawes, a widow, the principal support of Methodism in the town, received the preachers and fitted up a room for their accommodation; the first preaching place in Armagh was rented by Mrs Russell, Mrs Isabella Maxwell and Mrs Jane Justice in 1762, and there are many examples of women inviting preachers to make use of their homes.[21] Such women gave moral support and encouragement as well as practical aid to preachers. They also served as links between rural societies and the Methodist central leadership. Some corresponded with Wesley, for example, to comment and advise on individual preachers. In 1769, Mrs Bennis's request to Conference for the appointment of a specific itinerant to Limerick was noted by Crookshank as 'the earliest instance on record of the voice of the people being heard in connection with a preaching appointment'.[22]

Methodism's concern to draw in those on the periphery of society, the sick, the aged and the distressed, gave official recognition to traditional female duties, and endowed them with a more tangible moral authority. Piety and respectability were more important attributes for sick visitors and class leaders than finance, property or social status. The dynamics of female classes, which often seemed more durable than their male counterparts, provoked comment from many visiting itinerants, and kept the impetus going when initial enthusiasm had died down. Female prayer meetings were also noted as particularly successful examples of piety and devotion.[23]

One Methodist historian suggests that it was as class teachers and even preachers that women really 'transcended the stereotypical roles' of attendants and listeners to become active participants',[24] and it was as preachers that their activities proved most controversial. Although, in practical terms, this became the most contested area of women's contribution, it was not a new phenomenon. In the fifteenth century, the Lollards had proclaimed, 'why should not women be priested and enabled to celebrate and preach like men',[25] and the religious radicalism of the civil war period similarly gave encouragement to female preachers. The concept of spiritual equality was given most expression by the Quakers, with women appearing as the first Quaker preachers in London, in the universities, in Dublin and in the American colonies.[26] Quakers were however an ethnically distinct community. It was with the advent of Methodism that the phenomenon of women's preaching became more socially visible. Since most early Methodist preachers were not ordained, there was no official ban or prohibitive qualifications to deter female enthusiasts.[27] Methodism's flexible structure and overriding concern to spread the gospel message gave rise to a pragmatism which deployed all methods in the interests of moral reformation. This was reflected in Wesley's advice to aspiring female preachers which was cautious, but no different in essence from that given to men.[28] He advised Alice Cambridge, when dealing with critics to

> Give them all honour, and obey them in all things, as far as conscience permits. But it will not permit you to be silent when God commands you to speak; yet I would have you give as little offence as possible; and therefore I would advise you not to speak at any place where a preacher is speaking near you at the same time, lest you should draw away his hearers. Also avoid the first appearance of pride or magnifying yourself.[29]

Women, like men, were therefore regarded as instruments of divine providence to meet exceptional circumstances, an interpretation confirmed by their popularity. Blind and emotional Margaret Davidson drew large crowds with the 'fervour and fluency of her witness',[30] and Alice Cambridge attracted numbers 'amounting to eight or ten thousand persons' on a tour of Ulster at the beginning of the nineteenth century.[31]

However, early acceptance, or at least tolerance, soon gave way to caution and then condemnation, as women's position within Methodism reflected its growing respectability and organisational stability. The 1802 Conference decreed it 'contrary both to scripture and to prudence that women should preach or should exhort in public'.[32] It seems that this decision was not entirely effective, but by the mid-nineteenth century female preaching had had its day in Ireland, and in England also where it had been even more common.[33] In Ireland, it is plain that those preachers who most ardently supported their female counterparts were themselves 'enthusiasts' who frequently found themselves out of favour with an increasingly conservative Dublin leadership.[34] Those women who did continue the practice confined their activities to their own sex. Thus, while Alice Cambridge had addressed mixed congregations in the late eighteenth century, including a regiment of soldiers, together with their wives and children,[35] by the 1830s male followers of Anne Lutton were reduced to dressing in women's clothing in a vain attempt to hear her preach.[36]

Women's preaching should thus be seen as exceptional and transitional rather than officially sanctioned and accepted. Even at the peak of their influence women preachers were seen as itinerant supporters in virgin territory, as with the nineteenth-century overseas missionary movement, and were never accepted as regular preachers to settled congregations. The public activism of strong-willed individuals was only really possible in periods of disruption or innovation. Female Ranters, Congregationalists and Baptists similarly took advantage of hierarchical breakdown in the civil war period, but with the return to social and ecclesiastical stability, these 'anomalies' were removed. In the early nineteenth century, the new generation of Methodists, with property considerations and growing, established congregations, was eager to defend itself from accusations of hysteria and sentimentality. As the movement became more institutionalised and respectable, a denomination rather than a voluntary association, men took over the dominant positions and women again assumed supportive and background roles.[37]

It would also seem that, even when women did participate in religious life at this level, the traditional power structures remained unaffected. Even at the height of their involvement women never really succeeded, or indeed attempted, to alter the conventional relationships between men and women within religious communities.[38] For, while their opponents reviled them for casting off the virtues of their sex, their supporters were equally careful always to refer to them in terms of their womanhood. Thus they were portrayed as either exemplifying or denying their 'nature'. Anne Preston, her supporters said, lived a 'life of feeling'.[39] Alice Cambridge was neat, plain, and greatly opposed to evil-speaking.[40] When speaking of Anne Lutton, the Methodist historian, C.H. Crookshank, felt it necessary to explain how such a woman, 'of respectable parents and trained in fear of the Lord', overcame her 'natural' female reticence:

> Called of God to proclaim to her fellow countrywomen the love of Christ, had she consulted her own feelings merely, her natural diffidence, deep humility, and dislike to prominence would have presented an insurmountable barrier. But, believing that the Lord commanded, she dare not disobey, and He crowned her labours with abundant blessing.[41]

Anne Lutton's correspondence suggests that she shared these sentiments by balancing her deep spirituality and religious zeal with her ideas of the duties of womanhood.[42] The 'essential' nature of woman was thus accepted by both sides as determining the extent and nature of her activities. Modesty and humility precluded any prominent public role, and the predominance of

emotion over reason was regarded as a further limitation of the
value of her contribution. For example, the popular evangelist
Gideon Ouseley, a known supporter of female preaching,
remarked of a young woman preacher that while she was good
at recounting her own experience and blessings, 'her knowledge
was not equal to her zeal, and some of her remarks were confused
and incoherent'.[43] Wesley too felt that the exposition of texts was
a male preserve, requiring logic, reasoning and sustained argument; he advised a woman correspondent:

> With reference to women praying or giving short exhorta-
> tions in public. He advises them to keep as far from
> preaching as they can, never to take a text, and never to
> speak in a continued discourse without some break, above
> four or five minutes.[44]

These perceptions of male and female 'natural' attributes perpetuated the division of roles in areas other than the pastoral
office. Despite the Quaker theory of equality, for example, men's
meetings dealt with matters relating to property, including meeting houses and burial grounds, and with negotiations with the
state and the established church.[45] Generally speaking, matters
of policy, the intricacies of doctrine and public debate were
regarded as male concerns, while teaching, persuading, and
background supportive work were considered more appropriate for
women. It was only with the rise of voluntary religious agencies at
the beginning of the nineteenth century that opportunities in
these areas really opened up.[46] As patrons, fund-raisers, teachers
and energetic field-workers women extended their domestic
sphere to take in Sunday schools, foreign and domestic evangelistic missions, temperance, and Bible and tract distribution. The
various reports indicate that the areas in which their contribution
was most appreciated were teaching, sponsorship, promotion
and persuasion. Working-class men, it seemed, were more willing to purchase Bibles from lady visitors than from their male
counterparts,[47] and teaching rapidly became an acceptable occupation for women in many areas, particularly with the growth
of Sunday schools.[48] It was a leadership role which offered
an important outlay for piety as well as a position within
the community, but one which could also be regarded as an
extension of the traditional domestic duties of guidance and
teaching. A handbook for Sunday school teachers announced
that

> A woman's information influences the present comfort and
> future state of her family; if her house be well-ordered, the
> husband forsakes the ale-house, and where there would
> have been want there is plenty. It is the mother who instructs

the children, to her they look up for all they want, and in general as she is, so are they.[49]

It does seem that it was as wife and mother that women's influence was most obviously disseminated through society, and through which undramatic but pervasive contributions were made to the vitality and spread of popular Protestantism. A member of the Methodist New Connexion indicated the way in which mothers could exercise their power in the interests of their family's moral welfare:

> We must take our children with us on the Sabbath day. All the meetings are needed – public worship, class meetings, the Sabbath school and the prayer meetings; to keep the children fully employed leaving them no time to serve the devil.[50]

Responsibility for the spiritual guidance of the young gave women a degree of moral authority which religious leaders have always stressed as an important element in their campaign for the regeneration of society. But appreciation of this fact has usually been modified by simultaneous assertions of women's inherent weakness and emotional vulnerability, and this perception of the female sex also contributed to the growth of opposition to the Protestant sects. Those hostile to the popularity of itinerant preachers pointed derisively to the enthusiastic female response to their endeavours by suggesting both spiritual and physical exploitation.[51] Since it was almost always the woman of the house who first made contact with itinerants, and consequently she who most often introduced the rest of the family to meetings, this was not simply an academic point. One orthodox minister was scathing about the 'opportunism' of itinerant Methodist preachers, 'having a form of Godliness, they work on the minds of the unsteady and wavering, and of all who are given to change, they creep into houses; they lead captive silly women'.[52] The mob violence which so often accompanied early Methodist activities was frequently related to their success among the women of a family or community. In Fermanagh in 1768 the Henderson family, with a large mob in tow, besieged the Methodist Armstrongs for two days to starve out two preachers who had converted their daughter.[53] There are many such examples of evangelical preachers taking advantage of feminine weakness, and inevitably this was not always confined to mere persuasion.

The private minutes of the Methodist Conference suggests that relations between some itinerants and their female followers reached a degree of intimacy deemed 'unnatural' and unacceptable.[54] The connection between sexual and religious excitement was frequently made by contemporaries, and there is no doubt that some revivalist preachers were charismatic, romantic figures whose rhetorical appeals for submission provoked a less than orthodox response. The emotional nature of conversions, particularly during periods of revival, and the privacy and exclusiveness of class and band meetings added to local suspicions.[55] Dramatic conversion experiences, the intensity of religious ardour, and the repentant sinner's subsequent change of life style – all of which could be interpreted as 'unnatural' – also led to charges of madness, while the success of zealous preachers left them open to accusations of witchcraft.[56]

Clearly, in the context of the wider society, the ability of Protestant sects to attract large numbers of female adherents could have a negative as well as positive effect. Similarly, their emphasis on distinctiveness and separation from the world proved to be both their strength and their weakness. As already suggested, much energy was devoted to matters of dress and behaviour, with an emphasis on simplicity in the former and temperance and piety in the latter. Nor were the strictures of elders or of conferences merely advisory; failure to conform to strict discipline was closely investigated and could lead to expulsion from the Quaker, Methodist or Moravian society.[57]

In theory at least, the sect's distinctiveness and separateness was maintained, and the godly way of life perpetuated, by encouraging members to marry only 'godly' persons or even limiting relations to within the sect itself. The Methodist Conference decreed that parents were 'forbidden to encourage children to marry unawakened persons',[58] while in Quaker society individuals took their marriage plans to both men's and women's meetings for approval.[59] The Moravians at Gracehill, as an enclosed community, were even stricter, with marriage requests brought before the elders before being submitted to the Lot.[60] Religious conformity thus took precedence over social or sexual compatibility. Sexuality obviously created particular problems for these groups, and awareness of the power of sex was met by strict separation of unmarried males and females. Classes for prayer and worship were sexually segregated, and at Gracehill all casual intercourse between the sexes was strictly forbidden. One anecdote, referring to the admonition of a young boy in 1789, illustrates the extent to which this rule was enforced,

> the boy, John Carson, went to Mrs. O'Neill's himself to buy apples. He was called before the College of Overseers and told how sorry we were that he had taken such liberty without telling his labourer or room brother. Such steps lead to ruin![61]

In this same community, single women (always a particularly dangerous and vulnerable group) were not permitted to be seen after dark. It is not difficult to see how such severe strictures could have a negative effect. Whereas between 1776 and 1770 the number of 'single sisters' necessitated the appointment of an extra official to look after their welfare, a year later it was noted that 'many sisters have gone to the world'.[62]

It is difficult to gauge the success or failure of those groups which did not physically remove themselves from the wider society. It is likely that demographical considerations, and the vagaries of human nature, made the imposition of their restrictions extremely difficult, and there was consequently a gap between ideal and reality. Evidence suggests that within the family and the larger community religion could in fact be a divisive rather than a unifying factor, with the degree of conflict directly related to the intensity of faith. Alice Cambridge, following her conversion, reconsidered her relationship with a man 'to whom she was much attached, but who had given his heart to Jesus . . . she at once ended an engagement which was contrary to the Word of God, and could not be accompanied with the Divine Blessing'.[63] A magistrate in Clara, who objected to his wife and daughter attending Methodist services, hired 24 Roman Catholics to beat up the itinerant preacher; his wife, not suprisingly, later left his household.[64] Similar examples of domestic discord abound, especially in the early stages of Methodist penetration into Irish localities.

For those whose religious commitment led to family conflict, however, the class and band meetings of the local Methodist society could offer solace and support. At these gatherings, established members and hesitant newcomers alike could benefit, both from confessing their doubts, fears and sins, and from hearing the experiences of others. These communal soul-barings offered a system of mutual support which enhanced their cohesiveness and strengthened their sense of solidarity as they battled against the values and sins of the wider world.[65] In a parallel study of East Cheshire, Gail Malmgreen suggests that the daily life of the chapel and its close network of 'brothers and sisters in Christ', helps explain its particular attraction for adolescents and young adults and those for whom family relationships were undergoing strain or change.[66] Recent oral evidence from a later period similarly highlights the importance of intimacy and the ethos of 'homeliness' in recreating family virtues in a religious setting.[67]

In conclusion, it is clear that while women were to some extent able to extend their influence and range of activities within popular Protestant minorities, they neither sought nor were offered a fundamental shift in their relations with men. Despite the independence and assertiveness exhibited by some female preachers, the religion they embraced remained firmly conventional. For while evangelical leaders encouraged the participation of women in many areas, it was clear that their moral authority was to be used, not to break down the traditional boundaries, but as an instrument in the regeneration of the wider society. In this process, women did not necessarily regard themselves as victims of male control, but were generally willing participants in a religion which offered both domestic piety and new avenues of public service.

REFERENCES

1. K. Thomas, 'Women and The Civil War Sects' in *Past and Present*, no. 13 (April, 1958), pp. 42–62.
2. E.K. Brown, 'Women of Mr. Wesley's Methodism' in *Studies in Women and Religion*, Vol. II (New York, 1983); G. Malmgreen, 'Domestic Discords: Women and the Family in East Cheshire Methodism, 1750–1830', in J. Obelkevich, L. Roper and R. Samuel (eds), *Disciplines of Faith: Studies in Religion, Politics and Patriarchy* (London, 1987), pp. 55–70; N.F. Cott, 'Young Women in the Second Great Awakening', in *Feminist Studies*, Vol. III (1975), pp. 14–29.
3. Transcript of the Journal of John Cennick, Bristol Archives, Moravian Church House, London.
4. M. Weber, *Sociology of Religion* (London, 1966).
5. Thomas, *op. cit.*, p. 44; H. McLeod, *Religion and The People of Western Europe 1789–1970* (Oxford, 1981), pp. 28–35; See also C. Cross, 'He-Goats before the Flocks' in *Studies in Church History*, Vol. 8 (1972), pp. 195–202.
6. F.K. Brown, *Fathers of the Victorians* (Cambridge, 1961), p. 3.
7. C.H. Crookshank, *Memorable Women of Irish Methodism in the Last Century* (London, 1882), pp. 151–60.
8. A.C.H. Seymour, *The Life and Times of Selina, Countess of Huntingdon* (2 vols, London, 1844), Vol. 2, p. 196.
9. A. Stevens, *The Women of Methodism: Memoirs of Its Three Founders* (London, n.d.)
10. Seymour, *op. cit.*, Vol. 2, pp. 169, 202–27; it was noted by some observers that Lady Huntingdon's preachers, though pious, were not always well qualified. Surprise was expressed, for example, that one had formerly been a coachman. See Rev. Motherwell, *Memoir of Albert Blest, for Many Years Agent and Secretary for the London Hibernian Society* (Dublin, 1843), p. 40.
11. F.E. Bland, *How the Church Missionary Society Came to Ireland* (London, 1935); A.R. Acheson, 'The Evangelicals in the Church of Ireland' (Ph.D. thesis, Queen's University, Belfast, 1967); Proceedings of the Association for the Purpose of Discountenancing Vice and Promoting the Practice of Virtue and Religion (Representative Church Body Library, MS 174).
12. Seymour, *op. cit.*, p. 197.

13. M. Hill, 'Evangelicalism and The Churches in Ulster Society: 1770–1850' (Ph.D. thesis, Queen's University, Belfast, 1987), pp. 379–80.
14. Seymour, *op. cit.*, p. 183.
15. O. Goodbody, *Guide to Irish Quaker Records 1654–1860* (Dublin, 1967); I. Grubb, *Quakers in Ireland 1654–1900* (London, 1927). For an interesting discussion of Quakerism and early Methodism, see G.F. Nuttall, 'Early Quakerism and early Primitive Methodism' in *Friends' Quarterly*, Vol. 7 (1953), pp. 179–87.
16. *The Leadbeater Papers: A Selection From the Mss. and Correspondence of Mary Leadbeater* (2 vols, London, 1862), Vol. 1, p. 128.
17. D.E.C. Eversley, 'The Demography of the Irish Quakers, 1650–1850', in J.M. Goldstrom and L.A. Clarkson (eds), *Irish Population, Economy and Society* (Oxford, 1981), pp. 57–88; see also A. Gailey, 'The Ballyhagan Inventories 1716–1740', in *Folklife*, Vol. 15 (1977), pp. 37–64, 62.
18. D.N. Hempton, 'Religious Minorities', in P. Loughrey (ed.), *The People of Ireland* (Belfast, 1988), pp. 155–68, 164.
19. *The Leadbeater Papers*, Vol. 1.
20. Quaker Records, Public Record Office of Northern Ireland, Mic. 16.
21. C.H. Crookshank, *History of Methodism* (3 vols, London, 1885–1888), Vol. I, pp. 25, 58, 180, 203, 362; see also R. Haire, *Wesley's One and Twenty Visits to Ireland* (London, 1947), pp. 87, 117.
22. Crookshank, *History of Methodism*, Vol. 1, p. 229.
23. Crookshank, *History of Irish Methodism*, Vol. 1, pp. 189, 290–1, 383–4; Vol. 2, pp. 53, 296; Vol. 3, p. 138; and many examples in his *Memorable Women of Irish Methodism*.
24. Brown, 'Women of Mr. Wesley's Methodism'; see also E.K. Brown, 'Women in Church History: Stereotypes, Archetypes and Operational Modalities' in *Methodist History*, Vol. VXVIII (1980), pp. 109–32.
25. R.M. Haines, 'Wild Wittes and Wilfulness: John Swetsock's attack on those poyswunmongers, the Lollards' in *Studies in Church History*, Vol. 8 (1972), pp. 143–53, 152.
26. Thomas, *op. cit.*, p. 47.
27. While some Methodist preachers were ordained Anglican ministers, the ordination of its preachers did not become general Methodist policy until 1816. An indication of the difficulties caused by their ambiguous relationship to the established church can be found in M. Lanktee, *Biographical Narrative* (Belfast, 1836), p. 136.
28. E.K. Brown, 'Women of the Word', in H.E. Thomas and R. Skinner (eds), *Women in New Worlds* (Nashville, 1981), pp. 69–87.
29. Crookshank, *History of Methodism,*, Vol. 2, p. 31.
30. Crookshank, *Memorable Women of Irish Methodism*, p. 67; see also E. Smyth, *The Extraordinary Life and Christian Experience of Margaret Davidson* (Dublin, 1782).
31. Crookshank, *Memorable Women of Irish Methodism*, pp. 191–203; see also J.J. McGregor, *Memoir of Miss Alice Cambridge* (Dublin, 1832).
32. *Minutes of the Methodist Conferences in Ireland*, Vol. 1, p. 152.
33. D. Valenze, *Prophetic Sons and Daughters: Female Preaching and Popular Religion in Industrial England* (Princeton, 1985); W.F. Swift, 'The Women Itinerant Preachers of Early Methodism', in *Proceed-*

ings of the Wesley Historical Society, Vol. XXVIII (1951–2), pp. 89–94; Vol. XXIX (1953–4), pp. 76–83.

34. See letter from Zachariah Taft to Gideon Ouseley, 15 February 1823, (P.R.O.N.I., CR6/3).
35. Crookshank, *History of Methodism*, Vol. 2, p. 153.
36. E. Thomas, *Irish Methodist Reminiscences: Memorials of the Life and Labour of the Rev. S. Nicholson* (London, 1889), p. 10.
37. D.N. Hempton, 'Methodism in Irish Society 1770–1830' in *Transactions of the Royal Historical Society*, 5th series, Vol. 26 (1986), pp. 117–42.
38. Although dealing with a different profession and period, an interesting analysis on the gap between women's access to a profession, and equal opportunities within it, is provided in an essay by J.K. Conway, 'Politics, Pedagogy and Power' in *Daedalus* (1987), pp. 137–52.
39. H. Bingham, *The Life Story of Ann Preston* (Toronto, 1907), p. 33.
40. Crookshank, *History of Methodism*, Vol. 2, p. 31.
41. *Ibid.*, p. 405.
42. Letters of Anne Lutton of Moira; A volume of original letters of 'Holy Anne' Lutton, *c*. 1810–1840. We wish to thank Mr J. Gamble for making this available from his private collection.
43. Ouseley, 22 September 1802 (Ouseley Papers P.R.O.N.I., CR6/3); see also D.N. Hempton, 'Gideon Ouseley: Rural Revivalist 1791–1839' in *Studies in Church History*, Vol. 25 (1988), pp. 203–14.
44. N. Curnock (ed.), *The Journal of John Wesley, Enlarged from Original Ms. with Notes from Unpublished Diaries, Annotations, Maps and Illustrations* (8 vols, London, 1909), Vol. V, p. 306.
45. Goodbody, *op. cit.*, p. 4.
46. The best general assessment of women's involvement in voluntary religious agencies in this period is provided by F. Prochaska, *Women and Philanthropy in Nineteenth Century England* (Oxford, 1980).
47. *Report of the Hibernian Bible Society, 1822* (Dublin, 1822).
48. The Private Minutes of the Methodist Conferences in Ireland, 1794, notes that Sunday schools are to be established (P.R.O.N.I., Methodist Papers, CR6/3); in 1805 the Superintendents of every Methodist circuit were requested to form a Sunday school (*Minutes of The Methodist Conferences in Ireland*, p. 189); see also Sunday School Society for Ireland Records 1809–1971 (Representative Church Body Library, Ms. 182).
49. *Hints for Conducting Sunday Schools; Useful also for Day Schools and Families*, compiled by the Committee of the Sunday School Society for Ireland, (2nd edn. Dublin, 1819).
50. Thomas, *Irish Methodist Reminiscences*, p. 12.
51. J. Walsh, 'Methodism and the Mob' in *Studies in Church History* Vol. 8 (1972), pp. 213–37.
52. *An Address to the Clergy of the United Church in Ireland on the Present Crisis*, by an Aged Minister of the Gospel (Dublin, 1809).
53. Crookshank, *History of Methodism*, Vol. 1, pp. 218–19.
54. Private Minutes of the Methodist Conference in Ireland (Methodist Papers, P.R.O.N.I., CR6/3).
55. Walsh, *op. cit.*, p. 224.
56. C.H. Crookshank, *A Methodist Pioneer: The Life and Labours of John Smith* (London, 1881).

57. Goodbody, *op. cit.*, pp. 16–17; *Minutes of the Methodist Conferences in Ireland*, Vol. 1, p. xiv, Q.6; S.G. Hanna, 'The Origin and Nature of The Gracehill Moravian Settlement 1764–1855. With special reference to the work of John Cennick in Ireland 1746–1755' (M.A. thesis, Queen's University, Belfast, 1964), p. 109.
58. *Minutes of the Methodist Conferences in Ireland*, Vol. 1, p. 152.
59. Goodbody, *op. cit.*, p. 10.
60. Hanna, *op. cit.*, p. 109.
61. *Ibid.*, p. 168.
62. *Ibid.*, pp. 167–8.
63. Crookshank, *History of Methodism*, Vol. 1, pp. 353–4.
64. *Ibid.*, p. 340.
65. S.W. Christophers, *Class Meetings in relation to the design and success of Methodism* (1873); for specific illustrations of the importance of class meetings to hesitant newcomers, see the Early History of Gideon Ouseley, by J. Bonsall (P.R.O.N.I., Ouseley Papers, CR6/3, p. 13) and Crookshank, *History of Methodism*, Vol. 2, p. 14.
66. Malmgreen, 'Domestic Discords'.
67. H. McLeod, 'New Perspectives on Victorian Working-Class Religion: The Oral Evidence' in *Oral History*, Vol. 14, no. 1 (1986), pp. 31–49.

We wish to thank the Economic and Social Research Council for their financial assistance which facilitated the research for this essay.

13

Women and Religious Practice

PATRICK J. CORISH

The aim of this essay is to try to bring into some kind of focus the religious practice of Irish women as the Catholic Counter-Reformation developed into modern Ireland. In the concrete, that should mean trying to look primarily at two groups of people – Irish nuns and Irish mothers. There has always been a certain amount of writing on the Irish nun, and some recent studies are beginning to bring to bear the viewpoint of the late twentieth century on what had been perhaps less critical approaches, but just possibly more religious ones.[1] But the religion of the Irish mother has been rather neglected by historians – curiously, in view of the position of power so widely attributed to her, responsible, it would often be claimed, for all of both the good and evil in her children. In this short essay I would like to take a look at this less explored topic of the Irish Catholic mother. I will venture to overrun slightly the general dateline of 1800. In social and cultural history 1800 is not the decisive turning point so much as the Great Famine, and we are fortunate in having closely focused portraits of two Irish mothers who were young before that catastrophe. On this topic it might be too much to expect anything in the way of definite answers, but it might be hoped to pose a few questions, record a few reflections, and indicate a few directions where research might turn.

The topic is intangible in that historical investigation has to stop short of what religion claims to be really about, namely some kind of relationship between the human and the divine. The easiest historical approach to religion is to study it as some form of social control. This is indeed a very valid approach, so long as its limitations are recognised. The phrase 'religious practices' brings us closer to religion itself, probably as close as history can safely go, but even 'religious practice' will remain to some extent opaque to the historian, who is dependent on what is external-ised and what is recorded. Even externalised religious practice is likely to be heavily under-recorded except in so far as it is expressed in the community structures of what all Christian traditions are agreed in calling 'the Church'. Within these structures, the religious activities of those who did not hold functional office may be expected to be particularly under-recorded, and this of course is true of men as well as women. As a further complicating factor, for most of the time it is impossible to distinguish in any way neatly between religious practices proper to men and religious practices proper to women. As St Paul claimed, perhaps a little optimistically but with basic truth, among Christians there is to be 'neither Jew nor Greek, neither slave nor free, neither male nor female'. And finally, there are under-recorded even among the under-recorded, both men and women: it is a particularly difficult historical task to recover the religious practices of the illiterate poor.

The religious practices which developed out of the Catholic Counter-Reformation expressed themselves under the guidance of a male priesthood and were designed to be heavily concentrated in the parish church. While the Counter-Reformation priest was central to developments in Ireland as elsewhere, the second element – the parish church as the centre of religious practice – came much more slowly. Indeed well into the nineteenth century there were places which had no church at all, and many more where the church building was quite inadequate. This left religious practice centred on the home to an extent quite unparalleled among the Catholic countries of Europe. In Ireland, the great moments that Christians share with all humanity, the 'rites of passage' associated with birth, marriage and death, left the home for the church only through the nineteenth century. The central religious rite of the Catholic Counter-Reformation was the reception of the Eucharist after sacramental penance. Of its very nature it was church centred, but in Ireland it became home centred in the 'stations of confession'. Twice a year, in Lent and Advent, the priest visited designated houses in each district of his parish. The neighbours gathered and he heard their confessions and said mass. The practice seems to have developed naturally out of the conditions under which Irish Catholicism existed in the eighteenth century. Its origins are obscure, but we find it fully developed in the 1770s and 1780s. It had become so deeply rooted in Irish religious life that in parts of the country it resisted the determined attacks of nineteenth-century reformers, and survived into an age when the 'house mass' was once again orthodox and even fashionable.

The enduring strength which Irish Catholicism drew from this 'domestic' quality has been long recognised. It was brought into clear focus by John Bossy in a truly seminal essay, 'The Counter Reformation and the people of Catholic Ireland'.[2] Yet in the curiously tentative way that history makes its progress, we have been slow to draw what might seem to be the obvious inference, that a 'domestic' religion must be a religion very much influenced by women and especially by wives. Bossy makes this point in his major study of English Catholicism, though it seems to take him rather by surprise:[3]

> In *The England of Elizabeth* A.L. Rowse has advanced the view that English Catholicism was founded not in legitimate decisions made by responsible men but in a series of conjugal *coups d'état* mounted by aggressive wives, and allowed to take root because of the feeble resistance offered to their spouses by too many henpecked husbands. Rowse's portrait of a class victorious on the Narrow Seas but defeated in the kitchen and in the nursery is a comic invention of some power; it is surely also to a large degree true.

It would seem to be beyond question true, and it may be that in so far as it assumes the character of 'comic invention' this is due to a certain male chauvinism. As Steven Ozment has pointed out in what turns out to be an ironically titled book, *When Fathers Ruled*, the wife appears as a real partner in sixteenth-century literature, to such an extent that 'it would defy experience to believe that an age which wrote and taught so much about companionable marriage and the sharing of domestic responsibility utterly failed to practice what it preached'.[4]

In Ireland, we have not advanced beyond the stage of being able to point to examples, but the examples are certainly there. In the native Irish tradition, the use of the epithet *bean an tí* for the Blessed Virgin does seem to open up the riches of a *mentalité*:[5]

> Cia an bean do bhí mar Muire
> bean toighe í don uile . . .
>
> Gearr ó gach duine a dhightheach
> ceann guidhe na n-oileithreach . . .

It has often been noted how important the practices of almsgiving and hospitality were to the religious mind of Gaelic Ireland, and surely the religious significance of the *bean an tí* comes through very strikingly in this concept of Our Lady as the 'loaf-kneader' of Heaven: it appears to come close to what a more 'scholastic' approach would call 'mediatrix of all graces'.

The strong women of the Catholic Reformation in the English-speaking towns will have been already referred to, but a few of the most noteworthy may be briefly mentioned here. There was

Margaret Bermingham, daughter of Meath gentry, married to Bartholomew Ball, a wealthy merchant of Dublin, who left her a widow in her early fifties. Her house became a centre of recusancy in Dublin, a school for the education of young people, and a refuge for Catholic priests. She was arrested while a priest was celebrating mass, and both were marched to prison, the priest in his mass vestments. She appears to have been released fairly soon, but was arrested again in 1580, the tense time of the Nugent conspiracy and the Baltinglass rebellion. This time there was no release, and the old woman died in prison, probably in 1584. From two provincial towns just a little later come two women of the same stamp, whose names have been recorded, it is true, because their sons became bishops.[6] Joan Roche of New Ross was mother of John Roche, provided to the bishopric of Ferns in 1624. Those who testified to his suitability recalled his mother, a very devout Catholic, accustomed to give refuge to Catholic priests. Those who testified to the suitability of Thomas Walsh, provided to Cashel in 1626, spoke of his father Robert, who had suffered great persecution because of his recusancy and had died prematurely, and of his widow Anastasia, still alive in 1626, noted for her holiness of life and for the fact that her house was always open to the clergy and to the poor.

No historical revision can depict the devastation suffered in the 1650s by the Old English merchants and gentry as anything other than catastrophe. And yet the more we explore at the grassroots the more we come to realise that catastrophe is seldom complete. A very personal notebook kept by a Catholic bishop of merchant and gentry stock has chanced to survive from the end of the seventeenth century.[7] The bishop was Luke Wadding, of Wexford town and Ballycogley in the barony of Forth. The notebook began as a list of his books and ended up as a kind of last will and testament. Among the many things it tells us about the Catholics of Wexford town as they tried to rebuild after the catastrophe there are very human sidelights on a number of women who were clearly very close to him. His only sister, Nell, predeceased him. His most treasured keepsake was her rosary beads: he took care to note that on his own death it was to go to her sons, John and Frank. A brother, John Wadding, was making a life as a merchant in Drogheda. The bishop willed to his wife 'a fair pair of jet beads each grain having engraved the face of our Saviour'. He noted that he had given 'a fair amber pair from St Malos' to his 'good friend Mary Wiseman, God rest her soul'. It was with Mary and her husband Edward that he had lodged from the time he came to Wexford in 1674 until he was able to buy a house of his own in 1685 when he received a small pension from James II.

Two 'mixed marriages' show how he tried to keep the Catholics Catholic – in both cases it would seem unsuccessfully, for already property was heavily weighted towards Protestantism. A touch of the foreign seems to be associated with 'M. Christian Bor', who gave him 'ten pounds to be distributed [to the poor of Wexford] obliging me to silence which I did during his life, God rest his soul', and his wife, 'Madam Bor', where the bishop noted 'a silver chalice gilt with gold which I lent to Madam Bor I leave' – and then cancelled what followed: 'with her as my token of thanks . . . to her'. Now Christian Bor's father, also Christian, had come to Ireland from the Low Countries in the reign of James I and established himself successfully in business in Dublin. His namesake, a second son, set up in Wexford. His wife, however, was of the 'old stock', Ellen Hore, daughter of Philip Hore of Ballyhogue. The bishop's cancellation of the gift may be connected with the fact their six daughters married into the Protestant landed gentry. Then there was Ellen Bond, daughter of John Bond, also of old stock, who had survived the 1650s and was trying to re-establish himself in the 1660s. She had married John Shapland, a Protestant merchant whose family had settled in Wexford earlier in the century. The bishop willed his gardening tools to her, expecting that she 'will give the use of them to the Catholic priest who will serve as pastor in Wexford', assuming, it would seem, that everyone was interested in gardening. He noted too that the cithern in his possession belonged to 'Mrs Ellen Shapoland'. But the bishop and the lady had more serious concerns than gardens and music. He noted paying the considerable sum of 30 shillings for 'a *Holy Court* from London for Mrs Shapoland', five tomes of baroque spiritually written by the Jesuit confessor to Louis XIII of France, Nicholas Caussin. The marriage of Ellen Bond and the baptisms of her children are, of course, entered in the parish registers of the Church of Ireland, but they are also entered in the Catholic registers, in vain it would seem, for her daughter Elizabeth married Robert Carew in 1710 and brought considerable merchant wealth and the Shapland family name into this landed family which had first established itself in Wexford after the Restoration.

The last paragraphs go to show how easily an enquiry into religious practices can turn into an exploration of social history. Yet it will be obvious that the religious practices of these women, the rosaries, the reading (as well as the *Holy Court* for Ellen Shapland the bishop notes 'small books for Mrs Wiseman') cannot be appreciated unless they are rooted in a social context which fortunately can be supplied for Wexford town just at this time.[8] It is worth lingering over because it is nearly a century before our present knowledge allows a scene to come into such bright and sharp focus again. Yet, as Kevin Whelan has recently remarked of the eighteenth century, 'towns were also host to a Catholic "fifth column" hitherto obscure in the literature – women'. As yet we know next to nothing of them, he admits. All he can do is throw out a few indicators, such as the fact that 2527 of the 2980 members enlisted in the Third Order of St Francis in Wexford town between 1763 and 1824 were women.[9] And it was through this century that the house mass in the form of 'stations of confession' developed, in obscurity and out of dire necessity, fixing Irish Catholicism more firmly in the home and sustaining the role of the *bean an tí*.

What next comes into sharp focus is the organisation of catechesis in the second half of the eighteenth century. Both Catholic and Protestant Reformations had resulted in a 'religion of the book'. For the Catholics, this book was the catechism. In Catholic Europe from the sixteenth century catechesis was associated with the Confraternity of Christian Doctrine, an association of lay Catholics who in addition to the catechism could normally draw on the resources of a lending library of religious books. Because it depended on a stable parish system, it was slow to become established in Ireland. Its formal establishment may be attributed to two men, James O'Keefe, Bishop of Kildare and Leighlin from 1752 to 1787, and Daniel Delaney, appointed his coadjutor in 1783. Conditions were especially favourable in their relatively prosperous diocese, but they were improving everywhere, and the Confraternity spread rapidly. Its catechetical sessions in the chapel every Sunday absorbed but never entirely supplanted the previous pattern, which had been concentrated in the home and in the schoolroom: in 1824 in the parishes of Rhode and Edenderry, for instance, it was noted that

> in the country places, the sexes are taught in separate houses by pious persons, who in general belong to the Confraternity of Christian Doctrine.

Separate instruction of the sexes was an integral part of the system, and it is relevant to note that there was no shortage of suitable catechists, men or women. The woman well instructed in her faith would appear at least as common in the rural parishes of the diocese of Kildare and Leighlin in the 1780s as had been her counterpart in the town of Wexford a hundred years earlier. This is a significant fact, against which must be set the great expansion of congregations of nuns and brothers, beginning with Nano Nagle and the Presentation Sisters. Bishop Delaney himself founded two congregations, the Brigidine Sisters (1807) and the Patrician Brothers (1808).[10]

It would appear then that the new foundations which were to multiply so rapidly were much more in the nature of an organic development than of a 'new departure'. There has been a curious lack of stress on the fact that the better-off Irish Catholics had been sending their daughters to boarding schools kept by the few houses of nuns which had managed to survive in Galway and Dublin through the very difficult decades at the beginning of the eighteenth century, though the 1731 'Report on the state of Popery' quite casually and without any fuss refers to the 'boarding schools' kept by these nuns in these two cities.[11] However, as the new congregation developed, and as an Irish Catholic middle class grew in numbers, the prospect of a convent boarding school education extended itself to the daughters of more and more families. I should like to conclude this impressionistic sketch by looking at two products of the new catechesis and the new convent education, two who went on to become not nuns but mothers, one recalled by her son and the other by her daughter.

The son was Walter McDonald, professor of theology at Maynooth.[12] His caustic memoirs do not spare many of those he mentions, but his mother remained a bright memory. Walter was born in 1854 on a farm of about 100 acres in the very distinctive countryside of south Kilkenny. The fact that his father was an alcoholic threw a very heavy burden on his mother. 'I remember her', he said,

> always at work . . . I remember, above everything else, the reverent care with which she undressed us and put us to bed, reminding us of our guardian angels and how shocked they would be if they saw us do anything unseemly . . . She had been to the nuns in Mooncoin, who certainly trained her well. She kept in touch with them all her life . . . The most potent influence of all, however, was, curiously enough, the wife of a Protestant clergyman named Wills . . who . . . lived quite near . . . Such was my mother. Like my father, she was bilingual, speaking Irish quite as well as English, though we, their children, spoke English only.

Clearly, Walter McDonald saw his mother as at the heart of that 'certain family loyalty, love and pride, with the horror and dread thereby induced of doing anything to disgrace the family or give its members pain'.

The mother remembered by her daughter presided over a more comfortable household – 200 acres of the rich land of east Limerick.[13] Sissy O'Brien was born in 1858. Unlike Walter McDonald, she had a father who was a good and progressive farmer, indeed a bit of a patriarch not only to his own household out to the entire neighbourhood. But again it was the mother who was at the heart of the household:

> I remember my mother with fair hair and wistful blue eyes, she was fairly tall and had a fragile appearance which may have been due to the active life she led. She liked all kinds of work, whether in the kitchen, dairy or garden. I can see her now, sitting quietly at her sewing after a strenuous morning, or arranging flowers on a small altar in 'the children's bedroom, sitting beside a dying person in a poor cabin, binding up the leg of a lamb that had fallen from the rocks.

Sissy's appreciation of her mother deepened as she matured. Speaking of the time between her return from boarding school and her marriage she said:

> In those days I came very near to mother. She showed me a side of her character that I had not hitherto known. The practical, strong and reserved gave way to another, less certain, enquiring, wondering. It was Martha giving way to Mary . . . We dusted the Bible which had lain long unread and learnt the way from Bethlehem to Gethsemane.

Perhaps the most striking thing to emerge is the explicit comparison between her mother and the nuns of her boarding school, where the girls were 'educated by gentlewomen as gentlewomen'. While she felt that much of this was unreal, she was far from disliking the nuns: 'I learnt to respect them for their great goodness. One or two of them I loved'. Nevertheless, 'I knew that living with mother was to learn more of the ways of a gentlewoman than I could learn in a lifetime of convent etiquette'.

The main conclusion of these few impressionistic pages is how much we have yet to learn of that figure of power, the Irish Catholic mother. It should also, I feel, be clear that the learning cannot be rushed, but must emerge as part of a developing social and cultural history. It will be unnecessary to stress that the women who have surfaced in these pages come from the better off. Poorer people are hard to track precisely because they are not vocal. When they do surface it is as observed rather than as observers – the recipients of the catechetical programme as it took shape and reached down to them, for example, or, more immediately, the keenly observed maidservants in *The Farm by Lough Gur*, where catechesis, presumably thorough, seems to have only put a veneer of modernisation over older things: 'Although they were thankful for holydays and went to Mass, they were really more interested in the old Irish world where fairies, witches and banshees took the place of angels and saints'. Making real contact with such people will necessarily be very slow. No doubt folklore should have much to offer, but here as in many other approaches we are only at the beginning.[14]

REFERENCES

1. C. Clear, *Nuns in Nineteenth-Century Ireland* (Dublin, 1987); Tony Fahy, 'Nuns in the Catholic Church in Ireland in the Nineteenth Century' in Mary Cullen (ed.), *Girls Don't Do Honours* (Littlehampton, 1987).
2. Historical Studies, Vol. VIII (1971), 153–70.
3. *The English Catholic Community 1570–1850* (London, 1975), p. 153.
4. Harvard (1983), p. 55. The whole of Ch. 2 (pp. 50–99) is very relevant. It might be noted that the subtitle is neutral: *Family Life in Reformation Europe*.
5. Quoted by D. Ó Laoighaire, 'Mary in Irish Spirituality' in M. Maher (ed.), *Irish Spirituality* (Dublin, 1981), p. 53. See also P. O'Dwyer, *Mary: a History of Devotion in Ireland* (Dublin, 1988).
6. C. Giblin, 'The *Processus Datariae* and the Appointment of Irish bishops in the seventeenth century' in *Father Luke Wadding* (Dublin, 1957), pp. 522–4, 542–4; and p. 162 above.
7. P.J. Corish (ed.), 'Bishop Wadding's Notebook' in *Archivium Hibernicum*, Vol. XXIX (1970), pp. 49–114.
8. To supplement the bishop's 'Notebook' see the fascinating detail in P.H. Hore, *History of the Town and County of Wexford* (6 vols, London, 1900–11), Vol. V, pp. 305–408.
9. K. Whelan, 'The Regional Impact of Irish Catholicism' in W.J. Smyth and K. Whelan (eds), *Common Ground* (Cork, 1988), pp. 260–1.
10. M. Brenan, *Schools of Kildare and Leighlin A.D. 1775–1835* (Dublin, 1935).
11. Archivium Hibernicum, Vol. III (1914), pp. 126, 157; Vol. IV (1915), p. 147. See also Helena Concannon, *Irish Nuns in Penal Days* (London, 1931).
12. *Reminiscences of a Maynooth Professor* (London, 1926).
13. *The Farm by Lough Gur* (London, 1937).
14. See, for example, Pádraig Ó Héalaí 'Popular Morality in Irish Religious Tales' in M. Maher (ed.), *Irish Spirituality* (Dublin, 1981), pp. 71–87.

SECTION III

Family, Household and Health

14

No Scythians Here: Women and Marriage in Seventeenth-Century Ireland[1]

DAVID DICKSON

I

The new wave of research on early modern Ireland has done much to reconstruct the social, economic and intellectual transformation of the island, but although there have been heroic attempts to estimate the growth in population and settlement, regionally and nationally,[2] the prospects for a definitive account of Irish population behaviour in this period remain very poor.[3] The parish register evidence, so magnificently collected and analysed for early modern England and France, barely exists before the late seventeenth century for Ireland; fiscal data predating 1660 are very skimpy and the genealogical evidence from Gaelic and heraldic sources, while offering some promise of demographic information, will take a vast amount of research before it reveals its potential.[4]

The Gaelic genealogies are almost completely silent on women. And, whatever about the future delineation of the actual dimensions of Irish population in the early modern period, without information on the demography on women it is hard to see any line of enquiry that will illuminate the mechanisms of growth or will plot the changes in family structure. This is all the more regrettable as we can be confident that marriage and family composition were not unaffected by the wider world of war, Counter-Reformation, plantation, immigration and the intensification of a market economy.

Contemporary *literary* comment on what constitutes 'population behaviour' is another matter. All the major New English and Old English writers on Tudor and Stuart Ireland wrote colourfully on marriage, on Irish women, and on their success as procreators. MacLysaght, Quinn, Canny and, most recently, Laurence have surveyed various parts of this literature and have demonstrated the derivative nature of much of the writing, its credulous character, the parallel ethnographic writing in other colonial contexts –

North American and Hispanic – and the unquestioned cultural assumptions concerning English civility and the barbarism of all things fully Irish.[5] Some of these elements were truly ancient – forming part of the ideological baggage of Giraldus Cambrensis – but much of what concerns us here first appeared in Camden, Spenser or Moryson: the belief in the natural fecundity of Irish women and their large number of confinements, the ease with which they experienced childbirth, the relatively loose ties of marriage, the youthfulness of women at first motherhood. Such characteristics were presented not just as non-English but as positively non-European. The Scythian origins of the Irish, touched on by Spenser,[6] were being used to explain the cultural primitiveness of Irish women even in the Restoration period:[7]

> The women wear mantles, and a thing like [a] pettycoat round about them and under their mantles a kind of waist-coat, but in summer nothing but a smock of coarse un-whitened cloth which is often so wide that it serves the marryed couple for sheets, the husband creeping into his wife's smock and there being all night. The better sort of women are not distinguished from the meaner but by the fineness of their mantle, or linen, and by the tire of their heads, which is made up high, and capped at top very like that of the Turkish women, and not without reason they being all descended from the ancient Scythians and having many customs like the Tartars, sufficient to shew from whom they both descended . . . . The women generally have easy labours insomuch that they are often known to be brought to bed and go about their business presently after they have washed the child, and seldom lie in above three or four days. They are perfect slaves to their husbands, who will make their wives often carry them on their backs over the water pulling up their coats as high [as] the water comes nor much care they who see them in that posture, no more than in making water which they will come out to do in the street, without any concern.[7]

A very different perspective on Irish women comes from Catholic ecclesiastical sources. The Tridentine decree on marriage, *Tametsi* (1563), had given parish clergy the central role in witnessing and solemnising the match, and placed new sanctions against the arranged marriage. This decree, together with a restatement of the much older canonical prohibition on close marriages, formed the Counter-Reformation reform agenda as far as marriage was concerned. And while it may have taken over two centuries for *Tametsi* to be promulgated and enforced throughout Ireland, this was more because of the delicate position of Catholic priests in officiating at mixed marriages than because of any lay resistance.[8] The evidence of seventeenth-century Irish synodical decrees is in a negative way more telling: enforcement of ecclesiastical marriage regulations was *not* a primary area of concern for bishops, and although repeated references to the obligatory publication of banns to validate a marriage, and to the necessity for clergy to maintain registers of marriages and births suggests areas of omission, the impression is that the fundamentals of Christian marriage as defined by the Catholic Church were being widely observed by 1640, if perhaps not so obviously so in 1600.[9] The several rather sympathetic accounts we have of non-gentry weddings in the later seventeenth century, Rabelaisian affairs with strong clerical involvement, are quite unexceptional by contemporary European standards.[10] Ecclesiastical sources have probably much still to reveal on the degree to which the Counter-Reformation actually modified Irish social conventions; as of now, there seems a real tension between the general literary evidence of early, easy, unpoliced marriage, and the albeit fragmentary pastoral evidence from Catholic sources of a more formal rite of passage.[11]

II

In the recent demographic research on pre-industrial Europe, one of the most strongly based findings has been the discovery that the mean age of marriage for women in western Europe occurred many years after menarche and the arrival of the biological potential for conception. Hajnal, in his famous article of 1965, had speculated on the possibility of the historical existence of a distinctive west European pattern of late first marriage and of high female abstention from marriage (up to 20 per cent of the female population never marrying). By and large, family reconstitution studies in nearly a dozen countries, based on parish registers, have borne out his arguments. The never-marrieds have been found to vary between about 10 and 20 per cent of the population. The miniscule statistical evidence on marriage in eastern Europe suggests a mean bridal age well under 20, whereas the voluminous western European studies of the sixteenth, seventeenth and eighteenth centuries show a bridal age clustering around 25–26 years.[12] The importance of female marriage as a principal regulator of pre-industrial population (far ahead of fertility changes within marriage or of shifts in natural fecundity, for instance) has been emphatically demonstrated in these studies; the relatively late female marriage age in western Europe was the most important factor suppressing high levels of natural increase. A shift downwards of even one year in marriage

age would add the equivalent of a third of a child per family on average, and could make the difference between communal stagnation and population growth.[13]

The literary evidence for Ireland, as we have seen, suggests something positively non-west European in the Hajanal sense. Even Sir William Petty, pioneering an entirely new standard of social enquiry in the later seventeenth century that was inductive and empirical,[14] asserted that Irish women 'could marry upon their first capacity'.[15] Despite all his experiences as a social statistician, surveyor and land speculator, Petty's opinion in this area was not likely to have been formed by careful personal observation. Yet it is thanks to the administrative novelties of the Cromwellian regime in Ireland, Petty's first patrons, that we have some unique evidence on demographic structures in the 1650s.

Social statistics gathered in the wake of a civil war, a plague, and the Cromwellian re-annexation of Ireland are open to immediate objection that they offer peep holes onto a traumatised society, with high mortality and forced migration breaking up households, and institutional and ecclesiastical collapse undermining social and family conventions. Such is hinted at by the Reverend John Lynch, the Galway cleric in exile, in his rebuttal of Giraldus, when he conceded that long drawn-out war produced the greatest immorality.[16] Even the lesser traumas in contemporary England seemed to be connected with a noticeable downturn in population growth, occasioned by an upward movement in bridal age.[17]

This singularity of the 1650s makes it necessary to qualify any generalisation drawn from Cromwellian documentation. Yet such qualms have not stopped historians making profitable use of Boate, the Down Survey, or the '1659' census for example. The land settlement, together with the expulsion of the Catholic clergy and the attempted transplantation, threw up much novel social data, most of which was still extant in the Public Record Office in 1922.

One such document was the marriage register for the barony of Cashel liberties (and adjacent parishes) kept by one of the local JPs between 1654 and 1657: with the collapse of both Catholic Church and Episcoplian administration in 1651–1652, marriage registration was all but impossible until a statute of 1653 was passed which established regulations for civil marriage; JPs were empowered to publish banns and ordered to keep a register of marriages and burials. Apart from data for some Dublin parishes, the Cashel register (published in 1907) alone survives.[18] In the three-year period covered, over 200 marriages were recorded in south Tipperary, the great majority of them, to judge by the names, Catholic. Predating the earliest Catholic register (that for Wexford town) by nearly 20 years, this is the first serial record of Catholic marriages in Ireland. Addresses (but not ages) of the parties were recorded and some idea of the 'marriage field' is given: 24 per cent of the marriages were between partners from different parishes, a rather higher figure than later evidence would lead one to expect. This civil marriage system was evidently operating quite widely: a notice, published by an Ennis JP, announcing the banns for a County Clare couple in 1658 (Owen McConsidin, aged 19, and Una Clanchie, aged 20) survives in the descendants' possession.[19] After the Restoration the older system of ecclesiastical jurisdiction reappeared, with Catholic parties to marriage paying a fee to Church of Ireland ministers, and then being married before a Catholic priest.

A more remarkable if problematic Cromwellian source are the so-called transplantation certificates. These documents were also in the Public Record Office (hereafter P.R.O.) up to 1922, but now only transcripts or published extracts survive to tease us. The certificates were themselves seventeenth-century copies, made for the Revenue Commissioners; the originals were the sworn inventories by persons liable to be transplanted, together with their livestock, from Leinster or Munster to Connacht or Clare, arising from the government decision of October 1652 to clear all proprietors tainted with support for the confederacy from east of the Shannon.[20] Most of these certificates – or 'Shannon passports' – date from the early months of 1653. The P.R.O. copies varied very considerably as to the information they contained, some listing names and addresses of proprietors and the number of their dependants only, others giving crops and stock held by each family or group of families, and a minority giving physical details as to height, hair colour, age, occupation and the family relationship of all persons enumerated. One can assume the originals to have been consistently fuller, for entitlement to land in Connacht was calculated by the Loughrea commissioners on the information certified in these documents.[21] For Leinster counties, about 90 certificates per county were recorded and possibly more for Munster counties.[22] A transplanting proprietor or old freeholder was generally responsible for drawing up a certificate (quite often this might be a widow), and those named within the inventory were relatives, servants or tenants. In some of the extant transcripts, household groups are fairly clearly distinguished, but more often only a long string of names, with or without kin relationships, is given. According to Hardinge's count, made *c.* 1865, 26,444 persons were named in the Leinster and Munster certificates.[23] This may well be an underestimate of the personnel named, but is of course a considerable overestimate of the numbers who actually made the journey into Connacht.[24]

Numerous copies of certificates for three Munster counties in the South survive – Waterford, Tipperary and Limerick – and agricultural data extrapolated from Kerry and Wexford certificates are also extant.[25] In addition, a full transcript exists of a listing of inhabitants, Catholic and Protestant, of the baronies of Upper Cross and Newcastle, County Dublin.[26] This is variously dated by the transcriber as 1650 and 1652; it gives physical, occupational, age and kin-status information in most cases. The Dublin document lists some 3,000 names, but coverage is again inconsistent: for example, children were only included intermittently, a problem that also occurs with the Munster certificates. The circumstances surrounding the compilation of the Dublin survey have not yet been established, but because of the similarity in the type of information gathered, as well as internal evidence relating to particular families (e.g. the Sarsfields of Lucan), it can fairly confidently be assigned to the years 1652 or 1653. For present purposes, the Dublin and Munster documents are treated together.

The filtering of these lists through contemporary and modern transcribers is an obvious source of error. More disconcerting are obvious signs of 'age heaping' that only reflect the original depositions: the pronounced rounding of adult ages – notably around 30, 40, and 60 – presumably reflects the genuine ignorance of many illiterate adults of their age, or at least their lack of concern for precision. But if all persons with ages on the decennial year were to be removed, the sample size would be unacceptably contracted. The data in other words have a lot of 'noise'.

Two examples from the material, both cases where there were female heads of household, give some sense of its uniqueness and of its potential for illuminating family structure. The certificate of Margaret Heally, alias Creagh, relict of John Heally Esq., deceased, City of Limerick, listed 'the said Margaret, adged thirty years; flaxen hair; full face; middle size. Her substance, two cows, three ploughs of garrans, and two acres of barley and wheate sowen. John Neal, her servant, adged twenty-eight years; red haire; middle stature; full face. Gennet Comyn, one of her servants, adged twenty-four years; browne haire; slender face; of middle stature. Joan Keane, servant, adged thirtie-six years; brown haire; middle size; full face; and her little daughter, adged six yeares'.[27] And this can be compared with the first household entered for Dean Rath, County Dublin, which was also headed by a woman, Margaret Bourne: 'Margaret Bourne widow 40,

½,1, yellow hair; Joan Foster her daughter, 19, 4,3/4, yellow; Ann Hunter, servant 30, 5,3/4, brown; Alson Cleere, widow 60, 4½,1, gray; Ann Boylane widow, 26, 4½,3/4, gray'.[28]

The more homogeneous County Dublin surveys give information on 1,136 women and girls, but 204 of them were returned without any indication as to their relationship to the leading name in each group or household. The status of the remainder is summarised in Table 1.

The severe under-enumeration of children (principally the omission of children under 10) obscures perhaps the most interesting finding: the large numbers of unmarried servants, maids etc. in relation to wives and widows, standing at over one-third of the latter categories.

The relatively large number of female servants was no mere adolescent group; such a pool of unmarried women was a major factor affecting community fertility. An age analysis reveals that of the 934 women in the Dublin sample, only 79 per cent of those reportedly aged 30 were married (140 women), 81 per cent of those aged 28 (26 women), 64 per cent of those aged 26 (28), 54 per cent of those aged 25 (35), 48 per cent of those aged 24 (42), 28 per cent of those aged 22 (18), and 23 per cent of those aged 20 (69). The age-heaping, so clearly evident, does not detract from

Table 1. Female family status, County Dublin *c.* 1652 (relationship to leading name)

	Number	Per Cent
Wives	432 ⎫	57
Widows/mothers of leading name	106 ⎭	
Sisters/cousins	53 ⎫	17
Daughters/nieces	106 ⎭	
Maids/servants	197 ⎫	
Nurses, cooks, knitters, spinsters, dairymaids, 'housewives'	29 ⎭	24
Beggars	11	1
	934	

Table 2. Mean age of females, County Dublin *c.* 1652

Wives	33.7
Daughters/nieces	17.2
Widows/mothers	45.8
Maids/servants/nurses, etc.	26.0
Beggars	38.2

the fundamental point that here was no world of teenage brides or of universal marriage; service was responsible both for delaying female marriage and, in many cases it seems, for eliminating it altogether.

A more specific exercise to establish female marriage age is to take the minority of families where children's and mothers' ages were given in these documents. By assuming that the eldest child enumerated here was indeed the first conception and that marriage itself preceded the first-born by about one year, an upper-bound estimate of bridal age can be calculated (where miscarriage, death or migration has removed the first conceived from the reckoning, this will bias the estimated marriage age upwards). By this procedure, based on 103 cases for County Dublin,[29] a mean age of female marriage (reported age of mother (RAM) minus reported age of eldest child (RAEC) less one year) of 23.8 years is suggested and a median age of 23. The preponderance of mother-and-child observations relates to pre-1641 matches (two-thirds of the children were in fact 16 or over). In those marriages where the eldest reported child was 15 or under, a slightly younger mean age (23.0) is suggested. This is against what one might expect: that marital postponement and a fall in fertility would have accompanied the years of war and social breakdown.

This crude method of deriving an approximate age of female marriage has the merit of allowing comparison with the Munster certificates. Only in a small minority of cases (34) are mothers and children with their respective ages given in the Munster certificates,[30] but these are drawn from a socially fairly heterogenous group of families in Limerick, Waterford and Tipperary. Using the identical procedure (RAM − RAEC − 1), a mean age of female marriage of 22.6 is suggested, and a median age just below 22. With such a small Munster sample, it is perhaps rash to put too much emphasis on the disinctly lower Munster age, but it does at least fit in with later seventeenth- and early eighteenth-century evidence when hearth-tax figures indicate that population growth in the southern province was more pronounced than in most Leinster counties. Perhaps more important, however, is the fact that the Munster evidence broadly confirms the Dublin findings: a female marriage age in the 22–23 range which was thus at the bottom end of the west European spectrum, but by no means unique.

In Munster the prevalence of female servants and maids was somewhat less than in Dublin (there are problems in calculating this precisely). Male servants of all ages seem to have played a more central role, at least in the wealthier households in the outh. The median age of female servants is very similar in the two samples – 25 years for Dublin, 26 years for Munster – but age heaping in the case of servants was even more pronounced than in the case of married women.[31]

Another dimension of marriage that can be constructed is the age difference between spouses. In the Dublin sample of 421 marriages, the mean age difference was 6.4 years; in 56 Munster marriages the difference was very similar, 6.8 years. In 82 per cent of Dublin marriages the male partner was the same age or older; the comparable figure for Munster was 77 per cent. The mean difference in age between male and female spouses for Dublin was 5.0 years, compared with 5.4 years for Munster. The gender gap suggested here is high by later standards and if taken at face value suggests an Irish *male* age of marriage which was much closer to the late-20s European norm; such a wide differential contrasts with the modest 2.1 years seniority that English grooms had in the first half of the seventeenth century over their brides.[32]

III

The focus here has been on women and marriage in what were essentially Catholic communities in mid-seventeenth-century Ireland. The few strands of evidence on Protestant patterns in the seventeenth century also point in the direction of relatively early marriage. Gillespie's study of Antrim and Down before 1641 revealed nothing specifically on female marriage age, but his analysis of the age and marital status of male heirs at the time of their fathers' deaths showed that of 24 landed proprietors inheriting at ages up to 24 years, 21 were still single, whereas all 12 inheriting aged 25 or over were married.[33] Morgan's analysis of the late seventeenth- and early eighteenth-century Church of Ireland registers for Blaris, County Armagh, points to an even younger age of marriage for the women in her reconstituted sample than anything found for the 1650s – in the 18–19 range.[34] Eversley's investigation of Irish Quaker families from 1650, constructed on the solid foundations of Quaker genealogical records, has produced particularly striking results: Irish Quaker women were consistently marrying earlier than their English co-religionists and, more relevant in this context, their behaviour was very similar to what is suggested here for their Catholic neighbours: Eversley has calculated a female mean age of first marriage at 23.7 years, 5.0 years less than the mean age of Irish Quaker grooms.[35] The closeness of these results to those reported above is probably fortuitous, but the common pattern of Irish Catholic and Irish Quaker marriage is none the less an indicator

that explanations for the distinctiveness of Irish populatio
behaviour in the seventeenth century must be ecological rathe
than cultural, related to the volatile but expanding economy wit
its colonial and frontier characteristics, not to the archaic prim
tiveness of the indigenous population.

Connell's old assumption that the (presumed) late eighteentl
century take-off of Irish population was brought about by a majc
fall in female marriage age[36] becomes ever more difficult t
sustain as the seventeenth-century evidence on Irish fertilit
accumulates. Beyond reinforcing the case for a relatively low ag
of female marriage long before the Connell period, the 1650
sources have added one new element to the Irish demographi
debate: servants and maids, female and male, were very numer
ous and, it seems, largely celibate in non-gentry households i
mid-seventeenth-century Ireland. Even the 23-year-old brides ca
be assumed to have had some experience in service and, i
County Dublin at least, there were many maids and servant
much older than 23; the tasks they performed were not of cours
primarily domestic (in the modern sense), but craft an
agricultural,[37] although for all their statistical importance w
know precious little about their position in the household or thei
life style. In the eighteenth century unmarried servants an
maids, co-resident with farming families, were less common an
on average younger;[38] this shift towards a predominance o
married non-resident servants, i.e. tied cottiers, is hard to docu
ment directly, but we can assume that the dietary revolutio
associated with the potato, and the new cash income for wome
created by the spread of domestic textile work in the eighteentl
century together played a major part in transforming the natur
of servanthood, bringing forward the possibility of parenthoo
and child rearing for many poorer women and, by extension
contributing to the acceleration of Irish population growth.

REFERENCES

1. I am very grateful to Cormac Ó Gráda and W.S. Macafee who
   commented, in print and otherwise, on the original paper on
   which this chapter is based, 'A Note on the Cromwellian Transplantation Certificates' (1982).
2. L.M. Cullen, 'Population Trends in Seventeenth-Century Ireland',
   in *Economic & Social Review*, Vol. VI (1975), pp. 149–65; W.S.
   Macafee and V. Morgan, 'Population in Ulster 1660–1760', in P.
   Roebuck (ed.), *Plantation to Partition: Essays in Ulster History in
   Honour of J.L. McCracken* (Belfast, 1981), pp. 46–63, 257–9; S. Ellis,
   Tudor Ireland . . . (London, 1985), pp. 40, 50; R. Gillespie, *Colonial
   Ulster: The Settlement of East Ulster 1600–41* (Cork, 1985), Ch. III;
   M. MacCarthy-Morrogh, *The Munster Plantation: English Migration
   to Southern Ireland 1583–1641* (Oxford, 1986), pp. 108–19, 253–60;

A. Sheehan, 'Irish Towns in a Period of Change, 1558–1625' in C. Brady and R. Gillespie (eds), *Natives and Newcomers* . . . (Dublin, 1986), pp. 44–8.

3. M. O'Dowd, 'Gaelic Economy and Society', in Brady and Gillespie, *op. cit.*, p. 124.

4. Gearoid MacNiocaill, *Irish Population before Petty* ([Dublin, 1981]), pp. 7–9.

5. E. McLysaght, *Irish Life in the Seventeenth Century* (Cork, 1939); D.B. Quinn, *The Elizabethans and the Irish* (Ithaca, N.Y., 1966); N.P. Canny, 'The Ideology of English Colonization – from Ireland to America', in *William & Mary Quarterly*, Vol. XXX (1973), pp. 575–98; A. Laurence, 'The Cradle to the Grave: English Observation of Irish Social Customs in the Seventeenth Century' in *The Seventeenth Century*, Vol. III, 1 (1988), pp. 63–84.

6. E. Spenser, *View of Ireland*, quoted in Quinn, *op. cit.*, p. 83.

7. Paper entitled 'Of the Irish', *c.* 1680, (Bodleian Library, Oxford, Locke MS c. 31, ff. 37–9). I am grateful to my colleague Dr Patrick Kelly for drawing my attention to this document, and to the Bodleian Library for permission to quote from it.

8. P.J. Corish, *The Catholic Community in the Seventeenth and Eighteenth Centuries* (Dublin, 1981), p. 15; Corish, 'Catholic Marriage under the Penal Code' in A. Cosgrove (ed.), *Marriage in Ireland* (Dublin, 1985), pp. 72–4.

9. J. Bossy, 'The Counter-Reformation and the People of Catholic Ireland, 1596–1641', in *Historical Studies*, Vol. VIII (1971), pp. 161–2; Corish, *Catholic Community*, pp. 34–5, 69; Corish, 'Catholic Marriage', p. 69. *Cf.* McLysaght, *op. cit.*, p. 50; Laurence, *op. cit.*, p. 72.

10. For an excellent description of a Kildare wedding in the 1680s, highlighting the clerical role, see McLysaght, *op. cit.*, pp. 357–9. *Cf. ibid.*, p. 345; Corish, *Catholic Community*, pp. 94–5.

11. Even Catholic outsiders such as Rinnucini's aide, Dean Massari, could be a rather credulous witness: Massari wrote in 1645 of the very large families in Ireland, 'some have as many as thirty children, all living: not a few have fifteen or twenty . . .' (see *Irish Times*, 29 August, 1979).

12. J. Hajnal, 'European Marriage Patterns in Perspective', in D.V. Glass and D.E.C. Eversley (eds), *Population in History* (London, 1965), pp. 101–43; M. Flinn, *The European Demographic System 1500–1820* (Brighton, 1981), pp. 27–8, 124–7; M. Anderson, *Population Change in North-Western Europe 1750–1850* (London, 1988), pp. 49–51; Wally Seccombe, 'The Western European Marriage Pattern in Historical Perspective . . .', in *Journal of Historical Sociology*, Vol. III, 1 (1990), pp. 50–74.

13. Macafee, 'Pre-Famine Population in Ulster: Evidence from the Parish Register of Killyman', in P. O'Flanagan, P. Ferguson and K. Whelan (eds), *Rural Ireland: Modernization and Change 1600–1900* (Cork, 1987), p. 160.

14. For the empirical basis of some of Petty's population estimates, see T.C. Barnard, 'Sir William Petty, his Irish Estates, and Irish Population', in *Irish Economic & Social History*, Vol. VI (1979), pp. 64–9.

15. C.H. Hull (ed.), *The Economic Writings of Sir William Petty* (Cambridge, 1899), Vol. II, p. 608.

16. (Rev. John Lynch), *Cambrensis Eversus* . . . (?St Malo, 1662), quoted in McLysaght, *op. cit.*, pp. 48–9.

17. E.A. Wrigley and R.S. Schofield, *The Population History of England, 1541–1871: A Reconstruction* (Cambridge, 1981), p. 232.

18. J. Mills (ed.), *The Register of the Liberties of Cashel 1654–57* (Parish Register Society of Dublin, Exeter, 1907). *Cf.* St J.D. Seymour, *The Puritans in Ireland 1647–61* (Oxford, 1921), pp. 93–4.

19. A photocopy of this is in the National Library of Ireland, MS 25,017.

20. J.P. Prendergast, *The Cromwellian Settlement in Ireland* (3rd edn, Dublin, 1875), Ch. IV; R. Dunlop, *Ireland under the Commonwealth* (Manchester, 1913), Vol. II, pp. 474–5; R.C. Simington, *The Transplantation to Connacht, 1654–58* (Dublin, 1970), pp. vii–xiv.

21. Prendergast, *op. cit.*, pp. 103–6.

22. This calculation is extrapolated from figures given in J. O'Hart, *The Irish and Anglo-Irish Gentry when Cromwell Came to Ireland* (Dublin, 1884), pp. 328–58.

23. Simington, *op. cit.*, p. xxvii.

24. P.J. Corish, 'The Cromwellian Regime', in T.W. Moody, F.X. Martin and F.J. Byrne (eds), *A New History of Ireland, Vol. III: Early Modern Ireland, 1534–1691* (Oxford, 1976), pp. 361–70.

25. Transcripts (in whole or in part) of transplantation certificates can be found in the following: King's Inns Library, Dublin, Prendergast MSS, Vol. I, pp. 660–72, 678–82; P.R.O.I. Co/451 (newspaper cuttings of a number of certificates published in the *Dungarvan Observer*, July 1915, by R.C. Simington); Prendergast, *Cromwellian Settlement*, pp. 179–81, 363–76; M.A. Hickson, *Selections of Old Kerry Records*, 2nd series (London, 1874), pp. 32–5; W.P. Burke, *History of Clonmel* (Waterford, 1907), pp. 85–6; P.H. Hore, *History of the Town and County of Wexford* (London, 1911), Vol. VI, pp. 502–3; St J.D. Seymour, *The Diocese of Emly* (Dublin, 1913), pp. 220–2.

26. The Tenison Groves copy (P.R.O.I. MS 2467) is in pencil and now in a somewhat delicate condition; an accurate and more robust copy of Groves' transcript exists in P.R.O.N.I. (T808/15038A). The Tenison Groves copy (in slightly rearranged form) is currently being published by R. M. Flatman in *The Irish Genealogist*. The original MS was mentioned in the *Eighth Report from the Commissioners . . . respecting the Public Records of Ireland* (London, 1819).

27. Prendergast, *Cromwellian Settlement*, pp. 369–70.

28. P.R.O.N.I. T808/15038A, p. 35.

29. Cases where the mother's age at the presumed first conception turned out to be below 14 years or above 40 years have been eliminated (although their inclusion would make little statistical difference).

30. Cases have been excluded as in the Dublin document (see Note 29).

31. The mean age of female servants in Munster was 30.5 years, in Leinster 26.0 years.

32. R.M. Smith, 'Population and its Geography in England 1500–1730', in R.A. Dodgshon and R.A. Butlin (eds), *An Historical Geography of England and Wales* (London, 1978), p. 217.

33. Gillespie, *op. cit.*, pp. 53–4, 225.

34. Macafee and Morgan, *op. cit.*, p. 56.

35. Eversley, 'The Demography of the Irish Quakers, 1650–1850', in

J.M. Goldstrom and L.A. Clarkson (eds), *Irish Population, Economy and Society: Essays in Honour of the late K.H. Connell* (Oxford, 1981), p. 65. Note that Eversley found that the age of Irish Quaker women at *first* marriage was 22.7, with the 5-year gender difference remaining as in the case of all marriages.

36. K.H. Connell, *The Population of Ireland 1750–1845* (Oxford, 1950), p. 53. Connell never explicitly argued for a high female age of marriage before the 1770s, but it was an integral part of his model.

37. On servants and their demographic implications elsewhere, see A. Kussmaul, *Servants in Husbandry in Early Modern England* (Cambridge, 1981), Part I; Hajnal, 'Two Kinds of Pre-industrial Household Formation', in R. Wall (ed.), *Family Forms in Historic Europe* (Cambridge, 1983), pp. 92–9.

38. L.M. Cullen, *The Emergence of Modern Ireland 1600–1900* (London, 1981), p. 83.

15

Life after Death: Widows in Carrick-on-Suir, 1799

L. A. Clarkson and E. Margaret Crawford

Demographers have long been aware of two features of pre-industrial European communities shared with their post-industrial counterparts. These are that women commonly outnumber men and a large part of the female surplus is composed of widows. Today society provides for widows in a variety of ways ranging from pensions to old people's homes, Saga Tours to voluntary support groups, as well as through paid employment and the network of nuclear and extended families. But how did widows survive in eighteenth-century Ireland? There were 662 of them in Carrick-on-Suir in 1799, out of a population of just under 11,000, and an examination of their lives may provide an answer.

This essays falls into three parts. The first examines the main demographic features of widowhood in Carrick. The second considers the social groups in which widows lived and worked: their place in families and households and their position in society at large. Finally we explore the ways by which widows made their livings or, in the case of non-working widows, survived at a time when governments, national and local, provided almost no support for socially and economically vulnerable members of society.

I

The basic facts about widows in Carrick-on-Suir[1] are set out in Table 1. The absolute number of widows in the town made them a significant category. Even more striking, though, was that from the age of 20 widows formed one-fifth of the adult female population and outnumbered the number of single women (635). From age 60 onwards, widows constituted more than two-thirds of the female population. Almost one house in three contained at least one widow and every third person living in a house was a widow.

The youngest widow in Carrick was aged 20 and the oldest 98;

Table 1. Widows in Carrick-on-Suir, 1799[2]

Total number of widows in the population	662
Widows as a percentage of the whole population	6.1
Widows as a percentage of the female population	11.4
Widows as a percentage of females aged 20 plus	20.3
Widows as a percentage of females aged 60 plus	67.7

the average age was 53.5 years, although this particular statistic may be distorted by age heaping – the practice of declaring ages at round figures such as 40, 50, 60, etc. Table 2 presents the age of widows by five-year cohorts, both as originally given and also adjusted for heaping.[3] Whatever figures are used, it is clear that for widows in general life began at 40. Only 14 or 15 per cent of widows were aged between 20 and 39.

An examination of the age structure tells us something about the duration of widowhood. More than half of all widows were under 55 and some of these had obviously become widows at a still earlier age. The female crude death rate in Carrick has been calculated as 39.7 per 1000 and life expectancy at birth as 25.2 years. These demographic characteristics imply that women still alive in their early fifties could expect to live, on average, for another 15 or 16 years.[4] For many women, therefore, widowhood lasted longer than their experience of married life.[5]

The ages recorded in the census also hint at another characteristic. Collectively widows may have been more innumerate, more

Table 2. Age of widows in Carrick-on-Suir, 1799

Age	Unadjusted		Adjusted	
	Number	Per cent	Number	Per cent
20–4	6	0.9	6	0.9
25–9	19	2.9	20	3.0
30–4	31	4.7	29	4.4
35–9	37	5.6	43	6.5
40–4	88	13.2	72	10.9
45–9	61	9.2	74	11.2
50–4	79	11.9	72	10.9
55–9	71	10.9	83	12.5
60–4	137	20.7	104	15.7
65–9	33	5.0	58	8.8
70–4	50	7.6	43	6.5
75–9	26	3.9	30	4.5
80–4	18	2.7	17	2.6
85+	6	0.9	11	1.7

illiterate and poorer than married women. This hypothesi
emerges from the different patterns of age heaping apparen
among widows and married women, and from a consideration o
the reasons why heaping occurs in the first place.

The degree of age heaping can be shown by employing ar
index measuring the extent to which declared ages of adults aged
between 23 and 62 were concentrated on the nought and five
points. The index runs on a scale of 100 (no heaping) to 500 (tota
heaping).[6] Table 3 shows that heaping in Carrick was consider
ably greater among widows than among married women. The
simplest way of interpreting Table 3 is to say that almost half o
the ages declared by married women aged between 23 and 62
were concentrated on the nought and five points whereas for
widows the proportion was three in five.

Age heaping arises from two principal causes. The first, which
produces an error more properly described as age shifting, is the
deliberate declaring by an individual of an older or, more usually,
a younger age. Such deceit was noted by Morton Pitt, one of the
compilers of the Carrick census, who commented somewhat
ungallantly that 'many . . . especially females, were desirous of
representing themselves as younger than they were'. The second
reason is that in innumerate societies where there is no civil
registration of births, ages are frequently declared in round numbers.[7] An inability to count is often taken by demographers as a
proxy for illiteracy, and illiteracy interpreted as a sign of poverty.[8]

Which of these two reasons – deception or ignorance – explains
the high degree of heaping among widows in Carrick? Super-
ficially we might suppose that they shifted their ages downwards
in order to present themselves as desirable candidates for remarriage. But the supposition is not really sustainable. According
to Table 3 young widows indeed lied vigorously about their
ages, but those in their thirties and early forties abandoned the
strategy, only for it to be taken up again by women aged 45 and
over and adopted most enthusiastically by 60-year-old widows.
As a device for attracting husbands one would have thought that
age shifting would have had greater appeal for the under forties
than the over sixties. In any case such strategies were wasted on
three married census takers, a soldier, a gentleman and a school
master seeking demographic information and not brides.[9]

The main cause of age heaping among all women, whatever
their marital status, was in the words of Major Pitt, 'the inaccu-
rate knowledge a very large part of the lower classes, especially,
had of their ages . . .'. But why should widows be more innumerate than married women? Was it because they were chiefly from
the lower classes? There are no firm answers to these questions

Table 3. Index of age-heaping in Carrick-on-Suir, 1799

Age point	Married women	Widows
25	127	141
30	254	306
35	205	210
40	318	322
45	205	263
50	310	328
55	201	240
60	244	339
Population 23–62	240	298

but if we assume that women from the poorer ranks of society ran a greater risk of becoming widows than wealthier women because the age-specific mortality of their husbands was higher than that of the husbands of socially superior women, then we are some way towards an answer.[10] A further possibility is that when better-off women became widows they enjoyed greater opportunities to remarry than poor women.

Unfortunately evidence of remarriage is extremely sparse. James Ryan, who lived in Carrick and kept a chatty diary between 1787 and 1809, noted just six widows remarrying in the period. His catalogue of matrimonial events, though, is more eclectic than complete.[11] One of Ryan's references was to the marriage in April 1799 of 'the agreeable Mrs Hurley' to Mr James Power, a brewer. The groom in question was probably the brewer listed in the census as living in Waterford Road North, in Carrick Beg, aged 33. His wife, Ellen, was 25 (is this what made her agreeable?). Working in the house as a servant was one Patrick Harney aged 12. The surnames, Hurley and Harney, are sufficiently similar to make one suspect that either Ryan or the census taker had made a mistake with the names and that Ellen and Patrick were sister and brother-in-law. (Another possibility is that the former Mrs Hurley was engaging in age shifting of a particular extravagant kind and was really in her thirties and that Patrick was her son by her first marriage.)

Studies of remarrying widows in other communities are not much help. In the Berkshire town of Abingdon remarriage seemingly became less common between the sixteenth and eighteenth centuries; women of wealth and property were more likely to shun remarriage than poor women and were more able to survive economically without husbands. Similarly, in sixteenth century East Anglia it was poorer widows who had the greater incentive to remarry and the wealthier ones were more likely to remain widows. On the other hand, in the small Normandy town of Auffay at the end of the eighteenth century those widows most prone to remarry were those possessing property or jobs. Auffay was a textile town and cotton spinning provided women with employment. As domestic spinning declined in the first half of the nineteenth century so did the incidence of remarriage.[12] Carrick was also a textile town and at the end of the eighteenth century its industry was in decline and remarriage may also have been becoming more difficult.[13]

A further potential barrier to remarriage for all widows was the number of dependent children they had to support. The 662 Carrick widows had a total of 701 resident children; 304 widows had no children living with them. This does not mean, of course, that they were childless, merely that their children were not at home. The distribution of children among widows is shown in Table 4(a).

Nearly half of the widows with children at home had only a solitary child but at the other extreme one widow was left with a brood of eight. Part (b) of Table 4 shows the number of widows'

Table 4. Widows with resident children
(a) Distribution of children among widows

Number of children	Number of widows	Per cent
None	304	45.9
1	175	26.4
2	93	14.0
3	46	6.9
4	29	4.4
5	8	1.2
6	4	0.6
7	2	0.3
8	1	0.15

(b) Widows' children by age

Ages of children	Number of children	Per cent
10 and under	207	29.5
11–17	194	27.7
18 and over	300	42.8
Total	701	100.0

children by age. The groupings are based on an arbitrary judgment that up to the age of 10 children were a drain on the family budget, from 11 to 17 they contributed roughly the same as they cost to maintain, and from the age of 18 they made a net contribution to family income. On this basis more than a quarter of widows' children were an economic burden. Even more strikingly, the 207 children under 11 were shared among 150 mothers; over one-fifth of widows, that is, were left with one or more costly children.

Some widows with children did, of course remarry. Mrs James Ryan, for instance, triumphed over considerable odds in November 1787 when she married Mr Kennedy the subconstable:

> she has but 10 children by her former husband, and he 3 step-children by his former wife, and these 10, making in all but 13 step-children! tis remarkable his two wives were the widoes of 2 men that were killed.[14]

One further statistic is worth pondering. Widows outnumbered widowers by almost four to one; there were only 172 widowed men in Carrick. The discrepancy might be explained in a number of ways. For example, it could be that adult males experienced higher age-specific mortality than females. However, the reverse was almost certainly the true position, for during the age range 15–45 women ran a high risk of dying in childbirth.[15] A second possibility is that widowers moved away from Carrick in large numbers, or perhaps that widows came into the town from elsewhere. Many men migrated temporarily from Carrick at the end of the eighteenth century to the Newfoundland fisheries, to the army and navy, and to work in England, and there were presumably widowers among their number. We know nothing about female migration into Carrick, although some women, including widows, may have been attracted by the prospect of employment in the woollen industry or as domestic servants.[16] But the whole female population aged between 20 and 60 was only 26 per cent bigger than the male population, so migration clearly cannot explain more than a small fraction of the excess of widows over widowers. Most of the surplus, surely, was caused by the greater propensity of men to remarry. Apart from any obstacles to the remarriage of widows created by dependent children, the relative abundance of adult females in Carrick made the chances of remarriage greater for men than for women.

The proportion of widows in the Carrick population appears to be high compared with elsewhere. According to Peter Laslett widows accounted for 8.7 per cent of the female population of 100 English communities between 1574 and 1821.[17] Continental comparisons also suggest that the proportion of widows in

Carrick was high.[18] Turning to Ireland, there were 78 widows in Armagh in 1770 out of a population of 1948. They constituted just over 7 per cent of the female population and 17.3 per cent of the adult women.[19] In Lisburn in 1820–21 143 widows can be identified among a female population of 2914 (4.9 per cent). This is certainly too low a figure but the population listing does not permit a more accurate enumeration. Widows accounted for about 14 per cent of household heads, which was broadly comparable to the proportions found in Armagh and Carrick.[20]

How do we explain the high proportion of widows in Carrick? Just as high male mortality and emigration rates cannot explain satisfactorily the large number of widows in the town compared with widowers, so they cannot account for abundance of widows in Carrick compared to other communities. Further explanations have to be sought in the social groups in which widows lived and how they made their livings.

II

With the exception of 13 widows residing in Wadding's poor house – established by Thomas and Richard Wadding for 'destitute persons of the R.C. religion'[21] – all widows lived in domestic groups of some kind. Figure 1 summarises the size of these domestic units, based on a random sample of 300 of the widow population.

The most significant feature of Fig. 1 is that over one-quarter of all widows lived in domestic groups of 10 or more people; indeed, 9 per cent of widows lived in housefuls of at least 15 people. At the other extreme barely 10 per cent of widows lived in social groups containing fewer than four persons. The most common size was six and the mean houseful size was 8.00 which was significantly larger than for the population as a whole (6.27).

At this point we need to pause to explain the meaning of some technical terms. Historians of social structure have evolved a hierarchical classification of domestic groups into 'family', 'household' and 'houseful' in an attempt to escape from the ambiguities attaching to these seemingly simple words. The definitions fit together like a set of nesting dolls.[22] At the centre is the family, a grouping distinguished by kinship and location. The simple family (also known as the nuclear or conjugal family) consists of a married couple with resident offspring, or a widowed person with offspring, or a married couple without resident children. A widowed man or woman living without resident offspring does not, by him or herself, constitute a family unit. Children living away from home are not, on this definition, part of the simple family.

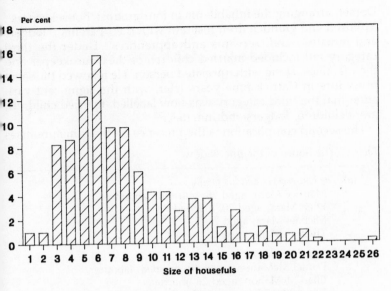

Figure 1. Proportion of widows living in housefuls

Simple families may be extended by the presence in the house of relations beyond the immediate conjugal group. Grandparents living in the same house are an upward extension, grandchildren a downward extension. Uncles and aunts form a lateral extension. Co-resident married brothers or sisters, with their own spouses and offspring, create a multiple family household.

Turning now to the household, this is a dwelling containing a person living alone, or a group of people not evidently related, or a simple or extended family, or a family supplemented by another person or persons, such as servants and apprentices, who contribute in some way to the household economy. To the distinguishing features of the family – kinship and location – is thus added the further characteristic of function. We might also include lodgers as part of the household since, presumably, in return for their board and lodging they made a contribution to the household budget.

The introduction of lodgers, however, raises two complications. The first is that lodgers were often related to the household head, although not part of the conjugal group, but not identifiable as relatives on population listings. This point was appreciated by contemporary observers of pre-industrial societies, not least by Morton Pitt, one of the compilers of the Carrick census. In 1790 he listed the population of his home town of Corfe Castle in

Dorset, arranging the inhabitants in four groups: 'housekeepers', 'children and grandchidren resident with their parents', 'lodgers and inmates', and 'servants and apprentices'. Under the third category Pitt included married children of the housekeeper and their families, along with unrelated person. He followed the same procedure in Carrick nine years later, with the significant variation that the third category was now labelled 'married children, grandchildren, lodgers and inmates'.[23]

The second complication is the presence on the same premises

Table 5. The house of the one widow

(a) *The housekeeper and his family*
Maurice Mara, aged 28, married, labourer
Ellen Mara, aged 20, married
Michael Mara, aged 2
Thomas Mara, aged 0

(b) *First lodging family*
Daniel McMahon, aged 40, married, labourer
Ellen McMahon, aged 26, married
James McMahon, aged 12
Winifred McMahon, aged 9
Daniel McMahon, aged 3

(c) *Second lodging family*
Dennis Hiffernan, aged 50, married, labourer
Johana Hiffernan, aged 30, married
John Hiffernan, aged 7
James Hiffernan aged 5
Patrick Hiffernan, aged 2

(d) *Third lodging family*
ANN COOK, aged 38, widow
Margaret Cook, aged 8
David Cook, aged 4

(e) *Fourth lodging family*
John McDonagh, aged 48, labourer, married
Mary McDonagh, aged 48, married
Annabella McDonagh, aged 24, single
Mary McDonagh, aged 16, single
Henry McDonagh, aged 8
James McDonagh, aged 6

(f) *Fifth lodging family*
Catherine Lewis, aged 26, single
Jillen Lewis, aged 19, single

(g) *No family*
Catherine Cavanagh, aged 22, single

Table 6. The house of the two widows

Housekeeper:	Bridget Walsh, aged 30, widow
Child:	Bridget Walsh, aged 2
Lodger:	Mary St John, aged, 60, widow

of other families in addition to that of the housekeeper but not obviously related to one another. Do these lodging families and the housekeeper's family form a single multi-family household or should they be regarded as entirely separate households located in a single dwelling? The point is relevant in Carrick where several of the large three-storey houses had been divided into tenements at the end of the eighteenth century and inhabited by two or more families.[24] It is to describe such an arrangement that the word 'houseful' has been coined, meaning 'all persons inhabiting the same set of premises'.[25]

Some examples will help to illustrate these definitions and demonstrate the complexities of domestic arrangements. In Carrick-on-Suir as a whole there were 10 907 people in 1799 living in 1738 houses, giving a mean *houseful* size of 6.27. However, the estimated mean *household* size – derived by splitting the houseful into separate family households – was 4.66, implying 2341 households. There were therefore approximately 1.3 households per house, although precise numbers depend on how we draw the boundaries around the various households in a particular house.[26]

The largest houseful containing a widow had 26 people in it although only one of them, Ann Cook, was a widow. It was composed as shown in Table 5. There is no evidence that these families were related in any way although they may have been. In terms of the definitions set out above we have here a houseful containing six family households plus Catherine Cavanagh as a lodger with one of the families.[27] We do not know whether the families shared anything more than the same premises. All the employed men were labourers but we cannot infer from that that the economy of the house rested on a collective effort.

A much smaller houseful, although containing two widows, is provided by our next example in Table 6. There are three ways of viewing this domestic group. It is obviously a houseful, but what else? If Mary St John were the mother of Bridget Walsh, then it was also an extended family consisting of mother, grandmother and child. If, on the other hand, Bridget and Mary were unrelated, then it was a conjugal family (mother and child) with a lodger, forming one household.

A final example (Table 7) considers a houseful of 16 people, five of whom were widows. This houseful presents some particularly ticklish problems of interpretation. The housekeeper, Ellen Noonan, might have been related to one or more of the other women in the house. She might, for instance, have been the mother of Ellen Barry, or alternatively of Ellen Kennedy (there are shared Christian names), and perhaps also of Mary and Catherine Hanrahan and Anne Neale. Catherine Hanrahan was probably the sister-in-law of Andrew Hanrahan, i.e. the widow of Andrew's deceased brother. If all these suppositions are correct we are looking at a houseful composed of a household containing a family extended vertically and laterally plus a couple of young children who seem to belong to nobody. If none of them be correct, the houseful was an amalgam of three households, one containing a solitary widow (a 'no family household'), one containing a family extended laterally, and the third consisting of a single nuclear family. The four 'no family' females could have been scattered throughout all three households or concentrated in one.

These examples could be multiplied extensively to reveal the complexities of domestic groupings in Carrick; but they all

Table 7. The house of the five widows

(a) *The housekeeper*
        (1) ELLEN NOONAN, aged 60, widow
        (no children apparently resident)

(b) *First lodging family*
        Andrew Hanrahan, aged 30, married, carrier
        Mary Hanrahan, aged 30, married
        William Hanrahan, aged 10
        Bridget Hanrahan, aged 1
        Andrew Hanrahan, aged 0
        (2) CATHERINE HANRAHAN, aged 32, widow
        Honora Hanrahan, aged 2

(c) *Second lodging family*
        William Kennedy, aged 50, married, boat builder
        Ellen Kennedy, aged 30, married
        Catherine Kennedy, aged 0

(d) *No family*
        (3) ANNE NEALE, aged 40, widow
        (4) MARY BRENNAN, aged 32, widow, charwoman
        (5) ELLEN BARRY, aged 26, widow
        Anty Maddock, aged 6
        Mary Sheary, aged 3

Table 8. Position of widows in families, households and housefuls

Position	Per cent
Head of houseful	28
Head of lodging household	25
Kin	13
Lodgers	30
Servants	4

demonstrate the more important point that widows were intimately integrated into the fabric of society.

Bearing in mind the difficulties of drawing precise boundaries within the houseful between families and households, Table 8, above, (based on all 662 cases) summarises the position of widows in the domestic groups. The distinction between kin and lodgers is particularly blurred and the proportions in the table are very approximate indeed. To put Table 8 into perspective, it should be remembered that widows headed 15 per cent of all households in Carrick (*households*, not housefuls), a proportion roughly similar to that found in other contemporary communities.[28]

We have already noted that very few widows in Carrick lived by themselves. Comparisons with other communities suggest that the solitary widows may have been more common elsewhere. In Armagh in 1770 widows were much more likely to live by themselves than in Carrick, or with dependent children or unrelated persons but not with other kin. In the small Normandy town of Auffay in 1796 a quarter of all widows lived alone and only 20 per cent lived with kin other than their dependent children. In Preston in 1851 22 per cent of widows lived either alone or with unrelated people and only 8 per cent with kin other than their children; in rural Lancashire in the same year the proportions were 35 per cent and 18 per cent.[29]

Carrick, unlike Armagh, was a desperately crowded town and the shortage of accommodation encouraged lodging and sharing. As in Preston half a century later, the textile industry may also have increased the extent of co-residence, although, paradoxically, in Auffay the employment opportunities offered by the cotton industry helped women to live by themselves.

III

The discussion has led us away from social groupings to a consideration of the ways whereby widows survived. It is already obvious that the great majority of widows found support among

their kith and kin. When we examine their employment pattern
(Table 9) it becomes even more clear that they depended vitall
on their families for their daily bread.

At first sight it appears that most widows relied on othe
people for their livelihoods since only 20 per cent of them had a
identifiable occupation. Nevertheless, the proportion of widow
in work was substantially higher than that for all women whicl
was only 15 per cent. Even so, there was apparently a smalle
proportion of working widows in Carrick than in Armagh where
30 years earlier, 32 per cent of widows had occupations.

The difference between Carrick and Armagh is probably mor
apparent than real since a large number of the widows listed o
the Carrick census without occupations was, in fact, engaged i
the manufacture of woollen cloth, either as employees of clothier
or, more likely, as unpaid family workers. In 1799 around 20 pe
cent of the adult population of Carrick was employed in th
woollen industry, including between 1100 and 1300 female
working as carders and spinners, none of whom were recorde
by the census takers as in employment. Probably, therefore
around 200 widows made their livings as carders and spinners.[3]

One or two widows were more prominent in the woolle
business, working, for example, as clothiers and responsible fo
the organisation of production and the marketing of the cloth
These included Mary Cahill, a 70-year-old widow who wa
matriach of a houseful comprising four males and six females
one of the males was a wool comber and one of the females wa
a servant. Mary Cahill may have been related to Edward Cahil
(perhaps his sister-in-law) who conducted a large cloth busines
in Carrick. Catherine McEniry, a clothier who subscribed to the

Table 9. Occupations or status of widows

Occupation or status	Frequency	Per cent
No stated occupation	498	75.2
Textiles	11	1.7
Dress	12	1.8
Food processing, selling	15	2.3
Drink processing, selling	17	2.6
Retailing	28	4.2
Domestic, personal service	42	6.3
Other	8	1.2
Lady	2	0.3
Pauper	29	4.4
	662	100.0

ıew Catholic chapel in 1804, was probably also a widow,
ılthough the Carrickman's diary is vague on this point. Another
ɔrominent widow was Honora Hayes, aged 56, who combined
he businesses of dyer and corn dealer. It is tempting to identify
ıer as the widow of James Hayes, proprietor of Hayes Quay,
_arrick, who died in December 1798. A son, William – 'without
ɛxception the best informed young man in Carrick' – had died in
November 1796. He, in turn, had introduced carding machines
nto Carrick.[31]

Mrs Cahill, Mrs McEniry and Mrs Power were widows carrying
ɔn their husbands' businesses; this was the most common route
for women into skilled trades in pre-industrial communities.[32] A
ɔarticularly prominent inheritor was Ellen Russell, aged 50, who
ƙept a shop in Main Street with the assistance of a clerk, two male
ƙervants and two female; the male servants were almost certainly
ƙhop workers. Ellen's husband, Garrett, had died in 1789, 'much
ƙegretted . . . much esteemed', leaving her with a son, also
_arrett, aged five, and a daughter, Anne, aged four. In April 1804
Mrs Russell was forced to close the shop for a week. At the time
there was a desperate shortage of acceptable coin throughout
Ireland which brought about a virtually complete stop of inland
trade and this was the probable cause of Mrs Russell's difficulties.
Two years later she was committed to Clonmel jail for debt,
prompting James Ryan, the Carrick diarist, to remark, 'wonder-
ful, tis well known there was [sic] no three shops in Carrick these
30 years did half the business as hers'.[33]

Not all widows were as fortunate as Mrs Russell in inheriting
ƚhe business interests of their husbands. By a will made in
February 1764, Alexander Reiley, a linen weaver (an unusual
ɔccupation for Carrick), left his wife Margaret £100, a house, a
feather bed, hangings, a table, chairs, the use of a chest of
drawers, a desk, small tea cups, saucers, tongs and tea spoons.
To his son, when of age, went 'all his substance, cash, leases,
goods, bills, notes'. His nephew was to get £12 and two linen
looms.[34] We simply do not have sufficient evidence for Ireland
to judge whether this was a usual arrangement, but it existed in
many variations in England from the Middle Ages to the nineteenth century.[35]

The great majority of widows, though, could probably expect
to receive very little from their husbands. Apart from those
widows employed in the woollen industry, they most commonly
worked as charwomen, washerwomen and petty traders such as
pedlars, hawkers and hucksters. We occasionally find a more
substantial trader such as Mrs Russell or her next door neighbour,
Mary Green, a tobacconist. The food and drink sellers – corn and

meal dealers, bread women, beer sellers, lodging house keepers
etc. – were also in a small way of business, except possibly fo
Mrs Ellen Quirk, a publican who had a clerk and a servant to help
her. Widows working in the clothing trades included dress
makers, seamstresses and mantua makers.

What of the widows who had no job? Perhaps there were really
no such creatures except among the very elderly and infirm, and
most widows had some task in the household economy, even i
it was only to look after grandchildren while the parents attended
to earning a living. But this is only another way of saying that
widows relied on other people, usually their relations, for their
day to day survival. They were a sizable number. Assuming that
200 of the 498 widows shown in Table 9 as having no occupation
were actually working as carders and spinners, we are still left
with almost exactly half of all widows in Carrick who apparently
had no employment. The burden of their upkeep weighed
heavily on a community afflicted by high food prices and a
woollen industry in distress.[36]

For 29 widows even the family support failed; these were the
ones recorded on the census as paupers. Most of them were
elderly – 17 were aged 70 or over – and 13 lived in Wadding's
poor house. The remainder depended on private charity which
they received in their own homes. Money for the purpose was
found in various ways. In January 1796, for example, the parish
priest of Carrick Mor preached a charity sermon which raised £44.
It was an eucumenical affair: 'there were many present of
different persuasions, and most of the collectors were of the
Church of Ireland'. In 1802 Mr Joseph Hearn, 'of charitable and
christian memory', bequeathed £500 to the poor of Carrick – and
12 warm riding coats to 12 poor men – to be administered by the
parish priest.[37] It is debatable whether the fact that fewer than 5
per cent of widows were living on charity in 1799 is an indication
of how little charity there was available in Carrick or whether it
was a measure of the ability of families to care for their own.

IV

The purpose of this essay has been to consider the economic and
social condition of widows in one Irish community at the end of
the eighteenth century. Given the nature of the evidence some
of the findings are conjectural but the broad picture is reasonably
clear. There seems to have been an unusually large proportion of
widows in Carrick. We have suggested that purely demographic
reasons cannot explain this but have argued that, essentially, the
social and economic structure of Carrick made it a safe haven for
widowed women. The town was large – by Irish standards – and

it had a busy woollen industry, although in 1799 it was poised on the edge of a calamitous decline. Nevertheless, there were jobs, either for the widows themselves or for their families, which provided them with the means to live. The social groups in Carrick – the housefuls – were large and quite complex. Widows therefore found their niches among their kith and kin. Perhaps this is not a very surprising conclusion, but it is worth knowing.

REFERENCES

1. Throughout this essay Carrick (or Carrick-on-Suir) refers to the twin communities of Carrick Mor in County Tipperary and Carrick Beg in County Waterford, separated by the river Suir but joined since medieval times by a bridge.

2. All the statistical evidence relating to widows in Carrick and all the household details come from a census taken in 1799. The original is in the British Library, Additional MS 11722. The document is discussed in L.A. Clarkson, 'The Demography of Carrick-on-Suir, 1799' in *Proceedings of the Royal Irish Academy*, Vol. 87, C, no. 2 (1987), pp. 13–36. The census has been analysed using the statistical package for the social sciences (SPSS).

3. To cope with the severe age heaping present in Carrick sophisticated smoothing techniques are required that cannot be applied to the truncated age distribution of widows. We have therefore adjusted the size of the widow cohorts derived from the original data proportionally in line with the adjusted size of the cohorts of all women obtained by smoothing the whole population. These adjustments are discussed in Clarkson, 'The Demography of Carrick-on-Suir, 1799', pp. 16–17. For a consideration of age heaping in general see H.S. Shryock and J.S. Siegal, *The Methods and Materials of Demography* (condensed edn E.G. Stockwell, New York, 1976), pp. 115–17; R. Pressat, *The Dictionary of Demography* (ed. Christopher Wilson, Oxford, 1985), pp. 4–5.

4. Clarkson, 'The Demography of Carrick-on-Suir, 1799', pp. 30–1. The estimates of crude death rates and life expectancies are based on the model life tables in A.J. Coale and P. Demeny, *Regional Model Life Tables and Stable Population* (Princeton, NJ, 1966).

5. For a consideration of the duration of marriage in pre-industrial societies see L.A. Tilly and J.W. Scott, *Women, Work and Family* (New York, 1978), pp. 28–9.

6. The index used here is the Whipple index which is described in Shryock and Siegel, *op. cit.*, pp. 115–17. See also Clarkson, 'The Demography of Carrick-on-Suir, 1799', p. 16.

7. Clarkson, 'The Demography of Carrick-on-Suir, 1799', p. 16; Shryock and Siegel, *op. cit.*, pp. 115–17; Pressat, *op. cit.*, pp. 4–5, 7.

8. E.g. by C. Ó Gráda, 'Across the Briny Ocean: Some Thoughts on Irish Emigration to America, 1800–1850' in T.M. Devine and D. Dickson (eds), *Ireland and Scotland 1600–1850* (Edinburgh, 1983), p. 122.

9. The soldier was Major William Pitt, the gentleman Mr Francis White and the schoolmaster Patrick Lynch. See Clarkson, 'The Demography of Carrick-on-Suir, 1799', pp. 14–15. Major Pitt's wife was described by Dorothea Herbert, daughter of the rector

of Carrick, as 'a dashing fashionable piece' (D. Herbert, *Retrospections* (new edn, Dublin, 1988), p. 379).

10. Embedded in this conjecture is yet another assumption, that age-specific mortality among males was higher than among females in the post-reproductive age cohorts. The Irish evidence is more tantalising than conclusive, but see R.E. Kennedy, *The Irish: Emigration, Marriage, and Fertility* (Berkeley, California, 1973), pp. 56–60.

11. P. Power (ed.), 'A Carrickman's Diary 1787–1809' in *Journal of the Waterford and South-East of Ireland Archaeological Society* (hereafter cited as *JWSEIAS*), Vol. XVI (1913), pp. 81–5. The Carrick parish registers might cast some light on remarriage, but a detailed analysis has so far not been possible.

12. B. Todd, 'The Remarrying Widow: a Stereotype Reconsidered' in Mary Power (ed.), *Women in English Society 1500–1800* (London, 1985), pp. 54–92; Margaret Spufford, *Contrasting Communities: English Villagers in the Sixteenth and Seventeenth Centuries* (Cambridge, 1974), pp. 113, 116–17; G.L. Gullickson, *Spinners and Weavers of Auffay* (Cambridge, 1986), pp. 166–77.

13. L.A. Clarkson, 'The Carrick-on-Suir Woollen Industry in the Eighteenth Century' in *Irish Economic and Social History*, Vol. XVI (1989), p. 31.

14. Power (ed.), 'A Carrickman's Diary, 1787–1809' in *JWSEIAS*, Vol. XVI (1913), p. 81.

15. Clarkson, 'The Demography of Carrick-on-Suir, 1799', p. 29. See also Tilly and Scott, *Women, Work, and Family*, pp. 28–9.

16. Clarkson, 'The Demography of Carrick-on-Suir, 1799', p. 27.

17. P. Laslett, 'Mean Household Size in England since the Sixteenth Century' in P. Laslett and R. Wall (eds), *Household and Family in Past Time* (Cambridge, 1972), p. 145.

18. See P. Laslett, 'Introduction: the History of the Family' in Laslett and Wall, *op. cit.*, pp. 74–5; A.M. van der Woude, 'Variations in the Size of the Household in the United Provinces of the Netherlands in the Seventeenth and Eighteenth Centuries' in Laslett and Wall, *op. cit.*, p. 313; Peter Laslett and Marilyn Clarke, 'Houseful and Household in an Eighteenth-century Balkan City. A Tabular Analysis of the Listing of the Serbian Sector of Belgrade in 1733–4' in Laslett and Wall, *op. cit.*, p. 382.

19. These figures come from 'A List of the Inhabitants of the Town of Armagh for the Use of his Grace the Lord Primate' compiled by the Rev. Dr William Lodge in 1770 and kept in the Armagh Public Library (G/5/20). It is analysed in L.A. Clarkson, 'Household and Family Structure in Armagh City, 1770' in *Local Population Studies*, no. 20 (Spring, 1978), pp. 14–31. Because of the structure of the document it is not possible to offer any precise calculations based on age cohorts.

20. The Lisburn figures come from local census compiled in 1820–1 by the Rev. Dr Cupples, the Church of Ireland rector and now in the Public Record Office of Northern Ireland, D10/1. The document is discussed in L.A. Clarkson and Brenda Collins, 'Proto-industrialization in an Irish Town: Lisburn, 1820–21' in Pierre Deyon and Franklin Mendels (eds), *La Protoindustrialisation: Theorie et Realitie*, VIIIth International Congress of Economic History (Budapest, 1982), tome 1, section 8.

21. S. Lewis, *A Topographical Dictionary of Ireland* (London, 1837), Vol. I, p. 277. Lewis refers to the founders as Thomas and Richard Wadden, but the name Wadding is still clearly inscribed over the door of the existing building.

22. The following account is based on Laslett, 'Introduction' in Laslett and Wall, *op. cit.*, pp. 28–39.

23. R. Wall, 'Mean Household Size in England from Printed Sources' in Laslett and Wall, *op. cit.*, p. 166. The Corfe Castle listing is reproduced, in part, in Osamu Saito, 'Who worked when: lifetime profiles of labour force participation in Cardington and Corfe Castle in the late eighteenth and mid-nineteenth centuries' in *Local Population Studies*, no. 22 (Spring, 1979), pp. 18–19. For the headings in the Carrick census see Clarkson, 'The Demography of Carrick-on-Suir, 1799', p. 34.

24. P.C. Power, *Carrick-on-Suir and its People* (Dun Laoghaire, 1976), p. 82. The division is also evident from the 1799 census.

25. Laslett, 'Introduction' in Laslett and Wall, *op. cit.*, p. 36. 'Premises' is further defined as 'accommodation provided by a building, or . . . a number of conjoined or contiguous buildings . . .'.

26. Clarkson, 'The Demography of Carrick-on-Suir, 1799', pp. 34–6.

27. The McMahon family, incidentally, illustrates some of the difficulties of interpreting the information in the census. Ellen is presumed to be the wife of Daniel McMahon but if her declared age (26) is correct she is very young to be the mother of John McMahon (aged 12) and possibly also Winifred (aged 9). Among the possibilities we have to consider are: (i) that she did indeed marry at the age of 13 or 14; (ii) that the declared ages are wrong; and (iii) that she is the second wife of Daniel McMahon and the stepmother of John and (perhaps) Winifred. If so, Daniel McMahon is an example of the remarrying widower.

28. Clarkson, 'The Demography of Carrick-on-Suir, 1799', p. 35.

29. Clarkson, 'Household and Family Structure in Armagh', pp. 16, 27–9; Gullickson, *Spinners and Weavers*, p. 175; Michael Anderson, 'Household Structure and the Industrial Revolution; Mid-Nineteenth-Century Preston in Comparative Perspective' in Laslett and Wall, *op. cit.*, p. 225.

30. L.A. Clarkson, 'An Anatomy of an Irish Town: the Economy of Armagh, 1770' in *Irish Economic and Social History*, Vol. V (1978), pp. 31–2; Clarkson, 'The Carrick-on-Suir Woollen Industry in the Eighteenth Century', p. 34.

31. Clarkson, 'The Carrick-on-Suir Woollen Industry in the Eighteenth Century', p. 36; Power (ed.), 'A Carrickman's Diary' in *JWSEIAS*, Vol. XV (1912), pp. 62–5, 133, 135; Vol. XVI (1913), p. 78.

32. See, for example, M. Prior, 'Women and the Urban Economy: Oxford 1500–1800' in Prior (ed.), *Women in English Society*, pp. 93–117.

33. Power (ed.), 'A Carrickman's Diary' in *JWSEIAS*, Vol. XV (1912), pp. 68, 131; Vol. XVII (1914), p. 124. For an account of the currency in 1804 see F.W. Fetter, *The Irish Pound, 1797–1826* (London, 1955), pp. 48–9.

34. I.R.B. Jennings, 'Old Wills (diocese of Waterford and Lismore)' in *JWSEIAS*, Vol. XVII (1914), p. 80.,

35. See the survey by E.P. Thompson, 'The Grid of Inheritance: a

Comment' in J. Goody, J. Thirsk, E.P. Thompson, *Family and Inheritance: Rural Society in Western Europe 1200–1800* (Cambridge, 1976), pp. 326–60.

36. Clarkson, 'The Demography of Carrick-on-Suir, 1799', p. 33; Clarkson, 'The Carrick-on-Suir Woollen Industry in the Eighteenth Century', pp. 31, 40.

37. Power (ed.), 'A Carrickman's Diary' in *JWSEIAS*, Vol. XV (1912), p. 136; Vol. XVI (1913), p. 22.

16

Women in the Domestic Linen Industry

W. H. CRAWFORD

Over these centuries in Ireland the preparation and spinning of both woollen and linen yarns by women in their own homes provided a major source of employment and income for many families. Women processed raw materials not only for the weaving of clothes and household furnishings for the Irish market but also for profitable export as yarn to thriving English textile manufacturing regions. Just as English wool had been exported to Flanders in great quantities by the twelfth and thirteenth centuries to supply the thriving textile industry there,[1] so Irish linen and woollen yarns were being exported to several regions of England by the sixteenth century.[2] By the end of the seventeenth century exports of wool and woollen yarns accounted for more than half the value of Irish exports to England and linen yarn for one-eighth. Because England could not produce sufficient yarns to service its own textile industries it had to pay good prices to attract yarns from Ireland. Although wool declined to less than 20 per cent by the mid-1720s it was replaced as a money earner by linen: whereas exports of linen yarn as a percentage of total exports peaked with worsted yarn before 1720, linen cloth provided two-thirds of the value of Irish exports as late as 1788.[3] In spite of this export trade Ireland was still able to clothe its people although it has to be admitted that most of the finer quality cloths were imported from England and the Continent. By the close of the eighteenth century, too, Ireland was producing at least one-third of all linens woven in the British Isles.

Although the woollen and linen trades in Ireland were both very important for Irish society and the economy, they developed in very different ways. The old nationalist tradition that the woollen industry suffered because the linen industry was promoted about 1700 by the London and Dublin governments at its expense, has been disproved. In general the home market continued to be dominated by Irish woollen cloth whereas the bulk of Irish linen was sold in the much more competitive English market along with large quantities of Irish linen and woollen yarns. Towards the close of the eighteenth century, however, as the home market came under heavier pressure from English industrialists, the Irish woollen industry was severely affected and hand-spun yarns became a thing of the past while the linen industry only survived by itself industrialising.[4]

In Ireland, as elsewhere, the domestic woollen industry had readily adapted to a 'putting out' system because it was possible for middlemen to buy up the raw material and prepare it for wage or piece-workers. By contrast the structure of the linen trade in Ireland made it difficult for middlemen to secure and exercise similar domination. The basis of this structure was confirmed by a clause in an act of 1719 (6 Geo I, c. 7) that declared:

> All linen-cloth and yarn shall be sold publicly in open markets or at lawful fairs, on the days such markets or fairs ought to be held, or within two days next preceding such fair-day; and all linen yarn shall be sold publicly at such markets or fairs without doors, between eight in the morning and eight in the evening; and if any person shall sell or expose to sale any such cloth or yarn except as aforesaid, all such cloth and yarn shall be forfeited.

Although this clause would have enabled middlemen to buy up flax for spinning into yarn, or yarn for weaving into linen, it acted as a strong encouragement both for those families who grew flax to convert it into yarn for sale in the public market, and for weavers to grow their own flax or purchase it in the yarn markets. Those weavers who could grow their own flax, have it prepared and spun by their own families, and weave it themselves, were liable to profit most in the public markets, especially if they were able, like those living in the Linen Triangle, to weave the finer quality linens. The system of public markets flourished and expanded with the support of the bleachers who had come to dominate the industry in the second half of the eighteenth century: they believed that if the linen markets were properly run with sealmasters to inspect the quality of the linens, they could obtain there for their bleachgreens the variety of linens that they needed to meet their orders from England.[5] The competition engendered by this system of marketing promoted independence among the weavers and their families and constrained them to organise the resources of the family to produce webs of cloth for the market.

Flax has always required an abundance of cheap labour and provided work for the whole family. Even the preparation of land was labour intensive. Flax usually followed a well-manured potato crop that put the land into good heart and cleansed it of weeds. After the land was ploughed several times to produce a good tilth, women picked up any remaining clods of earth and stone and dumped them at the foot of the banks that enclosed the fields. They weeded the crop by hand and when it was ripe they worked with men to pull it, a job that was very sore on their hands. With men they rippled it to save the seed. It was, however, the men who placed it in the lint-dams for retting so that the woody core of the flax stems could be softened. Working in the lint-dams was not women's work, perhaps because it was a very heavy and dirty job where women's clothing would have rendered them ineffectual as well as immodest. After the removal of the flax from the dam by the men, it was the women who spread it to dry, a process known as 'grassing'. Then the flax was ready for scutching to extract the fibre from its casing. Women beat it with a wooden 'beetle' to fragment this casing and then other women hung the flax over a block of wood and struck away the broken straw with long wooden blades.[6] The remnants of the straw, known locally as 'shives' or 'shous', were removed by passing handfuls of the fibre through an implement known as a 'clove'.[7]

The economic value of this work was calculated by several respondents for Arthur Young when he was touring Ulster in the summer of 1776. About this table, drawn up for him near Armagh, Young was careful to note:

> If let to a man who should farm flax, the labour would be much higher, as it is here reckoned only at the earning, which they could make by the manufacture, and not the rate at which they work for others.

The essence of Young's argument is that flax was an expensive crop to grow if labour had to be paid for, because fieldwork costs had to compete against spinning wages.

In the second half of the eighteenth century the scutching of flax had been mechanised using water power to turn the scutching blades in scutch mills. As a result flax was taken to the scutch mills where men carried out all the scutching processes. The employment of men in mills was traditional, probably because the operation of corn mills and tuck mills (for finishing locally produced woollen goods) could require considerable physical strength to manage cumbersome machinery or move heavy weights and bags. Many men were available for employment after the end of the grain harvest whereas women would be busy spinning yarn. Although it was reckoned about 1800 that a scutch mill serviced by men and boys could do more work than a dozen women,[9] it is probable that flax intended for the making of fine

Expense of an acre of land under flax[8]

Rent	£0	14	0
Seed bought from 10s. to 13s. a bushel, average 12s. : 3 bushels	1	16	0
One ploughing	0	7	0
Carrying off the clods and stones by their wives and children, 6 women, an acre a day	0	2	2
Weeding, 10 women an acre in a day, 4d.	0	3	4
Pulling by women and children, 12 at 4d.	0	4	0
Rippling by men and women, say 4 men at 10d.	0	3	4
Laying it in the water according to distance, say	0	5	0
Taking it out and spreading	0	5	0
Taking up, drying and beetling, 42 women a day at 4d.	0	14	0
Scutching 30 stone at 1s. 1d.	1	12	6
Total	£6	6	4
30 stone at 4s. 2d.	6	5	0

linens was scutched and hackled at home. Young was told in Portadown:

> In general they scutch it themselves and it is cheaper than the mills. Mr. Workman has paid 1s. 6d. for it by hand, and 1s. 1d. to the mills, and found the former cheaper; more flax from hand and much cleaner.[10]

This was said to be quite a common practice even as late as 1870.[11] Skilful hand scutching and hackling greatly reduced the amount of waste and best prepared the flax for spinning. For hackling it was reckoned worthwhile to employ a skilled craftsman and there were said to be many itinerant hacklers. One commentator remarked about the use of the hackling pins for combing out the fibres: 'The most experienced hands only attempt to work the finest hackle, which is very close, and a nice matter to perform well.' Spinning, however, was women's work. Many stories were told about the skill of famous women spinners and some of their achievements are recounted by McCall in the third edition of his book *Ireland and her Staple Manufactures* (Belfast, 1870): some specimens said to be much inferior to the finest yarns produced half a century earlier were awarded prizes at the Great Exhibition of 1851.[12]

Ireland had a long tradition of skill in spinning. In 1636 Lord Deputy Wentworth had observed that Irish women were 'naturally bred to spinning' and in 1673 Sir William Temple added: 'No women are apter to spin it well than the Irish'.[13] It was the ask of successive governments to enforce standards that would guarantee the length of the yarn exposed for sale. By an act of 1705 (2 Anne c. 2) flax yarn was to be reeled on a standard reel 2½ yards in circumference with 120 of these threads in a cut and 12 cuts in a hank so that each hank contained 3600 yards; four hanks made up a spangle. The act proved very difficult to enforce. In 1723 even the possession of unstatutable yarn was made a punishable offence but as late as the 1780s the transgression persisted.[14] The Linen Board as early as 1717 had regulated and patronised spinning schools to propagate skills and precepts throughout the country[15] but as early as 1724 it was decided that no more schools should be allowed in Ulster, except for the county of Fermanagh only, because 'the art of spinning had made so great a progress in the province of Ulster'.[16] Nevertheless, spinning was carried on in the 'charter schools' provided by the Incorporated Society for Promoting English Protestant Schools in Ireland, and provided much of the finance required to maintain the children and their teachers.[17] While the domestic spinning industry provided many families with an income or a supplement to it, it required them to meet government regulations and commercial standards. As women learned that they could earn more for quality yarns, output of them increased. Arthur Young noted that spinning and weaving for cambric (such as was used for making handkerchiefs) was being carried on around Lurgan.[18] Within 30 years it had spread to the surrounding towns of Lisburn, Banbridge, Tandragee and Dromore.[19] In 1822 the comment was made

> In the north of Ireland . . . the object of every person who has flax, is to have it of as fine quality as he can; and the spinner's object is to spin it as fine as they can, because it pays a better price; and the manufacturer's object is to weave the finest linen that he can; for which reason, the coarse article in the north of Ireland is made only of the refuse of the flax.[20]

Of every stone of flax that emerged from the rough hackling process it was reckoned that about a quarter could be spun into the fine yarn needed for the finest webs whereas about a half was fit to be woven into a medium quality linen. The remainder of the yarn, known as tow, was hackled again and spun into tow yarn that was woven and made into work shirts.[21]

Although it was the family that was idealised in contemporary literature as the unit of production, it would have been more accurate to talk in terms of the household. Many families employed and lodged in their homes young men as weavers and unmarried women or widows as spinsters. They required them

to carry out other duties in the house and around the farm. I
his tour through the northern counties of Ireland in the summe
of 1776 Arthur Young commented regularly on this phenomenon
South of Derry city he found: 'The spinners in a little farm ar
the daughters and a couple of maid-servants that are paid 30s
a half year, and the common bargain is to do a hank a day of
or 4 hank yarn.' Around Lisburn 'the spinners are generally hire
by the quarter, from 10s. to 12s. lodging and board and engage
to spin 5 hanks of 8 hank yarn in a week.' For such fine yarn
skilled spinster could earn up to 8d. per day but for the coarse
yarns 4d. to 6d. was more likely, while a girl of 12 could ear
1½d. or 2d. per day, and a girl of seven might get a penny. I
these cases, however, the spinster had to provide her own boar
and lodging.[22]

The relationship between 'the family' and 'the household' ir
this context is worth further scrutiny. Those members of the
household who were not also members of the nuclear family were
required to fill an economic vacancy in the family, that is to
undertake duties that would have been carried out if the family
had possessed someone with the relevant skills and experience.
Not only were women cheaper to employ: they were also more
versatile around the house and even the farm as long as heavy
work was not sustained or excessive. The ability of a family to
provide and manage the work of its own members depended
much on its economic base. Poor families had to labour for others
who could provide them with work and so they were likely to
shed their children early. There were, however, considerable
benefits to be gained by those families that could organise
themselves into an effective production team. They were usually
families that had managed to obtain a lease of their farm, no
matter how small, because the possession of a lease gave a family
status and self-confidence as well as an instrument for securing
loans. As the lease aged, the fixed rent became a smaller proportion of the family's expenditure because the value of land rose
steadily throughout the eighteenth century.[23] In such circumstances a family might sublet part of its farm to pay for the hire
of a cottier at the loom or in the field. In many districts throughout the north of Ireland women prepared and spun yarn for sale
in the market because their menfolk concentrated on their farming duties and would not weave. As the century progressed,
however, more men took up the weaving of coarse linens when
work on the farm was slack, or apprenticed their sons to the
trade.[24] It is probable, too, that many women engaged at busy
times in weaving. It was believed in the years before the fitting
of the flying shuttle to looms about 1815, that the loom was too

heavy for women especially as the weaver was required to stand and stoop over the cloth.

It may be that the greater widths of cloth required for the commercial markets made the task of weaving too strenuous for women. Yet it had long been the practice for women to weave the woollens and linens needed by their own families. Or it may be that the introduction of the lighter cotton loom equipped with the flying shuttle and using mill-spun yarn encouraged women to take up weaving. The absence of direct evidence for weaving by women throughout the eighteenth century probably has much to do with the fact that men were responsible for selling the webs as well as purchasing yarn in the markets. In parallel situations in Lancashire and in the American colonies women were to be found among the weavers.[25] Indeed the American case is especially interesting because, although the introduction to a recent exhibition refers to both male and females working in New England, all the specimens attributable to individuals were woven by women: they were probably made for use in the weavers' homes.[26] In general, however, in the Irish industry women concentrated on spinning to keep the weavers supplied and they would have to assist the weaver at the loom if there was no boy available.

In any consideration of the key role of the family and the family firm in the domestic linen industry, attention has to be paid to the family cycle. It has often been suggested that possession of skills in spinning and weaving enabled young people to marry early and set up home together. Their success, however, would depend to a great extent on the situation in their respective homes. It has to be remembered that these young people were in effect withdrawing from existing linen production units. If they had played their part at home and the omens were propitious, they might not only count on the goodwill of their parents but might even be given at least a subdivision of a parent's holding on which to build a dwelling, as well as a dowry with the bride to establish the new family. With these essentials and the continuing support of their families they stood a good chance of establishing a new family. Without them they were very vulnerable to misfortune especially in the aftermath of the birth of their first children, when the woman's earning capacity was seriously reduced, so that many slipped easily into debt that brought them into the clutches of moneylenders and unscrupulous dealers. At the same time it was still possible for poor families to work themselves up the social ladder. A landmark in their success would be the purchase of an interest in a lease because its possession provided both status and security.[27]

It is important to point out that much of the evidence presente
in this paper relates to the eighteenth century when the domesti
linen industry steadily increased until it came to dominate th
economy of the north of Ireland and seriously altered its socia
structure. The process in County Sligo was described in 1766 b
a local member of Parliament:

> . . . the present great price of land is principally owing to th
> cottage tenants, who being mostly Papists, have long live
> under the pressure of severe penal laws and have bee
> enured to want and misery. The linen manufactory in it
> progress opened to these such means of industry as wer
> only fitted to penurious economy. Three pence a day, th
> most that can be made by spinning, was an inducement f
> only to be held out to women so educated. The earning wa
> proportioned to their mode of living and became wealth t
> the family. In mountainous countries the grazier had for
> merly driven them [these people] to the unprofitable parts
> Here they placed themselves at easy rents for the deman
> for cattle in these days was not more than the good land
> could supply. The cottager, necessitated to try all means o
> drawing a support from his tenement, has in the course o
> his industry discovered that his mountain farm with th
> amelioration of limestone gravel, is productive both of cor
> and potatoes, and in succession afterwards of flax equal t
> the low grounds. But the labour of this is great and fit onl
> for people so trained to hardship. The home consumption o
> cattle increasing with the wealth of the country, the market
> of Great Britain open, and the colonies more extended an
> more populous, have multiplied the demand and given a
> last a value even to the mountains for pasture. But here th
> cottage tenant, abstemious and laborious, is enabled by th
> industry of his family to outbid the grazier. They cant each
> other and give to land the monstrous price it now bears. Bu
> from the inland countries where all the land is good the
> cottagers were early banished so that land only rises there in
> proportion to the additional demand for cattle. Besides that
> most lands in such countries are fitter for pasture than for
> tillage. Thus we flourish and land continues to bear its
> present price and will do so till an increase of wealth shall
> create new desires in the cottager, and that small profit
> which now gives excitement to his industry shall cease to be
> an object. Then the factors must be content with smaller
> profits, some new manufacture must succeed, or we must
> return to pasture and land fall to a lower price.[28]

The scale of these changes makes it very difficult to generalise about the social characteristics of earlier centuries. Even the importance of the family cannot be taken for granted. The same member of Parliament had commented in 1760 that as a result of the economic changes, 'A family now has a better bottom than formerly: residence is more assured and families are more numerous as increase of industry keeps them more together.'[29] It was this cohesion of the family that gave the mother status and authority both at home and in society. Without this role a woman's value was dependent on her earning ability within the community. Women did many of the everyday jobs that their physical strength allowed. They were not allowed by men to undertake strenuous work that might injure them. That reality deprived them of equal status in a world where physical strength was esteemed.

REFERENCES

1. M.M. Postan, *The Medieval Economy and Society* (London, 1972), pp. 190–2.
2. A.K. Longfield, *Anglo-Irish Trade in the Sixteenth Century* (London, 1929), pp. 77–93; A.P. Wadsworth and J. de L. Mann, *The Cotton Trade and Industrial Lancashire 1600–1780* (Manchester, 1931), pp. 5, 6, 11, 13, 46–7.
3. L.M. Cullen, *Anglo-Irish Trade 1660–1800* (Manchester, 1968), p. 50.
4. L.M. Cullen, *An Economic History of Ireland since 1660* (London, 1972), pp. 39–42, 59–66, 105–6.
5. W.H. Crawford, 'The Evolution of the Linen Trade in Ulster before Industrialisation' in *Irish Economic and Social History*, Vol. XV (1988), pp. 32–53.
6. W.H. Crawford, *The Irish Linen Industry* (Belfast, 1987), pp. 5–10.
7. A.T. Lucas, 'Flax Cloves' in *Ulster Folklife*, Vol. 32 (1986), pp. 16–36.
8. A.W. Hutton (ed.), *Arthur Young's Tour in Ireland (1776–1779)* (2 vols, London, 1892), Vol. I, p. 122.
9. Sir C. Coote, *A Statistical Survey of the County of Monaghan* (Dublin, 1801), pp. 197–8.
10. *Young's Tour*, Vol. I, p. 126.
11. H. McCall, *Ireland and her Staple Manufactures* (3rd edn, Belfast, 1870), p. 356.
12. *Ibid.*, pp. 366–8.
13. J. Horner, *The Linen Trade of Europe during the Spinning-Wheel Period* (Belfast, 1920), pp. 16, 22.
14. C. Gill, *The Rise of the Irish Linen Industry* (Oxford, 1925), p. 68.
15. *Ibid.*, pp. 75–6; J. Corry, *Precedents and Abstracts from the Journals of the Trustees of the Linen and Hempen Manufactures of Ireland* (Dublin, 1784), pp. 19–20.
16. Corry, *Precedents and Abstracts*, p. 70.
17. W. Harris, *The Antient and Present State of the County of Down* (Dublin, 1744), pp. 17, 77. See also Horner, *Linen Trade*, pp. 99–100 for a summary of a 1751 report on the spinning schools.
18. *Young's Tour*, Vol. I, p. 128.

19. Crawford, 'Evolution of the Linen Trade', pp. 37, 48.
20. *Ibid.*, p. 48.
21. *Young's Tour*, Vol. I, pp. 123, 126–7, 130, 139, 152, 161.
22. *Young's Tour*, Vol. I, pp. 122–204, especially 133, 174.
23. W.H. Crawford, 'Landlord–Tenant Relations in Ulster 1609–1820' in *Irish Economic and Social History*, Vol. II (1975), pp. 12–18.
24. J. McEvoy, *A Statistical Survey of the County of Tyrone* (Dublin, 1802), pp. 135–56.
25. Wadsworth and Mann, *Cotton Trade*, pp. 336–7.
26. *All Sorts of Good Sufficient Cloth: Linen-Making in New England 1640–1860* (Merrimack Valley Textile Museum, North Andover, Massachusetts, 1980): a catalogue for an exhibition.
27. *Cf.* the case argued in *Serious Considerations on the Present Alarming State of Agriculture and the Linen Trade, by a Farmer* (Dublin, 1773) in Vol. 377 of the Haliday Pamphlets in the Royal Irish Academy, Dublin; reprinted with a brief introduction in *Ulster Folklife*, Vol. 33 (1987), pp. 87–90.
28. National Library of Ireland, O'Hara papers. Some of this collection has been photocopied by the Public Record Office of Northern Ireland and this important manuscript is T. 2812/19: 'Charles O'Hara's account of Sligo'.
29. *Ibid.*

17

Women and the Preparation of Food in Eighteenth-Century Ireland

Nuala Cullen

From earliest times until the last quarter of the eighteenth century methods of cooking changed very little. The open fire was still the mainstay for the preparation of food for almost everyone. The open range, consisting of a raised fire box with bars in front, made its appearance towards the end of the century and came into use where coal was available, but where wood or turf were the customary fuel the open fire remained in use. The cost of adapting the fireplace, even where coal was available, was a deterrent to change for poorer households. There was also considerable prejudice against the smell of coal, the smell of turf being considered healthy: 'the coal smoke is so disgusting to the females, who have been used to turf that nothing can reconcile them to it' a clergyman noted in 1802 of the inhabitants of County Down.[1] The peat fire also had the advantage of ease of management, being easily kept in all night and rapidly rekindled for cooking by the use of bellows or wheel.

The actual cooking processes were characterised by the basic methods of boiling, baking and roasting, usually on a spit. Boiling was the most common of these and possibly the only method in the poorest homes. Boiling was carried out in an iron pot suspended over the fire, usually at this period by a chain. Baking could also be carried on in the pot and various recipes survive to the present using this method. A later development on the hanging chain was the crane, an iron bar which allowed the pot to be moved nearer or farther from the fire, but this was not in general use until the nineteenth century. In front of the fire, spits, in varying sizes, were used for roasting; small spits for birds and fowls, larger for joints. These were attached to fire dogs, or where there was a grate, to the bars. Trays were placed underneath the spits to catch the drippings and bread, or batter, could be cooked in the boiling drippings – Yorkshire pudding began life in this way, and the squares of fried bread still served under game birds today are a reminder of this system.

The most important addition to the basic fire was the bread oven. This was usually made of brick or earthenware and was either built into the side of the fireplace or in a side wall with its own flue. The oven was heated by burning twigs or wood, and when sufficiently hot, usually gauged by the changing colour of the interior, the embers were swept out and the bread put in. The largest items were placed at the back, smaller cakes at the front, then the door was sealed. The baking usually took two to three hours. Furze, which gives an intense heat, was frequently used to heat the bread oven, or added to an open fire when fast heat was required. In County Meath, where coal was available, the better-off families often burned coal in the parlours and bedrooms, but continued to use peat in the kitchen and furze in the bread ovens.[2]

The bread oven was mainly used for leavened wheat bread, which in turn was largely confined to better-off households and to districts where barm from brewing was available as a raising agent. Where a bread oven was in use it was the usual practice to do a large weekly baking. Any stale bread was in demand for toasting and making the 'sippits' and sops used to garnish dishes and mop up soups. Breadcrumbs were also in demand for thickening sauces or drinks such as ale caudle, a hot breakfast drink made with eggs and ale.

For families who could not afford wheat, oats and barley were the staple bread grains. These were more suitable for making flat breads, oat cakes, and these were usually baked on a bake stone, round flat stones heated in the hot embers. Decorative iron stands were later popular for oatcakes, which require more of a drying out process than actual baking. The flat iron griddle or girdle which could hang over the fire did not come into general use until the nineteenth century.

Breadmaking was important in the Irish household, (though only seasonally in the poorer families), as for at least one of the two post-breakfast meals bread was eaten. In rural areas particularly, bread making required a great deal of preparation as it frequently started with the grinding of the grain, either home produced or purchased, and not with bought flour. The grain was ground in the household quern and Humphrey O'Sullivan, in Callan, as late as 1827, mentions the whirling sound of the quern as something which could be heard by an attentive listener.[3] Bread was raised with barm, the yeasty froth on top of the beer or ale tub, and was easily available where brewing took place. Domestic brewing gradually declined, however, during the eighteenth century, except for some of the great houses where the self-sufficiency of an earlier period remained. The use of commercial baking powder did not become general until the last quarter of the nineteenth century, though bread soda was in use somewhat earlier.

For the eighteenth-century housewife, both rich and poor, the provision and preparation of food for the household was central to her daily life. At the higher levels of society the organisation of a large household, even with the aid of servants, was a time-consuming and very skilful occupation. On a lower level one of the great revolutions in women's domestic work in Ireland was that some aspects began to acquire a greater monetary value. One of the first instances of the change, most widespread in southern districts, was the sale of butter. Butter had long been made and consumed within the household but as it was a domestic staple there was little for sale. However, in the 1720s and 1730s market sales of butter spread rapidly and increasingly it became a cash commodity. Samuel Madden in 1738 related how formerly butter was sold 'by night and as privately as possible, thinking it disgraceful to make a profit of the industry of their wives'.[4] During the next 90 years, from 1730 to 1820, exports of butter quadrupled, suggesting a massive increase in the amount of cash acquired through women's labour. This in turn meant an increase in both manual and managerial demands in the dairy for the housewife and added to the number and value of female domestic servants in the dairy. Dairywork also began to enjoy a certain prestige, doubtless because it provided a cash return, and good dairy maids were treated with a degree of respect. The reality however, was that the work was merciless in its demands and required constant attention to hygiene. One of the frequent criticisms by outsiders was that dairies were not sufficiently clean, but with increasing butter sales exposing the product to external scrutiny, butter production developed more stringent standards than the lax ones formerly observed within the home by families unacquainted with outside constraints.

In more sophisticated homes the dairy was expected to produce a wide range of products including cheeses; all the creams and syllabubs of the period were also the province of the dairy. There is a suggestion that dairy maids were enjoying their position and sharing in a degree of prosperity in this acerbic comment from Mrs Delany in 1745 on a visit to Hollymount: 'I am very sorry to find here and everywhere people *out of character* and that *wine* and *tea* should enter where they have *no pretense to be* and usurp the rural food of syllabub, etc. But the dairymaids wear large hoops and velvet hoods instead of *the round tight petticoat* and *straw hat* and there is as much *foppery* introduced in the *food* as in the *dress – the purest simplicity of ye country is quite lost!*'[5]

In addition to the dairy, hens and fowl were widely kept in Ireland. Arthur Young commented on the number, and Meg Dods in her 'Cook and Housewife's Manual' referred rather patronisingly to the multiplicity of fowl as one of the features of poorer regions like Ireland or Lanquedoc in France.[6] Fowl were prized for their flesh but even more for the eggs. Eggs were used in staggering quantities in eighteenth-century cooking, and every household, rich and poor, could expect to produce most of its own eggs. For the farm wife or cottager the surplus eggs could be sold – carried to town on market days, or sold to inns and taverns – and while eggs had a hallowed place in the Irish diet there is surprisingly little knowledge about the trade in eggs. Passing references indicate that eggs were brought on carts to Dublin from as far away as the midlands, so egg buyers must have existed, which meant that housewives even far afield could count on a cash return for their produce. Fowl and eggs, like dairy produce, were the woman's province. Hence the housewife's place in the national and domestic economy greatly increased in the eighteenth century with much more cash passing through her hands than formerly, but it is impossible to say how much, if any, stuck. On the other hand, it meant much more work, either in a manual or managerial capacity, though the supplement in cash income would have been particularly important for poorer families and it may have represented, along with the income from pigs and from spinning, half the income of a farm labourer's family.

One of the aspects of the Irish table most commented on by visitors was the large quantity and variety of meat served at dinner. This reflected an earlier style and though common in England too, it had begun to change there quite early in the century, with the number of 'made' dishes increasing and the number of major joints of meat decreasing. However, this was very slow to change in Ireland. Mrs Delany gives a good example of this when, in the 1730s, she visited a gentleman in the west of Ireland who lived in a thatched cabin: 'it belongs to a gentleman of fifteen hundred pounds a year . . . He keeps a man cook and has given entertainments of 20 dishes of meat.'[7]

Given the social competitiveness of the times, this preponderance of meat, coupled with a certain ostentation, meant that in fashionable houses gargantuan meals were often served. The Lord Chief Justice Singleton at Drumcondra in 1750 gave an entertainment for 17–18 persons and 'Had a *vast* dinner and such a *vast* turbot as I never saw'.[8] When Mrs Delany returned to Ireland in the 1740s as mistress of Delville in Glasnevin she tried to adapt her menus to the newer style while still catering to the tastes of her guests. Of a dinner given in 1747 for the Lord rimate she wrote to her sister 'I give as *little hot meat* as possible, ut I think there could not be less, considering the grandees that re to be here; the invitation was 'to *beef stakes* which we are amous for'.[9] The menu in fact contained along with the 'beef takes' only one other joint of meat, a fillet of veal, the other 16 or o dishes comprising a fish, turkey, salmon both grilled and ickled, crab, rabbit, hare, little made dishes and vegetables. This vas a very modern dinner and reflected Mrs Delany's own reference for fish and interest in healthy eating. An old-time ountry gentleman, however, might have found it 'frippery'. Breakfast too was taken seriously and a 'chance visitor' calling on is acquaintance Sir Thomas Burke of Marble Hill, County Galway in 1802 and finding the house full of company was revailed upon to spend the night. He found that breakfast the ext morning was very much in the old style 'fish and flesh, tea, offee, marmalade, honey, usquebaugh, and mead, bread of all orts, white and brown, a large dish of stirabout on the sideoard, and beside it flourished another of mealy potatoes (with heir jackets on)'.[10]

The structure of the eighteenth-century formal dinner – two courses with anything from five to fifteen dishes in each course, vith all the dishes of each course laid on the table at once, equired a great deal of organisation and co-ordination in the kitchen, and well-trained servants for the removal of the first course and safe placement of the second, while the diners were seated. Great emphasis was placed on the symmetry with which the food was arranged, hence the uneven number of dishes in each course, the odd one being either a 'remove' such as soup, or destined for the centre. As a consequence, in order to balance the table, items which we would now consider condiments, such as flavoured butters or pickles, counted as dishes, thereby inflating the total number. The total number of dishes was a source of interest when friends reported on social events to each other and this was specially true of suppers. When the family of Dorothea Herbert, of Carrick-on-Suir, built a holiday villa at Bonmahon, County Waterford in 1793, it was all hands on deck for the housewarming party:

> We had Miss Bell Blunden and Miss Butlar in the House with us and the Young Blundens were quite at our command – we set all Hands to work, got our Pastry and Music from Carrick with every Rarity the Season afforded in Meats, Fruits or Vegetables – The two Blundens got us all Manner of fish and wildfowl – Miss Butlar, Miss Blunden and Fanny manufactored the Whips Jellies and Creams and I made a Central Arch of Pasteboard and Wild Heath with various

other Ornaments and Devices . . . Our Ball was followed b
one from Mrs Hayes who not being able to out do us i
Elegance resolved to Eclipse us in the Number of Suppe
Dishes – we had Sixty Nine and she had Seventy – Thi
caused much comment among the Neighbours – But m
famous Arch carried the Votes and was accounted worth
Shipload of Common Dainty Dishes.[11]

It was not the practice for everyone to partake of all the dishe
at dinner, the idea was more to offer a choice so that each dine
could find something to his taste, and due to the static positior
of the dishes, which were often quite heavy, diners wer
expected to help their companions to whatever was nearest t
them. This presented terrors for the socially gauche, and there
were many complaints from diners that they were not offered
their particular favourites. The host was expected to carve the
large joints of meat which were placed at his end of the table and
the hostess had the task of carving and dispensing the lighte
things such as birds or fish. Standing up to carve was no
considered quite 'genteel' but was often found to be necessary.

On a less formal level, when one considers everyday dinner ir
a comfortable family might consist of five dishes, usually includ
ing soup, fish meat or fowl, vegetables and tarts, all prepared on
above or in front of an open fire some idea of the skill anc
organisation required will be seen. As already mentioned, in rura
areas grain was ground for flour. Almonds, used in very large
quantities for the ever-present cheesecakes, pastries and creams
had to be pounded in a mortar to powder them, a difficult process
as they tended to oil – egg whites and cream were whipped with
a birch twig and took an hour, coffee was ground in a hand mill,
sugar, which was bought in a solid cone or loaf, had to be scraped
and pounded and for some purposes refined by boiling. Spices
of all kinds were used extensively and were also prepared in a
mortar. It will be easily seen that even simple culinary tasks were
time consuming and labour intensive in a way not understood
today and made several pairs of hands a necessity where there
was the slightest pretension to gentility.

The domestic burdens were of course eased in comfortable
households with the help of servants. Wages were on the whole
cheaper than in England and in consequence at a given level of
income more servants could be employed in Ireland. Arthur
Young noted that on £500 a year in Limerick a person could
maintain as well as a carriage and four horses, three men, three
maids, a nurse and a cook.[12] Dorothea Herbert, whose father was
rector at Carrick-on-Suir, recalled in her Retrospections that around
the years 1781–5 the family servants numbered two or three

nurses, a coachman, pantryboy, an apprentice boy, a dairy maid, housemaid, cook, a gardener, and a housekeeper who was 'a wonderfully clever Confectioner, Lady's Maid and Nursetender'.[13]

Even small farmers could afford to employ servants as well, and the Drummond Commission noted in 1838 that the employment of male servants, somewhat less widespread than female servants, was common in farms as small as 12 to 22 statute acres . . . as farm servants, young men from between 16 and 26 years of age . . . at remarkably low wages, seldom exceeding £1 per quarter'.[14] Larger farms were well provided with both domestic and outdoor servants and these were necessary as at this level the housewife was moving into what could be called a managerial role. The servants, usually coming from the poorest families, had the most rudimentary knowledge of cooking, hygiene and dairying, hence a larger responsibility devolved on the housewife to instruct in food preparation, dairying and house management. For the servants this was a means of learning the methods and standards of a wider world and the importance of this training function should not be underestimated for the servants of farm or great house alike. Such knowledge cannot but have been a recommendation to her suitor when a young servant came to marry – the heroine, Rose, in Mary Shackleton Leadbetter's *Cottage Dialogues* was modelled on her brother's cook, who was trained in the family.[15] Upper servants, governesses, were also much valued in proportion to any specialised knowledge they may have brought with them in areas such as confectionery and sugar boiling, and the new French cooking methods. Companions and poor relations often fitted into this category, sometimes acting as housekeepers, or taking charge of the baking and preserving and often working very hard indeed. An unmarried cousin of Lord Baltinglass, Molly Stratford, wrote to him in 1750 for a small sum of money due to her from her grandfather's will; '. . . when you seriously reflect on the many hardships that I have gone through, the Slave that I was in my Grandfather's house, sometimes from four o'clock in the morning till I went to Bed at Night, and this for near nine years, besides the uneasiness of his Temper withall, and his making me little or no return for my trouble in all that time'.[16] There are many references which suggest that Molly Stratford's experience was not an isolated one. The position of unmarried girls with no fortune of their own was often an unenviable one as there was no shortage of work to be found for an extra pair of hands.

Through this domestic instruction therefore, new and higher standards of housewifery were dispersed downwards through the population – something quite evident in the case of tea

drinking, and the taste for white bread, though the spread of te
drinking among the poorer classes is more a feature of the
nineteenth century. To demonstrate the superiority of a small and
poor tenant family which had been improved by association with
and past kindness from, the landlord and his family, Maria
Edgeworth describes in *The Absentee* (1812): 'The kettle was on the
fire, tea-things set, everything prepared for her guest by the
hospitable hostess, who thinking the gentleman would take tea
to his breakfast had sent off a *gossoon* by the *first light* to
Clonbrony for an ounce of tea, a *quarter of sugar*, and a loaf o
white bread; and there was on the little table good cream, milk
butter, eggs, – all the promise of an excellent breakfast'.[17] On the
evils of social pretension, in the same novel Miss Edgeworth has
this to say of Mrs Raffarty, upwardly mobile and out of her depth
in the matter of instructing servants and trying to give a dinner
which has two great faults – profusion and pretension '. . . she
was incessantly apologising, and fussing and fretting inwardly
and outwardly and directing and calling to her servants – striving
to make a butler who was deaf, and a boy who was harebrained,
do the business of five accomplished footmen of *parts and
figure*'.[18]

In this fraught area some help could be gained from the many
printed cookery books and household manuals which appeared
during the eighteenth century but by far the most important of
these was that of Hannah Glasse, first published in 1747 and
frequently reprinted thereafter.[19] It was certainly the most widely
read cookery book of the period both in Ireland as well as
England and it is likely that it was the only book to be found in
some homes. It also appeared peeping out of pockets or on
shelves in contemporary cartoons and prints. It would be difficult
to overestimate the influence of Hannah Glasse on the cooking
of the second half of the eighteenth century and while there were
many other printed cookery books circulating it is possible to see
her influence very clearly in the manuscript collections kept by
housewives and housekeepers of the period, and indeed much
later. Hannah Glasse was herself a professional cook and therefore had great practical appeal for those who ran their own
homes. Her influence could best be compared with that of
Elizabeth David on our own food during the past 40 years.

It is not to be supposed however, that a lady with sufficient
servants to sustain grand formal dinners actually stood in front
of the fire – some cookery books advised ladies to keep out of the
kitchen as the heat made the servants fractious – or ruined the
complexion – but it seems fairly certain that during the eighteenth
century she was able to perform culinary tasks herself, and cer-

ainly knew how they should be done correctly. Mary Shackleton Leadbetter's Aunt Carleton, a lady who when widowed lived in limited circumstances with one servant, was described by Mary as being well skilled in the science of cookery her little dinners were very comfortable. She perfectly understood the roasting of a pig or a hare'.[20] Wolfe Tone and his wife were no strangers to the culinary arts either. In 1790, when Mrs Tone was ordered to the seaside for her health, he took 'a little box of a house on the seaside at Irishtown' and 'I recall with transport the happy days, the delicious dinners – in the preparation of which my wife, Russell and myself were all engaged' and he recalled later when Russell was unexpectedly promoted to an Ensigncy how 'we set him to cook part of the dinner in a very fine suit of regimentals'.[21]

But where her circumstances were comfortable the role of the housewife would have been that of a co-ordinator, in conjunction with a housekeeper at the higher social levels, and her actual labour concentrated on the very important seasonal work of preserving. Houses of any size would have had the produce of a large garden to harvest and all the fruits, berries and vegetables had to be conserved in the most advantageous way. Auction notices of farms and houses of the period detail vegetable gardens, apple and cherry orchards, pigeon lofts, dairies and piggeries and the proper utilisation of this produce was vital to the economy and well-being of the family and servants and required a high degree of expertise and organisation to manage. The very wide range of meats, fruits, vegetables and nuts which appear routinely in the manuscript recipe books give some idea of what was available. Vegetables now considered luxuries such as asparagus and artichokes, apricots, peaches and cherries, provided seasonal diversity for our ancestors. On the highest social levels, where a great scientific interest was taken in growing exotic fruits, Mrs Delany was able to write to her sister in September 1750 that she had 'just been gleaning my autumn fruits – *melon, figs,* beury pears, *grapes, filberts* and *walnuts'*. All from her garden at Glasnevin![22] She grew orange trees in tubs too, commenting that 'Miss Hamilton is my confectioner to-day and is at this time making *orange-flower bread* of my own *orange flowers* – of which I am not a little proud'.[23] Miss Hamilton was the young daughter of one of her close friends.

For the great range of flavoured brandies and cordials so enjoyed in the eighteenth and nineteenth centuries the housewife also took full charge, often guarding her recipe for some speciality jealously. These were made by infusing fruits or berries with sugar in various spirits – sloe gin is one of the few examples still made today. Particular favourites such as orange shrub, made

with rum and Seville oranges, were so popular that they wer
made in commercial quantities by the spirit merchants or grocer:
who also offered the 'neat' brandy and rum, raisins of Corint
(currants), various sugars and spices necessary for home manu
facture of these cordials. Dorothea Herbert in her *Retrospectior*
recalls childhood pranks when the 'Whiskey Currants wer
thrown out when we were all as fuddled as Couple Beggars
Nay one time the Pigs, Servants and Children were reeling abou
the Yard where the heaps were thrown'.[24]

Tea, sugar and coffee (plantation and Turkey), along with th
spices and spirits tended in fact to be the cornerstone of th
grocer's stock and the items which appear most frequently ii
their advertisements, indicating how little was actually importe
into the household and how much it depended on its ow
resources. In an urban situation the domestic supplies wer
augmented by door to door pedlars, much fresh produce bein
distributed this way – in rural or provincial areas the weekl
market supplemented the supplies. Spices however usually ha
to be brought from large centres. *The Lady's Companion*, a popula
cookery book which ran through many editions, gives the follow
ing list in the 1751 edition:

> Things to be provided when any Family is going into th
> Country for a Summer; Nutmegs, Mace, Cinnamon, Cloves
> Sugar, Loaf, Lump, Sugar double-refined, Prunes, Oranges
> Lemons, Anchovies, Olives, Capers, Mangoes, Oil for Sal
> lads, Vinegar, Verjuice, Tea, Coffee, Chocolate, Almonds
> Chestnuts, *French* Pears, Sagoe, Truffles, Morels, Macaroni
> Vermicelli, Rice, Millet, Comforts, and Pistachoe Nuts.[25]

This list, while obviously reflecting the ideal, gives, I think, some
idea of the sophistication and variety of foods a comfortable
family could expect to eat, even if only on formal occasions.

It is important to remember also that the distinction betweer
the making of wines and cordials and the manufacture of purges
and physics was not separated as it is today. The care of the teeth
(a constant preoccupation), skin and general health of the family
was the housewife's lot as well, and every household recipe book
contains its physic recipes, frequently intermixed with cooking
instructions. Recipes for 'Plague Water, Soreness and distempers
of the Eyes, Cure for the Bite of a Mad Dog, Medicine for the
Stone', etc. reflect the ever-present worries of the human condition, and are rather affecting to read nowadays, when one can
sense the hope with which they were carefully attributed and
written down. Remedies in many cases may have been counter-
productive, such as the famous 'Cure for the Gout, published
by Thomas Swinford and Edward Gent, both of the City of
Kilkenny', which among other ingredients contained a 'pint of

the best Red-Port'. This recipe had a great vogue in the last quarter of the century appearing in several printed books as well as manuscript collections and seems a salutary note on which to end this look at the food and drink of our ancestors.[26]

REFERENCES

1. J. Dubourdieu, *Statistical Survey of the County of Down* . . . (Dublin, 1802), p. 216, cited in Caroline Davidson, *A Woman's Work is Never Done* (London, 1982), p. 216.
2. R. Thompson, *Statistical Survey of the County of Meath* (Dublin, 1902), p. 377, cited in Davidson, *op. cit.*, p. 73.
3. M. McGrath (ed.), *Cinnlae Amhlaoibh Ui Suilleabhain (The Diary of Humphrey O'Sullivan)* (4 vols, London, 1928–31), Vol. I, pp. 103, 147.
4. S. Madden, *Reflections and Resolutions Proper for the Gentlemen of Ireland* . . . (Dublin, 1738, reprinted 1746), p. 25.
5. Lady Llanover (ed.), *The Autobiography and Correspondence of Mary Granville, Mrs Delany* (1st series, 3 vols, London, 1861), Vol. II, p. 365.
6. M. Dods, *The Cook's and Housewife's Manual* (10th edn, Edinburgh, 1856), p. 617.
7. *The Autobiography and Correspondence of Mary Granville*, Vol. I, p. 351.
8. *Ibid.*, Vol. II, p. 555.
9. *Ibid.*, Vol. II, p. 468.
10. Letter dated 17 July 1850 in *Galway Vindicator and Connaught Advertiser*.
11. *Retrospections of Dorothea Herbert 1770–1806* (London, 1929–30, reprinted, Dublin, 1988), pp. 311–12.
12. A.W. Hutton (ed.), *Arthur Young's Tour in Ireland (1776–1779)* (2 vols, London, 1892), Vol. I, p. 395.
13. *Retrospections, op. cit.*
14. Drummond Commission as quoted in L.M. Cullen, *An Economic History of Ireland since 1660* (London 1987), p. 110.
15. M. Leadbetter, *Cottage Dialogues* (London, 1811).
16. E. Richardson, *Long Forgotten Days – Leading to Waterloo* (London, 1928), pp. 67–8.
17. M. Edgeworth, *Castle Rackrent* and *The Absentee* (London, 1910), p. 232.
18. *Ibid.*, p. 71.
19. Hannah Glasse, *The Art of Cookery Made Plain and Easy* (1st edn, London, 1747).
20. M. Shackleton Leadbetter, *The Annals of Ballitore* (Kildare, 1986), p. 194.
21. W.T.W. Wolfe Tone (ed.), *Life of Theobald Wolfe Tone* (Washington, 1826), Vol. I, p. 35.
22. *Autobiography and Correspondence of Mary Granville, Mrs Delany*, Vol. II, p. 584.
23. *Ibid.*, p. 571.
24. *Retrospections*, p. 37.
25. *The Lady's Companion* (2 vols, 5th edn, London, 1751), Vol. II, p. 392.
26. *Ibid.*, Vol. II, p. 419.

18

Family, Love and Marriage:
Some Evidence from the Early Eighteenth Century

S. J. CONNOLLY

This paper looks at the family life of some Irish women in the late seventeenth and early eighteenth centuries: the arrangement of their marriages, their relationships with their husbands, their experience of childbirth, and their attitudes towards their children. The women concerned are members of the propertied classes. The lives of the common people in this period, both men and women, are poorly documented; for them, it may never be feasible to say much on any of these topics. For those privileged groups that have left some record of the details of their daily lives, however, it should be possible to complement our steadily growing body of knowledge of the male-dominated worlds of politics and economics with some account of the experiences of the other half of propertied society.

If these experiences are worth reconstructing in themselves, the results may also help to cast light on a continuing historical controversy. On the one hand there are those historians who see the family life of the seventeenth and eighteenth centuries as radically different to that of the present day. Chief among them is Lawrence Stone, who has argued in a major study that the modern pattern of family relationships, with its norms of close emotional ties between husbands and wives, parents and children, developed only gradually from the end of the seventeenth century. Before that date – and for the majority of people long after it – marriage was generally a pragmatic arrangement, in which partners were chosen for the economic assets they brought with them, and close attachment or companionship between spouses was rare. Children too were viewed with a degree of detachment. Those of the wealthy were consigned almost entirely to the care of wet-nurses and servants, and their frequent deaths accepted with little emotion; those of the poor were often ill-treated, abandoned, or economically exploited. Miriam Slater, in a case study of the Verney family during the seventeenth century directly influenced by Stone's work, has presented a similar picture of family members tied to one another only by fairly weak emotional bonds. Elizabeth Badinter, in a study of seventeenth and eighteenth-century France intended to demolish the idea of an inbuilt maternal instinct, has offered evidence of widespread coldness towards children at all social levels. Other historians, however, have not been convinced. The apparent evidence of a growth in domestic affection during the eighteenth century, they have suggested, owes more to the rise of new modes of expression than to any real change in relationships. Studies of childhood that go for their evidence to the records of infanticide and desertion have chosen evidence that predetermines their conclusions. Sensationalised accounts of the widespread abandonment of children, or of the horrors associated with baby farming, have ignored or underestimated the economic pressures on lower class parents. Most of all the sceptics have been impressed by the counter-examples they have found of close emotional ties within families, and of grief and shock at the loss of spouses, parents or children, in periods long before such feelings are supposed to have emerged.[1]

A discussion of the family life of Irish women in the late seventeenth and early eighteenth centuries may in a small way help to offer a further test of these two rival views of the nature of the early modern family. But the Irish case is also of interest in another way. For Lawrence Stone the rise of new types of personal relationship, marked by a greater concern for the individual, was closely linked to the development of a market economy. Thus the new style of domestic affection that became evident from the later seventeenth century first appeared among sections of the mercantile elite, spreading only gradually to landed and provincial society. This view has been endorsed by Philip Jenkins's study of the gentry of Glamorgan, where the development of the companionate marriage and of a closer emotional involvement with children, occurring mainly after 1700, is seen as part of a spread of metropolitan values to this prosperous region of Wales.[2] Does anything similar seem to have happened in the family life of the Irish middle and upper classes?

There has been one earlier attempt to discuss these issues in an Irish context. This is Nicholas Canny's case study of the family life of Richard Boyle, first Earl of Cork (1566–1643).[3] Boyle's attitudes and practice seem at first sight to fit neatly into the pattern described by Stone and others. He regarded his wife as an intellectual inferior, and allowed her no part in major decisions. Children were brought up mainly outside the parental home, with wet-nurses and later in foster homes or at distant schools. While at Boyle's house at Lismore, they were left in the charge of tutors and servants. Boyle arranged marriages for his daughters, without consulting them, in which the sole purpose was to consolidate or develop social or political connections for himself. Sons were allowed a somewhat greater independence, but here too Boyle expected deference and obedience, and backed up his expectations with the threat of disinheritance. Yet these appearances, Canny argues, are to some extent deceptive. Although Boyle never regarded his wife as an equal, they had a close and apparently affectionate relationship, and her death appears to have left him genuinely distraught. He claimed an authoritarian control over his children's lives, yet he regarded each as an individual and took a close interest in what he regarded as their welfare. Indeed Canny argues that Boyle's main motive in keeping his children so much at a physical distance was in fact his fear, based on his puritan religious beliefs, that he might be tempted to over-indulge them. What Canny suggests, in other words, is that Stone and others have fairly accurately described the externals of family life among the seventeenth-century elite, but that they have misunderstood the psychological and emotional basis of such behaviour.

Let us begin with marriage. For the propertied classes of early modern societies, as indeed for the great majority of their social inferiors, this had major and inescapable economic implications. It provided heirs and could establish or consolidate valuable relationships; at the same time it created new claims and obligations, as well as requiring the immediate transfer of some assets and binding commitments regarding the future disposal of more. All this meant that marriage had to be approached in a purposeful spirit, not left to the accidents of casual encounter and developing individual preference. When Pole Cosby, only son of a Queen's County landowner, returned from the university of Leiden in 1724, at the age of 21, his father immediately began to open negotiations with the families of possible brides. When none of these bore fruit, he rented a house in Dublin for six months in the winter of 1725–6, and the entire family came to town 'to try and get a wife for me'. In 1771 word was being circulated in County Cork that Alderman Freeman of Youghal 'has three daughters ready to dispose of in marriage, and has £500 to give each', so that he was anxious to hear of suitable matches. On the other hand Thomas Knox of Dungannon was reported in 1700 to be reluctant to proceed with negotiations for the marriage of his eldest daughter and heir, 'by his expectation of his present wife's stepping off the stage in hopes to have a son for an heir with another'. A similar spirit of calculation appears in the comments of Bishop Ryder of Tuam on his forthcoming marriage in 1748:

> What has determined me in this affair is the approbation of
> it from both our families, and the high probability there
> appears to me that I shall have in her, what I cannot do
> without, a female friend to be interested with the care of my
> daughters, and instead of requitals to be made for it to such
> a friend, I shall have added to my income 800 a year.[4]

When marriages were arranged, they were invariably accompanied by financial negotiations. These, by their nature, were detailed, precise, and often conducted at least partly on paper. Consequently they remain highly visible to historians. The result has been to encourage the view that marriage at this social level was first and foremost a commercial transaction in which parents, or the parties themselves, concentrated on the assets bride or groom would bring with them. The shortcomings of such an interpretation have recently been subjected to devastating criticism by Dr A.P.W. Malcomson.[5] In so far as marriage was a financial arrangement, in the first place, it was an exchange between equals, in which there was generally no reason why either side should give more than it received. A bride would indeed bring with her a portion in cash or, less commonly, land. But this had to be matched by an equivalent provision, out of the husband's estate, for younger children of the marriage and for a jointure to the bride if she should survive her husband. There were thus few fortunes to be won by marriage. A satisfactory financial settlement was of course important, but it was a necessary precondition of an alliance rather than the end to be attained.

Since this was the case, even members of the aristocracy chose their partners for a range of reasons, of which personal attraction was at least one of the most important. The system did of course encourage endogamy: one married within one's own social group. But the same result is generally achieved today, by a less formal but nevertheless remarkably effective set of processes. And in fact Malcomson is able to produce a series of cases in which individuals were led by their preferences to make what were from the financial point of view unsuitable marriages, or indeed to marry outside their class entirely. Similar cases may be found in earlier decades. The future 3rd Baron Kingston is said to have been disinherited by his brother, in so far as family settlements permitted, for the triple offence of turning papist, supporting James II, and marrying the servant to his brother's poultry woman. Mary Delany noted in 1731 the case of Lord Meath, 'a man of good sense and great fortune', who had married his aunt's chambermaid. This had been a youthful indiscretion, and he never lived with the woman. When he was at length set free by her death, however, it was to marry, not a social equal, but the sister of Sir Thomas Prendergast, a woman of 'little or no fortune . . . [and] far from handsome', with whom he had been in love for several years. Other, less dramatic instances confirm that money was not the only consideration in choosing a partner. When Sir Emmanuel Moor brought his son to court the sister of Sir John Perceval of County Cork in 1683, the points noted in the suitor's favour were that he was 'a very virtuous, well humoured man, and one of good sense and understanding'; what counted against him was that 'he is low in stature and not so personable because his shoulders are a little round'. When Judge Michael Ward of County Down composed a letter of advice in 1738, to be given after his death to his son, he did not mention the financial aspects of marriage at all. What he warned against was the dangers of basing one's choice on 'a fair face', recommending instead the 'more lasting' virtues of 'good sense, health and cheerfulness'.[6]

Judge Ward, of course, was envisaging a choice to be made after his own death. Where fathers were alive, like Dudley Cosby or Thomas Knox, it seems to have been generally they who took the initiative in arranging their children's marriages. The freedom of choice left to sons or daughters in such a case must have varied with the circumstances and the temperaments of the parties concerned. But parental control was certainly not absolute. Lord Orrery was probably expressing a common view of how matters should be arranged when he observed in 1728 that '[as] soon as my father will find a woman whose person shall please me, and whose fortune will please him, she shall be heartily welcome to the arms of [the writer]'. Pole Cosby rejected a number of the possible brides his father selected for him, both in 1724 and during their stay in Dublin in 1725–6, at the cost of some friction between them. He did like one candidate, a Miss Mary Dowdall, but his father broke off negotiations because he was not satisfied with the financial provisions. For the next two years Cosby refused all matches proposed to him by his father, 'and told others he employed to speak to me that I would never marry any at all while he lived, unless it was Miss Dowdall'. In the end Cosby senior capitulated and resumed negotiations with Mary Dowdall's mother, this time successfully. A suitor for Thomas Knox's eldest daughter in 1700 was expected to visit, accompanied by a friend 'to make proposals for a match if the young people had a liking to [each] other'. Daughters, if English experience is anything to go by, would have had less independence than sons. But here too Thomas Knox, this time in 1704 in relation to a younger daughter, denied any claim to dictatorial power:

when I see a fit match for her I will do all for her that lies in
my power but were the fortune never so great that offered,
I should not press any of my children beyond their inclinations. I have reason to believe they will pay that deference
to my judgement as not to engage without my advice and
consent and I will be so just to them as not to force their
inclinations but allow them a vote in their own choice.[7]

What sort of marital relationships emerged from such arrangements? The tone of surviving correspondence between husband
and wife is generally informal and personal. Viscount Sarsfield
of Kilmallock, serving with King James's army in 1689, wrote to
his wife as 'My dear' or 'My dear life', concluding 'yours till
death', 'yours eternally'. 'My dear', he wrote on one occasion,
'until this day I never knew how much a separation like ours was
sensible; but I hope our meeting will be the more joyful'. Anne
Ward, in a routine letter to her husband Judge Michael Ward in
1756, began 'My dear' and ended 'Your own, A. Ward'. The wife
of another County Down landowner, Andrew Savage, wrote to
her absent husband around 1740 as 'My dearest life'. 'You can't
conceive how uneasy I was last night', ran one letter, 'having no
letter from you and hearing accidentally that my dearest was ill
of the measles I assure you I had like to have gone to Dublin.
You were very wrong that did not let me hear something from
you of it.' There is no guarantee, of course, that such sentiments
were always reciprocated. Certainly Margaret Savage, by the end
of the correspondence, was beginning to have doubts. 'I was
greatly surprised', the last letter from her begins, 'I had not the
satisfaction of a letter from you by last post, but as I am always
willing to put the best construction on every thing you do I was
thinking it might be miscarried and not my dearest's forgetful-
ness nor neglect of me in so short a time . . . Pray let me hear
every post from my dearest, though indeed I should not covet it
when you want being put in mind of it'. James Fitzgerald, Earl
of Kildare and later Duke of Leinster, and his wife Emily, whom
he married in 1747, addressed each other in their correspondence
as 'angel', 'my love', 'my dearest Emily' and 'my dearest Jemmy'.
Yet within one year of the Duke's death in 1773 Emily had
married their children's tutor William Ogilvie; even before then,
if contemporary gossip is to be believed, Ogilvie 'did his grace
the honour to get three or four bastards on the person of his
duchess'.[8] Even if the sentiments expressed in correspondence
between spouses cannot always be taken literally, however, the
prevailing tone seems to make two things clear. First there is no
trace, by the early eighteenth century at least, of the distant,
formal relations supposedly characteristic of Stone's familial
ancien régime. Secondly the marriage of affection was an ideal to

which couples clearly felt obliged to pay lip service, and to which at least some, like the possibly unfortunate Margaret Savage, genuinely aspired.

More concrete evidence of the existence of close emotional ties within marriage is found in reactions to the loss of a partner. Lord Orrery may have spoken of marriage in 1728 in a somewhat cynical spirit. Yet when his wife died four years later, he appears to have been genuinely grief-stricken. In 1736 he described himself as still lamenting her loss. Two years after his second wife's death in 1703 the Whig politician Alan Brodrick indignantly denied rumours that he was planning to marry again: 'I neither have nor had once since my dear Lucy's death a thought of any one of the sex but her self; my love to her was and is greater than any thing but her deserts and the anguish I stoop under since I lost her, which to tell you truth is inexpressible, and is hastening me after her apace. I struggle with my melancholy, but it is in vain; her image is always present to my mind and leaves no room there for a rival.' Brodrick did in fact marry again, 11 years later. In 1721 his third wife was believed to be dying. When he considered 'how well she hath deserved of me' for 'an inexhaustible tenderness and care', he told his brother, 'I must be ungrateful to the last degree, and ill natured beyond what I think I am, not to regret her misery and danger with all the veins of my heart'.[9] The tone, though dutiful and concerned, is rather different to that of 16 years before. It is a reminder that the emotional content of marriage, as in the present day, could vary widely, not only from couple to couple, but even within the experience of the same person.

Contemporary law, custom and attitude made women inferior to men: requiring a narrower and less rigorous education, completely excluded from political rights, forfeiting – if married – control of their property to their husbands. The extent to which this subordination was reproduced in the daily interaction of husband and wife depended on the personalities and outlook of those involved. It is clear that in many cases the relationship was more equal than contemporary theory would suggest. The most enduring monument to a wife's refusal to accept her husband's dictation is of course Castle Ward in County Down, built in the 1760s with two contrasting fronts, one classical as desired by Bernard Ward, the other gothic, as insisted on by his wife Lady Anne Magill. But there were other, less dramatic examples of equally assertive wives. Thus Pole Cosby's uncle, who died in 1727, would according to his nephew 'have been quite another sort of man had he not been too much governed by his wife, who had not the best of judgements and not half his sense'. Comment of this kind, of course, also illustrates the extent to which such husbands were seen as having failed to uphold their proper role. Emily, Lady Leinster and her husband discussed political events in their letters in detail and apparently as equals. But even she felt obliged to offer a deprecatory near apology, at the end of one such letter in 1755: 'My dear Jemmy has always used me to talk to him upon this subject and tell my mind freely, so I hope he don't think I have said too much'.[10]

In some cases economic circumstances gave a woman a greater than usual independence. A recent survey of Dublin trade directories in the second half of the eighteenth century has established that it was still common – in a way that it was not to be later – for a woman to take over the active management of a business from a deceased husband or father. Among the land-owning class too, a widow or the wife of an absent husband could take over the active management of an estate. Thus Lady Mary Shelburne was an efficient and assertive manager of the family property while her husband, Major General Henry Conyngham, was on active service from 1704. The Dowager Countess of Donegall, similarly, managed the family's affairs during the minority of her son between 1706 and 1715. In the 1750s, while the Duke of Leinster was away in London, his wife not only managed the household as normal but also supervised the running of the estate, including continuing building work on the house at Carton, County Kildare. In the same way the Dowager Marchioness Downshire was to take personal charge of the family's affairs, including a resumption of the long-standing duel with the Stewarts for dominance of County Down politics, during her son's minority between 1801 and 1809. Yet, despite such demonstrations of women's capacity, the assumption continued to be that these were men's affairs. Perhaps the most eloquent testimony to the strength of this assumption is that where a woman was a genuine heiress – in other words, the heir to actual landed property rather than the mere recipient of a marriage portion – the priority in negotiating her marriage was not to find a landowner of equal status, but rather to find a man who could undertake the essential tasks of estate and political management. From this point of view, in fact, a man of good family but with no lands of his own to distract him from the duties he would incur might actually be preferred to a more equal match with a man who was a proprietor in his own right.[11]

Beyond marriage lay, in most cases, the hazards and burdens of childbirth. According to William King, Church of Ireland Archbishop of Dublin, writing in 1712, 'when man and wife love one another in good earnest they commonly lie so close, that during the breeding age the poor woman has no respite'. Accordingly he planned to advise an acquaintance whose wife had just given birth to twins after a difficult labour to allow her 'a year or two to recruit . . . though I am afraid 'twill be in this case, as it has happened to me in many others, that neither of them will hearken to it'. It is difficult to know just how common an experience childbirth was. There were of course instances of very high marital fertility. Elizabeth, wife of Alexander Cosby of Stradbally, Queen's County, gave birth to 16 live children and one stillborn son between 1667 and 1689. Yet cases of this kind tend to stand out precisely because they were unusual. In the British and Irish peerages as a whole the completed family size of women married before 25 whose marriages lasted 25 years or longer varied between a high of 6.4 for those born in the third quarter of the seventeenth century, and a low of 5.2 for those born between 1700 and 1724. Mean family size among the Irish peers and their offspring was a little higher than among the English or Scottish nobility, but not dramatically so. Among those born in the last quarter of the seventeenth century, for example, the figures were respectively 3.86, 3.7 and 3.83.[12] On the other hand the Irish peerage – even if one excludes Englishmen and Scots with Irish titles – were the most cosmopolitan section of Irish society, and the work has simply not yet been done to allow us to say with certainty whether their experience was similar to or different from that of the Irish gentry and middle classes. All such figures, moreover, understate the true number of pregnancies and labours endured by women, because they exclude miscarriages and do not generally include stillbirths.

The main point of Archbishop King's comment, in any case, was less the total number of births than the physical burden imposed when they came in quick succession. Childbirth was undoubtedly arduous. Although a normal birth was not radically more dangerous to the mother than it is today, the mortality rate was pushed up by the lack of remedies for almost all serious complications, as well as by the risk of infection arising from such practices as the manual search of the womb after birth, to remove retained placenta and any obstructions to the contraction of the uterus. In sixteenth- and seventeenth-century England the maternal death rate has been estimated at around 25 per thousand births, compared with a modern figure of 0.12 per thousand.[13] Even what today would be considered minor complications could, given the lack of remedies, be very distressing. In 1702 Alan Brodrick's wife, in the late stages of pregnancy, was advised to drink water to relieve a headache. She then found herself unable to pass water for between four and five days, 'which put her into violent burnings . . . her skin being stretched and ready to burst'. All her doctors were able to do, however, was to reassure her that 'there is nothing of a dropsical humour in it, she not having any great drought on her'. The wife of John Savage of County Down, a week after giving birth in 1735, developed an infection of the right breast, which continued despite the attendance both of a doctor and of several local practitioners, including 'one of the best nurse-keepers in town, as also another experienced woman whose profession is sucking of gentlewomen's breasts'. After three weeks of treatment the patient, though considered to be recovering, was still in what her husband called 'the most exquisite, aching torture can be imagined'.[14] Even where there were no such complications it has been suggested that contemporary practice, with its emphasis on the dangers and painfulness of labour and its recommendation that women be kept physically inactive in hot, stuffy rooms, made childbirth more harrowing than it need have been, or indeed than it generally was for women of the poorer classes.

Probably the most striking feature of the attitudes portrayed by Lawrence Stone as typical of early modern society is the lack of emotional involvement of parents with their children. This Stone presents as partly another example of the general weakness of familial bonds, but also as a response to high levels of child mortality. Up to the middle of the eighteenth century between a quarter and a third of all children could be expected to die before they reached the age of 15. Mortality among under-fives was particularly high. It was only natural, Stone suggests, that parents should avoid becoming too deeply involved with children whose lives were so precarious. Other historians, however, have concluded that the bleak demographic prospects did not in fact deter parents from forming close emotional bonds. The Irish evidence would generally support this latter view. Some parents may well have wished that they could cultivate the detachment Stone suggests. 'I would not for the world but you loved me', Bishop Edward Synge of Elphin told his daughter in 1747, 'but you must love with discretion, and suffer not your fondness to be or grow such as to make you uneasy for what can't be avoided'. Yet Bishop Synge was unable to take his own advice. Three years earlier, when his son was dangerously ill, the most he could do was to refuse to listen to news of his condition, other than whether he was still alive. 'Were I to be tossed to and fro between hopes and fears', he wrote, again to his daughter, 'as I was yesterday and the day before, for a week to come, I might be destroyed, though your brother should be well at the conclusion'. When one of Emily, Lady Leinster's daughters died within

a few days of birth, she was surprised by the depth of her own
feelings. 'I did imagine', she wrote to her husband,

> you would be glad to hear that I was not too much affected
> with the death of our poor little child, which I have now quite
> got the better of, though I was much more grieved at first
> than I could have thought it possible to have been for an
> infant that I could know nothing of. It really convinces me
> there is a great deal more in what is called nature or instinct
> than I ever imagined before, for what else but such an
> impulse could make me feel so much for a poor little thing
> that does but just exist, as one may say.

It is of course true that the day-to-day care of children was
generally confided very much to servants. In 1791 Lord Shannon
complained that his son-in-law, Francis Bernard, expected his
wife to attend personally to the care of their four children,

> to attend their rising and going to bed, their dressing, meals,
> airings, and watching everything that goes into them or
> comes out of them. Nor does her task end with the day, for
> [the youngest's] bed is put close to hers and, he perpetually
> kicking off the clothes, she is disturbed every half hour to
> watch and cover him and answer his prattle when he wakes,
> for every word he says must be attended to, though she was
> dying for want of sleep.

This, however, was clearly exceptional. In fact Shannon was
outraged at seeing his daughter required to perform 'what in
every other family is the duty of a maid'. More typical was
Barbara Reilly of County Westmeath, who observed in 1744 that
her young son – presumably because his intercourse was almost
entirely with servants – 'speaks nothing but Irish, which I fear
will prevent his being a scholar so soon [as others]'. Yet this
reliance on servants did not necessarily mean a lack of concern
or affection. In August 1750, Emily, Duchess of Leinster, wrote
a long letter to her sister describing her children in terms which
leave no doubt either of her involvement with them or of her
perception of them as individuals. George, at just over two and
a half, was 'the most entertaining, comical arch little rogue that
ever was, chatters incessantly, is immensely fond of me and
coaxes me not a little . . . William [just under 18 months] is a
sweet little child, too, in a different way . . . He is vastly fond of
his nurse and does not care two pence for me; so, as you may
imagine, I cannot for my life be as fond of him (though in reality
I love him as well) as of George, who is always coaxing and
kissing me, and does not care for anybody else'. She also wrote
enthusiastically about her daughter Caroline, then aged six
weeks, who was to die at the age of four: 'she is in the first place

small, but fat and plump, has very fine dark long eyes . . . and her nose and mouth like my mother's, with a peeked chin like me'. Once again the clearest and most convincing evidence of parents' involvement with their children comes from cases of bereavement. While Pole Cosby and his wife were living in Bristol in 1734 their daughter, just under two years old, died 'to our most extreme great grief'. They returned 'her sweet corpse' to the family home at Stradbally and themselves moved back there, abandoning an earlier plan to live some years at Bristol, because of the associations the place now had for them.[15]

Inevitably the character of relations between parent and child, like that of relations within marriage, varied from case to case. Mothers may well have been more demonstrative than fathers. When John Vesey, Church of Ireland Archbishop of Tuam, wrote to his son Agmondisham in 1704, he began 'Dear Agmondisham' and ended 'Yours J[ohn] T[uam]'. His wife, on the same sheet, began 'My dearest dear child', ending 'your loving mother'. Where Vesey added in a postscript 'your little ones are very well and very good', his wife assured her son that 'your dear brats are the life of my house'. When Pole Cosby was at university in Leiden his father 'indeed seldom wrote me anything but grumbling scolding letters because he thought I did spend too much, but my dear mother was not so'. It is also possible to detect change over generations, or according to the position of children within a family. When Alan Brodrick, then in his early forties, wrote to his father in 1697, he addressed him as 'honoured sir', ending 'your dutiful son and servant'. Alan's eldest son St John, born around 1680, wrote to him in similar terms. Relations between Alan and the son of his second marriage, born in 1702 and also called Alan, appear to have been less formal. While Alan junior was in England, first at his uncle's house and then at school, his father addressed playful and affectionate letters to 'my little namesake'. 'Ever since I left my little boy,' he wrote on his return from a visit in 1706, 'I have wanted him every morning to kiss me and bid me open my eyes'. At 18 the younger Alan was still addressing his father, in rather cheeky letters, as 'dear papa'.[16] In other families too relationships, by the early eighteenth century at least, appear to have been generally informal. In the 1740s the adult daughters of the Nugent family of County Westmeath referred to their parents in family correspondence as 'mama' and 'dada', and to their grandfather, Lord Westmeath, as 'grandada'. Bishop Synge, around the same time, addressed his daughter in letters as 'my dear girl', 'huzzy', 'my dear giddy Brat' and 'mrs giddy-boots', and referred in his own letters to her as 'old Dad's prattle'.[17]

Not surprisingly, given the present underdeveloped state o
women's history in Ireland, this brief survey leaves many ques
tions unanswered. In particular there is room for a much mor
detailed exploration of the precise scope of the responsibilitie
which women undertook, both in domestic affairs and in th
management of land and business affairs, whether routinely o
in the absence of their husbands. More case studies are require
to illustrate the way in which marriages were arranged and th
character of relationships within families. Nothing has been sai
here, for example, about such matters as the incidence of adulter
and marital breakdown, or about the influence in Ireland of th
notorious 'double standard' of sexual behaviour. We also need t
know much more about medical practice, wet-nursing and
methods of child care, and about the theory and practice o
female education. In all of these areas, finally, there is scope fo
finer differentiation between social groups – between aristocracy
and gentry, between landed and commercial society, possibly
between Church of Ireland, Catholic and Presbyterian.

Nevertheless some conclusions at least can be suggested. A
comparison with Canny's case study of Richard Boyle indicates
that there had been major changes in the course of the seventeenth century. Relations between husbands and wives, parents
and children, if by no means egalitarian, had become less formal
and authoritarian and more overtly affectionate. Whether this
reflected a fundamental restructuring of people's emotions and
personal relationships, or only a change in manners and customs,
remains to be more fully explored, though Canny's conclusions
would certainly support the latter view. What we can say with
certainty is that there is little warrant for following Jenkins's
study of Glamorgan and seeing changes in Irish family relationships as reflecting a spread of metropolitan standards into provincial society. On the contrary the companionate marriage and a
close involvement between parents and their children seem to
have been well established in Ireland at a time when, according
to some accounts, they were only beginning to emerge in the
upper levels of English society. This may mean that Irish propertied society was more sophisticated and less provincial than has
generally been assumed. Alternatively it reinforces the suspicion,
already widely expressed, that both the extent and the significance of changes in the character of family relationships during
the early modern period have been greatly exaggerated.

REFERENCES

1. L. Stone, *The Family, Sex and Marriage in England 1500–1800* (London, 1977); M. Slater, *Family Life in the Seventeenth Century: The Verneys of Claydon House* (London 1984); E. Badinter, *The Myth of Motherhood: An Historical View of the Maternal Instinct* (London 1981); K. Wrightson, *English Society 1580–1680* (London, 1982), Ch. 4; R.A. Houlbrooke, *The English Family 1450–1750* (London, 1984); L. Pollock, *A Lasting Relationship: Parents and Children over Three Centuries* (London, 1987).

2. P. Jenkins, *The Making of a Ruling Class: The Glamorgan Gentry 1640–1790* (Cambridge, 1983), pp. 255–63.

3. N. Canny, *The Upstart Earl: A Study of the Social and Mental World of Richard Boyle, First Earl of Cork 1566–1643* (Cambridge, 1982), Ch. 5.

4. 'Autobiography of Pole Cosby of Stradbally, Queen's County' in *Kildare Archaeological and Historical Society Journal*, Vol. V (1906–8), p. 172; J. Busteed, 'Matchmaking in the 1700s' in *Cork Archaeological and Historical Society Journal*, Vol. LXX (1947), p. 188; T. Knox [of Killygordon, a relative] to John Murray, 31 May 1700 (P.R.O.N.I., D2860/4/8 – for this and other references to the Murray of Broughton papers I am indebted to Mr Graeme Kirkham); Ryder to Sir Dudley Ryder, 19 January 1748 (P.R.O.N.I., T3228/1/42).

5. A.P.W. Malcomson, *The Pursuit of the Heiress: Aristocratic Marriage in Ireland 1750–1820* (Belfast, 1982).

6. C.S. King (ed.), *A Great Archbishop of Dublin: William King 1650–1729* (London, 1906), p. 237n; Lady Llanover (ed.), *The Autobiography and Correspondence of Mary Granville, Mrs Delany*, series 1 (London, 1861), p. 330; *Report on the Manuscripts of the Earl of Egmont* (2 vols, Historical Manuscripts Commission, London, 1905, 1909), Vol. II, pp. 131–3; P.R.O.N.I., D2092/1/7/121.

7. Countess of Cork and Orrery, *The Orrery Papers* (London 1903), Vol. I, p. 63; 'Autobiography of Pole Cosby', pp. 170–5; Thomas Knox [of Dungannon] to Thomas Knox [of Killygordon], 24 January 1700 (P.R.O.N.I., D2860/4/6); same to same, 16 November 1704 (D2860/4/13).

8. J.G. Simms, 'Lord Kilmallock's Letters to his Wife' in *Journal of Royal Society of Antiquaries of Ireland*, Vol. LXXXVII (1957), pp. 135–40; Anne Ward to Michael Ward, 18 March 1756 (P.R.O.N.I., D2092/1/8/53); Margaret Savage to Andrew Savage, undated (*c.* 1738–40) (P.R.O.N.I., D552/A/2/9/8, 13); B. Fitzgerald (ed.), *Correspondence of Emily, Duchess of Leinster 1731–1814*, (Dublin, 1949–57); Malcomson, *Pursuit of the Heiress*, p. 10.

9. *Orrery Papers*, Vol. I, pp. 119–20, 174; Alan Brodrick to St John Brodrick, 5 January 1705 (Guildford Muniment Room, Midleton MS 1248/2 f. 161); same (now Lord Midleton) to Thomas Brodrick, 2 January 1721 (*Ibid.* 1248/4 f. 387)).

10. 'Autobiography of Pole Cosby', 176; *Corr. of Duchess of Leinster*, Vol. I, p. 14.

11. Imelda Brophy, 'Women in the Workforce' in D. Dickson (ed), *The Gorgeous Mask: Dublin 1700–1850* (Dublin, 1987), pp. 52–4. For Lady Shelburne see P.R.O.N.I., D2860. (Once again I owe this information to Mr Graeme Kirkham.) For Lady Downshire see W.A. Maguire, *The Downshire Estates in Ireland 1801–45* (Oxford,

1972), and for the marriages of heiresses Malcomsom, *Pursuit of the Heiress*, pp. 24–6.

12. King to Capt. Burgh, 4 November 1712 (Trinity College Dublin, MS 2532); 'Autobiography of Pole Cosby', p. 317; T. Hollingsworth, *The Demography of the British Peerage* (London: Supplement to *Population Studies*, Vol. XVIII, 2 (1964)), pp. 40, 96.

13. A. Eccles, *Obstetrics and Gynaecology in Tudor and Stuart England* (London, 1982), pp. 122–3; Houlbrooke, *The English Family*, p. 129.

14. Alan Brodrick to St John Brodrick, 7 January 1702 (Midleton MS 1248/2 f. 49); John Savage to ——, n.d. (*c.* 1735) (P.R.O.N.I., D552/A/2/2).

15. Edward Synge to Alicia Synge, 13 May 1747, n.d. (1744) (in the possession of Ms Mary-Lou Legg, London; I am most grateful to Ms Legg for permission to quote from typed copies prepared by her of this correspondence); *Corr. of Emily Duchess of Leinster*, Vol. I, pp. 16–17; E. Hewitt (ed.), *Lord Shannon's Letters to his Son* (Belfast, 1982), p. 27; Barbara Reilly to Andrew Savage, 21 August 1744 (P.R.O.N.I., D552/A/2/7/11); B. Fitzgerald, *Emily, Duchess of Leinster 1731–1814* (London, 1949), pp. 28–9; 'Autobiography of Pole Cosby' pp. 268–9.

16. P.R.O.I., Sarsfield Vesey Correspondence, no. 54 (14 May 1704); 'Autobiography of Pole Cosby', p. 165; Alan Brodrick to Sir St John Brodrick, 1 February 1697 (Midleton MS 1248/1 f. 293); St John Brodrick to Alan Brodrick, 14 June 1707 (*ibid.* 1248/2 f. 278v); Alan Brodrick to Alan Brodrick jr, 16 October 1706 (*ibid.* ff. 250–1); Alan Brodrick jr to Midleton, 7 October 1719, 10 September 1720 (*ibid.* 1248/4, ff. 164, 316).

17. Barbara O'Reilly to Margaret Savage, 23 June 1731 (P.R.O.N.I., D552/A/2/7/2); Margaret Savage to Andrew Savage, 25 June 1738, 5 December 1738 (P.R.O.N.I., D552/A/2/9/1,2); Edward to Alicia Synge (Ms Legg's transcripts).

I am grateful to Mavis Bracegirdle, Marianne Elliott, Graeme Kirkham and Peter Roebuck for their comments on earlier versions of this paper, and to Richard Connolly for his assistance in preparing the manuscript.

19

Images of 'Poor' Women in the Writings of Irish Men Midwives

JO MURPHY-LAWLESS

I

In 1671, James Wolveridge, an Englishman, who upon finishing his medical studies at Trinity College, Dublin had taken up the profession of man midwife in Cork, published a book on midwifery entitled *Speculum Matricis* or the *Expert Midwives Handmaid*. The *Speculum* was one of the earliest texts written in English in what was to become a floodtide of discourses on the pregnant female body that began in the seventeenth century.

The book takes the form of a dialogue between 'Dr Philadelphos' and the midwife 'Eutrapelia'. The latter is closely questioned by the former as to her knowledge of the correct conduct of a woman's labour and birth. Her answers, in relation to all manner of problems and difficulties which can arise, prove her competence as a midwife, albeit under the watchful eye of the male doctor. With this device, Wolveridge laid down his notions on pregnancy and birth as his contribution to the beginnings of the science of obstetrics.[1]

Wolveridge dedicated the book to 'the grave and serious matrons of England', explaining in his introduction that the book was meant to instruct women midwives in their important work which was particularly necessary for English women. The book was, he argued:

> never intended for the Irish . . . whose fruitfulness is such that there is scarce one barren among them and whose hardiness, and facility in bringing forth, is generally such as neither requires the nice Attendance of diligent, vigilant Nurse-keepers, or the Art of expert Anatomists or the unwearied pains and skill of dexterous midwives.[2]

The book represents the beginning of the colonisation of childbirth which proceeded steadily across both class and national lines and assumed increasing importance in the course of the eighteenth century as what is termed 'bio-politics' or demographic politics came into play.[3]

To justify the assertion that Irishwomen did not require midwives, Wolveridge included the following account in his introduction:

> And that this truth may gain the more Credit; mind a Story related by as Learned a Physician as our Age hath known who reports it (as he saith) from the mouth of the Lord Carew, Earl of Totness, and Lord President of Munster, for many years. . . . The Story is this; There was an Irish Woman, wife to a Common Souldier, who, though big with child, accompanied her Husband in the Camp; and whereas the Army daily was in motion, marching from place to place; it hapned, that by reason of sudden flood after a hasty rain, a small Brook began to swell so high, that it hindered the Armies marching for one hour: In which time of the Armies halting, the womans pains of child-bearing came upon her; insomuch, that she withdrawing her self to the next thicket of shrubs (without the help of any Midwife, or any other preparation of Babyclouts) there, all alone, brings forth Twins . . . both which she brought down to the River presently, and there washed both her self, and them; which done, she wraps them up (not swadled at all) in a course Irish mantle, and carries them at her back, marching with the Army the same day barefoot and barelegg'd (as she was) twelve miles, and that without the least prejudice to her health or to the lives of her children.[4]

This portrayal of an Irish woman giving birth in the seventeenth century raises the possibility of an intriguing glimpse into the life of a woman on the march with an army of the day. But given that there are few accounts of childbirth from the early modern period with social context and personal detail clearly set down, the obvious question to pose is whether or not it is 'real'? Does this particular account buried in a text, itself long-since forgotten by medical theorists of the female body, make an authentic contribution to restoring our sense of history as women and to better understanding our antecedents? Or, alternatively, in the words of Mireille Laget 'Does childbirth lie beyond the scope of history?'[5]

I would argue that stories like this do make a contribution but not in the sense of retrieving or rediscovering immediately a woman's experience which is part of our history. Indeed, although the attempt to make clear the shifting sets of historical realities surrounding childbirth is a valuable task within feminism, it is a problematic one, given the sources we have.

Laget, in reviewing the historical material on childbirth available in France – manuals on midwifery practice; learned papers o obstetrical societies; pamphlets written to advise women midwives and mothers; archival material relating to the regulation of women midwives – concludes that in the attempt to write the history of childbirth in the seventeenth and eighteenth centuries: 'the greatest difficulty for anyone who tries to understand is the total lack of first hand testimony'.[6]

Laget's emphasis on the importance of first-hand testimony implicates an area of continuing concern for many feminist scholars. The lack of any extensive material dating from the early modern period written by women themselves inevitably frustrates the search for a women's history grounded in observations at the crucial level of the ordinary and commonplace.

Limitations like these are increasingly pushing feminist historians like Schiebinger to state that it is no longer sufficient to be involved in retrieving or rescuing women from the obscurity of the past. We have moved away from what she sees as the 'simple celebration' of women to a closer examination of the social processes which have alternately encouraged or denied women's participation in so many spheres.[7] The trend to this mode of analysis is evident in the papers which were presented at the International Conference on Women's History in Amsterdam, 1986. In her overview of that conference, Leydesdorff defines the current direction of feminist historiography as a 'searching out the story behind the sources' to examine how the ideologies of male and female have been constituted in any given period. She makes the plea for a historiography of what 'is not immediately visible' in the overall task of recovering our history.[8]

Certainly, in relation to childbirth, there is the stark reality that the immediately accessible detail from women of every class is seldom available. Whether one then attempts to utilise the descriptions of women that occur in the writings of seventeenth- and eighteenth-century obstetricians which, as Laget states, are mostly what we have left, depends on where, as feminist scholars, each of us stands on the issue of 'the real' and how we define the demand for authenticity in reading women's pasts. If we abandon our desire for those unattainable first-hand accounts, we can still argue that the historical experiences of childbirth are not beyond reach. But we have to deal instead with the problem of the representation of women in the texts of male midwives. An analysis of these texts begs the question of how certain images of women are being constructed and why.

II

In making sense of the story from Wolveridge's manuscript, for instance, the first requirement is to locate the account contextually.

Wolveridge has taken it, he tells his readers in a note, from the treatise *De Generatione Animarum* by the English physician William Harvey, published in 1653. That the story has already been passed on to Harvey suggests that the political preoccupation of the English with the 'wild Irish' extended to the scientific domain during this period.

But in this instance, colonial knowledges of one sort are used to buttress another form of colonisation, that of the pregnant woman. At the outset, it is a colonisation concerned exclusively with upper class women. Eccles notes that it was a common assertion amongst men midwives in the seventeenth century 'that nothing like the same pain and danger attended childbirth for women from any other class or background. The notion that 'hardy Scots, wild Irish, working countrywomen, whores and doxies all had nearly painless labours' was really the other side of the argument that upper class women were delicate by contrast.[9] In establishing that it was these women who required the skilled assistance and special regime that men midwives alone could provide, or so they argued, the latter benefited by considerable financial rewards and increasing status.

Stories like the one Wolveridge lifted from Harvey's text served the professional interests of men midwives as they sought to legitimate their claim that their superior knowledge was vital for such women. So even if the story is apocryphal, its representation of a lower class Irish woman undergoing childbirth is an important benchmark with which to measure subsequent images of women in texts on the female body in pregnancy.

Simon, in her analysis of Renaissance portraiture, has argued that the way women are 'framed' or represented by male portrait painters enables us to 'examine relationships between the sexes' and how gender as an area or field of power relations comes into play.[10]

In a similar manner, the details and definitions about women that arise in the texts of men midwives illustrate how medical theories of childbirth established the context in which the specificity of the female body in childbirth is substantially redefined and women become passive bodies. The images men midwives choose to convey above all concentrate on the incapacity of women to deal with the pain and danger of childbirth.

Elsewhere, I have focused on how this textual construction of female incompetence created a new field of power relations around the female body as obstetrics established itself in the eighteenth century. I have argued that the same notion of female incompetence continues to play a key role in how contemporary obstetric science determines women's relationship to their bodies n pregnancy and childbirth. Here, I want to consider the specific nanner in which women who belong to 'the lowest ranks' of Irish ociety appear in these texts.[11]

III

The phrase 'the lowest ranks' is found in the sermon which was vritten by the preacher, Dr Lawson, to be delivered at the public opening of the chapel of Great Britain Street Lying-in Hospital in 759. Subsequently known as the Rotunda, the hospital even now prides itself as having been the first lying-in hospital for vomen in the British Isles.[12] But its foundation as a charity for he impoverished women of Dublin was inseparable from the ntervention it sought to make in demographic politics.

Extensive documentation supported its establishment – from the petition presented by its initiator, the man midwife Bartholomew Mosse, to the Irish House of Commons in 1755 to its royal charter ssued in 1756 to the periodic references in newspapers like *Faulkner's Dublin Journal* and the *Dublin Newsletter*. What is notable is that these women were specifically targeted and their bodies invested with political significance.[13] The usefulness of preserving women from dying in childbirth and their children along with them was manifest to any contemporary observer, according to *Faulkner's Dublin Journal* (see e.g. 23–26 March 1745; 5–8 July 1746) and it was on this basis, touching on some of the concerns of mercantilism, that the Rotunda was underwritten financially by the state. As Lawson baldly summarised the argument in his sermon:

> For the chief foundation of the prosperity of the state is the multitude of inhabitants, it grows usually in wealth and power as it becomes populous . . . the increase of inhabitants most to be desired is among the lowest ranks; those of condition or such as effect to live like those of condition above labour being perhaps numerous enough. Now the direct influence of this charity is this increase; to supply hands for tillage . . . for the carrying on of manufactures, for doing the labourious part and drudgery of mechanics, for maintaining the safety and glory of the nation in the war-like forces of both elements, sometimes at present filled up not without difficulty . . . in supporting this scheme we contribute to the national advantage.[14]

The distinctive relationship between the rise of this institutional form which opens up a new field of operation focusing exclusively on labouring women and the discourses which argued the necessity for total control of their bodies is reflected in the increasing size of the texts themselves. Erickson argues that 'as

the midwife treatises become more learned, advanced an
philosophical, they become larger weightier objects'.[15]

By the mid-eighteenth century, the male science of childbirt
had begun to develop a hegemonic account of the female body
centring on the soft and fragile nature of the reproductive organs
The very weakness and unreliability of these organs define th
female body as suffering inherent incapacities which require th
controlling agency of male midwifery. In epistemological terms
there are subtle and not so subtle interplays here betwee
medical writing on the body and the broader interests c
Enlightenment philosophy in defining the social position c
women. It was a mutually beneficial development that th
argument about 'Delicate, Tender, Feeble women' of the uppe
classes, as the English man midwife James McNath refers t
them, came to apply to all women in both the medical an
philosophical arenas.[16] The way was now open to apply th
medical notion of female sensibility and women's greater emc
tional lability as a result of their reproductive organs to buildin;
an entire social experience around women's need for protection
Hagstrum in her study of sex and sensibility in the eighteent}
century, observes that sensibility, itself invoking suffering, pai
and passivity became strongly associated with pity and compas
sion in response to that suffering.[17] In gender terms, thi
relationship between female pathos and male compassion was a
extraordinarily powerful device in the social control of women.

For, not only did the initial medical version of the argumen
about women's incapacity move down the class spectrum, it alsc
extended across national lines to include Irish women as well. Ir
just under 70 years, Wolveridge's image of hardy able-bodiec
Irish women giving birth with facility was replaced by the 'poo
suffering' women from the slums of Georgian Dublin wh(
required both male midwives and the hospital they controlled
Indeed women from this background came to occupy something
of a privileged place in the annals of obstetrics, so frequently wer(
they cited.

When Fielding Ould, who was to become second master of th(
Rotunda, published his treatise in 1742, he commented that 'th(
poor who are by much the greater number [are] most subject tc
misfortunes in childbearing'.[18] Mosse, the founder of th(
Rotunda, first as a private hospital in 1745 and then as a large1
venture, wrote of Dublin's working poor giving birth:

> . . . their lodgings are generally cold garrets open to every
> wind, or in damp cellars subject to flash floods from
> excessive floods, themselves destitute of attendance, medi-
> cine and often proper foods, by which hundreds perish with

their little infants and the community is at once robbed of both mother and child.[19]

This is the fertile ground where the state's interest in the growing discourse on the social body and its bio-political function happily intersected with the direction male midwifery takes.[20] In presenting case after case drawn from the background of the labouring poor, something of a conceptual slide occurs. The bodies of hundreds of poor women in Dublin's dank backstreets merged with the theoretical concerns of male midwifery, resulting in the creation of the 'poor suffering woman' in labour.

IV

These two phrases, 'poor woman' and 'poor suffering woman', are the predominant images presented in the texts. They can follow on from one another in reference to the same woman, and only the context then explains whether the terms refer to the social class background of the women being written up or the condition of extreme suffering to which all women in labour are reduced, according to the men midwives.

In Ould's text for example, there is a case history describing the first time he used his newly designed instrument, the *terebra occulta*, 'being a piercer to perforate the Head of an Infant, in order to lessen the Size of it':[21]

> In December 1739, I was conducted to a poor Woman in Stephen street, who had been in labour six days; inquiring for the Woman who attended her, I was informed that she had not been there for two Days before, having left the Patient on Account of her Pains easing, desiring that she might be sent for when they returned; which not happening during the space of two Days, they sent for me.[22]

He goes on to describe how he deals with this prolonged or dystocic labour, where as he discovers the baby has died in the womb. The 'external Parts of Generation' were 'so prodigiously swelled' he records 'that it was with Difficulty I could find a Passage for my Finger' so as to examine the position of the baby. When he concludes that the baby's head is impacted, that is, stuck in such a way that it cannot be freed by manual version and that the woman must be delivered instrumentally, he operates with the *terebra occulta* to 'lessen the Size of the Head'. He then writes:

> From the long Continuance of this Woman's Labour, her Weakness, and the prodigious foetid Smell of her Uterine discharge, I thought it impossible for her to live many Days; in about eight Hours after her Delivery, I found her perfectly easy, having slept almost two hours; but her Urine came

away insensibly; the next Visit, I was told that both Stool and
Urine came away insensibly . . . which confirmed me in the
Opinion that all the Parts contiguous to the child's Head
were mortified; in this wretched loathsome manner did this
poor Creature live for the Space of Six Weeks.[23]

It is clear from these two passages how the conceptual slide
between poor women and their social realities and the poor
suffering woman who became the focus of obstetric attention
takes shape. Beginning with the social context, Ould designates
the woman as coming from the poorer class in Dublin. As with
other men midwives of the period, he almost always mentions
place names and sometimes includes a note on the husband's
trade as well when presenting his exemplary cases. Remember
that at this mid-century mark, just before the creation of the
lying-in hospital, men midwives were engaged in the active
pursuit of establishing their science which necessarily had them
seeking out cases amongst poorer women who form the most
numerous portion of the childbearing population as Ould himself
declared. He refers to the 'Women who attended her', meaning
a woman midwife although unusually in this instance, he is not
explicitly attacking her for not returning to see the woman in
labour.[24] The phrase 'they sent for me' is part of his argument
about possessing superior professional competence so that he is
called in to redeem a situation beyond the skill of a woman
midwife.

However, social context is superceded quickly by the details of
the case itself. The next two pages are a minute clinical description of a complication met with by the pregnant body in labour
and of Ould's judgements on how to treat that body. Clinical
cases like these, in which their different modes of practice are
explained and justified through the representation of women as
a fragmented body, form the core of the texts by men midwives.

Coming to the end of his account of the craniotomy operation,
Ould turns away from the external and internal parts of her
reproductive organs to which the woman has been reduced, and
she appears briefly in the text one more time as a person in her
entirety. She sleeps, she appears to be recovering but she is
overwhelmed by injury and infection and lives for only another
six weeks, in great misery, the apotheosis of the 'poor suffering
woman'.[25]

A story about her is created within a discursive context that
builds itself on the sense of female suffering and passivity. It is
inherent in the way obstetric texts function that her 'poor' body,
with connotations of being 'inadequate' rapidly becomes 'out of
health' and 'unwell' (Oxford English Dictionary). This story

comes to represent the reality of all women in pregnancy and childbirth. By the middle of the eighteenth century, the female body is itself inadequate, regardless of class, in the texts of men midwives. Thus, it is the target for male pity and compassion and of course, control. The irony of the argument is that it is being built on the bodies of the urban labouring poor who, as they become increasingly numerous in Dublin (and certainly increasingly visible), most probably are 'out of health'.[26]

Thus Ould recounts the history of a widow who is also seen as poor in both senses:

> In August 1740, I delivered a Woman in the Brick-field, between Ring's-End and Merion, whose husband died about six weeks before, on which Account she was obliged to attend a Horse, by whose Labour she had her daily Support; carrying a large two-handled Tub of Water for this Horse to drink, between her Hands, the whole Weight lying on her Belly, killed the Child in the womb, which she discovered by the Contusion on her Belly, and the Foetus ceasing to stir from that Time.[27]

Again, this case history is an account of an operative delivery in which Ould struggles for some time with his *terebra occulta* to release the dead child from the uterus. He has to repeat the operation having failed the first time 'at which I was a good deal mortified' he admits. Yet 'this poor Woman recovered and in six weeks walked to Town to return me Thanks for her Delivery'.[28] In summarising her story, the woman is now designated 'poor woman' because of what she has undergone in labour, her economic position notwithstanding. As for the reference to her walking six miles to give grateful thanks, this fits into the model of dependent female pathos/male compassion which is part of the legitimating strategy of male midwifery, in spite of what it inadvertently says about the woman's physical strength and capacity.

The conceptual slide was complete when regardless of class and economic considerations, all pregnant women became 'poor'. We can see this transformation when Ould is called to see a 'Gentlewoman' who begins labour in her eighth month in March, 1738. After yet another ordeal, as Ould reports it, in which he works for hours over her body to perform a manual version, the woman is exhausted, not surprisingly, and Ould refers to her as 'our poor Patient'.[29]

The same construction recurs in the discourses of later Irish men midwives like Jebb (1770, 1772), MacBride (1776) and Dease (1783) and the 'poor suffering woman' remained even after the creation of the hospital.[30] Once its institutional domain was

secured and with it the clinical material it required, obstetrics was
no longer quite as concerned with portraying itself as a charitable
effort for impoverished women. But the social control of their
bodies was maintained by the constant reinvention of female
weakness so that the 'poor woman' is still a potent image and
can be recognised in obstetric texts far removed in time from the
streets of eighteenth century Dublin.[31]

VI

These discourses of Irish men midwives reveal some of the
problems involved in retrieving the historically specific circumstances of women. In Leydesdorff's terms, what we are examining is not the story behind the sources but how the sources create
the story.

Already, in Wolveridge's text, despite his notional courting of
women as capable midwives and childbearers, they were in a
position of subordination to him and his knowledge. More tell-
ingly, the female body was becoming a problematic, abstracted
entity. Wolveridge wrote first of the process of pregnancy and
birth and then of the woman as the sum of the process. By the
eighteenth century, this mode of reference dominated the texts.
When women made an appearance, however brief, as themselves
rather than their bodies, they were 'poor'. These 'poor' women
represent women of all classes whose bodies were overtaken by
the scientific enterprise of obstetrics.

By the twentieth century, even these images vanished completely from obstetric texts and, now, the social context of women
outside the hospital field is irrelevant to the practice of obstetrics.
The female body in childbirth has been rewritten and inserted
into obstetric discourses in such a way that the lives of women
are overwritten or overdetermined by the discursive reality.

In her analysis of the 'technologies of gender', that is, the
production of gendered representations of women, de Lauretis
argues that in spite of feminism (and indeed sometimes within
feminism), the construction of gender is as prolific an activity as
it was a hundred years ago. The representation of woman
continues to impinge on us even as we attempt to view ourselves
as 'historical subjects governed by real social relations'. She
argues that this is due to the 'logical' and 'irreconcilable' contradiction of women being simultaneously inside and outside representation and goes on to assert that such an ambiguous situation
cannot be resolved by 'desexualising' gender and concludes that
it is just a metaphor, something that is reducible to a pattern of
'purely discursive effects'.[32]

I am arguing that the problematic of reading women's past is not so much the task of recovering ourselves as historical subjects but of critically examining the extent to which women's lives have been concretely shaped by dominant discourses, in this instance, male medical discourse. Retrieving our history in this context to produce a radical transformation of our present realities involves getting at and uncovering the relationship between the writers of the male midwifery texts and the bodies of the women about which they write. One might also say that the subject of obstetrics permits a woman's subjectivity only by a fragmentation of her 'Parts'.

REFERENCES

1. A. Eccles, *Obstetrics and Gynecology in Tudor and Stuart England* (London, 1982) describes Wolveridge's book as largely plagiarised from other treatises and presenting no original material on midwifery practices and medical theories.
2. 'The author to the reader' in J. Wolveridge, *Speculum Matricis* (Dublin, 1671). In his preface, Wolveridge refers to the 'art and skill of Obstetricie (commonly called Midwifery)' but it takes another three centuries for the word obstetrics to become common currency.
3. M. Foucault, *The History of Sexuality Volume One: An Introduction* (Harmondsworth, 1981).
4. 'The author to the reader'.
5. M. Laget, 'Childbirth in Seventeenth and Eighteenth Century France: Obstetrical Practices and Collective Attitudes' in R. Forster and O. Ronum (eds), *Medicine and Society in France Selections from the Annales Économies Sociétiés, Civilisations, Volume 6* (Baltimore, 1980), p. 137.
6. *Ibid.*
7. L. Scheibinger, 'The Clash Between Guild Traditions and Professional Science' in A. Angerman, G. Binnema, G. Keunen *et al.* (eds), *Current Issues in Women's History* (London, 1989), p. 21.
8. S. Leydesdorff, 'Politics, Identification and the Writing of Women's History' in *ibid.*, pp. 18–19.
9. A. Eccles, *Obstetrics and Gynecology in Tudor and Stuart Ireland*, p. 86.
10. P. Simon, 'Women in Frames: the Eye, the Gaze, the Profile in Renaissance Portraiture' in *History Workshop, a Journal of Socialist and Feminist Historians*, Vol. 25 (1988), p. 7.
11. J. Murphy-Lawless, 'Women and Childbirth: Male Medical Discourse and the Invention of Female Incompetence' (Ph.D thesis, University of Dublin, Trinity College, 1987); 'Male Texts and Female Bodies' in B. Torode (ed.), *Text and Talk as Social Practice* (Dordrecht, The Netherlands, 1989), pp. 25–48; 'The Central Drama of Their Lives: Reading Birth and Death Through Obstetric Practice' in Society for the History of Women (ed.), *'As Equal Comrades, Not as Serfs': Women in Modern Ireland* (forthcoming).
12. I.C. Ross, 'The Early Years of the Dublin Lying-in Hospital' in I.C. Ross (ed.), *Public Virtue, Public Love: the Early Years of the Rotunda Lying-in Hospital* (Dublin, 1986).

13. The 1755 petition by Mosse was accompanied by recommendations from Protestant clergy in Dublin parishes supporting the Rotunda because it prevented disruption to the 'habitation of the working poor' which took place if women gave birth in the home: when the wife is in labour . . . the work of that room must be suspended whereby not only the ordinary expenses must be continued but even extraordinary must accrue . . . and yet no work is carried out to support them for fear of disturbing the woman which frequently throws poor families as objects of distress on the parish . . . therefore this hospital besides the humanity of relief may continue workmen at their employment . . . and remove one common cause for idleness. (W. Wilde, 'Illustrious Physicians and Surgeons in Ireland. No. 11: Bartholomew Moss, Founder of the Dublin Lying-in Hospital' in *Dublin Quarterly Journal of Medical Science* (November, 1986), pp. 565–96).

14. J. Lawson, *A Sermon Intended to Have Been Preached at the Publick Opening of the Chapel of the Lying-in Hospital in Great Britain Street Dublin* (1759).

15. R.A. Erickson, 'The "Books of Generation": Some Observations on the Style of British Midwife Books, 1671–1764' in P. Boucé (ed.), *Sexuality in Eighteenth Century Britain* (Manchester, 1982), p. 83.

16. *Ibid.*, p. 82; L.J. Jordanova, 'Natural Facts: a Historical Perspective on Science and Sexuality' in C. MacCormack and M. Strathern (eds), *Nature, Culture and Gender* (Cambridge, 1980), pp. 42–69; M. and J. Bloch, 'Women and the Dialectics of Nature in Eighteenth-Century Thought' in *ibid.*, pp. 25–41.

17. J. Hagstrum, *Sex and Sensibility: Ideal and Erotic Love from Milton to Mozart* (Chicago, 1980).

18. F. Ould, *A Treatise of Midwifry in Three Parts* (Dublin, 1742), p. 79.

19. Quoted in W. Wilde, 'Illustrious Physicians and Surgeons in Ireland', p. 569.

20. M. Foucault, *The History of Sexuality Volume One*, p. 26.

21. F. Ould, *A Treatise of Midwifry*, p. 167. This kind of instrumental delivery, also known as a craniotomy, was common in instances where the labour was impacted and the baby could not be born. At a time when Caesarian section almost certainly entailed death for the woman, the craniotomy might preserve her life at the expense of the baby's.

22. F. Ould, *A Treatise of Midwifry*, p. 169.

23. *Ibid.*, p. 172.

24. The lack of censure is a rarity. The usual charge would be that the midwife had abandoned a hopeless case which Ould then sought to rescue against all the odds. Offensive designations of women midwives become the norm in the texts of men midwives from the early eighteenth century onward as men midwives seek to assert the superiority of their own knowledge over that of women midwives (see J. Murphy-Lawless, 'Male Texts and Female Bodies' in B. Torode (ed.), *Text and Talk as Social Practice*; J. Donnison, *Midwives and Medical Men* (London, 1977)).

25. Whatever the cause of dystocia, and there could be a number, ranging from the woman having a rachitic pelvis to the baby having an unusual presentation at the onset of labour or even having an enlarged hydrocephalic head, if a woman had to be

delivered instrumentally, the chances of her dying because of infection were greatly increased. There would also have been a greater probability of anaerobic infection setting in because of the prolonged pressure of the baby's head in the birth canal over several days. This is possibly indicated by the foetid smell of her urine that Ould reports. However, whether she sees her physical suffering and impending death in Ould's terms, and whether indeed she would not have had an easier death without his mechanical interventions which lead to further damage and pain, is what we do not know. E. Shorter, *A History of Women's Bodies* (London, 1983), in his descriptions of pain and death in childbirth, includes a number of accounts from Germany, France and Switzerland, that he claims are verbatim records, in which the women actively choose to die rather than submit themselves to obstetric intervention. The passive aspect of their suffering capitalised on by men midwives is therefore entirely absent.

26. A. Eccles, *Obstetrics and Gynecology in Tudor and Stuart England* argues that there was a substantial increase in the phenomenon of rickets from the seventeenth century and that it can be linked to the specific living conditions generated by urban poverty and the ever greater numbers of people subject to those conditions. A rachitic pelvis with its attendant complications substantially increased a woman's risk of dying in childbirth.

27. F. Ould, *A Treatise of Midwifery in Three Parts*, p. 186.

28. *Ibid.*, p. 188.

29. *Ibid.*, p. 121.

30. F. Jebb, *A Physiological Enquiry into the Process of Labour and an Attempt to Ascertain the Determining Cause of it* (Dublin, 1770); 'Of an Hemorrhage Occasioned by the Adhesion of the Placenta to the Os Uteri'in *Transactions, Medical and Philosophical Memoirs*, Vol. III, 3 December 1772 (Medico-Philosophical Society, Dublin), pp. 45–9; D. MacBride, 'An Account of Two Extraordinary Cases of Delivery' in *Medical Observations and Enquiries*, Vol. 5 reprinted in F. Churchill (ed.), *Collected Essays on Puerperal Fever* (London, 1849); W. Dease, *Observations in Midwifery Particularly on the Different Methods of Assisting Women in Tedious and Difficult Labours* (Dublin, 1783).

31. J. Murphy-Lawless, 'The Obstetric View of Feminine Identity' in A. Todd and S. Fisher (eds), *Gender and Discourse: the Power of Talk* (Norwood, New Jersey, 1988); 'Let's Hear it from Bartholomew and the Boys' in *Women's Studies International Forum*, Vol. 11, no. 4 (1988), pp. 293–8.

32. T. de Lauretis, *Technologies of Gender: Essays on Theory, Film and Fiction* (Bloomington and Indianapolis, 1987), pp. 9–11.

20

Women in Irish Folklore:
The Testimony Regarding Illegitimacy,
Abortion and Infanticide

ANNE O'CONNOR

In examining women in Irish folklore, and in particular the testimony regarding illegitimacy, abortion and infanticide, the primary interest is to elucidate deeply rooted beliefs and attitudes in Ireland as revealed by what is called the Irish child murderess and dead child traditions.[1] There is a vast amount of material relevant to the exploration of this subject, ranging from historical documentary sources through to primary and secondary folklore sources, in Ireland and elsewhere.[2] For present purposes I will present an overview of this subject as treated in Irish folklore scholarship, and with reference to the evidence of Irish social historical research. Although it is primarily the early modern period which is of concern here nevertheless reference to both earlier and later material will be made: folklore material does not always allow distinct periodisation.

Child murderess traditions are concerned with the super-natural manifestations of women, who as mothers have killed their own children, or as midwives have taken the lives of the children of others. Dead child traditions are concerned with the supernatural manifestations of the souls of children who have died without baptism (whether aborted or miscarried foeti, stillborn infants or those who have prematurely died of natural causes immediately after birth, or murdered children). A strong and widespread child murderess tradition contrasts with a weak and limited dead child tradition in Ireland. These traditions are distinctly religious in character and they reflect the teachings of the Roman Catholic Church predominantly. In this paper the focus will be upon the social and historical context of these traditions as they have developed in Ireland, particularly in the early modern period, rather than upon the nature and function of the traditions themselves.

I

Folklore concerning illegitimacy, abortion and infanticide has much more to do with personal and collective beliefs and customs than it has to do with the actual recording of historical instances and cases. The analysis of folklore yields valuable insights, not only into the actual details of daily living but also into the belief and value systems operating upon individuals and communities at particular places and at particular times. This immediately raises the perennial debate between folklore and history: the central question usually raised concerns the trustworthiness or reliability of folklore material for history.[3]

Without entering upon what is a vast area of scholarly discourse, suffice to say for the present purposes that traditional folk history has been constructed through the interaction of very particular forces and circumstances. Historical 'truth' and 'facts' are also so formed, but often unsubstantiated material may be dismissed as merely 'folklore', meaning that it is not worthy of equal consideration from an historical point of view. The search for documentary evidence is posited as opposed to that of the oral tradition. No such opposition necessarily exists, and arguably the sources for both folklore and history are far more similar than dissimilar. Folklore, however, may reveal more about what people in a particular place and at a particular time have taken and passed on as *traditional* history, sometimes indicating more about people's allegiances and hopes than actual happenings. This has often been at the heart of the folklore/history debate: to what extent can we take folklore to be 'true' or representative of actual events and happenings? The response from folklorists must acknowledge that folk history is not necessarily the same as 'official' history, but that nevertheless folklore provides insights into human response and behaviour which would otherwise be totally lacking in the straighforward documented historical account. This is readily apparent in any example from Irish historical tradition, whether Daniel O'Connell, the famine, or the Battle of the Boyne are cited. The folklorist is concerned to establish that what she or he is collecting or analysing is truly traditional, that is, that it belongs to a common and generally attested store of oral material, and that it is not merely an idiosyncratic or personal account. In this way, folklore and oral history (often conflated) are significantly different in both their objects and methods of investigation. A process of collective selection is evident in folk history: Jan Vansina has suggested that[4]

Each type of society has in fact chosen to preserve the kind

of historical traditions suited to its particular type of structure, and the historical information to be obtained by study-
ing these traditions is limited by the framework of reference
constructed by the society in question

which is similar to Richard Dorson's contention that 'it is not so
much a matter of fact versus fiction [history versus folklore] so
much as the social acceptance of traditional history'.[5] Folklore
scholarship provides the criteria and means of assessing not only
the historical content of traditions, but also the traditional context
of history.

In approaching the traditions of the child murderess in Ireland
therefore, it is apparent that a wide range of cultural and
historical phenomena and occurrences must be taken into
account in order to attain an understanding of the processes and
significance of the oral tradition surrounding the subjects of
illegitimacy, abortion and infanticide. Ireland in the broader
European context must also be scrutinised, and significant simi-
larities and differences with other countries and communities
across Europe must be appreciated. Only from such a complex
and integrated approach will the importance of these traditions
in the construction of Irish cultural and religious values be
understood.

II

By the beginning of the sixteenth century all of Europe had been
Christianised to a certain extent and the old proscriptions against
the exposure (abandonment) of unwanted children (as is evident
from northern Europe[6]), abortion[7] and infanticide by overlying
(smothering) or other means,[8] had become part of the secular and
ecclesiastical law in most, if not all, of the countries of north-
western Europe and the European mainland. The religious
upheavals of the Reformation and Counter-Reformation and their
social and historical consequences were also to have some effect
upon the phenomenon of child killing.[9] In England, laws regarding child killing were in operation at this period,[10] and acts
concerning the status of, and providing for 'bastard children'
were also passed from the time of Elizabeth onwards.[11] Thus a
concern for the provision of illegitimate children is evident in
England in the sixteenth century, developing into the following
centuries. In 1623 an act 'to prevent the destroying and murther-
ing of bastard children' was passed in England,[12] which was the
government's response to the 'frequent killings of illegitimate
infants';[13] the same act was passed in Scotland in 1690,[14] and in
1707, the sixth year of the reign of Queen Anne, this same act
was passed by the Irish parliament.[15] This infanticide act was

singular in that the burden of proof was on the defendant, not on the Crown: the woman who secretly gave birth to an illegitimate child must herself prove her innocence by proving that the baby was stillborn.[16] This statute was not repealed until 1803 when Lord Ellenborough's act reinstated the common law presumption of stillbirth,[17] and provided legal protection to the foetus at any stage of pregnancy.[18] The act, passed in 1707 by the Irish Parliament, is worthy of quotation in the present context:

> Whereas many lewd women, who have been delivered of bastard children, to avoid their shame, and to escape punishment, do secretly bury or conceal the death of their children, and after, if the child be found dead; whereas it falleth out sometimes (although hardly is it proved) that the said child or children were murthered by the said women, their lewd mothers, or by their assent or procurement: for the prevention therefore of this great mischief, be it enacted by the Queen's most excellent Majesty, by and with the advice and consent of the lords spiritual and temporal and commons in this present Parliament assembled, and by the authority of the same, That if any woman after the first day of November, which shall be in this present year one thousand seven hundred and seven, be delivered of any issue of her body, male or female, which, being born alive, should by the laws of this realm be a bastard, and that she endeavour privately, either by drowning or by secret burying thereof, or any other way, either by herself, or the procuring of others, so to conceal the death thereof as that it may not come to light, whether it were born alive or not, but be concealed; in every such case the mother so offending shall suffer death, as in the case of murther, except such mother can make by one witness at the least, that the said child, whose death was by her so intended to be concealed, was born dead.[19]

It could be inferred that some need precipitated the passing of such a law in Ireland at the beginning of the eighteenth century in accordance with the English (and Scottish) legislation; however it is not possible to definitely ascertain the particular reasons for this from the material which has so far come to light. Further research may reveal more information in this regard.

The European (and later North-American) experience of the witch craze, in which *inter alia* the killing of newborn infants was cited as a predilection of 'witch-midwives',[20] must not be forgotten in the analysis of the way in which concern for illegitimate children, abortion and infanticide developed during the sixteenth and seventeenth centuries in Europe.[21] The Irish history of witchcraft and witch trials, such as it is,[22] unfortunately casts little light on the development of practices of child killing in this country (that is taking witchcraft in the terms of the witch craze, and not referring merely to the practice of witchcraft; the use of sorcery and magic for both good and ill purposes).[23] A developing consciousness of reproduction, midwifery and infant mortality, and their demographic consequences, is apparent in later seventeenth-century and eighteenth-century thinking, as Jo Murphy-Lawless's contribution to this volume indicates.[24] In northern Europe, Juha Pentikäinen[25] has suggested that an intensification of interest in the subject of child killing occurred during the eighteenth century: he linked this 'high-point in the history of dead child traditions' manifest in trials for child murder in seventeenth- and eighteenth-century Scandinavia, to the fact that witch trials 'had flourished in the Nordic countries up to the seventeenth century', stating that 'many of the migratory legends which spread quickly throughout the Nordic countries can be traced to this very period. It is interesting that the supernatural revelation of the child murderess is a central motif in these legends'.[26]

Throughout eighteenth-century Europe legislation regulating illegitimacy and infanticide became common.[27] Concern with 'foundlings' grew as more and more illegitimate (and probably legitimate) children were abandoned.[28] Complex demographic and social circumstances were evidently influential in the concern which developed during this period in relation to illegitimacy, abortion, infanticide, child abandonment and all such 'immoralities'.[29] Such themes were also reflected in the literature of the period.[30] In Ireland too these issues came to be of increasing concern to the authorities.[31] By the first decades of the nineteenth century, government controls began to become more stringent in dealing with what was now an acknowledged social 'problem',[32] although, as we have seen, some relaxation in the English laws in the definition of 'infanticide' occurred at this time. Illegitimacy, or 'bastardy' as it was termed, was taken account of,[33] as for instance the 'Bastardy Clauses' in the English poor laws[34] and the initiation of state statistics of illegitimacy and similar practices[35] all indicate. The incidence of abortion, or an account thereof, began to be noted during the nineteenth century also.[36] Public opinion seems to have taken a more lenient attitude towards these offences than that suggested by the legislation,[37] and few prosecutions actually occurred. The history of illegitimacy, abortion and infanticide in the nineteenth century is, however, outside the scope of the present discussion. The developments of the seventeenth and eighteenth centuries formed the basis upon which the sudden explosion of interest in these subjects which is so noticeable in nineteenth- and twentieth-century developments, was constructed.

III

That illegitimacy and child killing were social as well as 'official' problems, or crimes, during the period up to the nineteenth century is more difficult to establish. In this respect the evidence of folklore may be of paramount importance. Arguably, and interestingly, it is the fact that taking the life of a newborn infant would thereby deprive its soul of an eternally blissful afterlife that was evidently most prevalent in popular religion and imagination. It is apparent that infanticide rather than abortion was the most general means of disposing of the life of an unwanted child. Methods of causing abortion have indeed been recorded in Irish and international folk tradition,[38] but there is much evidence to indicate that while trying to cause an abortion endangered both the life of the mother and the infant, the practice of killing the newborn infant, by whatever means available, would only result in the death of one person. The reasons for doing away with unwanted children are obviously complex, ranging from social, religious, economic and psychological to personal factors, and the ways in which societies judge this act have of course varied over time and place in history. As mentioned above, the fact that an unwanted baby was deprived of baptism, and therefore of an eternally blissful afterlife (in Roman Catholic terms), was the central issue of concern in Irish folk tradition. Child murderess and dead child traditions in Ireland are profoundly *religious* in character; this cannot be interpreted as meaning that child killing was viewed solely as a religious issue, but rather that the popular perception of the woman who takes the life of either her own or another woman's newborn child is that of a demonic and unrepentant murderer. This observation is based upon the folklore material available for analysis in Ireland and elsewhere regarding this subject.[39]

Child murderess traditions have a long history in Europe and this theme has been explored in international folk legend and balladry, as well as in medieval religious *exempla* and other writings. Indeed strong medieval preoccupations with sin and repentance, purity and impurity are evident in these traditions. Traces of these themes and motifs are also discernible in some sixteenth- and seventeenth-century Irish literary texts.[40] Such written texts provide a useful means of comparison with orally transmitted narratives collected in twentieth century Ireland concerning the child murderess figure. These Irish traditions have been discussed in detail elsewhere.[41] However in order to appreciate the context in which such traditions (legends, beliefs, ballads) would have been circulating in Ireland, certainly by the nineteenth century and most probably beforehand (if the evidence from Irish literary sources of the sixteenth and seventeenth centuries can be taken to indicate some familiarity among religious writers with these themes and motifs), then it is essential that an attempt be made to reconstruct the social and historical circumstances which would have allowed their introduction and dissemination in Ireland.

The traditions themselves, of which much could be made, can only be very summarily described in this paper.[42] Child murderess and dead child traditions in Irish folklore constitute a corpus of religious legends, folk ballads and popular belief and custom. Legends of an unrepentant child murderess figure have been collected from a variety of locations throughout the country, but primarily, as already stated, from the southern and southwestern areas. The name spirits of 'Petticoat Loose', 'Moll Shaughnessy' and 'Máire Gaelach' together with their unnamed counterparts (in Kerry and in the western parts of Ireland) have attracted to themselves narratives which tell of a woman who has killed her unbaptised child (children) and does not repent of this deed even though a priest confronts her tormented spirit. This was the deed which damned her and denied her any happiness in the afterlife. In the legends the woman spirit is subdued by the priest, who exorcises and banishes the spirit away from the place she has been frequenting (usually to the detriment of men travelling the roads late at night) to Bay Lough, in the Knockmealdown mountains, or to the Red Sea, where she is instructed to accomplish some impossible task, such as making ropes of sand or emptying the waters with a thimble, until the last day of judgement.[43] The child murderess figure in these legends is represented as a diabolical character for whom no mercy may be granted. Of central importance is the fact that she does not repent of her sin of denying baptism to a newborn child. By contrast, legends which treat the supernatural manifestation of the souls of unbaptised children evince far more complex issues of moral and religious import, where a Mary Magdalene figure who is a sinner-saint emerges in contrast to a priest who is seen to have been afflicted by pride and degradation. Two opposing images of women in Irish folklore emerge from an analysis of these two legend types, both inextricably related to each other, and both evidence of a very particular evolution of traditions of this nature in Ireland. Ballads which deal with the theme of child murder, and in particular the killing of newborn children by their mother,

ave also been recorded in Ireland[44] and are still well known at
he present time. In general the image of woman as evil, a killer
f children without thought for the child's unending misery by
ts separation from God, and consigned to dwell in limbo until
he day of judgement,[45] is clearly apparent. The importance of
eliefs in the afterlife and the power of such precepts in regulat-
ng social and personal behaviour may only be supposed.
However, there is sufficient evidence to indicate that these
raditions were current among Irish people, certainly during the
ineteenth century and up to the 1950s and later, especially in
he south, south-east and south-west of Ireland. Versions of the
child murderess legends and the 'cruel mother' ballads, and their
associated types, have been collected in the 1970s and 1980s. It
s not easy to correlate social and personal behaviour with social
elief and custom and folk narrative; the fact that particular
stories are told by people does not indicate that the stories may
be taken to be evidence of real problems or issues in that society:
it may be argued, however, that the currency of particular
narratives in a society indicates at least an interest in, or preoccupation with, the subjects concerned. Given the realities of life,
rural as well as urban, and particularly the pressures upon people
to observe social norms and regulations, the fact that women
conceive, and give birth to, children outside of matrimony, can
have serious implications in social and economic as well as
religious terms for the person or persons involved. The folklore
evidence indicates both an understanding on the one hand, and
a fear and rejection on the other, of the woman who would find
herself in this predicament.

Thus a complexity of opposing images and opinions is evident.
The intention in briefly summarising some of the material regarding child murderess and dead child traditions in Ireland has been
to indicate that Irish religious legends dealing with the subject of
women taking the lives of their newborn (and unborn) infants
reveals something of the nature of popular beliefs and attitudes
regarding the practices of abortion and infanticide. This material
stands as a complementary, if also somewhat obscure, witness to
the factual historical evidence which is available for research into
these issues. The Irish child murderess and dead child traditions
have been constructed through the interaction of many different
(and sometimes opposing) forces and influences, and, as we have
seen, have found expression in different ways at different times,
even up to the present.

Folklore is historically situated by a comparative method, and
by association with known historically documented events and
facts on the one hand, and by the accumulated evidence and

knowledge of a collectively communicated body of oral tradition on the other. In examining Irish folklore, or any regional folklore it is also essential to situate that material within a wider inter national context. Regarding child murderess and dead child traditions for example, by such an analysis the uniqueness of the Irish traditions becomes readily apparent, and points to a unique concurrence of force and circumstance in creating the social and historical context in which such traditions should have devel oped. Thus the intricate tapestry of historical truths may be examined, strand by strand, and the interrelationship, and com plementarity, of folklore and history may yield enriching insights into human experience.

REFERENCES

1. *Cf.* A. O'Connor, 'Child Murderess and Dead Child Traditions. A Comparative Study' (Ph.D thesis, National University of Ireland, 1987), to be published by Folklore Fellows Communications.
2. *Cf.* J. Pentikäinen, *The Nordic Dead-Child Tradition, Nordic Dead Child-Beings. A Study in Comparative Religion* (Folklore Fellows Communications, Helsinki, 1968), pp. 101–27; Anne O'Connor, *op. cit.*, pp. 12ff.
3. R. Dorson, 'The Debate over the Trustworthiness of Oral and Traditional History' in R. Dorson (ed.), *Folklore: Selected Essays* (Bloomington, 1972).
4. J. Vansina, *Oral Tradition: A Study in Historical Methodology* (London, 1965), p. 43.
5. Dorson, *op. cit.*
6. *Cf.* Pentikäinen, *op. cit*: O'Connor, *op. cit.*, pp. 59–60; B. Almqvist, 'Folk Beliefs and Philology' in *Arv* (1971), pp. 69–75; 'Nida(n)grisur, The Faroese Dead-Child Being' in *Arv* (1971), pp. 97–120; 'Norska utburdsagner i västerled' in *Norveg*, Vol. 21 (1978), pp. 109–19.
7. O'Connor, *op. cit.*, pp. 56ff.
8. *Ibid.* See also C. Damme, 'Infanticide' in *Medical History*, Vol. 22 (1978), pp. 1–24.
9. O'Connor, *op. cit.*; K. Thomas, *Religion and the Decline of Magic. Studies in Popular Beliefs in Sixteenth and Seventeenth Century England* (London, 1971).
10. O'Connor, *op. cit.*, p. 62; Damme, *op. cit.*, pp. 10ff; *cf.* D. Seabourne-Davies, 'Child-Killing in English Law' in *English Studies in Criminal Science*, Vol. IV (1945), pp. 301–43.
11. See U.R.Q. Henriques, 'Bastardy and the New Poor Law' in *Past and Present*, Vol. 37 (1967), pp. 103–29 regarding an act of 18 Elizabeth, 3, 2 in which weekly payments to illegitimate children are specified. Apparently this act was not very effective and further acts were passed to regulate social behaviour (*ibid.*, pp. 103–4).
12. 21 Jac. I c. 27; *cf.* Damme, 'Infanticide', p. 12; Seaborne-Davies, *op. cit.*, p. 312f; R. Sauer, 'Infanticide and Abortion in Nineteenth Century Britain' in *Population Studies*, Vol. 32 (1978), pp. 81–93; R.W. Malcolmson, 'Infanticide in the Eighteenth Century' in

J. Cockburn (ed.), *Crime in England 1550–1800* (London, 1977), p. 196.

13. Damme, 'Infanticide', p. 12.
14. *Cf.* Sauer, *op. cit.*, p. 82.
15. *The Statutes At Large Passed in the Parliaments Held in Ireland* (Dublin, 1786), Vol. IV, p. 120.
16. Sauer, 'Infanticide and Abortion in Nineteenth Century Britain', p. 82; Damme, 'Infanticide', p. 13.
17. *Ibid.*; 43 George 3, c. 58, s. 3; Seaborne-Davies, 'Child Killing in English Law', p. 312n.
18. Sauer, *op. cit.*, p. 84.
19. As noted under note 15 above.
20. *Cf.* O'Connor, 'Child Murderess and Dead Child Traditions', pp. 60–2; Anne O'Connor, 'Images of the Evil Women in Irish Folklore: a Preliminary Survey' in *Women's Studies International Forum*, Vol. II, 4 (1988), pp. 281–5.
21. *Ibid.*, K. Thomas, *Religion and the Decline of Magic.*
22. O'Connor, 'Child Murderess and Dead Child Traditions' pp. 60–2, 77 note 66. See also St John Seymour, *Irish Witchcraft and Demonology* (Dublin, 1913); A. Neary, 'The Origins and Character of the Kilkenny Witchcraft Case of 1324' in *Proceedings of the Royal Irish Academy*, C, 83, 13 (1983), pp. 333–50.
23. O'Connor, 'Images of the Evil Woman in Irish Folklore'.
24. Thomas, *Religion and the Decline of Magic*; O'Connor, 'Child Murderess and Dead Child Traditions'.
25. Pentikäinen, *The Nordic Dead-Child Tradition*, p. 98.
26. *Ibid.*
27. O'Connor, 'Child Murderess and Dead Child Traditions, pp. 63ff. See also P. Laslett, K. Oosterveen and R.E. Smith (eds), *Bastardy and its Comparative History. Studies in the History of Illegitimacy and Marital Nonconformism in Britain, France, Germany, Sweden, North America, Jamaica and Japan* (London, 1980); Sauer, 'Infanticide and Abortion in Nineteenth Century Britain; Malcolmson, 'Infanticide in the Eighteenth Century'; C. Delasselle, 'Abandoned Children in Eighteenth Century Paris' in R. Forster and O. Ranum (eds), *Deviants and the Abandoned in French Society. Selections from the Annales Économies, Sociétés, Civilisations*, Vol. IV (Baltimore and London, 1978), pp. 47–82; L. Rose, *Massacre of the Innocents, Infanticide in Great Britain 1800–1939* (London, 1986); J. Eliassen and S. Sogner (eds), *Boteller Bryllup, Ugifte Mødre og gravide bruder i det gamle samfunnet* (Oslo, 1981); J. Frykman, *Horan i bondesamhallet* (Lund, 1977).
28. *Ibid.*
29. See Malcolmson, 'Infanticide in the Eighteenth Century' regarding Malthusian philosophy.
30. *Ibid.*, p. 189 quoting H.L. Wagner's *Child Murderess* (1775), Schillee's poem 'The Infanticide' (1781) and George Eliot's *Adam Bede* (1851); the theme is also evident in Goethe's *Faust*.
31. *Cf.* O'Connor, 'Child Murderess and Dead Child Traditions', pp. 66–7; *cf.* also J. Robbins, *The Lost Children. A Study of Charity Children in Ireland, 1700–1900* (Dublin, 1980).
32. O'Connor, 'Child Murderess and Dead Child Traditions, pp. 63ff; Rose, *Massacre of the Innocents*; Sauer, 'Infanticide and Abortion in Nineteenth Century Britain'; Henriques, 'Bastardy and the New Poor Law'; P. Knight, 'Women and Abortion in Victorian and

Edwardian England' in *History Workshop Journal*, Vol. 4 (1977), pp. 67–70; J. Weeks, *Sex, Politics and Society. The Regulation of Sexuality Since 1800* (London and New York, 1981).

33. Laslett, Oosterveen and Smith (eds); *Bastardy and Its Comparative History*; Henriques, *op. cit.*; Rose, *op. cit.*; G.R. Quaife, *Wanton Wenches and Wayward Wives. Peasants and Illicit Sex in Early Seventeenth Century England* (London, 1979); M. Kischke, review of Michel Mitterauer, *Ledige Mutter, Zur Geschichte Umehelicher Geburten in Europa* in *Frankfurter Rundschau*, 17 February 1984; R.D. Storch (ed.), *Popular Culture and Custom in Nineteenth Century England* (London and Canberra, 1982).

34. *Cf.* Henriques, 'Bastardy and the New Poor Law'.

35. Official statistics on rates of illegitimate births were initiated under the English and Scottish civil registration acts of 1836 and 1854, respectively, but these statistics must be treated with caution (see Rose, *Massacre of the Innocents*, pp. 22ff). See also S.J. Connolly, 'Illegitimacy and Pre-Nuptial Pregnancy in Ireland Before 1864: the Evidence of Some Catholic Parish Registers' in *Irish Economic and Social History Journal*, Vol. VI, pp. 5–23; *Priests and People in Pre-Famine Ireland* (Dublin, 1982); K.H. Connell, *The Population of Ireland, 1750–1845* (Oxford, 1950).

36. Sauer, 'Infanticide and Abortion in Nineteenth Century Britain'; Rose, *Massacre of the Innocents*; Knight, 'Women and Abortion in Victorian and Edwardian England'.

37. Sauer, *op. cit.*, p. 84.

38. S. Ó Suilleabháin, *A Handbook of Irish Folklore* (Dublin, 1942) and material in the Irish Folklore Collections, housed at the Department of Irish Folklore, University College, Dublin; M. Chamberlain, *Old Wives' Tales, Their History, Remedies and Spells* (London, 1981); *cf.* J. Camp, *Magic Myth and Medicine* (London, 1973); G. Greer, *Sex and Destiny, The Politics of Human Fertility* (London, 1984).

39. O'Connor, 'Child Murderess and Dead Child Traditions'.

40. *Ibid.*, pp. 221ff; L. McKenna (ed.), *Dánta Do Chum Aonghus Fionn Ó Dalaigh* (Dublin and London, 1919), pp. 67–8; L. Ó Caithnia, 'An Apológ i bhFilíócht Shiollach na Gaeilge 1200–1650' (M.A. thesis, National University of Ireland, 1964); F.C. Tubach, *Index Exemplorum* (Folklore Fellows Communications, 204, Helsinki, 1969), p. 79; C. O Maonaigh, O.F.M. (eag.), *Sgáthán Shacramuinte na hAithridhe* (Dublin, 1952), pp. 82–3.

41. O'Connor, 'Child Murderess and Dead Child Traditions'.

42. For examples of both types see appendix.

43. O'Connor, 'Child Murderess and Dead Child Traditions, pp. 221ff. See also appendix below.

44. O'Connor, *op. cit.*, pp. 210ff; F.J. Child, *The English and Scottish Popular Ballads*, Vol. I (London, 1987), pp. 225ff.

45. O'Connor, *op. cit.*, pp. 22ff; O'Connor, 'Images of the Evil Woman in Irish Folklore: A Preliminary Survey' in *Women's Studies International Forum*, Vol. II, 4 (1988).

APPENDIX A: EXAMPLE OF CHILD MURDERESS LEGEND

SÉAMUS O'BOUGE AND 'MÁIRE GAELACH'

It is nearly close on two centuries ago since Máire Gaelach used to be seen in the southern side of this parish. She was an evil spirit and would appear anywhere from Kilmeen Cross to the Ahahan Cross, that would be about half ways across the parish. There was one man whom she made a set on, his name was Séamus O'Bouge. On nights when he would be coming home from fair or market after daylight had passed, one of his own family or some neighbour should go out to meet him and take a scythe.

One night he was returning home with his horse and cart. A neighbour met him and sat into the cart behind him. As they travelled the horse began to sweat and lag as if he had a ton weight behind him.
'Máire is on the cart,' said Séamus, and he turned around and saw her sitting on the heel.
'Strike the heel,' says he to his friend, 'she's on it.'
The man drew a blow of the scythe and she had to go from the steel. She attacked him all the way home, on the wheel she'd be sometimes, on the horse's back another time, but only Séamus himself could see her. And a blow from the scythe would send her off.

One night Séamus was caught out alone, but he hadn't far to get to his own house. As he was walking along Máire came before him.
'Is it Séamus O'Bouge I have' she said.
'Go nine times around Kilmalooda', says he, 'and then you'll know who you have.'
Máire vanished and Séamus ran. He was only closing the door behind him when she was at his heels.
'It was well for you' said she.

The people of the parish were so terrified that the priest decided to banish her. One night he went out on horseback along the road that she was frequenting. Three times he called her, and at the third call she came.
'Where were you when I called first?' he asked her.
'In hell' she replied.
'And where were you when I called the second time?' he asked.
'I was untying the chains that bound me' she said.
'And at my third call?' he asked.
'I came as fast as the devil would let me' she answered.
'What damned you?' asked the priest.
'I murdered my husband, and my two step-children when they slept' she said.
'What more?' asked the priest.
'I murdered an unbaptised infant for hire and I died without repenting it' was her answer.
'I banish you now from these haunts to the shores of the Red Sea' the priest commanded.
'I will wreck every ship that passes that way' she threatened.
'You cannot', said the priest, 'for I will set you a task. Go, take a cockle

shell and with it draw out the waters of the sea until it is empty.'

That was the end of Máire on the road, but the priest's boy got a fright that very same night. When the priest returned home the boy took his horse and led him to the stable. When he had the horse in his stall he ran in and told the priest that a cow had come in after the horse, that he couldn't put her out.

'Never mind,' said the priest, 'that cow can do no harm, and she will be gone in the morning.'

(Recorded in 1947 (Irish Folklore Collections 1015:379–82))

APPENDIX B: EXAMPLE OF DEAD CHILD LEGEND

THE NINE LIGHTS IN THE PRESENCE OF THE PRIEST

There was a woman in *Páirc an tSléibhe*, ten miles on the west side of *Cathair Uibh Ráthaigh*. She was never married. She had nine children, and no two of them were by the same father. The parish priest kept her on the move out of the parish and he said that anyone who would give her the lodgings of the night would be cursed from the altar of God. Nobody would give her lodging. She went and after a year she came in [to the townland] again, in the autumn when they were putting in the hay. She was inside in a farmer's garden near a cock of hay when they came from the meadow with a load of hay. The old person saw the sick woman, and he went in to the woman [his wife] and he said that there was such and such a woman outside and to bring her in.

'I won't,' said she, 'the priest will be cursing us.'

Ah, don't mind,' said he, 'what the priest does, she's not a donkey, she'll have to come in.'

She came in and was given a drink. She said to her son to go and get the old woman who was in the place, the handywoman [midwife] she used be called. He went and when he came to the woman she would not come to her because she was afraid of the priest. The old man went on horseback and he called her and he didn't come off the horse.

'Are you inside?' said he.

'I am,' said she.

'Come out here,' said he, 'and if I come off the horse,' said he, 'you won't see the door of the garden out [you'll come out very very quickly].'

She was afraid, she came out and she went to the house with the old man. She was doing no good, there was no child being born, and at the dead hour of night she said to the man of the house to call for the priest. He did and when he [the priest] found out who it was, he wouldn't allow the coadjutor to come to her.

'Well,' said the coadjutor, 'I'll go there.'

'You'll go to eat your fill' said he.

'It's not to eat my fill that I took this sutane that I'm wearing, but only to save the souls of people, and I will go now,' said he, 'in spite of you.'

'If you go,' said he, 'you needn't come back.'

'If I don't,' said the coadjutor, 'I'll have some other house.'

He went and he found the woman ready and the woman died in his arms, and the child was born dead.

'Well now,' said the priest, 'it is too late to go home, and it's no good for me going home because the door will be locked before me. Nevertheless,' said he, 'we'll go in another little while.' They left.

'I see a light before me,' said the priest, 'and the light is no evil thing,' said he, 'but nevertheless walk behind me,' said he, 'one at a time.'

They did that and when they went another piece along the road they saw ten lighting candles coming against them. Who was there but the Glorious Virgin and nine children with her, they were baptised, and she said to him [the priest]:

'You've done good work tonight.'

'Well I did my best anyhow.'

'You did,' said she, 'and the children there,' said she, 'are mine,' said she, 'and they don't belong to the woman who said they were hers. Do you see the small light,' said she, 'in the house,'

'I do' said he.

'That is the child,' said she, 'who was born a while ago. Baptise it,' said she, 'and I and the boy over there will stand for him,' said she, 'as godmother and godfather,'

He baptised the child on the spot and the candle lit up.

'Be going now,' said she, 'you're doing well,'

'It's no good for me,' said he, 'the door will be locked before me.'

'The door is open before you,' said she, 'because I went to the house,' said she, 'and I opened the door, and himself is asleep.'

'I'll get a lot of his tongue [he will be giving out to me]' said he.

'If you do' said she 'don't say anything.'

She gave him a ring.

'If he's going too hard on you,' said she, 'put this before him and let him look at it.'

When the coadjutor got up in the morning, the parish priest started the scolding and he let him be for a good while, then he brought forward the ring and he put it in the light. He [parish priest] saw something in the ring and he began to perspire. He got sick and he took to the bed. He didn't leave the bed until he died, and the coadjutor had the parish. (Translated from the Irish original recorded in 1949 (Irish Folklore Collections 1152:317–21))

* Reproduced by kind permission of the Department of Irish Folklore, University College, Dublin.

21

Women and Madness in Ireland, 1600–1850

ELIZABETH MALCOLM

It has been a commonplace of male thought since classical Greek times, if not earlier, that women are particularly prone to mental illness and that this propensity results from the 'peculiarities' of their physiology, notably their sexual and reproductive systems.[1] Although this basic premise has been widely accepted, the details of exactly how women's sexual characteristics shape their states of mind have proved far more controversial, and a variety of explanations have been advanced over the centuries by male doctors, philosophers and clergymen. Much of this literature, as we shall see, however, tells us more about male attitudes, and indeed male fears, regarding women than it does about the real problems that led to female mental breadown. It is only when we reach the nineteenth century in fact that, using surviving patient records from mental hospitals, we can gain a clearer insight into the vexed issue of female mental health and escape, to some degree at least, the all-pervasive effects of male prejudice.

From medieval times into the seventeenth century in Ireland, as in much of the rest of Europe, madness in women was commonly regarded as the result of thwarted sexual desire. Unlike nineteenth century bourgeois society, which tended to deny the very existence of female sexuality, earlier centuries had been all too aware of its reality and indeed of its power. Thus, despite the strictures of Christianity, Irish vernacular stories and songs often centred on the problems – sometimes funny, sometimes tragic – created by female lust.[2] But perhaps the most influential attempt to link female sexuality and madness is to be found in Robert Burton's *The Anatomy of Melancholy*, first published in Oxford in 1621. Burton, a middle-aged, unmarried, Oxford scholar and clergyman, largely focused his discussion on male 'melancholy': what we would probably call today neurosis. But, in passing, he had some striking things to say about women. He believed that several distinct groups of women were especially liable to disorders of the mind, notably young, unmarried girls, 'ancient maids', widows and nuns – in other words, women, both young and old, who lacked husbands. Nor was Burton in any doubt why such women were likely to be so afflicted. In an oft-quoted sentence, he asked: 'Of women's unnatural, unsatiable lust, what Country, what Village doth not complain?'[3] Like many of his male contemporaries and forebears, Burton believed that women's sexual appetites were far greater than men's and, if they should happen not to be satisfied, then disorder and havoc would be the inevitable outcome. In young girls the 'green sickness', as the problems associated with adolescent sexuality were termed in the seventeenth century, could be cured relatively easily by marriage.[4] Burton thought that a 'very sparing' diet, blood-letting and 'physick' could help girls suffering from the 'green sickness', but 'the best and surest remedy of all is to see them well placed, and married to good husbands in due time; . . . this [is] the ready cure, to give them content to their desires'.[5]

Contenting the sexual desires of young women was one thing, however, satisfying those of older women was rather a different matter. Burton demonstrated a distaste for, if not a positive horror of, old women, typical both of his sex and of his era.[6] If 'burning Lust' and its resulting 'Disease, Phrensy, Madness, Hell' was to be condemned when found among the hot-blooded young, how much worse was lust among the old. For 'an old fool to dote, to see an old lecher, what more odious, what can be more absurd?' scoffed Burton. But the worst 'old lecher' was a female one:

> Worse it is in women than in men, [Burton went on] when she is . . . an old widow, a mother so long since . . . she doth very unseemly seek to marry, yet whilst she is so old a crone, a beldam, she can neither see, nor hear, go nor stand, a mere carcass, a witch, and scarce feel; she catterwauls, and must have a stallion, a champion . . .[7]

The key to Burton's intense reaction against the sexuality of older women is to be found in his use of the word 'witch'. For centuries the witch had commonly been portrayed as an elderly, single woman and her dealings with Satan and his usually male cohorts had had strong sexual overtones. Typically the witch undertook to carry out Satan's orders in return for sexual favours, often of a bizarre kind. Thus, the insatiable demands of female sexuality not only provoked madness, but they also provided the devil with a ready means of wrecking havoc in human affairs.[8] It is probably no coincidence that the most famous accusation of witchcraft made in Ireland was levelled in the fourteenth century against

Alice Kyteler, a wealthy Kilkenny woman, who had been widowed four times.

But at least witches and women maddened by insatiable lust were figures of power, and indeed of considerable menace. As belief in demonology went into eclipse in the seventeenth and eighteenth centuries, however, so the mad were seen less as demoniacs or wild beasts and more as the child-like victims of faulty social conditioning or of physical irregularities. This was particularly true of women, who came to be regarded as the helpless prey of their own inherently weak physical and emotional make-ups.[9]

Greek medicine had identified displacement of the uterus, or the 'wandering womb' as it was popularly known, as the underlying cause of many female mental disorders. In *Timaeus* Plato had argued that the womb in women

> is a living creature within them which longs to bear children. And if it is left unfertilized long beyond the normal time, it causes extreme unrest, strays about the body, blocks the channels of the breath and causes in consequence acute distress and disorders of all kinds.[10]

Sixteenth- and seventeenth-century medical writers were still employing this bizarre, ancient theory to explain what was termed 'fits of the mother' or 'hysteria'. The 'mother' in this instance was a popular term for the womb, while the word 'hysteria', which came into use in English in the seventeenth century, was derived from the Greek word for womb.[11] In addition to the womb, menstruation was also frequently singled out as a feature of women's physiology liable to disturb their minds. Burton again stressed that menstruation was particularly problematical in unmarried women. He believed that menstrual blood gave off 'vicious', 'black', 'smoky' and 'putrid' vapours and in unmarried women this 'fuliginous exhalation of corrupt seed, [troubled] the brain, heart, and mind', producing 'care, sorrow, and anxiety, obfuscation of spirits, agony, desperation and the like . . .'[12]

The general thrust of male writing on the subject of female madness during the seventeenth century was clearly in the direction of the notion that marriage, sexual satisfaction and childbirth were the cures for most of the troubles that afflicted women. If madness largely arose out of women's failure to exercise their 'natural' sexual and reproductive functions, then marriage was the obvious panacea.

But even during the seventeenth century, more mechanistic theories regarding the operations of both the mind and the body were developing and these were given an enormous fillip at the end of the century by the educational theories of John Locke and by the researches into optics and gravity of Isaac Newton. Such theories led to a significant shift in attitudes to women. Already in the 1660s Thomas Willis, one of the pioneers of modern neurology, had rejected notions of humours or vapours in favour of a theory which focused on the nerves. Willis believed that nerves carrying fluids or spirits around the body were keys to both mental and physical health.[13] How exactly the nerves functioned was much debated, but one fact of which Willis and his followers were convinced was that women had weaker nerves than men. Willis was particularly interested in hysteria, but to him it had nothing to do with discontented wombs or frustrated sexuality; it was a nervous disorder: a defect of the nervous spirit. Thomas Sydenham, a follower of Willis who published an influential account of hysteria in 1682, wrote that women

> are more frequently afflicted with this disease than men, because they have receiv'd from nature a finer and more delicate constitution of body, being designed for an easier life and the pleasure of men, who were made robust, that they might be able to cultivate the earth, hunt and kill wild beasts for food, and undergo violent exercises.[14]

The earlier notion of female madness being brought about by unsatisfied sexual desire was giving way to an idea of madness as resulting from weakness, or more flatteringly, delicacy, of the body and particularly of the senses. This process went hand in hand with a growing tendency to deny women's sexuality altogether. Admittedly the process was never fully completed, for it was applied more commonly to women of the middle and upper classes than to women of the working classes. Male writers on women and madness in fact largely ignored working-class women, believing, like Burton, that the 'hired servant . . . poor handmaid . . . [or] coarse country wench . . . kept hard to her work and bodily labour' was seldom troubled in the mind. Far more vulnerable were 'Noble Virgins, nice Gentlewomen, such as are solitary and idle, live at ease, lead a life out of action and employment . . .'.[15] Certainly in the eighteenth century leisure, as well as extreme physical delicacy and an acute mental sensibility, was considered an essential attribute of the hysterical woman.[16]

Little of substance regarding women and madness appears to have been written in Ireland before the eighteenth and nineteenth centuries. Giraldus Cambrensis, following his visits in the late twelfth century, concluded that the Irish were exceptionally healthy and that their climate was particularly good for those suffering from nervous disorders.[17] But, whatever the situation

in the twelfth century, certainly by the seventeenth and eighteenth centuries there was a growing concern about the problems
posed to society by the mentally ill. Mad people seem either to
have been confined at home, allowed to wander the countryside
as beggars, or else committed to prisons and later to workhouses
and hospitals. In 1817 Denis Browne, MP for County Mayo, told
a select committee investigating the plight of the lunatic poor in
Ireland that traditionally there had been 'nothing so shocking as
madness in the cabin of the peasant, where the man is out
labouring in the fields for his bread, and the care of the woman
of the house is scarcely sufficient for the attendance on the
children'. For the rural poor 'the only way . . . to manage' this
'human calamity', according to Browne, was to imprison the mad
person in a hole in the cabin floor. The 'wretched being' stayed
there till he or she died.[18] Among the middle and gentry classes
the mad also seem generally to have been confined at home, for
Ireland lacked the many small, expensive, private asylums that
sprang up in England in the eighteeenth century.[19] But even
greater numbers of lunatics appear simply to have wandered the
countryside as part of the large army of vagrants and beggars that
was so characteristic of eighteenth-century Ireland. Certainly
when attempts were made to establish workhouses to control
vagrancy, first at the beginning of the century and again in the
1770s, they quickly attracted large numbers of mentally ill
inmates.[20] Prisons also housed lunatics. In 1684, for instance, the
keeper of the Dublin house of correction petitioned the corporation for money with which to maintain a 'madd woman', who
had been committed in the previous year by the lord mayor. After
a similar petition in 1701, the corporation agreed to pay a regular
sum towards the upkeep of imprisoned lunatics.[21]

The institutionalisation of the mad, which began in Ireland on
a small scale in the seventeenth century, continued rather hap-
hazardly in the eighteenth century and during the nineteenth
century gained such momentum that by 1914 an astonishing one
person in every two hundred was resident in a public mental
hospital.[22] The collecting together of large numbers of mad
people had several important implications, not least of these was
that it provided doctors, for the first time, with an opportunity to
study mental illness in large groups over long periods. Generally,
however, it was not until the second half of the nineteenth
century that the Irish medical profession showed much interest
in the problems of the mentally ill, most doctors preferring to
treat the body rather than the mind. But there was an important
exception to this state of affairs in the person of Dr William
Saunders Hallaran, the first Irish doctor to write a major book on

madness. His *Practical Observations on the Causes and Cure of Insanity* was published in Cork in 1810 and appeared again in 1818 in an expanded edition. Hallaran had received his medical education in Edinburgh under Dr William Cullen, one of the most noted eighteenth-century medical teachers and a leading proponent of the nervous theories of Willis and Sydenham. But Hallaran's views on mental illness did not come from lectures or textbooks alone; as he liked to stress, they were 'practical', that is based on his long personal experience of managing asylums. From the early 1790s till his death in 1826, Hallaran was physician to the Cork County and City Workhouse and Asylum, as well as operating his own small, private asylum near the city. The Cork workhouse had been opened in 1777 and in 1791–2 a special block was built for the accommodation of 24 lunatics. By the time of Hallaran's death the asylum had the capacity to house nearly 300 lunatics and was the largest institution of its kind in Ireland.[23]

Although in some respects Hallaran's attitude to mental illness was very enlightened for the period, he nevertheless was thoroughly imbued with the traditional view as to women's greater suspectibility to insanity.

This cannot be wondered at [he wrote] when we take into account the many exciting causes to which females are more particularly exposed: such as those arising from difficult parturition; the sudden retrocession of the milk, immediately on delivery; the irresistible force of sudden terror, – or of severe disappointment, producing grief; or of unexpected fortune, – excessive joy, or surprise.[24]

Later Hallaran added menopause to this list of predisposing factors. But, among men, the situation was decidedly different.

Amongst males, on the contrary, [wrote Hallaran] though the proclivity as to temperament be equally strong, it is observed, even on exposure to that description of excitement to which they are obnoxious, that their superior powers of resistence will continue until, with the exception of a few particularities, the impulse ceases to be observed.[25]

So, even when as predisposed to insanity as women, perhaps through hereditary factors, men were far better equipped by their stronger constitutions to resist disturbing influences.

In the second edition of his book Hallaran included a fascinating table, listing the numbers of both men and women admitted to the Cork asylum between 1798 and 1818, with the causes of their illnesses. Nearly fourteen hundred people appear on this list, almost exactly 50 per cent of whom are women. Although Hallaran had claimed that women were more prone to mental illness than men, he argued that men were more likely to be committed to asylums by their families. And indeed, throughout the nineteenth century, men outnumbered women in Irish public asylums, though in English asylums women were coming increasingly to predominate.[26] These figures are somewhat problematical, however, as many public asylums provided equal amounts of accommodation for both sexes, regardless of demand; and this seems to have been the case in Cork under Hallaran. Asylum population figures are thus of dubious value in assessing levels of mental illness among men and women.

Hallaran's table shows that the most common causes of insanity in women were: excess in drinking; terror from the rebellion; heredity; disappointment; difficult parturition; grief; and loss of property. We perhaps need to bear in mind when analysing this information that the period it covers was one of considerable political and economic dislocation, including, for example, the 1798 rebellion and French invasion, the Napoleonic wars and the severe post-war depression. These years were also ones of rapidly rising whiskey consumption.[27] With regard to men too, drink and the rebellion were the most common causes of illness listed, though male victims of drink outnumbered female ones by nearly two to one. After these causes came: loss of property, in which men also significantly outnumbered women; heredity; and epilepsy. Men were admitted as well far more commonly

Hallaran's 'Table of the Causes of Insanity', 1798–1818[28]

	Male	Female
Terror from the Rebellion	61	47
Jealousy	20	25
Pride	1	9
Grief	6	34
Fever	3	5
Epilepsy	33	24
Religious Zeal	11	9
Loss of Property	51	33
Excess in Drinking	103	57
Disappointment	10	37
Lues Venerea	12	1
Consumption	6	2
Injury on the Head	19	2
Heredity	41	38
Palsy	6	7
Difficult Parturition	–	36
Unknown	295	328
Total	678	694

than women for insanity resulting from venereal disease, tuberculosis and head injuries. One of the most intriguing aspects of Hallaran's work is the stress he places on contemporary events as important determinants of mental health. He was convinced that anxiety and insecurity resulting from the rebellion, plus the increase in spirit consumption, were leading to many more cases of mental breakdown. These views were quoted by witnesses appearing before the 1817 select committee on pauper lunatics and they almost certainly played a part in the government's decision to embark on a large-scale programme of public asylum building in Ireland.[29]

But it is what Hallaran's data tells us about perceived differences between men and women that is more germane to this article. Hallaran believed that there were two basic types of insanity: one arising from physical disorders and the other the product of mental or emotional disturbances. In his treatment of the sexes it is clear that he felt men to be more prone to insanity resulting from bodily illnesses or disabilities, like venereal disease or tuberculosis, while in women emotional factors, like romantic disappointments or grief at the death of a loved one, loomed much larger. Difficulties in childbirth and menopause certainly were physical events in a woman's life, which, in Hallaran's view, were likely to produce mental disorders. But it is interesting to note that he, unlike some earlier male writers, has nothing to say regarding the problems of women's sexuality. Of course the reliability of Hallaran's figures and the picture that emerges from them must be open to question. Hallaran essentially argues that women are more prone to insanity than men, even though female patients did not significantly outnumber male ones in his own asylum in Cork. His statistics certainly suggest that women became ill for more varied reasons than men. But one cannot help wondering if Hallaran's theories regarding the greater vulnerability of women were formulated on the basis of his experience of women asylum patients, or if his perception of women's problems was really determined by his pre-existing views as to the nature of women. Either way, his book – the first major statement on mental illness by an Irishman – strongly endorsed long-established male opinions regarding women's basic mental instability.

Hallaran, unfortunately, only gives details of a few of his actual cases and these on the whole relate more to questions of treatment than to the circumstances of the patient. Thus, if we want accounts of the lives of Irish women admitted to asylums, we need to venture further into the nineteenth century and to shift our focus to Dublin. St Patrick's Hospital, on the corner of

Steevens and Bow Lanes, is the oldest mental hospital in Ireland and one of the oldest such purpose-built institutions in the world. It had been erected with money provided under the will of Jonathan Swift and opened to receive its first patients in 1757.[30] But patient records are sketchy and incomplete up to the 1830s and it is only from the 1840s that admission application forms survive. These, however, often provide a wealth of information about individual patients and especially so when accompanied by letters from relatives. As we shall soon see, the picture that emerges from a survey of the women admitted to St Patrick's in the 1840s is far more complex, and indeed compelling, than the rather crude caricature presented in much of the theoretical literature relating to women and madness.

A number of interesting points emerge from the table below and from the admission forms generally. By the 1840s St Patrick's patients were predominantly male and Protestant and also predominantly middle class and Dublin resident. The erection of

An Analysis of Admission Forms of St Patrick's Hospital, Dublin, 1841–50[31]

Total admissions	256	
Surviving forms (%)	69	
Male patients (%)	61	
Female patients (%)	39	
Protestants (%)	75	
Catholics (%)	25	
Marital status	Male (%)	Female (%)
Married	40	19
Single	54	75
Widowed	6	6
Age between 20 and 40	64	61
Committed by		
Father	19	19
Mother	15	19
Brother	25	23
Sister	3	10
Husband	–	13
Wife	20	–
Other	18	16
Length of stay more than 5 years	29	43

Discharged		
Recovered	27	26
Relieved	18	24
Unrelieved	11	6
Fate unknown	6	7
Died in the hospital	38	37
Cause of illness		
Not known or given	30	44
Overwork or study	13	3
Financial reverses	10	4
Ill health	7	13
Natal or menstrual problems	–	7
Drink	13	1
Drugs	1	1
Religion	5	6
Grief	1	6
Romantic or domestic	4	4
Heredity	6	2
Anxiety or nervousness	5	6
Hysteria	–	2
Mental excitement	5	1

public asylums throughout the country, beginning in the 1820s, plus the appearance of a handful of expensive, private asylums, meant that St Patrick's was catering less and less for either the very poor or the very rich, or for those living outside the city and county of Dublin. Some 90 per cent of the hospital's male patients were employed; most in occupations like medicine, the law, the army, the church, business, commerce and administration. University students, shopkeepers, skilled tradesmen and farmers were also well represented. In contrast, among women patients admitted in the 1840s, only about a quarter had some form of paid employment. Most of these were governesses or teachers, especially music teachers, with a sprinkling of dressmakers, shopkeepers or assistants, and postmistresses; and with one workhouse matron. Women patients were also overwhelmingly single, unlike the men, a significant proportion of whom were married. In terms of age, both groups were largely young to middle aged, though the number of elderly female patients was on the increase. Most also were committed by a close relative, but it is interesting to note that the group most likely to commit were brothers, rather than fathers, mothers, husbands or wives. In terms of length of stay in the hospital, there was again a significant difference between the sexes, with women being far more likely than men to spend long periods in the institution. Men, however, were as likely as women to die there, though the death rate among men was falling more rapidly than that among women.

On the admission forms both the cause and the nature of the illness had to be given. This appears generally to have been done by relatives, perhaps at times with advice from the two doctors who signed the accompanying medical certificate. Unfortunately however, the categories used to describe 'nature of illness' are so inexact as to be almost meaningless. Commonly used terms are 'mania', 'melancholia', 'monomania', 'insanity', 'moral insanity' 'derangement', 'dementia' and 'lunacy', while 'irritability', 'constant talking', 'selfishness' and 'quiet' also appear. More precise and more detailed descriptions tend, however, to appear under the heading 'cause of illness' and so I have chosen to analyse these instead. Though even here, as can be seen in the table, for about a third of cases no cause was given or the cause was listed as unknown. This probably reflected genuine popular ignorance about mental illness, but it may also very well have reflected a reluctance on the part of relatives to publicise embarrassing family secrets. Keeping in mind that the figures are by no means complete, let alone reliable, we can at least deduce from the above table that employment and financial difficulties, followed by drunkenness, were far and away the most common causes given for male mental breakdown. With regard to women, ignorance or unwillingness to impart information was even greater, but such figures as we do have suggest that physical ill health and grief were the factors most likely to produce mental illness.

Some families do seem to have been more prepared than most to provide St Patrick's with detailed information on the nature and cause of the patient's illness. A number of admission forms were accompanied by letters or petitions explaining the reasons for seeking admission or requesting free admission. An examination of such correspondence helps put a little more flesh on the bones of the data contained in the table above. Three women admitted to St Patrick's at this time offer good examples of the sorts of backgrounds from which female patients came. Below are brief accounts of their cases.

Mary Anne Hickey was born in 1819, the eldest of five daughters of a Dublin brewer and publican, Charles Hickey of New Market. Her father and mother both died around 1837, when Mary Anne was 18, leaving her and her sisters with an income between them of a mere £70 per annum, derived from an interest that Charles Hickey had had in two public houses. In

November 1837 Mary Anne was admitted to St Patrick's Hospital
as a free patient, which suggests that she was too poor to pay
any fee. She stayed for a year, being removed in December 1838
as convalescent by her uncle and aunt, Denis and Julia Ford of
Castle Street. For over two years she was 'perfectly well', according to the Fords. But in April 1841 she was readmitted to St
Patrick's suffering, according to the medical certificate accompanying the admission form, from insanity caused by anxiety
about her health. More information on her situation was,
however, contained in a memorial from the Fords attached to the
application. This stated that the small income on which the
Hickey sisters relied had been wiped out in consequence of Fr
Mathew's temperance crusade, which had forced many public
houses to close. Mary Anne was thus 'without any means of
support whatsoever'. What happened to her younger sisters is
not disclosed in the hospital's records, but they do show that she
remained a free patient until her death from tuberculosis in
1863.[32]

Our second example of a woman admitted to St Patrick's in the
1840s is Euphemia Nickson. She was born in 1803, one of five
children of Michael Nickson, a linen draper with a prosperous
business in Grafton Street. Michael Nickson, however, lost all his
money when he invested heavily in a flour mill and he died in
1841 leaving his children penniless. By 1842 the two brothers and
three sisters were, as they themselves described it, maintaining
'an unequal struggle against adversity for personal support'. The
eldest son Michael, a flour miller with a 'numerous family', was
out of work: the other son had had a job as a clerk in the post
office, but had lost it due to reductions in staff: while the three
sisters ran a school, which they were having difficulty in getting
enough pupils to make viable. Euphemia, who was described on
her admission form as a governess, appears to have broken down
shortly after her father's death, for in mid-1841 she was admitted
to a private asylum in Finglas at a cost of £60 per annum. Clearly,
however, her brothers and sisters could not afford this fee for
long; equally clearly, though, they did not want to commit her as
a pauper to a public asylum. Instead, in November 1842, they
successfully petitioned St. Patrick's to take her as a free patient;
and there she stayed till her death from a haemorrhage in 1863.[33]

Our third case is Eleanor Murray, born in 1825, the daughter
of John and Elizabeth Murray of Sligo. John Murray, an apoth-
ecary, died in 1835 of a fever, leaving his widow to bring up seven
children, ranging in age from 11 months to 11 years. She was
assisted financially by her two brothers and also by her brother-
in-law, Denis Murray, an army surgeon who had served in the

East Indies for many years. In the mid-1840s, however, the famil
was hit by a series of disasters. One of Elizabeth Murray'
brothers died, as did one of her sons after a long illness. Eleanor
the eldest daughter who was 22, also became seriously ill. Thi
occurred during the black famine year of 1847: a tragic time fo
many Irish families. Eleanor did recover, but, according to he
uncle Surgeon Murray, she was immediately afflicted witl
'dementia'. For two years her mother looked after her at home
By May 1850, however, she had become so unmanageable tha
she had to be committed to the county jail as a dangerous lunatic
and from there in October she was transferred to St Patrick's. She
was admitted as the highest category of paying patient, with a
fee of 40 guineas a year, for although she had no resources of her
own, she was entitled to £400 upon her mother's death. But in
1854 Surgeon Murray, who was then living on half pay in
Enniskerry, County Wicklow, petitioned the hospital to have his
niece's fee reduced 'to the cheapest class of paid patient'. After
consideration, the governors agreed to reduce the sum to £30 a
year. In his petition the surgeon said that he had hoped St
Patrick's might be able to cure Eleanor, but, on the contrary, 'the
complaint appears to have settled down into confirmed idiocy
leaving no room for hope of recovery'. Eleanor Murray died in
St. Patrick's of 'senile decay' in 1903. Casebooks, begun in 1899,
record her as suffering from 'melancholia and dementia' and as
living 'a very automatic life': eating when food was placed in front
of her, sleeping when put to bed, and spending most days sitting
beside the fire staring vacantly in front of her. After 53 years in
the institution, it is hardly to be wondered at that Eleanor
Murray's life had become 'automatic'.[34]

These three women are typical of female patients admitted to
St Patrick's during the 1840s in a number of respects, notably in
the fact that they all experienced a family breakdown resulting in
financial hardship. Such cases would seem to underline the
crucial role of the father in the nineteenth-century, Irish, middle-
class family and to suggest that the younger, female members
were utterly unprepared to cope with the consequences of his
unexpected death. These women were not expected nor trained
to work and only undertook employment when forced to do so
by dire necessity. But jobs like governessing, music teaching or
dressmaking, though relatively 'respectable', were insecure and
poorly paid and hardly amounted to a satisfying career. The
accounts of the lives of governesses contained in the hospital
admission forms particularly portray loneliness, poverty and
uncertainty.[35] If an orphaned young woman did not work,
however, then she became a financial burden upon her family.

Fathers of course were expected to support unmarried daughters, but other relatives were less willing, and often less able, to do so. Brothers, for instance, demonstrated a greater readiness than any other single relative to commit family members to St Patrick's. Among the admission documentation surviving from the 1840s are letters from the brothers of female patients, complaining of the financial difficulties attendant upon raising their own families while having, at the same time, to support a mad sister.[36] On the other hand, however, there are a few cases which look suspiciously as though brothers were trying to rid themselves of unwanted female dependants by having them committed. Admittedly the evidence is suggestive rather than conclusive, but wrongful committals certainly were a problem in nineteenth-century private asylums.[37]

What emerges most forcefully though from the correspondence accompanying admission forms is a picture of women struggling to cope with familial and economic misfortune, with insecurity and with powerlessness in a society that allowed them little scope for self-expression or independence. These letters and petitions reveal a complex and problematical socio-economic context which is almost totally absent from the theoretical literature on the subject. One inevitably wonders what a study of the surviving admission forms from the public asylums would reveal about the lives and problems of Irish rural and working-class women. Unfortunately to date, except for one brief article, no such study has been attempted.[38]

In the middle-class family it was clearly the unmarried daughters who were in the most vulnerable position if the family fell upon hard times. They, probably more than mothers or sons, were the ones who broke down when the family was under stress. Both mothers and sons had accepted roles, indeed vital roles, in the event of a crisis. The mother had to support and bring up the children in place of the father. Having completed this task, however, older widows then became more vulnerable. In the 1870s and 1880s, for instance, when the female population of St Patrick's had come to outnumber the male, widows in their fifties and sixties comprised 15 per cent of female patients. Sons also had clearly defined roles. When old enough they had to get work or pursue a career, though the obligation to support an aging mother and unmarried sisters must have become a severe burden when a son wished to marry and start a family of his own. Only daughters had little or no role outside marriage; and a daughter from a family which had fallen on hard times was not a very attractive marriage prospect. Small wonder then that far more women than men were admitted to St Partick's suffering from the effects of grief at the death of a close relative. It is not always possible to identify this relative, but it does indeed appear that in many cases it was a father.

The St Patrick's admission forms thus suggest that orphaned younger women, plus middle-aged single women and older widows, were most likely to find themselves committed to asylums. These of course were much the same groups that Burton had identified back in the 1620s as particularly susceptible to madness. But his simple explanation of frustrated sexuality, although more convincing than earlier notions of displaced wombs, is still not adequate to account for the plight of such women. Daughter, wife and mother were the three accepted female roles, particularly among the middle and upper classes. It is therefore no coincidence that most of the women committed to St Patrick's in the 1840s, and later in the century as well, did not fill any of these roles. In this sense they were social misfits and for this reason, rather than because their disorders were any more serious than those of men, they were liable to spend long periods in the hospital. Male patients had social roles to return to; often they had jobs or careers which could be resumed. They were also more likely to have close relatives who wanted them back, who may in fact have needed them as breadwinners. As the above table shows, families were a good deal more willing to take back male patients who had not improved in the hospital than they were to take back women in the same circumstances.

It is thus only when we extract women from male medical treatises and observe them in the contexts of their own lives that we have some chance of understanding why certain of them suffered from mental disorders. The learned medical tracts discussed in the first half of this article generally tell us more about men's fears and misconceptions than they do about women's problems, mental or otherwise. But, unfortunately, scholarly works by eminent male clergymen, doctors and philosophers are far more readily available in libraries and archives than is material illustrative of the daily lives and problems of working- or middle-class women. Yet, in Ireland for the late eighteenth and nineteenth centuries at least, the records of hospitals like St Patrick's and also of prisons, workhouses, nunneries and other institutions which housed significant numbers of women, are beginning to be tapped; and although their analysis is often complex and time consuming, they promise a rich harvest to the dedicated student of women's history.[39]

REFERENCES

1. H. King, 'Bound to Bleed: Artemis and Greek Women' in A. Cameron and A. Kuhrt (eds), *Images of Women in Antiquity* (London and Canberra, 1983), p. 113.
2. See, for example, Séathrún Céitinn, 'A bhean lán de stuaim' in S. Ó Tuama and T. Kinsella (eds). *An Duanaire, 1600–1900: Poems of the Dispossessed* (Portlaoise, 1981), pp. 86–9.
3. R. Burton, *The Anatomy of Melancholy*, ed. A.R. Shilleto (London, 1896), Vol. III, p. 61.
4. A. Fraser, *The Weaker Vessel: Woman's Lot in Seventeenth-Century England* (London, 1985), pp. 51, 56.
5. Burton, *Anatomy*, Vol. I, p. 479.
6. Fraser, *op. cit.*, pp. 110–15.
7. Burton, *Anatomy*, Vol. III, pp. 54, 61–2.
8. K. Thomas, *Religion and the Decline of Magic: Studies in Popular Beliefs in Sixteenth- and Seventeenth-Century England* (Harmondsworth, 1973), pp. 678–9; G. Rosen, *Madness in Society: Chapters in the Historical Sociology of Mental Illness* (Chicago and London, 1968), pp. 13–14, 238–41; R. Padel, 'Women: Model for Possession by Greek Daemons' in Cameron and Kuhrt (eds), *op. cit.*, pp. 12–14.
9. R. Porter, *Mind-Forg'd Manacles: A History of Madness in England from the Restoration to the Regency* (London, 1987), p. 105.
10. Plato, *Timaeus and Critias*, trans. Desmond Lee (rev. edn Harmondsworth, 1977), p. 123.
11. Thomas, *op cit.*, pp. 15–16; Vieda Skultans, *English Madness: Ideas on Insanity, 1580–1890* (London, Boston and Henley, 1979), pp. 83–4.
12. Burton, *Anatomy*, Vol. I, pp. 476–7.
13. Porter, *op. cit.*, pp. 176–7; K. Doerner, *Madmen and the Bourgeoisie: A Social History of Insanity and Psychiatry*, trans. Joachim Neugroschel and Jean Steinberg (Oxford, 1981), pp. 24–5.
14. Quoted in Doerner, *op. cit.*, pp. 26–7.
15. Burton, *Anatomy*, Vol. I, p. 479.
16. Porter, *op. cit.*, pp. 105–8.
17. Gerald of Wales, *The History and Topography of Ireland*, trans, J.J. O'Meara (Harmondsworth, 1982), pp. 53–4.
18. *Report from the Select Committee on the Lunatic Poor in Ireland*, p. 23, H.C. 1817 (430), Vol. VIII, p. 55.
19. W.L. Parry-Jones, *The Trade in Lunacy: A Study of Private Madhouses in England in the Eighteenth and Nineteenth Centuries* (London and Toronto, 1972).
20. Sir W. Fownes to Swift, 9 September 1732 in H. Williams (ed.), *The Correspondence of Jonathan Swift* (Oxford, 1965), Vol. IV, pp. 65–70.
21. J.T. Gilbert (ed.), *Calendar of Ancient Records of Dublin* (Dublin, 1895), Vol. V, p. 321; (Dublin, 1896), Vol. VI, p. 257.
22. M. Finnane, *Insanity and the Insane in Post-Famine Ireland* (London, 1981), p. 233.
23. *Copies of All Correspondence . . . on the Subject of Public Lunatic Asylums*, pp. 17–18. H.C. 1828 (234), Vol. XXII, pp. 239–40.
24. W.S. Hallaran, *Practical Observations on the Causes and Cure of Insanity* (2nd edn, Cork, 1818), p. 50.
25. *Ibid.*, p. 51.

26. Finnane, *op. cit.*, pp. 130–1; E. Showalter, *The Female Malady: Women, Madness and English Culture, 1830–1980* (London, 1985), pp. 51–3.

27. Elizabeth Malcolm, *'Ireland Sober, Ireland Free': Drink and Temperance in Nineteenth-Century Ireland* (Dublin, 1986), pp. 22–4.

28. Hallaran, *op. cit.*, page not numbered.

29. *Report from the Select Committee on the Lunatic Poor in Ireland*, p. 12, H.C. 1817 (430), Vol. VIII, p. 44; Hallaran, *op. cit.*, pp. 46–9.

30. For more details of St Patrick's history, see Elizabeth Malcolm, *Swift's Hospital: A History of St Patrick's Hospital, Dublin, 1746–1989* (Dublin, 1989).

31. Admission Forms, Nos 300–599, 1841–53 (St Patrick's Hospital, Dublin, uncatalogued).

32. Mary Anne Hickey, Admission Form No. 311, 23 April 1841 (St Partick's Hospital, Dublin, uncatalogued).

33. Euphemia Nickson, Admission Form No. 349, 31 October 1842 (St Patrick's Hospital, Dublin, uncatalogued).

34. Eleanor Murray, Admission Form No. 551, 17 September 1850; Casebook-Female-1899, p. 86 (St Patrick's Hospital, Dublin, uncatalogued).

35. See, for example, Anne Barter, Admission Form No. 348, 4 July 1842 (St Patrick's Hospital Dublin, uncatalogued).

36. See, for example, Mary Anne Medlicott, Admission Form No. 327, 4 December 1841 (St Patrick's Hospital, Dublin, uncatalogued).

37. See, for example, Elizabeth Julia Grove Grady and Susanna Grove Grady, Admission Forms Nos 419 and 420, 12 May 1845 (St Patrick's Hospital, Dublin, uncatalogued): for a discussion of the problem in England, see P. McCandless, 'Liberty and Lunacy: The Victorians and Wrongful Confinement' in A. Scull (ed.), *Madhouses, Mad-Doctors, and Madmen: The Social History of Psychiatry in the Victorian Era* (London, 1981), pp. 339–62; for a fictional treatment of the wrongful confinement of women in the eighteenth century, see Mary Wollstonecraft, *Mary and The Wrongs of Woman*, ed. G. Kelly (Oxford and New York, 1976).

38. For a comparison of admissions to nineteenth-century public asylums in both Ireland and New South Wales, see M. Finnane, 'Asylums, Families and the State' in *History Workshop*, no. 20 (Autumn 1985), pp. 134–48.

39. For some recent interesting studies of Irish women and institutions, see C. Clear, *Nuns in Nineteenth-Century Ireland* (Dublin and Washington, DC, 1987) and H. Burke, *The People and the Poor Law in 19th Century Ireland* (Dublin, 1987).

Index

abortion, 305ff
agnatic succession customs, 26–7
alehouses, keeping of, 50–1, 54, 60
annals, 148ff; women's obituaries in,
  148–52; *Annals of Connacht*, 148;
  Annals of Inisfallen, 32; *Annals of
  Loch Ce*, 38, 70, 148; *Annals of the
  Four Masters*, 37; *Annals of Ulster*,
  148–9; *see also* Gaelic literature
Appleby, John C, 5, 11, 53ff
Armagh, 95, 97, 201, 247
Askeaton castle, 161
Athlone, 94, 106, 169

Badinter, Elizabeth, 277
Baker, Deborah, 184
bardic literature, 32–5, 70–1, 87, 134ff,
  147; ideal women, 70, 148–9;
  bardic schools exclude women,
  152; *see also* Gaelic literature
Barnewall, Margery, 188
bean an tí, 8, 214, 217
Beaton, Cardinal David, 21
Belfast, 44, 138, 139
Benedictine nuns, 169
Bermingham, Margaret, 162, 214
Bethlehem convent, 191–2
Binchy, D A (ed.)
  Studies in Early Irish Law (1936), 1
Bingham, Sir Richard, 57–8, 79
Blagdon, Barbara, 182, 183–4
Bolton, Richard
  Justice of the Peace for Ireland (1638), 46
Bom Sucesso convent, 117, 169, 191
Bonny, Anne, 53ff, 64–6
Book of Howth, 72–3
Book of Leinster, 33
Book of O Conor Don, 36
Book of the Dean of Lismore, 33, 34–5

Boyle, Richard, earl of Cork, 47, 167,
  277–8; on the education of his
  children, 170–3
Brady, Ciaran, 5, 6, 69ff
brehon law *see* Gaelic law and customs
brideprice, 20
Britanny, trade with, 118
Brodrick, Alan, 282, 287
Burke, Honora, countess of Clanrickard,
  77
Burke, Síle, 36, 40
Burton, Robert
  Anatomy of Melancholy (1621), 318
Butler, Eleanor, countess of Desmond,
  79–81
Butler, Joan, countess of Desmond, 164
Butlers of Ormond, 76

Calvinism, 165, 166, 199–200
Cambrensis, Giraldus, 224, 321
Cambridge, Alice, 202, 207
Campbell, Agnes, 35, 38, 78–9
Campion, Edmund, 161–2
Canny, Nicholas, 277–8
Carrick-on-Suir, 11–12; widows in,
  236ff
Cashel marriage registers, 226
Casway, Jerrold, 7, 112ff
Catholic Church, 7–8, 213ff; canonical
  portion of death duty, 19; clerical
  arbitration, 47; women in, 7, 117,
  189, 193–212, 224
cess, 58
childbirth, 291ff
child murder, 304ff
Church of Ireland, 8, 46, 165, 167, 170,
  179, 193, 200
Churchyard, Thomas, 71
Clarkson, L A, 11, 236ff

Concannon, Helena, 1
Connolly, S J, 7, 13, 276ff
convents *see* nuns
Cooke, Lucretia, 185
cookery books, 272, 275
cooking methods, 265ff; *see also* food
  preparation
Corish, P J, 7, 212ff
Cork, 186; asylum 323
Cosby of Stradbally, Pole, 278, 280,
  282, 287
Counter-Reformation, 8, 32, 167, 188,
  212
Country Cork Presentment (1576), 25
Crawford, E M, 11, 236ff
Crawford, W H, 11, 255ff
crime, 43ff; records, 4–5; female per-
  centage of total crime, 48, 51; female
  receivers of stolen goods, 49, 55,
  66
Cromwell, Oliver, 192
Crookshank, C H, 201, 203
Cúchonnacht Og *see* Maguire
Cullen, Mary, 2
Cullen, Nuala, 10, 11, 265ff
Cunningham, Bernadette, 5, 9, 10,
  147ff
Curran, Sarah, 2
Curtin, Nancy J, 6, 9, 133ff
Cusack, Abbess Mary, 164
Cusacke, Margaret, 78

Davies, Sir John, 17
Defoe, Daniel, 55, 63–4
Delany, Mary, 267, 268, 273, 279
Derry, 135
Desmond, house of, 76, 80
de Sales, St Francis, 156
De Valera, Eamon, 2
Dickson, David, 12, 223ff
disguise, 65, 72; in female congregations, 202
Dowdall, Lady Elizabeth, 92–3
dowry payments 20–1, 22, 25–6; repayment sureties, 22–4; subscriptions
  towards, 25; dowry 'tax', 26
Drennan, William, 143
Drogheda, 94, 169, 189, 191
Dublin, male/female population ratios,
  50–1; women traders, 54; women
  refugees in the 1640s, 99, 100;
  convents, 169, 191; preachers, 182;
  childbirth among Dublin poor,
  296–300; provision for insane,
  325–32

Dublin Castle, 6
ducking stools, 44
Dudley, Robert, earl of Leicester, 84, 85

Edgeworth, Maria
  The Absentee (1812), 272
Edmundson, William, 180, 181, 184,
  188
education, 9, 10, 32, 157, 160ff; bardic
  orders, 32–3; scholarship, 33–4;
  Scottish parallels, 34–5; 18th
  century ideas, 139–40; Tudor
  attitudes, 161–3; libraries, 161;
  Ulster schools, 170, 259
Elizabeth I of England, 6, 83–6, 161,
  163, 164
employment, domestic, 265ff; in the
  linen industry, 255ff
emigration, 112ff; seasonal labour to
  England, 114; plight of
  Irishwomen in English cities, 116;
  to Bordeaux, 119; to Spain, 121;
  regimental camp followers, 124–5;
  political refugees, 119, 121, 125;
  press gangs, 126; to the Caribbean,
  127; Scotch-Irish, 113, 128–9;
  'temporary bondage', 128–9
English common law, 4, 7; of property,
  17, 39, 104; inheritance, 18, 26, 27;
  jointure, 24–5; spread of, 75
English policy in Ireland, 75, 81
English viceroys, 6, 75, 82
Erasmus, 155–6, 160

Falkland, Viscount Henry, Lord
  Deputy, 165, 170
family life, 276ff
female sexuality, 318ff
feminist historiography, 3, 293
Fingal, Benedictine monastery, 164
fishing industry, 54
Fitzgerald, Brigid, 35–6, 87, 120
Fitzgerald, Lady, 92
Fitzsimons, Henry, 188–9
Fitzwilliam, Lady Anne, 82–3
Fitzwilliam, Sir William, 86
Fletcher, Elizabeth, 182, 184
folklore, 304ff; infanticide in, 306
food preparation, 265ff; bread ovens,
  266; butter-making, 267; hen and
  fowl raising, 267; social
  entertaining, 268–9; table
  arrangement, 269–70; use of
  servants, 270–1; household
  management, 271; tea-drinking, 272

Forbes, Lady Jane, 92
Fox, George, 184, 187–8
Franciscans, Observantines, 37;
    convents, 169, 189

Gaelic law and custom, 4, of property,
    17; inheritance, 18, 26; legal status
    of women, 19, 56–7; brideprice, 20;
    legal rights of women, 37, 38–9;
    chiefly women, 70–1; *see also*
    inheritance laws
Gaelic literature, 9, 35–6, 147ff; poetry
    of exile, 130; annal obituaries,
    148–9; women patrons, 148ff;
    women authors, 152–4; women as
    subjects in, 154–7; genealogies,
    223; *see also* annals, bardic
    literature
Galway, 95–6, 21, 167, 169
Geashill castle, Co Offaly, 92
Gillespie, Raymond, 4, 11, 43ff
Glasse, Hannah, 272
Godwin, William, 139
Gooch, Steve
    The Women Pirates, 55
Gráinne ni Mháille *see* O'Malley,
    Grainne
Green, Alice Stopford, 1

Hajnal, J, 225
Hallaran, William Saunders
    *Practical Observations on the Causes and
    Cure of Insanity* (1810), 322–5
Harvey, William, 294
Hayden, Mary, 1
Hempton, David, 8, 197ff
Henry VIII, 84, 162
Herbert, William, 170
Hill, Myrtle, 8, 197ff
Huntingdon, Lady, 199

illegitimacy, 305
import/export trade, 118
infanticide, 304ff
inheritance laws, 26–7; *see also* Gaelic
    law and custom
International Federation for Research
    in Women's History, 3
Irish Feminist History Forum, 3
Irish republicanism, 133ff; influence of
    French and American
    republicanism, 137; literature and
    poetry, 137

Jesuits, 163, 168, 188, 190

Kildare, house of, 76, 190
Kilkenny, 97, 101
Kilroy, Phil, 8, 179ff
King, Archbishop William, 283, 284
Knott, Eleanor, 1

Laget, Mireille, 292–3
land settlement, 108; surrender and
    regrant, 85; transplantation of
    Connacht, 103–8
law *see* English common law; Gaelic
    law and custom
Leslie, Henry, bishop of Down and
    Connor, 179
Limerick, 25, 106, 182, 218
Lindon, Molly, 152–3, 157
linen industry, 255ff
Lismullin, Co Meath, Augustinian
    nunnery, 164
literacy, 166
literature *see* Gaelic literature
Loftus, Adam, archbishop of Armagh,
    37
Longfield, Ada K, 1
love and marriage, 276ff; *see also*
    marriage
Lutton, Anne, 202, 203
Lynch, Sir Henry, 21

Mac a Liondain, Padraig, 152
McCracken, Mary Anne, 6, 12, 138–43
MacCurtain, Margaret, 2, 3, 8, 9, 160ff
Mac Dáire, Tadhg, 36
McDonald, Walter, 218
MacDonnell, Fionuala (Inion Dubh), 78
McLoughlin, Katherine, 184
Machiavelli, 69, 74
madness, 318ff; provision for mental
    illness, 322ff
Magdalene Chapel, Dublin, 199
Magennis, Catherine, countess of
    Tyrone, 120, 165
Magrath, Miler, 37–8
Maguire, Cuchonnacht Og, 35–6, 87,
    149–50
Malby, Sir Nicholas, 79
Malcolm, Elizabeth, 12, 318ff
Malcolmson, A W P, 13, 279
Markievicz, Constance, 2
marriage, 223ff; marriage laws, 21, 39;
    redeemable marriage settlements,
    24; jointures, 24, 279; age at, 225–
    32; Cashel registers, 226–7; and
    family life, 276ff; economic
    importance, 278

Mary Queen of Scots, 149
Maxwell, Constantia, 1
Maynooth castle, 161
mental illness *see* madness
Merici, Angela, 163, 168
Methodist Church, 8–9, 197ff
midwives, 291ff
Mitchel, Susan, 185–6
monasteries, dissolution of, 164, 188
Moravians, 197ff
More, Thomas, 160
mortality of children, 285
Moryson, Fynes, 71, 77, 224
mothers, 212ff
Murphy-Lawless, Jo, 13, 14, 291ff

National Archives of Ireland *see* Public
    Record Office of Ireland
Nicholls, K W, 3, 5, 17ff, 40
Nugent, Francis Lavalin, 163
nuns, 164, 168, 188–92, 212ff, 218–9;
    convents, 117, 169

obituaries *see* annals *and* Gaelic
    literature
Offaly, Lady Lettice, 92
Orange order, 135
Ormond, earls of 6, 85–6, 103
Ould, Fielding, 296–9

O'Brien, Donnchadh, 4th earl of
    Thomond, 36
O'Brien, Sissy, 218–19
O'Brien, Una, countess of Thomond,
    77
Ó Bruadair, Daibhi, 151
O'Carroll, Margaret, 78
Ó Colmáin, Donal, 155–6
O'Connor, Anne, 304ff
Ó Corráin, Donncha, 2, 3
Ó Doirnín, Peadar, 153
O'Dowd, Mary, 6, 91ff
O'Gallagher, Caecilla, 121
O'Keefe, James, bishop of Kildare and
    Leighlin, 217
O'Malley, Grainne (Gráinne ní
    Mháille), 2, 22, 38, 53ff, 55, 79, 164
O'Neill, Hugh, earl of Tyrone, 85
O'Neill, Owen Roe, 101, 124
O'Neill, Shane, 35, 39, 70, 82; at court
    of Queen Elizabeth, 85
O'Neill, Sir Turlough, 120
O'Rourke, Dervogilla, 2, 73
O'Shea, Katherine, 2
O'Sullivan, Mary Donovan, 1

Paine, Tom, 139
Pale, 7, 9–10, 24, 26, 70, 83, 105;
    education in, 162
Parliament na mBan, 155–6, 174
Parnell, Anna, 2
Pearse, Patrick, 2
Perrot, Sir John, 78, 79, 86
Petty, Sir William, 226
piracy, 53ff; economic background, 55;
    in Munster and the south west, 59;
    Turkish pirates, 62; *see also*
    O'Malley, Grainne, *and* Bonny,
    Anne
plantation of Ireland, 43, 47; *see also*
    transplanation
Poor Clares, 117, 190–1
population: statistical analysis
    problems, 12–13; population
    change, 43, 223; male/female
    ratios in 17th century Dublin, 50–1;
    emigrations from Ireland, 113;
    numbers of Irish in England, 116;
    numbers emigrating to Caribbean
    and North America, 127; widows
    as a proportion of the total
    population of Carrick-on-Suir,
    236ff
Presbyterian Church, 10;
    Templepatrick, Co Antrim,
    session records deal with domestic
    disputes, 44, 47; session records of
    drunkenness, 49–50; and
    education, 166, 170; and the
    Establishment, 179
press gangs, 126
Preston, Lady Elizabeth, 103
prostitution, 50, 54, 60, 62–3, 115
Protestant churches: in the 17th
    century, 8, 179ff; in the 18th
    century, 197ff
Public Record Office of Ireland (PROI),
    3, 47
punishment for petty crime, 43ff;
    manor courts, session books and
    ducking stools, 44

Quakers, 8–9; in the 17th century, 180–
    8, 192; in the 18th century, 197ff

Rathkeale, Co Limerick, 161
Read, Mary, 55, 64–6
Rebellion of 1641, 91ff; repatriation of
    Protestants to England and
    Scotland, 99–100; land grants,
    102–3; transplantation, 103–4

eformation, 165–7, 179ff; recusancy
167–8
estoration of 1660, 107
tich, Barnaby, 50, 71, 76
inncini, G B, 101
Roche, Joan, 215
Rose of Ross, 72
Rotunda Lying-in Hospital, Dublin,
295

t Leger, Lady, 82
t Leger, Sir Anthony, 83
t Patrick's Cathedral, Dublin, 172
t Patrick's Hospital, Dublin, 325–32
Sarsfield, Patrick, 120
schools, 170, 259; *see also* education
Scotch-Irish migrations, 113, 128–9
Scottish Gaelic poetry, 154
Scroop, Sir Stephen, 73
session records *see* Presbyterian
Church
Sidney, Lady Mary, 82
Sidney, Sir Henry, 57, 78, 79, 82, 84,
85, 86
Silken, Thomas, 162
Simms, Katharine, 4, 9, 10, 32ff
Slater, Miriam, 276–7
Sligo, linen in, 262
Smith, Elizabeth, 182
Smith, Erasmus, 170
soldiers *see* women soldiers
sorcery, 46; *see also* witchcraft
Spenser, Edmund, 76, 224
Spottiswood, James, bishop of
Clogher, 47
Stanihurst, Margaret, 165
Stanihurst, Richard, 71–2, 162
Statute of Distributions (1696), 18
Stone, Lawrence, 276, 277, 278, 281,
285
Strafford, Thomas, earl of Wentworth,
170, 179
surrender and regrant *see* land
settlement
Sussex, Thomas, Earl of, 84, 85, 86
Sydenham, Thomas, 321

Táin Bó Cuailnge 32–3
tea drinking, 272
Thirsk, Joan, 9
Tipperary, 97; assize records, 48–9
tithes, 180, 181, 186–7
Tone, Theobald Wolfe, 273
Transatlantic crossings, mortality rates,
126

transplantation: of Connacht, 103–8,
227; to North America, 126–7;
certificates, 227
Trent, Council of, 8, 165
Trinity College Dublin, 1, 163, 166, 167,
172, 291
Tudor strategies in Ireland: extension
of English common law, 26, 75;
establishing an Irish kingdom
(1541), 81, 163; conquest and
reform, 87; church reform in the
Pale, 162

Ulster Goal, delivery rolls, 46–8
Ulster schools, 170, 259
United Irishmen, 6, 133; lack of
interest in women's suffrage, 134;
recruitment, 135; their role in
defending women-as-victims, 136
United Irishwomen, 134ff; Orange
hostility, 135
University College Dublin, 1
University College Galway, 1
Urban VIII, Pope, 168
Ursuline nuns, 168; educational
reforms, 163
Usher, Henry, archbishop of Armagh,
189
Ussher, James, archbishop of Armagh,
165, 166, 172

viceroys, 81–2
Vincent de Paul, St, 168
Vesey, John, archbishop of Tuam, 287

Wadding, Luke, 215–6
Walsh, Anastasia, 215
Ward, Mary, 8, 168, 190
Ward, Judge Michael, 280, 281
Weber, Max, 198
Wenworth, Thomas *see* Strafford, earl
of
Wesley, John, 201, 202, 204
Waterford, 167, 169
Wexford, 215–6
widowhood, 236ff; age structures, 237–
8; remarriage, 239–41; livelihoods,
243, 248–9
'wild geese', 108, 112; *see also*
emigration, Casway, J, *and*
O'Dowd, Mary
Willis, Thomas, 321
witchcraft, 44–6, 183, 206, 319; trials,
45; and infanticide, 307–8
Wollstonescraft, Mary, 139

Wolveridge, James
  Speculum Matricis (1671), 291–4
women preachers, 9, 181, 182, 201–4
women soldiers, 94–5
women's movement in Ireland, 2–3
women's obituaries *see* annals
women's sexuality, 318–21, 325
Women's Studies Forum, 3
women's work and the Irish economy,
  10–12; in maritime trades, 54–5; a
  transplanted landowners, 104; as
  factory employers, 141; as nuns,
  166ff; at Carrick-on-Suir, 248; in
  the linen industry, 255ff

Youghal, corporation records, 44, 45,
  48; Quakers at, 182
Young, Arthur, 257, 258, 259–60, 268